Pivotal Deterrence

A volume in the series

CORNELL STUDIES IN SECURITY AFFAIRS

edited by Robert J. Art, Robert Jervis, and Stephen M. Walt

A full list of titles in the series appears at the end of the book.

Pivotal Deterrence

Third-Party Statecraft and the Pursuit of Peace

TIMOTHY W. CRAWFORD

Cornell University Press

ITHACA AND LONDON

First published 2003 by Cornell University Press

Printed in the United States of America

Library of Congress Cataloging-in-Publication Data

Crawford, Timothy W.
   Pivotal deterrence : third-party statecraft and the pursuit of peace/ Timothy W. Crawford.
      p. cm.—(Cornell studies in security affairs)
   Includes bibliographical references and index.
   ISBN 0-8014-4097-1 (cloth : alk. paper)
   1. Balance of power. 2. Conflict management. 3. Great powers. 4. Deterrence (Strategy). 5. Intervention (International law). 6. Third parties (International law). I. Title. II. Series
   JZ1312.C73 2003
   327.1'17'0973—dc21   2003007980

Cornell University Press strives to use environmentally responsible suppliers and materials to the fullest extent possible in the publishing of its books. Such materials include vegetable-based, low-VOC inks and acid-free papers that are recycled, totally chlorine-free, or partly composed of nonwood fibers. For further information, visit our website at www.cornellpress.cornell.edu.

Cloth printing   10 9 8 7 6 5 4 3 2 1

For my parents,
Arthur Wallace and Mabel Wren Crawford

Contents

Acknowledgments

This book began as a gnawing question: How can you deter two sides in a conflict? I thank John Ruggie for encouraging me, early on, to explore the obscure question in depth. My greatest intellectual debt is to Robert Jervis, who showed me why the question was not so obscure after all (indeed, that he had written a thing or two about it). Richard Betts also deserves credit, for what started me thinking about the question was his well-known argument in *Foreign Affairs* that it is often better to choose sides when intervening in conflicts. My thanks to Jervis and Betts for reading and critiquing my work; to Page Fortna, Kenneth Waltz, and Kimberly Zisk, who also gave valuable comments; and to Robert Art, Glenn Snyder, Mark Sheetz, and Keir Lieber, who all reviewed later versions of the manuscript and suggested improvements in content and form. I am also grateful to Roger Haydon, Ange Romeo-Hall, and Cathi Reinfelder at Cornell University Press for expert guidance throughout the editorial process.

Others who deserve thanks for feedback on the project include Nora Bensahel, Chris Ball, Robin Bhatty, Mia Bloom, Derek Chollet, Tom Christensen, Stephen Cohen, Ivo Daalder, Sumit Ganguly, Bates Gill, Stacie Goddard, Talbot Imlay, Peter Jakobsen, Colin Kahl, Ron Krebs, Aaron Lobel, Jon Mercer, Dinshaw Mistry, Michael O'Hanlon, Robert Rauchhaus, Matthew Rendall, Evan Resnick, Jeff Ritter, Stephen Rosen, Robert Ross, Jordan Seng, Jeremy Shapiro, Jack Snyder, Marc Trachtenberg, Leslie Vinajamuri, Jon Western, Richard Wilcox, and Micah Zenko. I also owe a debt to many others who participated in seminars at Brookings Foreign Policy Studies, Columbia's Institute of War and Peace Studies, Harvard's Olin Institute of Strategic Studies, Yale's International Security Studies program, and the Boston College Department of Political Science.

Two research institutions provided crucial support for the bulk of my work: I thank Sam Huntington and Stephen Rosen for a fellowship at Harvard's Olin Institute of Strategic Studies; and Richard Haass and James Steinberg for a fellowship in Foreign Policy Studies at the Brookings Institution. The final draft was completed while I was a Visiting Fellow at Princeton's Center of International Studies, and a Visiting Scholar at the Institute for European, Russian, and Eurasian Studies at George Washington University. I am grateful to Richard Ullman, Aaron Friedberg, and Jim Goldgeier for this support.

I am also indebted to teachers and mentors who did much to shape my thinking about international politics: David Baldwin, Jeff Knopf, Vidya Nadkarni, Leanne Otto, Susan Peterson, Warner Schilling, and Randy Willoughby.

Portions of Chapter 6 and 7 are extracted from articles reprinted with the permission of *India Review*, Vol. 1, No. 3 (July 2002): 1–38, and *Political Science Quarterly*, Vol. 116 (winter 2001): 499–523.

This book is dedicated to my parents. I have been emboldened to take chances in life by their steadfast assurances. My brother John Crawford, the Mishan-Mizrahi-Wiesenfeld-Blank clan, Oliver Wright and Leslie Vinjamuri, and Danny and Amy Reich supplied crucial relief and reinforcement as I worked on this book. Orly Mishan, my wonderful wife, made my life complete and contributed much to this book as reader, editor, and critic.

T. W. C.

Pivotal Deterrence

Introduction

A Prince is . . . esteemed who is a staunch friend and a thorough foe . . . who without reserve openly declares for one against another, this being always a more advantageous course than to stand neutral. . . . it will always be well for you to declare yourself, and join in frankly with one side or other.

Niccolò Machiavelli, *The Prince*

Machiavelli's counsel against equivocating and avoiding commitment when conflicts between others appear to force a choice invoked a lesson at least as old as Aesop.[1] Down the years, many serious political thinkers have endorsed it. Yet the annals of statecraft are filled with examples of powers that, possessing the leverage and flexibility of a central position, have tried to deter others from war without choosing sides. They have not always failed. I call this form of statecraft *pivotal deterrence*. In the last century and a half, some of the most praiseworthy diplomatic feats, and notorious foreign policy failures, involved pivotal deterrence. In the 1870s Bismarck famously deflected Russia and Austria-Hungary from coming to blows in the Balkans. Sir Edward Grey, Britain's foreign minister, tried to do the same with Germany and France before 1914, with catastrophic results.[2] Why did Bismarck's policy succeed and Grey's fail? In the 1960s the United States pursued similar policies toward the rivalries between India and Pakistan and Greece and Turkey. Its efforts were largely successful in the Greco-Turkish dispute, defusing near-war crises in 1964 and 1967. In South Asia, on the other hand, U.S. policy failed, culminating in the bloody 1965 Kashmir war. Why did U.S. policy work in one case and not the other?

This book posits a simple but powerful answer. Pivotal deterrence tends to work when the adversaries have bad alignment options, or none at all, and it tends to fail when they have good alignment options. Bismarck's policy swayed Austria and Russia because they had no reliable allies to turn to. Grey's policy was handicapped by the fact that France and Germany were both attached to committed allies with whom Britain simply could not compete. Similarly, in the Greco-Turkish crises, neither side had attractive alignment options other than the United States. While the Soviets could have done more to interfere with U.S. policy, they did not want Cyprus to be suborned by either member of the North Atlantic Treaty Organization (NATO). So in the heat of crises, Moscow left the United States an open field in which to play the pivot. But in South Asia, India and Pakistan had alignment options in the Soviet Union and China that were eager to compete with each other, and with the United States, for influence in the region. This undercut America's efforts to avert war.

The questions how and under which conditions pivotal deterrence works carry a great deal of relevance for U.S. foreign policy today. In recent years, repeated near-war crises between nuclear-armed India and Pakistan have made deterrence a paramount U.S. goal, as Washington has been repeatedly forced behind the scenes to restrain both sides from dangerous escalation.[3] The continuing rivalry between China and Taiwan, likewise, presents the United States with a major challenge involving important features of pivotal deterrence. On another front, as recently as 1996, the United States had to act to prevent its allies, Greece and Turkey, from coming to blows. Elsewhere the United States has, with varying success, attempted pivotal deterrence in disputes involving Serbia and Kosovo, Serbia and Montenegro, and the Macedonian government and ethnic Albanian guerilla.[4] The list goes on, running from failed U.S. efforts to broker peace in the Israel-Palestinian conflict and to quell war between Ethiopia and Eritrea, to more successful albeit less taxing efforts to nip budding conflicts between Spain and Morocco, and Russia and Georgia.[5] In Afghanistan and Iraq today, the United States is deeply implicated in efforts to prevent open warfare among feuding factions, which require it to oppose and deter the ambitions of many sides at once.[6] In short, pivotal deterrence is part of the warp and woof of many of the conflicts engaging America today.

This book builds on and speaks to traditions in the field of international security. There is a strong analytical and substantive parallel between this research and scholarship on international mediation. But pivotal deterrence should not be conflated with mediation. Although the two may sometimes merge in what has been called "muscular mediation" they are not the same, and they need not go together.[7] Mediation, say I. William Zartman and Saadia Touval, "must be acceptable to the adversaries . . . who cooperate diplomatically" with the mediator, who is "restricted to diplomatic involvement" and "may not employ violence."[8] Pivotal deterrence, as we shall see, is often pursued against the wishes and without the cooperation of one or both sides, and it involves coercion—threats to use force or to refrain from using it, and thus expose the weak to the strong. It is this attempt to prevent war by making potential belligerents *fear the costs* that makes pivotal deterrence, above all else, a form of deterrence.

Deterrence theory, which addresses strategic studies' "most thoroughly considered power relationship," has had strikingly little to say about the problem at hand.[9] The reasons are not hard to divine. Modern deterrence theory was hatched during the Cold War, when the most pressing issues confronting scholars and practitioners of national security policy involved political situations in which the lines of amity and enmity were clearly drawn. Its tried and true models of "basic" and "extended" deterrence have imposed an unfortunate path dependence on the evolution of thinking about deterrence. Consequently, that rich intellectual tradition speaks with less probity to many deterrence problems today than it did in decades past.[10]

Robert Jervis, in a short essay in 1994, was perhaps alone among deterrence theorists to explicitly pose the generic problem of deterring "two countries or factions that are in conflict with one another." The nub of this problem of "dual deterrence," as he called it, is that "complex, conditional threats and promises" are much harder "to make credible" than the typically one-sided threats of extended deterrence.[11] Jervis highlighted a few key central questions: How to avoid signaling unconditional hostility to the adversaries, without also appearing weak? How to check two-way aggression without unduly freezing the status quo and discouraging peaceful change? How, and whether, to identify a primary party to be deterred? Jervis posed these questions but did not answer them, and in a telling indication of the dearth of research on the subject, did not refer to any sources that did.[12]

In keeping with the times, a major focus of security studies in the 1990s was peacemaking in regional and civil wars, and the linked problems of intervention, termination, and peacekeeping. At the high-water mark of this research program, Barbara Walter demonstrated that a credible enforcement commitment from an outside party is critical to the success of negotiated civil war settlements.[13] Here, the conundrum Jervis raised cries out for an answer. A credible third party commitment that will assure adversaries they can disarm must be sufficient to deter them from attacking each other. Yet the inner workings of such third party deterrence, and the conditions under which it is likely to thrive, remain undeveloped by scholarship in this vein.[14] Similarly, Joshua Goldstein, Jon Pevehouse, and their colleagues have examined the relationship between "cooperative" and "bullying" interventions by outside powers and the level of cooperative or antagonistic reciprocity within regional conflicts. This important research suggests that by inducing "triangular" reciprocity, outside powers can moderate regional conflicts. But the results are not well supported by a theory that explains why cooperative strategies by outsiders sometimes produce moderation among regional rivals and sometimes do not.[15]

More broadly, since the early 1990s, scholars of U.S. foreign policy have debated the need for American "leadership" and "forward engagement," which almost by definition, involves deterring wars among other powers and regional partners.[16] Much of this debate has revolved around the questions of "whether" and "why," while the more mundane (but less obvious) questions of "how do we do it?" and "when is it likely to work?" are short-changed. This is unfortunate because pivotal deterrence is not simply a matter of will power, and preponderance, as we shall see, does not guarantee success. Because deterring wars between adversaries without choosing sides will remain an important goal of U.S. foreign policy, we need a clear conceptualization and description of pivotal deterrence, a theory of how it works and when it works, and an empirical analysis to back it up. Those are the purposes of this book.

[1]

The Problem and Theory of Pivotal Deterrence

Perhaps the real mark of statesmanship is to avoid the horns of a dilemma, to find a third path at the traditional "fork in the road" where our anxious guides bid us make a choice between two obvious forks.

Reinhold Niebuhr, *World Politics*, April 1950

Pivotal deterrence involves the manipulation of threats and promises in order to prevent war. Like other forms of deterrence, it tries to prevent war by making potential belligerents fear the costs, by confronting them with risks they do not want to run. There are two other important dimensions of the concept. First, the deterrer must hold a "pivotal" position between the adversaries, which means that it can more easily align with either side than they can align with each other and that it can significantly influence who will win in a war between them. Second, a pivotal deterrer will try to maintain flexibility and avoid consistent alignment in relation to the adversaries, and therefore avoid firm commitments to either side.[1] The point here is not merely that the pivot remains flexible in a fluid political situation. More than that, the pivot strives to maintain and use flexibility that others—because of the conflict between them—do not have. Thus, by playing both sides against the middle, leaving them uncertain and afraid of what it may do if they go to war, a pivot may use its flexibility to deter them from fighting and to encourage them to compromise.

THREE PIVOTAL DETERRENCE SCENARIOS

All pivotal deterrence policies aim to address one of three basic "triangular" dilemmas. In each the pivot's best response is to avoid making firm

[5]

public commitments to either side. Below I illustrate these scenarios using a simple three-actor model. The basic model describes the adversaries' preferences about the pivot's alignment in the triad. Each variation of the model gives a snapshot of the pivot's beliefs about the two adversaries' motives and intentions. In all the models, there is a Pivot and two adversaries (A1 and A2), and the Pivot has three options, to align with either of the two adversaries (P_{A1} or P_{A2}) or to remain neutral (P_N).

The Basic Model

$$A1: P_{A1} > P_N > P_{A2}$$
$$A2: P_{A2} > P_N > P_{A1}$$

This model simply says that each adversary would rather the pivot were aligned with it than anything else, and would rather the pivot were neutral than aligned against it. Now in order to show the logic behind different deterrence strategies, we must plug in some assumptions about the adversaries' intentions. Specifically, we must state the conditions under which the adversaries would be willing (or rather, are believed by the pivot to be willing) to launch a war against the other side. Preferences with an asterisk (e.g., $P_{A1}{}^*$) will indicate these conditions in each player's order of preferences.

To use the basic model to describe the three pivotal deterrence scenarios, we must assume that the pivot believes that both sides harbor aggressive aims toward the other, and that under some more or less favorable condition they would use force to achieve them. Chapter 2 lays the deductive foundations for this premise; for now, let it stand on its own. We must also assume that under some set of conditions within the model, the pivot can deter the adversaries: There are no revisionists "at any cost" here. Each of the three pivotal deterrence scenarios, therefore, describes a different pattern of the adversaries' aggressive—but not hopelessly belligerent—intentions.

Scenario 1: Janus-Faced Foe (JFF)

$$A1: P_{A1}{}^* > P_N{}^* > P_{A2}$$
$$A2: P_{A2}{}^* > P_N{}^* > P_{A1}$$

"The Iranians are flying, the Iraqis are flying, and we are warning both of them that it is not acceptable." This is how a U.S. official described U.S. efforts in October 1997 to deter combat between Iranian and Iraqi air forces over the southern "no-fly" zone of Iraq.[2] In Shakespeare's *Henry V*, Lieutenant Bardolph made this sort of threat to his fellow soldiers, Nim and Pistol, as they faced each other with daggers drawn: "[H]e that strikes the first stroke, I'll run him up to the hilts . . . he that makes the first thrust, I'll kill him . . . thou wilt be friends [or] be enemies with me too."[3] Similarly, in July 1870, as France and Germany teetered on the brink of war, Britain warned each side not to violate Belgian neutrality, threatening to align against that side if it did, and wrested from both Paris and Berlin formal treaties guaranteeing Belgian neutrality.[4] Here the pivot used its leverage to limit the scope of the war rather than prevent it altogether, but the basic logic of conditional two-way threats is the same.

In this scenario, then, the assumption is that each adversary will be deterred if (and only if) it thinks that the pivot will align against it. And the trick for the pivot is to convince both sides—or at least make them worry—that it will join their rival and fight against them. To express the logic in terms of the model, the pivot will try to make A1 fear P_{A_2}, and A2 fear P_{A_1}.

To do this successfully the pivot must not make a commitment that will embolden either side—but must also avoid giving the impression that it will stand aside if they go to war. This is the crux of the dilemma, and this is what makes the JFF strategy so hard to pull off. For by refusing to choose sides ex ante (which it must do to avoid egging on one side or the other), the pivot sends a signal that can easily be misconstrued (or rightly construed) as an indication that it will not intervene ex post. Attempts to strengthen the conditionality of the threat, and the commitment to carry it out, through formal pacts, treaties, and declarations, will not resolve this catch-22. The bane of collective security schemes—the difficulty and subjectivity associated with identifying an "aggressor"—rears its head here. And if the pivot decides that it does not want to intervene, it can de-commit with a "pox on both your houses" policy that brands both sides aggressors or argue that because the situation is too close to call, the *causus foederis* remains moot. There is simply no way to eliminate the ambiguity embodied in the JFF strategy: not on paper and not through public declarations or other costly signals. This does not mean that the strategy cannot work. Rather, it means that the strategy works *because of,* not in spite of, the essential ambiguity at its core.

Scenario 2: Fair-Weather Friend (FWF)

A1: $P_{A_1}{}^* > P_N > P_{A_2}$
A2: $P_{A_2}{}^* > P_N > P_{A_1}$

In the second scenario, each adversary will escalate if (and only if) it has the pivot's firm allegiance. Here the pivot may deter them simply by denying them any assurance of support in the event of war. As we will see in Chapter 3, Bismarck's policy toward Austria-Hungary and Russia during the Eastern Crisis of the mid-1870s in many ways fits this scenario. Publicly,

[7]

Bismarck adopted an attitude of neutrality, saying that he would support anything Austria and Russia could agree on. Privately, at the two key junctures (in the fall of 1876 and the winter of 1878) where German policy demonstrably derailed the adversaries' war plans, Bismarck warned them that Germany could not be counted on to come to their aid in a war against the other side. Since both sides wanted to score a cheap and limited victory, underwritten by German allegiance, they were deterred by Bismarck's unwillingness to commit.[5]

Putting the logic in formal terms, here the pivot will try to immobilize A1 with the prospect of $\sim P_{A_1}$ if war breaks out, and A2 with the prospect of $\sim P_{A_2}$. All else being equal, this is the scenario in which pivotal deterrence is easiest. Here the pivot can even adopt a public attitude of clear-cut neutrality and still effectively deter. Indeed, this may be the pivot's dominant strategy given that it entails no need for deception about or obfuscation of its position.

Scenario 3: The Straddle Strategy (SS)

A1: $P_{A_1}^* > P_N^* > P_{A_2}$
A2: $P_{A_2}^* > P_N > P_{A_1}$

Finally, in this scenario, one adversary (A1) will go to war if the pivot is neutral, but the other (A2) will not go to war without the pivot's firm allegiance.[6] The ambiguity in the pivot's policy does not disappear, but the range of possible strategies is narrowed. The pivot swings between neutrality and allegiance to one side. Here, as Machiavelli put it, "the one who is not your friend will want you to remain neutral, and the one who is your friend will [want] you to declare yourself by taking arms."[7] In Chapter 4, we shall see how Britain faced this dilemma in July of 1914, with respect to France and Germany. Sir Edward Grey, Britain's foreign minister, worried that France held aggressive aims vis-à-vis Germany—especially in the Alsace-Lorraine— and that it would pursue them if it had a solid commitment from Britain. He also thought that Germany would attack France if it thought Britain would stand aside, but not if it believed that Britain would side with France. So Grey tried to restrain France with the threat of British neutrality, and to deter Germany with the threat to fight alongside France and Russia. America's enduring policy of "strategic ambiguity" toward the China-Taiwan conflict has a similar ring to it. The United States will not commit to defending Taiwan under all circumstances, and refuses to support independence, in order to deter provocations from Taipei. At the same time, it is committed to insuring a "peaceful" solution to the conflict and to helping Taiwan defend itself against an unprovoked mainland attack; in other words, to deterring China.[8]

The central problem here is that the pivot must instill contradictory fears

[8]

in the adversaries. To the one who would not choose war without the pivot's support (A2), the pivot will hold out the threat of neutrality (P_N). To the one who would go to war if the pivot were neutral (A1), it will hold out the threat of an alliance with its enemy (P_{A_2}). A firm public commitment to either course of action, however, would destroy the pivot's leverage over one side, so again, the pivot's position must remain ambiguous.

Summary

The key element in these three scenarios is the need for the pivot to avoid firm commitments to either side. Because the pivot must sometimes lead different sides to fear different (indeed contradictory) things, ambiguity is also often an important ingredient in its best response to the problem. In short, the pivot must not publicly commit to one side, and must often be vague and elusive about its intentions, if it is going to deter both sides from going to war.

Finally, it is worth noting that the pivot has the most leverage in the Fair-Weather Friend scenario. In this sense, the FWF scenario is the "ideal" pivotal deterrence situation, the one where neither side feels it can act without firm support from the pivot. Here, a declared policy of neutrality is enough to prevent war. In the rough-and-tumble of real-world diplomacy, pivot states can rarely attain much less sustain this ideal situation, but the model is powerful heuristically because it captures the essence of what pivot states strive for in their diplomacy, even if they rarely get there and end up instead in a Janus-Faced Foe or Straddle Strategy.

SOURCES OF PIVOTAL DETERRENCE THEORY

Deterrence Theory

In trying to prevent war by manipulating the potential belligerents' expected costs of war, pivotal deterrence joins the broader corpus of deterrence theory. Because it is a third-party effort, it is more specifically a form of "extended deterrence."[9] However, what makes pivotal deterrence different from the orthodox notion of extended deterrence is that the "defender" (i.e., the pivot) does not simply commit to one side (the "protégé") in order to deter the other (the adversary). Instead, the pivot tries to obscure its ultimate allegiances in order to restrain both sides. There are other differences worth probing.

Extended Deterrence vs. Pivotal Deterrence
The basic logic and prescriptions of pivotal deterrence depart from orthodox extended deterrence in a number of ways. In extended deterrence,

the defender tries to create widespread certainty about its future behavior. It therefore surrenders freedom of action, stakes its reputation on public threats and promises, and closely coordinates war plans with allies: These are the hallmarks of extended deterrence. In pivotal deterrence, on the other hand, the pivot is better off leaving some uncertainty about its future behavior. Benjamin Franklin's advice to "let no man know thee thoroughly [for] men freely ford that see the shallows" captures the logic well. Here maintaining freedom of action and keeping leverage over both sides is the goal; avoiding public commitments—and when they are necessary, making them as ambiguous and vague as possible—is the name of the game. This basic difference between the two types of deterrence carries implications for the timing, clarity, and publicity of commitments.

Extended deterrence works best when commitments are made early. There are a variety of reasons for this. First if one waits too long to make a deterrent threat, the adversary may have already become politically committed to the undesired action. John Foster Dulles put it succinctly: "if you draw a line in advance then you serve notice on the enemy. At the same time you give him an opportunity to retreat or stay his hand which is not open . . . if you intervene in a war that is already under way."[10] Second, a deterrent threat made in the midst of a crisis may be more destabilizing than it would be if it were made before the crisis. As Austen Chamberlain, Britain's foreign minister in 1925, once said, "The only way of making a [defense] pact of this kind is to make it when the danger is not yet acute, not to leave it till the moment when it is almost as menacing and provocative . . . as an act of mobilization."[11] Third, an early commitment allows the defender and protégé to coordinate war plans and to conduct maneuvers, which not only improves their ability to prevail if deterrence fails, but sends a strong signal to the adversary.

In contrast, in pivotal deterrence one tries to avoid making firm commitments to either side, and failing that, to delay making that commitment as long as possible. The first and most obvious reason is that surrendering freedom of action prematurely and coming down decisively on one side of a heated conflict that is not your own is politically costly.[12] But more specifically, refraining from commitment—even to a party you know you will fight for—can give you more leverage over them. This, in other words, is the simple truth that you may have more control over those who need you by playing hard to get.[13] Winston Churchill (then chancellor of the exchequer) put forward exactly this view to challenge Chamberlain's position (quoted above) in the 1925 Cabinet debates over whether to make a formal alliance with France against Germany:

Will we have more influence over [France] . . . if we are bound to her or if we are independent of her? . . . Should we not have just as great an influence, or perhaps an even greater influence, over her if we had still to be won, if she had still . . . to convince us of her own rectitude and moderation? . . . [I]t is by standing aloof and not by offering ourselves that we will ascertain the degree of importance which France really attaches to our troth . . . I am sure we would do better, for the present at any rate, to keep ourselves free.[14]

Finally, avoiding a premature commitment may also allow you to negotiate with the other adversary—the one you would ultimately fight against— more effectively. For example, in the Quemoy and Matsu crisis of August 1958, President Eisenhower came under intense pressure to specify immediately how U.S. forces would be used to prevent China from taking the islands from Chiang's Nationalist army, which was deployed on them. He refused to do so, saying "you simply cannot make military decisions until the event reaches you." This statement is hard to reconcile with the decisive signaling logic of extended deterrence, but makes sense given what we know were his goals in the crisis: to deflate the ambitions of the Nationalist forces on the islands and to negotiate *with* mainland China to produce a compromise that impelled the Nationalists to withdraw.[15]

Another typical view of deterrence is that it is more credible, and thus more likely to work, when governments "define their commitment clearly." Robert Rothgreb says "the most effective communications [of threat] involve a situation in which an actor states clearly what it wishes the target to do, is explicit about the penalties it will apply for non-compliance, and is definite about how it will react if the target does not go along." Similarly, Phil Williams argues that "the clearer, more salient, and less ambiguous the line a potential aggressor must not cross, the more successful is deterrence likely to be." In the same vein, Lawrence Freedman notes that "[w]hen statements by one actor as to what he might do become no more than hints and are couched in vague terms then a deterrence strategy will become feeble and unconvincing." Paul Lauren agrees: "the specificity and clarity generally associated with . . . [threats] have frequently facilitated the effectiveness of coercive diplomacy, by defining the precise obligations to be fulfilled and by informing the opponent what is *not* being required of him."[16]

But, as a bit of reading in diplomatic history will show, "delphic" utterances and equivocation figure as much if not more in the fabric of coercive diplomacy as bold and crisp declarations. Accordingly, there is also a rich vein of theoretical work in international relations pointing to the importance of ambiguity in deterrence. A key insight—that someone will be cautious when faced with an uncertain situation in which a costly outcome is possible—appears especially in classic works by Glenn Snyder, Thomas Schelling, Alexander George and Richard Smoke, and Patrick Morgan.[17] The logic of pivotal deterrence taps into this vein. A related line of argument suggests that in some situations it may be "advantageous not to make one's demands too specific or too precise" because "a vague or ambiguous threat may . . . reduce the costs to the target of complying with the conditions of the threat."[18] Vague and ambiguous threats are a common feature of pivotal deterrence for this reason too. The pivot's leverage comes from having better relations with the adversaries than they have with each other; leverage that would be sacrificed if the pivot adopted as threatening a posture toward one adversary as that adversary's principal rival. Ambiguity is one way to do this. Opaque threats may be seen as less threatening and hostile than pointed ones.

Finally, extended deterrence puts a premium on public communication of threats. Because the interests of the defender and the protégé are not usually identical—that is, because the defender may be less threatened by the adversary than the protégé—the defender usually needs to take steps to enhance his "resolve" to fight for the protégé. And as many deterrence theorists have emphasized, threats that are communicated in public are more costly and therefore more credible signals of resolve than private communications.[19] Nevertheless, as even Schelling, the don of commitment logic, noted, it is sometimes better "not being too explicit or too open about precisely what is demanded, if the demands can be communicated privately and noncommittally."[20] In pivotal deterrence this is often the case. That is partly because commitments made secretly are less binding and give the pivot more flexibility. Moreover, private threats and promises are often *necessary* in pivotal deterrence because the pivot must lead the adversaries to fear contradictory things about what he will do if they go to war. For example, in the July 1914 crisis, Grey tried to restrain France by privately hinting that Britain would remain neutral and to deter Germany with private warnings that Britain would fight. To have expressed either of these positions clearly, forcefully, and publicly would have undercut the other entirely.

To sum up, it is typically assumed that the best way to achieve deterrence is to make your threats and promises early, clearly, and publicly. But these are *tactics* not necessary conditions of deterrence strategy. When the problem of pivotal deterrence arises, flexibility, ambiguity, private communications, and the avoidance of firm commitment are often useful ways to make potential belligerents fear the costs of war and therefore avoid it.

General and Immediate Pivotal Deterrence

Like basic and extended deterrence, pivotal deterrence can be conceived in both "general" and "immediate" forms. *General pivotal deterrence* occurs when (1) there is an ongoing rivalry between two states in which the use of force to alter the status quo between them is likely; (2) there is a pivot state with the ability to significantly influence the outcome of a war between

[12]

them; and (3) the rivals do not attack each other because they know that (2) is the case and do not want to risk the pivot intervening against them. *Immediate pivotal deterrence* occurs when (1) a crisis erupts between the two rivals causing each to actively consider attacking the other; (2) the pivot state undertakes efforts to deter them, but does not firmly align with either side; and (3) neither side attacks as a consequence of the pivot's actions.[21] Both forms of pivotal deterrence figure in the theoretical and empirical concerns of this book.

Holding the Balance

There is a close affinity between pivotal deterrence and the power policy known as "holding the balance."[22] Edward Vose Gulick tells us that the latter phrase describes "the role of a third party interested in preserving a simple balance between two other powers or two other blocs of powers. When one side threatens the security and survival of the other, the third party steps in on the side of the weaker and sees that a balance between independent powers is restored."[23] Here a pivotal deterrence policy is implicit in the logic of balancing in a system of three equal powers. As Martin Wight described it, if "the first attacks the second . . . the third power cannot afford to see the second so decisively crushed that it becomes threatened itself; therefore if [the third] is farsighted it 'throws its weight into the lighter scale of the balance' by supporting the second power."[24] Now if the first and second powers anticipate that the third will intervene against whichever side is winning, and so refrain from going to war, then we have a pure instance of general pivotal deterrence, one that flows naturally from the adversaries' expectation that logic of balancing will operate.

More broadly, it is also true that those conditions that allow one to hold the balance must be in place if one is to pursue a policy of pivotal deterrence. In other words, to hold the balance is to occupy a power *position* that permits a range of power *policies*, one of which is pivotal deterrence. The leverage that drives pivotal deterrence stems from both the pattern of political relations and the pattern of capabilities that must obtain if one is to hold the balance. "A balancer cannot perform," writes Henry Kissinger, "unless the differences among the other powers are greater than their collective differences with the balancer."[25] When such political conditions exist, the forces that a pivotal deterrence policy strives to harness may be set in motion. When faced with a balancer "isolated by its own choice," writes Hans Morgenthau, "the [adversaries] must vie with each other to add its weight to theirs . . . since its support or lack of support is the decisive factor . . . [it] is able to extract the highest price from those whom it supports."[26] Here, then, the balance holder's patrimony is undeniable. But there is far more to pivotal deterrence than holding the balance.

Preventing War vs. Inciting and Exploiting War

A balancer may be an "abettor" who seeks not to keep peace but to "instigate conflict between the other[s] . . . for its own purposes," what John Mearsheimer calls a "bait and bleed" strategy.[27] Three millennia ago, the Athenian turncoat general Alcibiades recommended to his Persian protector that he do just that against the Greeks: "he advised the satrap neither to help the Spartans whole-heartedly nor yet to finish off the Athenians," instead he should "cause difficulties to both sides and gradually wear them down and so render them an easy prey . . . when they had wasted their strength on one another."[28] Similarly, Frederick the Great, a virtuoso of statecraft in the central position, aggrandized Prussia "by inflaming the passions of both [Austria and France], by pretending to serve both, and by deserting both" in the War of the Austrian Succession.[29] Going further, a balancer may play the *tertius gaudens* (laughing third) who goads others to war in order to extract "an exploitative price for its support."[30] Pivotal deterrence does not stoop to these forms of incitement. It uses the leverage of a balancer to keep the peace between adversaries and impel them to compromise, not to foment war between them and make gains at their expense.

Deterrence vs. Win-the-War Strategy

Less cynically, holding the balance is also often associated with a prudent strategy for winning wars that you did not start but can not sit out. As Wight put it, the goal is to let the belligerents "grind down each other's strength . . . and batter each other to pieces" before picking a side and ending the war decisively.[31] The logic here is similar to what Norman Mailer dubbed "the old rule of many a Victorian crazy house: Let the madmen duke it out, then jump the one or two who are left."[32] For the notorious Confederate general, Nathan Bedford Forrest, the recipe for winning battles was to get there "the fustest with the mostest." The balance holder's war-winning formula is just the opposite: to get there last with the least. Again, Great Britain, with its "English Channel behind which to assess developing events and across which to interfere at the moment of maximum advantage" is the archetype for this strategy of war termination.[33] To the extent that such a war-winning strategy contributes to "stability," that term must be understood to pertain to system stability, not peace *per se*. Michael Sheehan makes the point: "The purpose of the balancer was at all times to ensure the survival of a particular political system, the system of independent states, by resisting hegemonic aspirations of expansionist powers. It was not part of the balancer's function to avert war, any more than balance-of-power systems generally . . . aimed to prevent war."[34]

In contrast, pivotal deterrence strives to prevent war. The distinction here is familiar to deterrence theorist: Strategies that are good for deterring wars (e.g., Mutual Assured Destruction) often depart, logically and practically, from ones that are good for fighting wars after deterrence fails.[35] Similar differences arise between strategies of holding the balance that allow the balancer to win wars cheaply and those that try to deter wars in the first place.[36]

Strategic Dependence vs. Strategic Independence

Finally, insularity, "aloofness," and a large margin of "strategic security" are thought to favor a balance-holding policy. These assumptions, of course, are inferred from Great Britain's balancing policy toward the Continent. Thus, for Gulick, Britain's geographic position was "ideal" for holding the balance because its "location as an island, separate from the Continent and yet close to it, gave her security, aloofness, and flexibility."[37] Similarly, Morgenthau argued that as a balancer, Britain made "its beneficial contributions to peace and stability only because it was geographically remote from the centers of friction and conflict, because it had no vital interests in the stakes of these conflicts as such."[38] Likewise for George Liska, for whom Britain's "aloofness and ability to withdraw from the balance were required for the necessarily elusive and flexible operations" of its balancer policy.[39]

This body of wisdom is misleading when it comes to pivotal deterrence. Geographic insularity and the strategic independence that attends it may improve a balancer's ability to incite and win wars that exhaust others. But they do not necessarily improve a pivot's ability to deter wars in the first place. Indeed, they tend to undercut pivotal deterrence, just as they do any other type of extended deterrence. Paul Schroeder makes the point succinctly: "The state best suited [to play the pivot] is not one whose power and position render it fairly independent of the system, able to live without it, but the power dependent on it, compelled by its central position and vulnerability to be a prime investor in stability and survival."[40]

Strategic Triangles

Pivotal deterrence involves a triangular relationship between the pivot and two adversaries or groups of adversaries (i.e., alliances)—in other words, a triad. This calls forth a rich and varied line of research on "triads." The path-breaking sociology of triads came from Georg Simmel, whose insights were developed and tested more rigorously by Theodore Caplow in the 1960s. Simmel's key points were (1) that a third party can wield a disproportionate share of bargaining power in a triad by maintaining the flexibility to choose between two antagonists, so long as it has a portion of power sufficient to determine who wins in the end; and (2) that triads tend to become "segregated" into a pair and an isolated party.[41] Caplow, many years later, coined the phrase "two-against-one" to describe this second tendency.[42]

The emerging field of game theory used abstract models to formalize some of these basic truths about the nature of interaction in strategic triads. Game theory pioneers John Von Neumann and Oskar Morgenstern produced a three-person game that showed that when each of two parties (A and B) will gain more benefits by forming a "couple" with a third (C) than by forming a couple with each other, "one must expect that this will lead to a competitive bidding for [C's] cooperation."[43] As game theory developed, the two-against-one tendency identified by Simmel thus became a convenient *initial assumption* about both the preferences and the goals of the actors in three-player games. As Von Neumann and Morgenstern described their zero-sum three-person game, where the two parties who form a coalition win everything, and the cornered party losses all, "coalitions are the only thing that matters, and the only conceivable aim of all players."[44]

Formal international relations (IR) theorists studying strategic triangles tend to do either of two things. For the sake of "tractability," they may, as Robert Powell puts it, "finesse the problem by formalizing the situation so that bargaining only occurs between two actors."[45] Or, more often, they use *n*-person game theory, assuming that each player is in a zero-sum game against the others and that each one aims to form a coalition with one of the others that will maximize its gains (conceived as the resources acquired from the cornered player divided up among the members of the winning coalition).[46] James Morrow thus stresses that "coalitions are central to any *n*-person game," and, according to T. Clifton Morgan, "much of coalition analysis centers on the free-for-all competition for membership in a decisive coalition."[47] These basic assumptions limit the insight into pivotal deterrence that can be gleaned from formal models that use them. Such models may detract from our understanding by turning a *strategy* into a preference over an outcome. Coalitions are often better seen as means not ends: they reflect *one* strategy that states may use to achieve their goals, and their goals may vary depending on their preferences and their beliefs about the preferences of others.[48] Pivotal deterrence is a strategy for preventing war and maintaining the status quo between others: In choosing that strategy, the pivot does not try to gain territory or resources at the expense of the others, and it explicitly tries to avoid firm alignment with either side.

Powell's formal model of alignment in a triad is a partial exception to this line of criticism because it embraces the possibility that a third party may benefit from "waiting" (i.e., remain neutral or abandon an ally) when one of the other two players goes to war with the second.[49] But even here, Powell assumes that the third party's decision whether to align with one side or to "wait" once a war breaks out will be determined by which option promises to maximize its benefits when the war ends and one side is eliminated (as must happen in the context of the model) and the victim's territory is portioned out to the remaining two players. The goals motivating pivotal deterrence are very different from those attributed to the bystander in Powell's model. Unlike his "waiting" state, a pivotal deterrer does not avoid alignment in order to maximize the territory that it will gain or retain in the wake of war between the other two. It avoids alignment in order to prevent war between the adversaries in the first place, to preserve the status quo or at least ensure that it is changed peacefully. In sum, by often limiting actor strategies to forming coalitions, and by positing that their only—and common—aim is to gain at the expense of others, the austere assumptions of most formal work on alignment in triads tend to exclude the strategic interaction we are most interested in here.[50]

Still, a less formal game-theoretical work is quite revealing for our purposes. Namely, Lowell Dittmer's study of strategic triangles.[51] Like many China specialists, he focused on the U.S.-China-Soviet triangle. But Dittmer's work was unique in that it developed a typology of *different* strategic triangles: (1) a "ménage à trois", (2) a "Stable Marriage", and (3) a "Romantic Triangle." The first two need little discussion. A pattern of three-way cooperation, the ménage à trois will "preserve the balance and provide incentives to all three for continued cooperation at low costs." The second, a stable marriage, is a consistent system of "symmetrical amity between two players and enmity between these two and a third." There is a close affinity here among a stable marriage, a two-against-one coalition, and the basic logic of extended deterrence. So we turn then to Dittmer's third strategic triangle—the "romantic triangle."

In a romantic triangle one player (the pivot) seeks to maintain "amity with [the] two other players [while] they have an enmity with each other." Here "each of the 'wing' players [adversaries] is placed in a position of considerable uncertainty: unable to form an amity with the rival . . . and dependent exclusively on amity with the pivot . . ."[52] Dittmer's romantic triangle evokes key features of pivotal deterrence. First, the adversaries view each other as greater threats than the pivot. Second, the adversaries' are met with *uncertainty* about the pivot's allegiance, which is a source of its power over them. Third, the adversaries are "dependent exclusively on amity with the pivot." An important insight comes from relaxing this last assumption. When the adversaries need not exclusively depend on the pivot's friendship, the pivot's leverage over them is greatly diminished.

Which leads us to another important effort to model two-way deterrence dynamics, Glenn Snyder's seminal work on the "composite security dilemma" (CSD).[53] The CSD captures the interlocking dilemmas that grip a state that seeks to restrain both its ally and its adversary. A state trying to restrain both its ally and its adversary will have to parlay a combustible mix of threats and inducements to both sides. Buttressing an ally with commitments that are too firm may provoke a defensive reaction from the adversary and embolden the ally to run risks. Restraining an ally with the threat to abandon it may invite depredations from the adversary or even cause the ally to bolt to his side.[54]

Snyder's "straddle strategy" is an attempt to balance the cross-pressures of the CSD.[55] Here the statesman straddles between his ally and adversary: he tries to restrain the ally by threatening to abandon her, and to deter the enemy by threatening to oppose him. This approach to the CSD dovetails with—and is the namesake for—the third scenario of pivotal deterrence described earlier. The deductive logic that Snyder uses to get there is different than mine.[56] But the end point is the same. The weakness in Snyder's formulation of the straddle strategy is that it unnecessarily posits two different games: an "alliance game" between the pivot and one side, and an "adversarial" game between the pivot and the other side. But pivotal deterrence often involves avoiding alliances with the adversaries, or, similarly, maintaining alliances with both of them at the same time despite their antagonism. In these cases it becomes very hard to make heads or tails of the situation. With whom is the pivot playing the alliance game, and with whom is he playing the adversary game? Still, what makes Snyder's CSD so useful for understanding the dynamics of third-party deterrence is that it includes healthy doses of ambiguity, uncertainty, and "moral hazard," which I will say more about below.

Finally, on the subject of strategic triangles, we should turn to Robert Jervis' discussion of the role of the pivot in international relations. "In some triangles," he writes, a "state is able to gain a pivotal position [when it has] the ability to align with either of the other two who lack this flexibility."[57] Henry Kissinger marshaled this logic in crafting U.S. diplomacy toward China and the Soviet Union during the Nixon administration: "Our relationships . . . should be such . . . that our options toward both of them are always greater than their options toward each other . . . The hostility between China and the Soviet Union served our purposes best if we maintained closer relations with each side than they did with each other."[58] Count Andrássy, Austria-Hungary's foreign minister in the 1870s, used similar terms to describe his country's best strategy within the Three Emperors League of Austria, Russia, and Germany: "we must first of all strive to occupy the middle of the triangle which the three imperial powers formed in their alliance, so that neither of the other allies could stand nearer to each other than to us."[59]

The key point here is that—besides material capabilities—a source of the pivot's flexibility and leverage over the others is the rivalry between them. As Jervis puts it: "what is important is the relative conflict of interests and antagonism among the states . . . a state that has sharp conflicts with the two others may still be [a pivot] if the other two are divided by differences even less bridgeable."[60] This adds an important qualification to the romantic triangle model, where the pivot has "amity" with the adversaries and they have "enmity" with each other. We need not assume that amity with the adversaries is necessary for pivotal deterrence to work. In the Civil War, Abraham Lincoln understood this intuitively when he advised a general who was trying to suppress both rebels and abolitionist militias in Missouri, "if both factions, or neither, shall abuse you, you will probably be about right. Beware of being assailed by one, and praised by the other."[61] Nor must we assume that the pivot does not perceive them to be threats; it is only necessary that neither one is so threatening that the pivot must firmly close ranks with the other. Finally, there is no need to assume the adversaries are unremittingly hostile toward each other. They may even in some respects share common security goals. It is only necessary that there is less amity in their relations with each other than in their relations with the pivot. An obvious instance of this appears in the case of "intra-alliance" pivotal deterrence, such as that between the United States and Greece and Turkey, all NATO allies.[62]

Jervis also notes that "states that have freedom of action can use it to generate or at least reward moderation [in others]."[63] This point is important for two reasons. First, it goes back to our earlier reservations about the concept of "holding the balance." Some pivotal policies are designed to incite fighting among adversaries; others are designed to inhibit it. If we do not distinguish between such policies, we will not grasp a great deal about when and how pivotal deterrence works. Second, Jervis's observation about the pivot's ability to "generate" and "reward" moderation alludes to a key causal mechanism of pivotal deterrence theory, one that allows the pivot to draw concessions from the adversaries that may keep the peace between them. I will discuss this mechanism fully in the next section.

Finally, Jervis affirms the basic insight that "states gain and lose bargaining leverage . . . in rough proportion to the alternatives available to them . . . power is a function not only of the relative strengths of the actors and the relationships between them, but also of the existing and possible relations between each of them and third parties."[64] This takes us directly to the matter of alignment options. Much of the pivot's leverage stems from the adversaries' need for its support (or at least their need for it *not* to support the other side).[65] As the adversaries' dependence decreases—that is, as their alignment options improve—so too will decrease the pivot's leverage, and the deterrent effect of their concerns about what it will do if they go to war.

THEORY OF PIVOTAL DETERRENCE

How does pivotal deterrence work? How can what we have described as a pivotal deterrence policy cause peace between adversaries who would otherwise go to war. In this section I will answer those questions in two ways. First, I will draw out the peace-causing mechanisms of pivotal deterrence theory. Next, I will discuss the assumptions about the actors that underpin and drive the theory. Finally, to illustrate the relationship between the actor assumptions and the causal mechanisms, I will draw some parallels between pivotal deterrence theory and the way insurance markets work.

Struggle to Avoid Isolation

Our theory rests on a bedrock assumption: "every decision to wage war is influenced by predictions of how outside nations will affect the course of the war."[66] In international politics truly isolated enemy "dyads" are very rare, and in the diplomatic jostling that usually leads up to war (or its avoidance), adversaries often take positions that are crafted more to "impact on third parties" than to directly influence their enemy.[67] If a bystander can significantly affect the outcome of a war, the adversaries should pay close attention to whether it is likely to intervene and if so, on whose behalf or to whose benefit, when they choose between war and peace. From their concern about the pivot's attitude—and the jockeying for position that results—springs the causal logic of pivotal deterrence.

When rivals square off before a bystander who can decide who wins, and they are uncertain about what it will do if they go to war, the logic of "isolation avoidance" will loom large in their decision making.[68] At bottom, this struggle between the adversaries to avoid isolation is the catalyst of pivotal deterrence. As Saul Bellow's Augie March once lamented, "while any wish lives, it lives in the face of its negative."[69] Pivotal deterrence capitalizes on this essential truth, playing on the adversaries' hopes and fears—their desire for support, their dread of isolation—in order to make them more cautious and willing to compromise.

Inducing Caution: The Uncertainty Effect

Let us call the first peace-causing mechanism the "uncertainty effect." I distilled the workings of the uncertainty effect in the three pivotal deterrence scenarios at the beginning of this chapter. Thus, the uncertainty effect of the Fair-Weather Friend scenario is brought out by Samuel Huntington: "if . . . the support of a third party is essential to the victory of either of two [adversaries], neither side is likely to risk war until it is assured of the support."[70] Likewise for the Janus-Faced Foe strategy: when each side will lose if the pivot supports their enemy, both adversaries should avoid war as long as they are uncertain about whether the pivot will oppose them. There is a similar dimension to the Straddle Strategy scenario. If one adversary believes that he needs the pivot's support to achieve victory, but the other believes that the pivot's neutrality is sufficient to ensure hers, then he should not risk war unless he knows the pivot will support him, and she should not risk war unless she knows the pivot will remain neutral. In each of these scenarios, the peace-causing logic of the uncertainty effect is straightforward—uncertainty induces caution. By leaving open the possibility that it will choose a course of action that will mean their defeat—whether it be to oppose them or to remain neutral—the pivot may deter the adversaries from stepping off the brink into war.

Producing Concessions: The Ingratiation Effect

When the pivot's position is in doubt, both adversaries should not only be cautious about *starting* a war but also should worry about doing things short of war that might alienate the pivot and drive it into their adversary's camp. For example, to defend London's ambiguous policy during the Balkans crisis of 1912, a British diplomat used this logic with his Russian interlocutors: "the fact that we were only a friend who might be turned into [Russia's] ally should Germany and Austria force a war on Russia made [Germany and Austria] much more ready to listen to us."[71] The pressure to avoid isolation should also lead the adversaries to make concessions in order to attract the pivot's support. This is the "ingratiation effect" of pivotal deterrence.[72] With the pivot hovering between them, both sides should engage in this kind of ingratiating behavior, and the result may be a "virtuous"—if also incremental—competition in concessions. A pivot that wants to prevent war and impel a settlement may demand that those concessions be paid in the coin of moderation and compromise toward the other adversary. In 1963, U.S. Secretary of State Dean Rusk used this logic to describe his attempt to orchestrate a Kashmir settlement between India and Pakistan:

[Our] tactics should be to offer friendly off-stage encouragement [to India and Pakistan] that they *out-vie each other in forthcomingness.* We should clearly indicate on both sides that [the] outcome [of Kashmir talks] will have a genuine impact on U.S. [support]. Hence, both parties have a vested interest in demonstrating a disposition to compromise.[73]

These, then, are two peace-causing mechanisms of pivotal deterrence theory. Because the adversaries are uncertain about what the pivot will do if they go to war, and because what the pivot will do may determine the outcome, they will work hard to avoid isolation when tensions rise. Thus, they will be cautious, avoiding provocations that are likely to alienate the pivot. And they will be solicitous, trying to woo the pivot's allegiance (or neutrality) with concessions. The trick for the pivot is to extract concessions from the adversaries that narrow the differences between them.

[21]

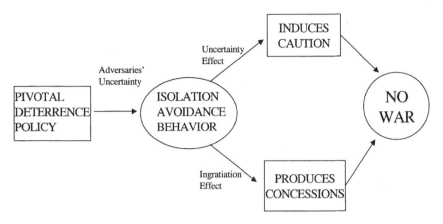

Figure 1. The Casual Logic of Pivotal Deterrence Theory

What Drives the Theory: Moral Hazard, Uncertainty, and Risk Aversion

Consistent with the basic principles of deterrence, our theory assumes unitary actors who are in a "thin" sense rational. In other words, actors who "when faced with several courses of action . . . will usually do what they believe is likely to have the best overall outcome."[74] An important qualification, however, is that they are "risk-averse." They will shy away from decisions that risk a wide variance of outcomes in favor of ones that may promise fewer potential benefits but also fewer potential losses. When confronted with a choice between two alternatives, $50 for sure, and a lottery with a 50 percent chance of getting either $100 dollars or nothing, risk averters will take the $50.[75]

To better understand how this assumption drives the dynamics of pivotal deterrence, it is helpful to draw an analogy to insurance markets and two pathologies of them, moral hazard and adverse selection. Insurance allows firms (households, people) to engage in risky but potentially profitable activities that, in the absence of insurance, they would not undertake. The insurer has more cushion and resources for managing risk and takes on some of the exposure of those who are less risk-tolerant, for a price (i.e., a premium). Insurers, however, do not want to encourage their customers to become too risky, or to sell insurance to customers who are already especially risk-prone. They could not stay in business if they did. These are the problems of "adverse selection" and "moral hazard." *Adverse selection* arises when the insurance for sale *attracts* customers who intend to take very high risks, and who want the insurer to absorb the downside costs of their behavior while they reap the profits. *Moral hazard* arises when insurance encourages those who have it to behave more recklessly than they would without insurance. For example, the moral hazard of a property insurance policy that promises to pay back "more than the value of the premises" is that it may become "an inducement to arson or at least to carelessness."[76] For these reasons, insurers will not sell to some classes of high-risk customers, and there are some markets so inherently risky—and the likelihood of adverse selection so high—that insurance is simply not available.

Pivotal deterrers act like insurers do in markets where adverse selection and moral hazard prevail: They do not sell. There are two dimensions to this. First, the pivot wants to keep the peace between the adversaries, but believes they both are aggressive. Second, the adversaries threaten each other more than the pivot threatens them, and therefore they try to align with it. Therein lie the problems of moral hazard and adverse selection. Both adversaries want to ally with the pivot, so it will absorb some of the risk associated with their aggressive goals. But if the pivot firmly aligns with either side—that is, insures them—it will embolden them to pursue policies contrary to its interests.[77]

In this sense, Dean Rusk justified to President Johnson the need for hedging U.S. commitments to India and Pakistan: "we could never fully support the policy goals of either India or Pakistan. The best protection of American interests rests in maintaining adequate, though probably not intimate, links with both."[78] This unwillingness to "fully support" (and thereby encourage) the ambitions of the adversaries is a central reason why a pivot will avoid firmly aligning with either side as long as it can, in the hope of restraining both.

Again, the key assumption here is that the adversaries will recoil from big risks, from choices that pose a "wide variance" of potential outcomes, including very bad ones. They would both choose war if there was a good chance of victory and no chance of catastrophic defeat, prospects that a firm alliance with the pivot could provide. But they will avoid war if there is a plausible chance that doing so will cause the pivot to oppose them or leave them in the lurch, and thus make a galling defeat likely. This type of risk-averse reasoning lies at the heart of the theory of pivotal deterrence. Thus, the moral hazard logic driving pivotal deterrence theory expects that those who wish to engage in behavior contrary to the pivot's interests will be more likely to do so if the pivot insures them against the risks of that behavior and will be less likely to do so if the pivot does not.

Finally, as we will see in the next chapter, the moral hazard logic of pivotal deterrence dovetails with the hypothesis that pivotal deterrence is more likely to fail when the adversaries have alignment options. Alignment options reduce the adversaries dependence on the pivot, giving them other avenues for shifting risks. Thus, alignment options stymie the ingratiation incentive of pivotal deterrence and diminish the risks to the adversaries of acting without the pivot's support.

[23]

This chapter presented the conceptual groundwork and the rudimentary theory for our study. We defined the concept of pivotal deterrence and introduced three models to describe the various permutations of it. Then we reviewed the literature that informs the concept of pivotal deterrence and sheds light on its essential characteristics. Finally, we presented the theory *of* pivotal deterrence, which explains how states that pursue such a policy may cause peace between states that might otherwise go to war. After describing the two basic peace-causing mechanisms in this theory, we reviewed the underlying assumptions about the actors that are required to make the theory work. Finally, we drew a parallel between the operation of insurance markets and pivotal deterrence in order to illustrate how the assumption about actors' risk propensity underpins the explanation. Now, before we begin to test this theory, we need to resolve a more focused set of questions: What are the *necessary* conditions for pivotal deterrence to be attempted? What conditions make it *more likely* to be attempted? What conditions make it more likely to succeed? The next chapter introduces answers to these three questions.

[2]

Power, Interests, and Alignment Options:

FRAMING THE INQUIRY

Any theory or model or paradigm propounding that there are only two possibilities—disaster or one particular road to salvation—should be *prima facie* suspect. After all, there *is*, at least temporarily, such a place as purgatory!
Albert O. Hirschman, *World Politics*, April 1970

WHEN IS PIVOTAL DETERRENCE POSSIBLE?

Pivotal deterrence policies go against the grain of "strong and widespread" pressures toward consistency in alignment in the international system.[1] For this reason, systemic realism, which focuses on the structural pressures that impel conformity in state behavior, has little to say directly about the origins of pivotal deterrence. Still, useful clues about when, and why, a state will adopt a policy of pivotal deterrence can be inferred from the sort of systemic realism that is sensitive to differences in actor preferences. What follows, therefore, is a tightly focused application of insights from systemic realist theories that explain how states' relative capabilities, their perceptions of threat, and their preferences for the status quo or revision combine to determine their alignment choices.[2] These theories help us to grasp when pivotal deterrence will be *attempted* by clarifying the conditions in international politics that normally call forth *different* strategies.

As Stephen Walt reminded us, states do more than balance against other powerful states, they balance against threatening states.[3] Threat assessments involve perceptions of both an actor's intentions and its ability to carry them out. By this logic then, a pivotal deterrence policy can only occur if the adversaries view each other as more threatening than the pivot (otherwise the adversaries would join together and balance against the pivot). When such conditions hold in a triad, "balance-of-threat" theory also tells us that the adversaries will each try to lure the pivot into an alliance against the other. Their desire to do so is a source of the pivot's leverage over them.

Although the leverage that comes from flexibility is an important reason why states try to maintain it, Randall Schweller's work on alliances suggests an additional reason why a pivot may want to avoid alignment with either side. Schweller argues that alignment choices are strongly determined by whether or not states and their potential partners support the status quo or want to change it.[4] Status quo states will flock together, while revisionist states will bandwagon with other revisionists. This linkage between state preferences and macro alliance patterns in the international system is suggestive: It points to three conditions that would seem to be necessary for pivotal deterrence to be attempted at the micro level of the triad.

First, the pivot must prefer the status quo between the adversaries or that they change it peacefully. Second, the pivot must believe that the adversaries are "reciprocal revisionists"—that each seeks gains at the other's expense and will use force to achieve them if conditions permit. Third, each adversary must believe that the other is aggressive and inclined to use force against it, and that the pivot is less menacing in this respect. In short, the adversaries must perceive each other to be more threatening than the pivot.[5]

Behind all of this is a basic thesis: Power relations are not synonymous, nor must they co-vary, with perceptions of threat. Rarely can we predict alignment patterns among states simply by looking at their relative power positions. One very important implication is this: If we hold the distribution of power constant across triads, status quo pivots will act differently than revisionist pivots. Conversely, pivots with the same preferences, but with different degrees of relative power, will in many circumstances act similarly. To expand on this point more concretely, let us examine some triads with varying distributions of power and preferences.

Start with a simple triad in which only the actors' preferences are known. Assume first that the pivot prefers the status quo. If the pivot believes that the other parties both prefer the status quo but are in a fearful spiral, it will adopt a policy of pivotal assurance, promising to defend both. In this instance, the pivot tries to create a condition of defense dominance in the triad, which will mute the risk of a war caused by misperceived intentions among the other status quo powers. This strategy would appear in the sort of strategic triangle called a *ménage à trois* by Dittmer, where all three parties seek cooperation with the others. A similar logic is invoked by those who described the U.S. role in NATO as a "security blanket" that allows its Western European partners to cooperate more easily.[6]

If the pivot believes that just one of the two adversaries prefers the status quo, then the pivot should form an alliance with that state and pursue extended deterrence against the other (the revisionist). This is why, logically, *for a policy of pivotal deterrence to be attempted, it is necessary that the pivot believe both sides are revisionist.* For if the pivot does not believe this, it should firmly align with the side it thinks supports the status quo.

Finally, if we assume the pivot is a revisionist, then regardless of the others' preferences, its policy should be one of "divide and conquer," not pivotal deterrence. Divide and conquer strategies include an offensive alliance with another revisionist in the triad, at the expense of the status quo state (e.g., the Nazi-Soviet "Non-Aggression" Pact); or, if both are status quo states, a "wedge" strategy that inhibits them from forming a balancing coalition or encourages buck-passing, so that they can be picked off sequentially; or, if all three are revisionists, a strategy of inciting war between the other two in order to reap the spoils.[7] The arguments are summarized in Table 1.

Now fix the preferences in the triad: assume that the pivot prefers the status quo between the adversaries, while they do not. What pivot strategies follow from different patterns of relative power? First, if the pivot is much weaker than the others, it should not attempt pivotal deterrence, the logic of self-preservation dictating a more prudent lower profile policy, what Paul Schroeder calls "hiding" and Schweller "distancing."[8] If the "puny" pivot is so weak that it will not significantly increase one side's prospects for victory by joining it, then it is also too weak to hope for protection from either side. Neither adversary will be likely to defend it if failing to do so will not jeopardize their prospects against each other. Thus, to pursue a policy of pivotal deterrence a state must be at least powerful enough to significantly influence the outcome of a war between the adversaries.[9]

Second, in a triad where power is distributed about equally, we would expect to find the pivot pursuing pivotal deterrence. Third, in a triad where one revisionist is roughly the pivot's equal, and the other is much weaker, the pivot may try extended deterrence, or it may do nothing, depending on its stakes in the weaker side's survival. If the strong revisionist will be better able to threaten the pivot after conquering the weak one, then the survival motive should override the pivot's inhibition against aligning with and emboldening a revisionist. Here the pivot should side firmly with the weaker revisionist in order to deter the stronger from attacking it.

Fourth, and finally, is a triad in which the status quo pivot dominates the combined capabilities of the revisionists. When "offensive" realists see a preponderant state, they tend to assume that it will, as Martin Wight put it, "take part in the rivalries of small powers, simultaneously encouraging and controlling them, on the principle of 'divide and rule.' "[10] But divide and rule does not ineluctably follow from preponderant power or, for that mat-

Table 1. Pivot's Preferences and Perceptions of Adversaries' Intentions

Pivot	Adversary 1	Adversary 2	Pivot Strategy
Status Quo	Status Quo	Status Quo	Pivotal Assurance
Status Quo	Status Quo	Revisionist	Extended Deterrence with Adversary 1
Revisionist	Status Quo	Status Quo	Divide and Conquer (wedge)
Revisionist	Revisionist	Status Quo	Divide and Conquer (offensive)
Revisionist	Revisionist	Revisionist	Divide and Conquer (incitement)

ter, from the theory of "offensive realism." Though a policy of divide and rule is not incompatible with preponderance, neither is it determined by the structure of the situation or by the logic of self-preservation. And even an offensive realist must concede that states that stir up conflict and seek conquest in one part of the world may work to promote peace elsewhere, if only to stabilize their flanks and better concentrate their expansionist energies. In short, even preponderant power, as William T. R. Fox observed, "can be used to protect as well as to enslave."[11] Thus, the preponderance scenario central to this study arises when a dominant pivot seeks to preserve the status quo or promote peaceful change among weaker states that wish to aggress against each other. Here, the presence of conflict among the weak states is not *the consequence* of the preponderant power's machinations, but instead, the reason for it adopting a policy of pivotal deterrence. These arguments are summarized in Table 2.

In sum, I have deduced four necessary conditions for pivotal deterrence to be attempted. They are:

1. The pivot must possess power at least roughly equal to the adversaries.
2. The pivot must prefer the status quo between the adversaries or that any change to the status quo is made peacefully.
3. The pivot must believe that both adversaries hold revisionist aims toward each other and that they will risk war to achieve those aims if they are assured of its support or acquiescence.
4. The adversaries must perceive each other to be more threatening than the pivot.

Power, Interests, and Pivotal Deterrence Outcomes

There is an old debate among deterrence theorists over which is more important—capabilities or interests—but most agree that together the balance

Table 2. Preferences Fixed, Relative Power Varies

Status Quo Pivot	Revisionist 1	Revisionist 2	Pivot Strategy
1	3	3	Hiding
3	3	3	Pivotal Deterrence
3	1	3	Extended Deterrence with Revisionist 1
3	1	1	Pivotal Deterrence

of capabilities and interests is the most important determinant of deterrence outcomes.[12] We should start, therefore, with such matters if we want to know when and explain why pivotal deterrence is likely to succeed or fail. For if we do not control for the effects of relative power and interest, we cannot properly assess the influence of alignment options on outcomes. Let us begin then with this question: When will the balance of power and interest alone be likely to determine the outcome of pivotal deterrence?

A simple typology provides an answer to that question. In the typology, power and interest are represented by two variables: (A) the distribution of capabilities among the pivot and the adversaries; and (B) the intensity of the pivot's interests at stake in the potential conflict. The typology shows (1) when pivotal deterrence is likely to be determined by the balance of power and interests; (2) when it is not; and, consequently, (3) when it *is more likely* to be attempted. The hypotheses associated with these variables are described below.

Relative Power and Pivotal Deterrence

The cornerstone of deterrence theory is a simple proposition: The more the balance of military power favors the deterrer, the more likely deterrence will succeed.[13] Thus, *ceteris paribus,* pivotal deterrence is more likely to succeed the more the military balance favors the pivot over the adversaries. In the section above we deduced that a necessary condition for pivotal deterrence is that the pivot be at least a peer to if not preponderant over the adversaries. This deduction allows us to narrow the range of possible power configurations in a triad to those that are most relevant to this study. All pivotal deterrence pivots will fall somewhere between rough equality—"peerdom" if you will—and preponderance. Below we will give a bit more precision to the concepts of a peer and a preponderant pivot, the two ends of a continuous variable measuring the pivot's relative military power in our typology.

Definition of a Peer Pivot

A peer pivot is roughly equal to the adversaries in terms of military power. It is strong enough so that by joining one side, it can significantly influence the outcome of a war between them, but not so strong that it could dominate both sides if they combined. In a peer-pivot triad, *none* of the actors will be so powerful that it can overwhelm the other two in combination—that is what is meant by "roughly equal." If it is to significantly influence the outcome of the war, the peer pivot must intervene *in time* and *in concert* with one side in order to defeat the other. The peer's leverage may evaporate if it does not have the capability to join the fight before the outcome is decided.

Definition of a Preponderant Pivot

A preponderant pivot, on the other hand, can outmatch the adversaries, even if they combine. The preponderant pivot, therefore, does not need to join with one side in order to defeat the other. Even if one adversary conquered the other and fully absorbed its capabilities, the victor would still be weaker than the preponderant pivot.

THE BASIC POWER HYPOTHESIS
Ceteris paribus, the more preponderant a pivot, the more likely it is to succeed; the closer to peerdom a pivot, the more likely it is to fail.

Interest Intensity and Pivotal Deterrence

But superior capabilities do not always determine the outcome of deterrence. Context matters. Often what will determine the credibility of a threat is the target's beliefs about the interests motivating it.[14] As George Washington put it, "No nation is to be trusted farther than it is bound by its interest."[15] Although in policy debates and even scholarship, the concept of national interests is imprecise and much abused, we are not, as Bernard Brodie put it, "talking about mere gossamer . . . some interests will be vital beyond any shadow of doubt" and some will not.[16] Rough and reasonable measures of the intensity of a state's interests are not hard to come by. If we start with the basic assumption that states (even aggressive ones) at a minimum seek survival, or as Nicholas Spykman put it, the "preservation of territorial integrity and political independence," we can make some generalizations about the conditions under which they are more likely to find their survival threatened.[17] And it is fair to say that states do assess the intensity of each other's interests in this way, even if this is not the only way they do.[18]

Accordingly, we can construct a continuous variable representing a pivot's interests at stake in a policy of pivotal deterrence, with vital interests at one end and secondary interests at the other. No doubt, in many other contexts, such blunt conceptualizations will do more to obfuscate than clarify issues. But here they are useful. They allow us to easily grasp when adversaries will be more or less attentive to the pivot's attitude, and thus, when pivotal deterrence is more or less likely to succeed. Let us define vital and secondary interests more concisely.

Definition of Vital Interests

The pivot's most vital interests involve its self-preservation, political independence, and, by extension, "defense of strategically vital areas." In other words, vital interests may not only involve the immediate political and territorial integrity of the state but also extend to contiguous or otherwise critical territory. When does contiguous (or otherwise critical) territory count as a vital interest? This is a crucial question. If we are not careful about how we answer it, the concept of vital interest can be emptied of meaning. In this study, contiguous (or otherwise critical) territory will involve a pivot's vital interest if and only if "[a] major threat to [its] own territorial integrity might materialize through [those] lands."[19] This is a fairly conservative definition of vital interests. I adopt it for two reasons. First, self-preservation provides a fairly powerful benchmark for inferring the intensity of a state's interest, provided we keep the concept limited.[20] Second and closely related, it is in situations involving their self-preservation, narrowly defined, that states are more likely to assess the intensity of each other's interests similarly.

Definition of Secondary Interests

If one adopts a conservative definition of vital interests, as I have above, then what counts as secondary interests at the other end of the spectrum will vary greatly. They may range from very important interests, such as maintaining trade routes, the safety of your allies, and even national "prestige," to much more ephemeral ones, such as having your team win the World Cup in soccer. Where these goals rank vis-à-vis *each other* in the hierarchy of a state's interests and, as importantly, where others will think they rank, is something we cannot derive from our rudimentary assumptions. But we can say that they should rank lower, and be perceived by others to rank lower, than interests pertaining directly to national self-preservation. For our purposes that is good enough.

Pivotal deterrence in areas of secondary interest to the pivot will be less likely to succeed than in areas of vital interest. Whereas secondary interests are at stake for the pivot in these contexts, vital interests remain at issue between the adversaries.[21] Thus, pivotal deterrence in areas of secondary interests will always put the pivot at the weak end of a "motivational asymmetry" vis-à-vis the adversaries.

THE BASIC INTEREST HYPOTHESIS
A pivotal deterrence policy will be more likely to succeed the more intensely it is motivated by the pivot's vital interests.

When Will Power and Interests Determine Pivotal Deterrence Outcomes?

Figure 2 arranges the foregoing arguments in a typology. On the horizontal axis is the variable measuring the pivot's relative power (i.e., power). On the vertical axis is the variable measuring the intensity of the pivot's interests at stake.[22]

This typology shows, first of all, when pivotal deterrence outcomes are likely to be overdetermined by the combination of power and interests. This category includes cases in which a peer pivot has secondary interests at stake and failure is overdetermined (A) and cases in which a preponderant pivot has vital interests at stake and success is overdetermined (D). Conversely, the typology also captures situations in which the effect of the balance of power and interests on pivotal deterrence is indeterminant (cells B, C).

When Are Pivotal Deterrence Policies More Likely to Occur?

The conditions of overdetermination will exert a selection bias on the types of pivotal deterrence crises that occur.[23] When the combination of power and interests "loads the dice" in favor of an outcome, we should see few instance of overt pivotal deterrence. Where power and interest both favor success, we should not find *immediate* pivotal deterrence attempted often because those conditions will shape the expectations of others and suppress crises in the first place. In other words, cases of *immediate* pivotal deterrence will be rare because *general* pivotal deterrence will usually work. On the other hand, where power and interests both point toward failure, we should not find pivotal deterrence attempted often because the pivot anticipates that it will fail. Figure 3 represents this frequency distribution.

The typology—and the selection effect it captures—relays crucial information about how to proceed with our analysis.[24] It tells us what types of pivotal deterrence are most likely to occur and most need explaining. It suggests that the vast majority of pivotal deterrence cases will cluster around and between (B) and (C). Therefore, we will get the most analytical mileage from testing our theory and hypotheses in cases that fit the basic characteristics of those two contingencies, which I refer to as "Type I" and "Type II" pivotal deterrence. Type I cases involve a peer pivot with vital in-

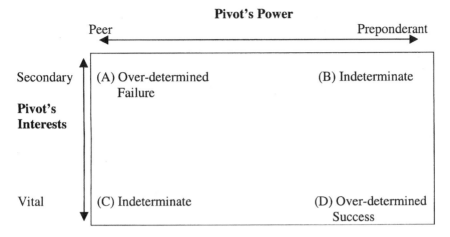

Figure 2. Typology: Pivot's Power and Interests and Expected Outcomes

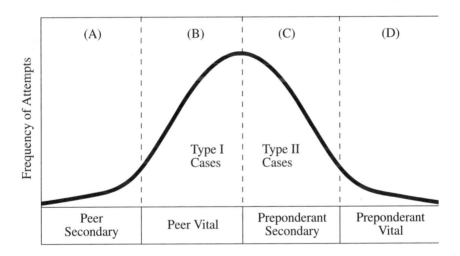

Figure 3. Expected Frequency of Pivotal Deterrence Attempts

terests at stake. Type II cases involve a preponderant pivot with secondary interests at stake.

The typology helps to control for alternative explanations, but it does not predict the outcomes of Type I and Type II cases. In each, the predictions of power and interests hypotheses cut against each other, and because they do, we cannot infer from their conjunction which Type I and Type II cases are likely to succeed and which to fail. However, because power and interests cut against each other differently in Type I and Type II cases, they should give rise to predictably different dilemmas and dynamics of interaction within each Type. Thus, we can deduce a few expectations about the behavioral patterns likely to appear in the two Types of cases. Although these deductions do not tell us when pivotal deterrence in Type I and Type II cases will succeed or fail, they do tell us *how* it is likely to fail, and *how* it is likely to succeed, in the different cases. They tell us both what we should expect to see and what we *should not* expect to see when pivotal deterrence succeeds or fails in the two Types of cases. Thus, they give us a way to test both positively and negatively the strength of the explanations.

Type I Cases: Peer Pivots with Vital Interests at Stake

With vital interests at stake, the credibility problem for the peer is less likely to be one of intentions or resolve than of military effectiveness. The adversaries are likely to believe that the pivot will be vitally interested if war breaks out between them. But they may doubt its ability to defend those interests militarily. The margin for error is much smaller for a peer pivot than for a preponderant pivot. If the pivot delays too long and fails to prevent one side from defeating the other, it may be faced with a fait accompli that it cannot undo and forced to contend with a much more powerful adversary than before. Thus, the peer pivot's relative weakness in the overall balance of power puts a high premium on its position vis-à-vis the adversaries in terms of *relative military capabilities*. Specifically, I mean here its forces "in being" and the military missions they can perform directly in relation to the adversaries.[25] Two things will condition the pivotal deterrence effect of a peer's military capabilities: the need to commit them *in time* and *in concert* with one side if they are to be decisive. The more capable the pivot is of engaging its forces promptly and effectively, before one side defeats the other, the more attentive to its position the adversaries should be.

But this raises a key dilemma for the peer pivot. To maintain the adversaries' uncertainty about its probable alignment, it must forgo the boost in military capabilities that comes from closely coordinating doctrine and operations with one side. This in turn reduces the certainty with which the pivot can threaten to defeat or derail the adversaries. Prewar planning among allies is a "force-multiplier"—it creates a situation in which the whole is greater than the sum of the parts. Since pivots cannot do these things the way firm allies do, their capabilities will be less threatening, and therefore deter less effectively, than they would otherwise.

The crucial problem facing a peer pivot in Type I cases, therefore, is how to maintain military effectiveness vis-à-vis the adversaries without altogether diluting their uncertainty about its alignment. Two principles are at work in the solution to this dilemma. First, the peer pivot's forces must be invulnerable or difficult to pin down in a surprise attack. As long as they are, neither of the adversaries can, with any confidence, count on eliminating them before they begin an attack against each other. Second, the pivot's forces must be mobile and capable of promptly engaging the adversaries beyond the pivot's borders. In other words, they must be offensive.

This reveals a kink in the conventional wisdom of offense-defense theory—that offensive forces are destabilizing—by showing that a status quo power must have offensive forces to maintain stability between aggressive states or, for that matter, to dampen the security dilemma between status quo adversaries who fear each other.[26] In order to succeed at pivotal deterrence, the peer pivot must be capable (or perceived to be capable) of joining the fight early enough to prevent the adversaries from achieving a decisive victory and thereby amassing a tremendous military advantage. These points suggest that when peer-pivotal deterrence fails, a part of the story will be the adversaries' doubts about whether the pivot's military capabilities can be brought to bear soon enough, or to a location critical enough, to determine the outcome of the war. In a failed case of Type I pivotal deterrence, we should not expect to find that the adversaries believed the pivot's military capabilities could be brought to bear quickly and forcefully enough to determine the outcome. And in a successful case of Type I pivotal deterrence, we should not expect to find that the adversaries doubted the pivot's military capabilities in this regard.

When Type I pivotal deterrence succeeds we should also see some other salient patterns. If the adversaries do not doubt the pivot's military capacity, then they should both try explicitly to secure the pivot's support—or at least its acquiescence—in the event of war, which will put the peer pivot in a strong bargaining position. We also know that by denying the adversaries such assurances in a crisis, the peer pivot can dampen their willingness to fight, especially if they *initially expected* to receive the pivot's support when the crisis began. So when Type I pivotal deterrence succeeds, we would expect to find that adversaries tried hard to secure the pivot's support or neutrality in a war between them. Although we might also find this sort of behavior in a failed case of Type I pivotal deterrence, we would be very surprised if we *did not* find this pattern of behavior in a successful case. In other words, it will be necessary but not sufficient.

Type II Cases: Preponderant Pivots with Secondary Interests

Without vital interests at stake, the preponderant pivot's great strength is also a source of weakness. Because the adversaries, even in combination, do not have enough capabilities to menace the preponderant pivot, it will have difficulty convincing them of its motivation to prevent war. For even if one side quickly conquered the other, the victor still could not overpower the preponderant pivot. That is why we cannot assume that the preponderant pivot in a Type II case will be more likely to succeed than a peer pivot will in a Type I case.In spite of its much superior capabilities, the preponderant pivot may be in a weaker political position than the peer to keep the adversaries apart. In a Type II case the adversaries are likely to believe that the pivot's interests at stake are weak, and thus they will not greatly fear or expect its interference. Before the pivot can bring to bear the looming costs represented by it capabilities, and exploit the adversaries' concerns about its alignment, it must first remedy their low estimates of its interests at stake. This raises the fundamental dilemma for the preponderant pivot in a Type II crisis.

The most reliable way for it to signal a strong interest would be to choose a side and remove any uncertainty about its allegiance. Alliance commitments are the method par excellence for demonstrating and *creating* an interest in fighting over stakes that would otherwise be less than vital. Alliance commitments do not merely "reveal" existing interests, they create new ones, by incurring reputation costs, by "system effects" that turn your ally's enemies (and their friends) into your enemies, by creating security "asset-specificities" that cannot be easily replaced, and so on.[27] Thus, a preponderant power that wishes to sustain a policy of pivotal deterrence will have trouble sending the sorts of signals that are most useful for shaping other's beliefs about its interests at stake.

How then may a preponderant power in a Type II crisis signal to the adversaries that its interests are engaged, though not so much as to warrant a firm commitment to one side? Is pivotal deterrence impossible in these situations? It is not impossible; it is just much harder to do. Deterrence theory's banal prescription is that the pivot should make a "costly commitment" by making valuable assets (military or otherwise) hostage to the adversaries, and in that way diminish the attractiveness of doing nothing if they go to war. This is hard to do militarily without choosing sides.[28] One can think of examples in which it has been tried with apparent success (e.g.,

U.S. forces deployed in the Sinai between Israel and Egypt), but these often turn out to be instances more of pivotal assurance and confidence building, in the spirit of traditional United Nations (UN) peacekeeping, than of pivotal deterrence of two adversaries hell-bent on war.[29] So the direct deployment of the pivot's active military forces may figure less prominently in Type II pivotal deterrence, even though the pivot's military preponderance casts a long shadow over the bargaining context. Instead, the pivot may use its preponderance to transfer to both sides "security values"—military aid or political assurances—that do not commit it to fighting for one side if they both go to war.[30] These offsetting security values are not merely "costly signals." They do more than merely indicate that the pivot may have an interest in acting if the adversaries go to war. More important, they are levers. Once expectations of continuing support have been set, the pivot may threaten to withhold support from whomever does not cooperate.[31] Or, what is much the same, it may promise to increase support to whomever is more willing to compromise. When pivotal deterrence works in these Type II situations, we are likely to find that the adversaries wanted to get (or keep) what the pivot could give (or take away) more than what they wanted to take from their rival.

There are two key problems with a policy that sinks offsetting security values into both sides of a rivalry. First, such investments—especially military aid—tend to debase each other, and so their value as signals of the pivot's interests is subject to cycles of inflation. Each new investment in one side renders the prior investment in the other side symbolically, if not operationally, less valuable. Pivot's who use this strategy may feel great pressure to keep "feeding the pot" just to maintain their current leverage. Second, and more important, as instruments of leverage, the investments themselves must be something that the adversaries need badly and cannot easily find elsewhere. The utility of these offsetting investments—both for the pivot and for the adversaries—will be strongly influenced by the availability of alternatives. They become less valuable to the adversaries, and therefore less useful as tools of the pivot's deterrence policy, to the extent that substitutes are or become available elsewhere. Which takes us to alignment options.

ALIGNMENT OPTIONS AND PIVOTAL DETERRENCE

Though the patterns outlined above describe key features of Type I and II cases, they do not predict when or explain why pivotal deterrence of either type is likely to succeed or fail. For that we need our "prime" hypothesis, which focuses on the adversaries' alignment options. The key to the pivot's bargaining power is its flexibility vis-à-vis the adversaries—flexibility that, because of the conflict between them, the adversaries do not have. To pose it as simply as possible, when the pivot has two alternatives (align with one or the other adversary), the adversaries only have one (align with the pivot). Thus Jervis's basic point that "states gain and lose bargaining leverage . . . in rough proportion to the alternatives available to them."[32]

This simple truth is hardly unique to international relations. The same logic explains why price is a function of not just demand but also of supply, why scarcity increases price (leverage) and abundance decreases it. It is why we pay much more for diamonds than for water, though we need water much more than we need diamonds.[33] It is why Plato wrote that "Only what is rare is valuable," and why the Talmud teaches that "when thou art the only purchaser, then buy, [but] when others are present, be thou nobody."[34] And it is why pivotal deterrence is likely to fail when the adversaries have good alignment options.

The adversaries' access to alignment options will vary within and across cases. Some situations closely approximate a "closed" triad—the alignment options are much weaker than the pivot, much farther away, or simply do not exist. In others, the adversaries are each blessed with powerful and proximate alignment options. Let us begin, then, with the rudimentary hypothesis.

ALIGNMENT OPTIONS HYPOTHESIS
Pivotal deterrence is more likely to succeed when the adversaries' alignment options are scarce, and more likely to fail when their alignment options are abundant.

Defining and Operationalizing Alignment Options

Alignment, according to Glenn Snyder, is the "expectations of states about whether they will be supported or opposed by other states in future interactions."[35] This is a good working definition, but how do we operationalize the variable? When I say that an adversary has an alignment *option,* I mean that she expects to receive support, in the form of security values, from a bystanding state, in the context of her relations with her adversary and the pivot. The option may be an ongoing or potential supporter, but in either case, the adversary must see it as such at the time.[36] It makes no sense to attribute alignment options to states that, at the time, did not conceive of them in that way.

Furthermore, the bystander must not only be historically plausible but also powerful. Alignment options, just like the pivot, must possess military capabilities roughly equal to, or greater than, the adversaries, and the adversaries must see them in this way. This does not mean that the adversaries will not seek, or already have, supporters who are much weaker than they are; but so long as those supporters cannot compete with the pivot, or neutralize its ability to play "king-maker," their influence on the central dynamic of pivotal deterrence will be marginal.

Finally, an alignment option must proffer security values that are similar to or substitutable for what the pivot can (or does) provide. *Security values*, in the simplest terms, reduce to arms or alliances, or the promise of them. As with all interactions in the security domain, weapons and "forces in being" can substitute for commitments by others to fight for or with you, and vice versa.[37] In the same way that there is "internal" balancing (building arms) and "external" balancing (making alliances), pivotal deterrence manipulates both material security values (giving or deploying arms) and expectations of meaningful military and diplomatic support (giving or withholding assurances, making or withdrawing threats). This is the stock in trade of pivotal deterrence, and bystanders who cannot do the business will not count as alignment options.

Few instances of pivotal deterrence occur in which the adversaries have *no* other avenues of support save the pivot. Just the same, few instances of pivotal deterrence occur in which the adversaries have *many* alignment options. Both a completely closed triad, and an open one with a crowded market of alignment options, are analytical abstractions. However, Type I and Type II cases vary in the degree to which they approximate the conditions captured in the two models. In some cases the adversaries have, at best, weak and unattractive alignment options. In other cases, both adversaries have attractive alignment options. That is enough variation for us to test the explanatory power of the alignment options hypothesis.

Drawing from the logic of relative abundance and scarcity, we will use a simple dichotomous variable. When both adversaries have a good alignment option other than the pivot, there are really three alignment options (two plus the pivot) at play among the two adversaries. Thus, in cases that have two or more alignment options, alignment options are "chasing" adversaries—they are "abundant." In cases with one alignment option or less, adversaries are chasing alignment options—here alignment options are "scarce." The bargaining power of the pivot should vary accordingly.

Alignment Options and the Causal Mechanisms of Pivotal Deterrence Failure

"Swamping" of the Pivot's Relative Capabilities

The simplest reason why pivotal deterrence may fail when the adversaries have alignment options has to do with relative military capabilities. In short, in some situations, when the alignment options' capabilities are combined with the adversaries', the pivot's relative military capabilities will decline significantly. Here, the pivot's weak bargaining power is a straightforward consequence of relative military weakness. This is most likely to happen in Type I cases. Here a peer pivot may become a "puny" one once the adversaries' alignment options are taken into account. Consequently, the adversaries may seriously doubt whether the pivot possesses the quantity or quality of military power needed to significantly influence the outcome of a war. The location of the adversaries' alignment options may also throw into question the peer pivot's ability to join the fight before the outcome is settled and the pivot must accept a fait accompli. And if the adversaries have doubts about those two issues, then they will also have reason to doubt that the pivot will intervene, which will further undermine its bargaining leverage.

Diversification of the Adversaries' Risks

Alignment options may allow the adversaries to control the risks associated with going to war by diversifying their potential sources of security values. *Diversify* here means more than just increase. When its sources of support are diversified, an adversary has relationships with alignment options that are likely to move in a different direction than its relationship with the pivot. Thus, if his support from the pivot decreases, then his support from the alignment option is likely to increase; if the pivot moves closer to him, then the alignment option will probably move farther away.[38] This pattern of alignment options controls the adversaries' risk by reducing the costs of the worst outcome, depending on the scenario (i.e., the pivot aligning against or abandoning them).

We can draw another helpful analogy here to the economics of insurance. In markets where insurance is not available, diversification is the next-best response to uncertainty.[39] A farmer who lives in an area where weather is unpredictable and depends on his produce to survive will not plant just one crop in a season. Instead, he will plant a variety of crops, each of which is likely to thrive under different conditions. The overall bounty is less than it would be if he had planted all of his land with an optimal crop, but he has also reduced the chances that he will starve. Similarly, in the stock market, where the payoff for risk taking can be enormous, moral hazard and adverse selection make insurance unavailable. Consequently, investors who want to reap the benefits of taking risks with their money, but want to eliminate the chance of catastrophic losses, will hold diversified portfolios with stocks (and other instruments) that are likely to perform differently depending on economic conditions.

As I argued before, a policy of pivotal deterrence is essentially an attempt by the pivot to deny the adversaries insurance, in the hope that doing so will cause them to be more cautious and more attentive to the pivot's concerns. But the adversaries may be able to neutralize the pivot's policy through their own policy of diversification. Obviously, they cannot do so if they have no other options. But when they do have alignment options, they are likely to diversify, especially after the pivot uses their dependence on it as a lever over their policy.[40] The adversaries can best do this when there are preexisting antagonisms between the pivot and their alliance options. And when they believe that they can offset the pivot's opposition or abandonment with increased support from others, they will be more likely to pursue aggressive policies, and pivotal deterrence will be likely to fail.

Bidding Wars

The condition that favors diversification for the adversaries—antagonism between the pivot and their alignment options—also makes bidding wars between the latter two likely. Bidding wars benefit the adversaries by hoisting the pivot on its own petard. They put the pivot in the position of competing with the adversaries' alignment options. For example, if in return for its support to Adversary B, the Pivot demands that B make concessions to Adversary C, B may force the Pivot to reduce those demands by threatening to turn to Alignment Option D for support instead.[41]

This dynamic is at work in both Type I and Type II cases, but it will be most salient and easy to observe in Type II cases where the use of offsetting military aid (and the threat to curtail it) is usually a key source of the pivot's leverage. When the adversaries can get from others what the pivot offers, for the same political price but with more certainty or with the same uncertainty but for a lower price, pivotal deterrence will be likely to fail. The overall argument is summarized in figure 4.

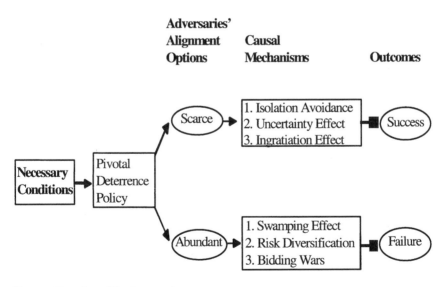

Figure 4. Overview of the Argument

CASE SELECTION AND RESEARCH METHODOLOGY

We will examine four cases, a pair of Type I cases and a pair of Type II cases, in the following four chapters. In each pair, alignment options are scarce in one case and abundant in the other. Table 3 shows the coding of variables and outcomes in the cases. Below are the four empirical cases, with the pivot (P) listed first in each.

The Empirical Cases

1. Germany (P), Russia and Austria-Hungary, 1875–78
2. Britain (P), France and Germany, July 1914
3. United States (P), Turkey and Greece, 1963–67
4. United States (P), India and Pakistan, 1962–65

This research design permits a variety of tests of my arguments. First, we can test most of the hypotheses about the necessary conditions for pivotal deterrence attempts. Second, we can test the prime hypothesis about alignment options. Below I will discuss each of these in turn.

Testing the Necessary Condition Hypotheses

Earlier, I laid out four necessary conditions for a policy of pivotal deterrence to be attempted.

1. The pivot must posses power at least roughly equal to the adversaries.
2. The pivot must prefer the status quo between the adversaries or that any change to the status quo is made peacefully.
3. The pivot must believe that both adversaries hold revisionist aims toward each other and that they will risk war to achieve those aims if they are assured of its support or acquiescence.
4. The adversaries must perceive each other to be more threatening than the pivot.

Table 3. Research Design: Coding of Case Variables and Outcomes

Case #	Relative Power	Intensity of Interests	Type	Alignment Options	Outcome
(1)	Peer	Vital	I	Scarce	Success
(2)	Peer	Vital	I	Abundant	Failure
(3)	Preponderant	Secondary	II	Scarce	Success
(4)	Preponderant	Secondary	II	Abundant	Failure

Note that these conditions do not address whether the policy of pivotal de-terrence is likely to *succeed*—only whether it will be *attempted*. Now, al-though many have criticized research designs that select on a dependent variable, it is nevertheless true that "selecting on the dependent variable is perfectly admissible if one is evaluating necessary (as opposed to suffi-cient) conditions."[42] Indeed, using a "most different systems" method—where multiple cases have the same value on the dependent variable but "vary on many other dimensions"—is a powerful way to test necessary conditions.

Our research design is configured to allow this sort of test for conditions 2, 3, and 4 above. Condition 1 describes a lower threshold of the pivot's rel-ative power. Below that threshold, I argued, pivotal deterrence will not be attempted, and above it, pivotal deterrence *may* be attempted. Because I use this as a reason to examine only cases above the threshold, it remains an untested assumption in the research design. It is a fairly benign assump-tion. Of the four necessary conditions listed above, it impinges the least on the core logic of pivotal deterrence.

In each of the four cases pivotal deterrence *was attempted*. But the four are also quite different from each other on important dimensions; namely, in terms of the pivot's relative power and interests, and the adversaries' align-ment options. Thus, each case, to use Adam Pzeworski and Henry Teune's terminology, represents a logically distinct "different system."[43] If, in spite of these differences, conditions 2, 3, and 4 do hold true in each of the cases, then my hypotheses will be supported. If, however, any of three conditions is not evident *in any one* of the four cases then the particular hypothesis cor-responding to the missing condition will be disconfirmed.[44]

Testing the Alignment Option Hypothesis

The research design is also configured to test the alignment options hy-pothesis. By combining the method of difference and the method of agree-ment, it forces clear expectations about the outcomes of four different piv-otal deterrence contingencies. We expect that different Type cases with similar values on the alignment options variable will have similar out-comes. And we expect that similar Type cases with different values on the alignment options variable will have different outcomes.[45] These correlative predictions are confirmed by the outcomes of the cases. The correlations are an important first cut, but alone they do not convincingly demonstrate the causal role of alignment options. So we will go much deeper into the cases, using two different methods of causal analysis that are both possible and useful in fine-grained historical case studies: (1) process tracing and (2) within-case congruence procedures.

Process Tracing

Process tracing seeks to reveal and describe the causal chain or mechanism connecting an independent variable or variables to the outcome of the dependent variable.[46] By tracking the causal chain over time and in detail, this technique allows us to increase the number of observations of the effect of causal variables, and thus the number of hypothesis tests in our cases.

Each of the four main case studies captures one of four different contingencies in which *most* instances of pivotal deterrence are likely to occur. If my hypotheses are right, three things should happen. First, in cases of the same Type, similar initial typological conditions should lead to similar strategic dilemmas and observable patterns of interaction. Second, in cases where alignment options are scarce, the adversaries' decisions to avoid war and accept compromise should be observably influenced by one or more of the causal mechanisms that make pivotal deterrence work (isolation avoidance, uncertainty effect, ingratiation effect). Third, in cases where alignment options are abundant, the pivot's policy should observably fail because of the operation of one or more of the causal mechanisms associated with abundant alignment options (swamping of capabilities, risk diversification, bidding wars).

These convergent and divergent patterns should be readily apparent in the four cases. The sequence of events and the relevant decision-making process should unfold in the ways my hypotheses suggest they will. Just as important, political leaders should speak, write, behave, and appear to reason in ways consistent with my hypotheses. If they do not, we should doubt whether the hypotheses capture the most important features of pivotal deterrence.

Because process-tracing requires attention to historical texture and detail, it may also bring into view other factors in a case that should be accounted for in the explanation of its outcome.[47] Such accounting is particularly important in the cases of pivotal deterrence success. For in order to properly assess the importance of scarce alignment options in the success of the pivot's policy, we need to do more than confirm through process tracing that the causal mechanisms associated with scarcity operated as expected. We also need to identify and weigh the influence of other things about the situation that may have led the adversaries to avert war, such as the contours of the stakes and the military balance between them. Accordingly, chapters 3 and 5, which examine instances of pivotal deterrence success, will conclude with a discussion of other aspects of the cases that may have also contributed to peace.

Congruence Procedures

Another way to test the hypotheses is to use within-case congruence procedures. These assess the extent to which *diachronic* change (i.e., change over time) in an independent variable within a case produces expected changes in the dependent variable.[48] If, for example, the pivot's relative power and the adversaries' alignment options remained constant in a case, but the pivot's stakes increased over time—from secondary to vital interests—we would expect to see the adversaries' beliefs about the prospects of the pivot intervening also change dramatically. Or, for another example, if at the beginning of a case, an adversary has what it thinks is an alignment option, but the option is later eliminated, we would expect the adversary to become more cautious and to make more concessions to win the pivot's support as a consequence.

Overview of Case-Study Format

The four major case studies below follow a similar format. Each begins with a brief review of key questions and controversies relating to the case at hand and then presents an overview of the main argument addressing them. Next is a description of the values obtaining on the main variables in our framework: the distribution of power and interest, and the availability of alignment options. Following that is an in-depth narrative, describing the sequence of events and the relevant causal mechanisms at work in the case. Finally, we conclude with an assessment of the implications of the case for our theoretical framework and, in the instances of pivotal deterrence success (Chapters 3 and 5), of potentially confounding causes that have been brought out by the analysis but are not captured in the theoretical framework.

[3]

Pivotal Deterrence in the Eastern Crisis, 1875–78:

WHY BISMARCK HAD IT EASY

I have two powerful dogs by their collars . . . I am holding them apart: first to keep them from tearing each other to pieces; second to keep them from coming to an understanding at our expense. I believe I am performing a service not only to each of them, but also to Germany and Europe.

Otto von Bismarck, September 1875

Bismarck has never before held in his hands so much power for good or evil . . . if any country can thus save the world from a tremendous war, it is Germany.

The Times (London), October 16, 1876

Imperial Chancellor of Germany Otto von Bismarck steered his country through wars of unification in 1864, 1866, and 1870. He then began twenty years of conservative diplomacy seeking to keep the peace in Europe, and with it, Germany's favorable position. His two preeminent goals were to isolate France so it could not wage a war of revenge and to prevent Austria and Russia from fighting in the Balkans. A war between them would force Germany to choose sides and would give France the ally it could not wage war without. To this day, debates continue over whether World War I was the logical consequence of Bismarck's policy of *realpolitik* or of his political demise and replacement by "lesser" German statesmen who lacked "his sure touch and almost artistic sensitivity" in international politics.[1] But few would argue that his diplomacy was not an important cause of peace in Europe between 1871 and 1890.

[46]

Bismarck's conservative statecraft is held up by some today as a model for U.S. grand strategy in the post–Cold War world. The United States, so the argument goes, should put itself at the center of a "hub and spokes" alliance system, where it can play the pivot and prevent war between its allies, like Germany did a century before.[2] The analogy is appealing, but just how did Bismarck's system work? Why did his pivotal strategy succeed when similar strategies attempted by others have failed? Until we answer those questions, it is difficult to know whether Bismarck's strategy would serve U.S. interests today.

WHICH BISMARCK IS BETTER?

There is an additional problem. While Bismarck's goals of isolating France and preventing war between Austria and Russia remained constant between 1871 and 1890, his peace strategy changed radically after 1879.[3] This is often overlooked today amid calls for a Bismarckian style of U.S. foreign policy. Before 1879, Bismarck pursued a fluid strategy of vague commitments with Russia and Austria, keeping the peace by pivoting within the orbit of the conservative Three Emperors League of 1873. The Three Emperors League was a weak association for promoting solidarity among the three monarchical powers (Austria, Russia, and Germany) in case one were attacked by an outsider. Within the *Dreikaiserbund*, as the League was called, Bismarck sought to "play the benevolent third so long as Russia and Austria-Hungary were working together" and to "support only what had been agreed by his two allies."[4] Bismarck would refuse "to act as umpire between Austria and Russia" and strive to avoid "the appearance of a deliberate choice between our more or less intimate friends."[5] The League did not commit the parties to anything more than consultation in the event of conflict among them, least of all Germany. Yet it was in this gray area of consultation that Bismarck worked his strategy of pivotal deterrence. He followed two simple rules: He refused to support either side if they tried to pursue aims that were likely to lead to war with the other, and, should they go to war anyway, he subtly threatened to align against whomever had too much success on the battlefield.

After 1879, Bismarck's diplomacy changed to one firmly anchored in a formal defensive alliance with Austria. At the Congress of Berlin in 1878, where the European Great Powers convened to settle the Russo-Turkish War, Bismarck refused to take sides between Austria and Russia. This resulted in revisions to the Treaty of San Stefano that dramatically reduced Russia's gains against Turkey. After the Congress, Germany's relations with Russia soured. Czar Alexander II judged the meeting to have been "a European coalition against Russia under the leadership of Prince Bismarck."[6] In

February 1879, Austria agreed to abrogate Article V of the Treaty of Prague (1866), which required Germany to hold a plebiscite in Schleswig. Now Germany could annex Schleswig completely; to Russians this looked like Austria's payback to Germany for Bismarck's support at the Berlin Congress.[7] Their suspicions were strengthened as the implementation of the Treaty of Berlin went forward, and German commissioners cast repeated votes against Russian positions.[8] In the spring and summer of 1879, the czar made his disaffection with Germany felt. There were major troop movements in Poland, which increased the Russian military presence on Germany's border by about 400,000 men.[9] The Russian press unleashed virulent attacks against Germany. Germany reciprocated the ill-will in the press, and adopted a stringent trade quarantine to halt the spread of plague from Russia.[10] The czar complained to the German ambassador to St. Petersburg about German favoritism toward Austria, and warned, "If you want our hundred year friendship to continue, then this should change."[11] Of the press war between Russia and Germany, he said "this will end in a very serious way."[12] And he wrote to the German kaiser, Wilhelm I, to call his attention to the peril of the situation and to caution him not to forget Russia's loyalty in 1870, or "the consequences may be disastrous for our two countries."[13] That, in turn, led Bismarck to conclude that "the alliance of three emperors has, unfortunately, ceased to exist."[14]

Bismarck signed a defensive pact with Austria in 1879.[15] This alliance was the first node in an alliance system that would expand over the next decade to include Serbia (1881), Italy (1882), and Rumania (1883) as formal partners and would even draw in Great Britain as a silent partner via the Second Mediterranean agreement (1887). Thus 1879 marks a "decisive change" in Bismarck's diplomacy.[16] Putting aside his aversion to making alliance commitments during peacetime, Bismarck built up a web of formal alliances with Germany standing at the center.[17] He managed to rekindle the Three Emperors League in 1882, and in 1887, after it expired, he tried again with Russia in the Reinsurance Treaty.[18] These were efforts, as always, to keep Russia and France apart and to promote Austrian and Russian cooperation. The Reinsurance Treaty committed Germany to neutrality if Austria attacked Russia, and Russia to neutrality if France attacked Germany. However, it did not dilute the central reality of extended deterrence embodied in the Dual Alliance between Germany and Austria. By 1880, Austria could not and would not contemplate war against Russia alone, and only Russia continued to harbor revisionist aims in the Balkans. Thus, after entering into the Dual Alliance, Bismarck moved away from pivotal deterrence and opted instead for extended deterrence against Russia. Ideally, the firm defensive commitment with Austria would deter Russia and assure Austria, while giving Germany maximum control over its ally.[19]

In short, though Germany did not escape its central position between

Austria and Russia, Bismarck did reject pivotal deterrence as a strategy for managing that relationship after 1879. Before then, Bismarck avoided firm commitments to either side and wielded German influence flexibly between Austria and Russia. After 1879, Bismarck took sides, adopting a formal defensive alliance with the Dual Monarchy of Austria-Hungary. Which is not to say that he no longer tried to restrain Austria or conciliate Russia, but there was not now any question about German loyalties in a pinch. Therefore, in order to understand how and why Bismarck's strategy of pivotal deterrence worked, we will do best to look at his diplomacy before 1879.

Overview of the Case

During the Eastern Crisis of the mid-1870s, Germany was a peer pivot. It was centrally located between Russia and Austria, and it had an army that could mobilize sooner and move by rail faster than either of them. A major war between Russia and Austria in the 1870s would have harmed Germany, putting in danger its territorial integrity and internal stability. Thus, Austria and Russia both needed to secure German support before embarking on such a war. Neither of them had a good alignment option. Russia had no option at all. Austria had a weak and wavering one in Britain. British policy toward the Eastern Crisis seesawed back and forth, and even if London had steered a course that Vienna could count on, the fact remained that Her Majesty's fleet could not determine the outcome of a war between land armies in the Balkans. And Turkey, whose gradual internal collapse was an immediate cause of clashing Austro-Russian interests, was perhaps the least attractive and reliable option of all.

Bismarck's policy of pivotal deterrence worked well in the Eastern Crisis of 1875–78. Relations soured between Russia and Austria in 1876 as Russia prepared to intervene in support of the South Slavs and to wage war against Turkey. Austria had no interest in seeing the South Slavs strengthened or in the creation of a large Slavic state near its borders; thus the Dual Monarchy and Russia were at cross-purposes. The Russians at first showed little regard for Austrian concerns because the czar was convinced that Bismarck would support him against Vienna. Indeed, the Russian foreign minister was so optimistic as to believe that a German army would march with the Russian if war between Vienna and St. Petersburg broke out. Bismarck banished such notions in St. Petersburg, and thereby pushed the czar into seeking accommodation with Vienna. Russia simply could not contemplate fighting both Turkey and Austria at the same time by itself.

But to insure that Austria was not emboldened to take a hard line against Russia, Bismarck also pointedly turned down a number of Austrian bids to enlist Germany in a war against Russia. Austria could not risk war with

Russia without the assurance of active German support, and so Bismarck's denial of such a commitment was enough to derail war-talk in Vienna. This pattern would repeat itself in a number of crises over the next two years, with the same results. Though they contemplated war against each other, Austria and Russia were unwilling to do so without German allegiance; in its absence, they were left with no alternative but to reach for accommodation along the lines Bismarck preferred.

DESCRIPTION OF SITUATIONAL VARIABLES

The Balance of Capabilities

The conventional wisdom among historians is that between 1870 and 1879 Germany was the dominant military power in Europe. James Joll argues that after the Franco-Prussian War, Germany achieved "preponderance in the new balance of power in Europe" and became "the strongest military and potentially the strongest industrial power on the Continent."[20] According to Raymond Sontag, the victories against Austria and France in the wars of unification "gave Continental hegemony to Prussian Germany."[21] William Langer, echoing Disraeli's famous hyperbole, wrote that Germany's victory against France "completely destroyed the balance of power in Europe."[22] Even Otto Pflanze, the preeminent biographer of Bismarck who *doubts* that Germany's victory over France destroyed the European balance of power, says that in the 1870s, "there could be little doubt about German hegemony in Europe."[23]

The conventional wisdom is misleading for our purposes. In relation to Austria and Russia, Germany was not a preponderant pivot. What the historians mean by terms like hegemony, predominance, and preponderance is that Germany was more powerful than any other European, or Continental, great power at the time. This may be debatable (see below), but whether or not it is true is beside the point. For *preponderance* means more than that in our conceptual framework. It means that the pivot has military capabilities that dominate the combined capabilities of those it is trying to prevent from fighting. A peer pivot falls short of this standard. In a peer-pivot triad, no single actor can decisively outmatch the other two combined.

In the decade after 1871, Germany was not preponderant over Russia and Austria; it was a peer. The measure of relative capabilities I use to make this determination is composed of three, equally weighted elements: number of military personnel, military expenditures, and number of ironclad warships. That index is rough and no doubt excludes many important components of national military power (e.g., geography, legitimacy, population, natural resources, wealth, and industrial output). But for our purposes it is sufficient because there is a rather wide margin for error in the distinction

[50]

between peer and preponderant power: We are looking for order-of-magnitude differences, not to split hairs. For that, a ballpark measure of the military capabilities among them works well enough.

Table 4 shows that, by this index, between 1870 and 1880, Germany never possessed capabilities outweighing the combined capabilities of Russia and Austria. Although there is clearly secular change, Germany remained in the middle rank between a dominant Russia and a steadily weakening Austria. That, by this index, Russian capabilities always outweigh the sum of German and Austrian capabilities by a sliver of percentage points *does* present a quandary, if we adhere strictly to the numbers at the expense of common sense. Common sense suggests, among other things, that this overhang—and much more than that—was consumed by deployments in the vast reaches of the Russian empire in East and Central Asia. Capabilities, in other words, that could not easily be converted into military power in Europe.

Before we move on, we should also consider the qualitative dimension of German military power. After 1870, Germany's professional military prowess was well established. A critical element of Germany's capabilities, not captured in the index above, was the rapid mobilization system and rail network that allowed it to move forces quickly into battle around its borders. The efficacy of this system was clearly demonstrated in 1866 against Austria and in 1870 against France—two countries with reasonably well-developed rail nets of their own—and was vastly superior to the Russian system in Poland and the Southern Districts.[24] This meant that Germany would be able to move quickly against Russia—or Austria, if necessary—to prevent either side from handing the other a catastrophic defeat. Germany's

Table 4. Relative Military Capabilities among European Powers, 1870–1880

Years	Germany	Britain	Russia	Austria	France	Italy
1870–73	9.7	19.6	24.7	9.2	26.6	10.2
1873–75	12.7	20.7	24.5	9.2	24.7	8.2
1874–76	13.2	21.3	24.3	9.2	24.6	7.3
1875–77	13.7	20.7	24.5	9.2	24.5	7.5
1876–78	14.0	21.3	24.1	9.1	23.7	7.8
1877–79	14.3	21.0	24.1	9.0	23.6	7.9
1878–80	14.0	21.0	24.0	9.3	23.6	7.9

Source: Alan Alexandroff, *The Logic of Diplomacy* (Beverly Hills, Calif.: Sage, 1981), 184, table B.8.

Note: Military capabilities are measured as a composite of three equally weighted indicators: number of military personnel, military expenditures, and number of ironclad warships.

central geographic position, rapid mobilization system, and superior rail net gave it a sound military basis for pursuing pivotal deterrence as a peer pivot poised between Russia and Austria.

The Distribution of Interests and Intentions

After 1871, Germany was a status quo power in Europe. After taking the Alsace-Lorraine in the Franco-Prussian War, Bismarck believed that Germany, "no longer had any objective that could profitably be attained by war."[25] And, "realizing the unease and jealousy which the Second Reich's sudden emergence had caused . . . [Bismarck] strove after 1871 to convince the other Great Powers (especially the flank powers of Russia and Britain) that Germany had no further territorial ambitions."[26] Both sides of the status quo coin—keeping what you have, and not taking more—were important to Germany after 1871. Thus, Bismarck sought not only to preserve the fruits of German victories but to assure the other Great Powers that Germany did not want more—at least not in Europe. These two goals were not unrelated, for the only power in Europe who clearly wished to deprive Germany of her position was, of course, France; but she could not do it alone, and if Bismarck could convince the rest of Europe that Germany was both satisfied with her gains and willing to fight hard to keep them, none would have much cause, or incentive, to aid French revanche.

If Bismarck became a staunch defender of the status quo after 1871, this applied to territorial settlement at the heart of Europe and more specifically to the preservation of Germany's existing borders. This caveat is important, for in relation to the Eastern Question—how to deal with the erosion of Ottoman control over European possessions—and the larger fate of the Ottoman Empire, Bismarck did not want so much to preserve the status quo there as to preserve peace between Austria and Russia. Indeed, on many occasions he made it clear that he thought dismembering the Ottoman Empire for the sake of peace between the other Great Powers would be a good thing. In Bismarck's view, not only were the Balkans not worth the bones of a Pomeranian grenadier, but "the whole Ottoman Empire as a political institution was not of sufficient value to justify the civilized people of Europe in ruining themselves by wars to uphold it."[27] Germany's vital interests were only engaged in the Eastern Question because of the dangers to Germany that would arise from a general war between Britain, Austria, and Russia over Turkey.[28] To avoid such a calamity, Bismarck would not hesitate to settle the Eastern Question at Turkey's expense.

Germany's vital interest in preventing war between Russia and Austria flowed from three distinct strategic rationales, which, in practice, were mutually reinforcing. The first followed from unvarnished balance of power logic: Germany could not afford to see either Russia or Austria cease to function as a European Great Power. The dramatic weakening of either would require Germany to expend far greater energy propping up one and containing the other. Thus, Bismarck noted in his memoirs: "We could indeed endure that our friends should lose or win battles against each other, but not that one of the two should be so severely wounded and injured that its position as an independent great power . . . would be endangered."[29] From this perspective, there would appear to be a certain tolerance for error in Bismarck's pivotal policy. Germany did not need to prevent war between Austria and Russia altogether or to intervene in a limited war between them. It was only imperative that Germany did not let one seriously weaken the other.

But the picture was more complicated than that. There were more pressing reasons why Germany needed peace between Russia and Austria, and why even a limited war would imperil Germany. With Austria, there was the "German problem." "One crushing defeat," Bismarck believed, "would mean the end of Austria and of the Habsburg dynasty."[30] Then Germany could be impelled to absorb Austria's Germanic (and Catholic) populations, if not Slavs too, and that would wreak disastrous internal consequences upon Germany. With Russia, there was the "Polish problem." Russia, Germany, and Austria were partners in the partition and annexation of Poland, and each had absorbed great populations of Poles in the process. Poles under Russian rule had revolted four times since 1815: in 1830, 1846, 1848, and 1863. The weakening of Russian power in the West would undoubtedly spark another Polish rebellion, which could easily spread to Silesia, Posen, and West Prussia, thus undoing Bismarck's efforts to "Germanize" and integrate these territories.[31] So if Austria was less resilient than Russia to military misfortune, it was also true that Germany's vital interests would be endangered by any loss of Russian control in Poland, something likely to occur if Austria and Russia went to war. Undoubtedly, Russia would survive a limited military defeat by Austria in the Balkans, but this would be small comfort to Germany now confronted with a Polish uprising or liberation on its eastern borders.

Finally, Germany had a vital interest in preventing an Austro-Russian war because of its enmity with France. Even a limited war between Russia and Austria would create political conditions that could be exploited by France. For the reasons stated above, even a limited war between Russia and Austria could impel Germany to take sides, and if France did not "strike just as soon as Germany was deeply engaged in the East," then at a minimum it "could demand the restitution of Alsace-Lorraine as the price of neutrality."[32] In short, Germany's stakes in a war between Austria and Russia could not be divorced from the threat of French *revanche*. For Germany, the key to maintaining its western borders lay in preventing war in the East.[33]

Austria-Hungary's Contingent Revisionism

Sontag argues that during the 1870s "Austria . . . was a satiated state, desiring only the preservation of the status quo."[34] This is not quite true. It may accurately describe the most sincere wishes of Emperor Francis Joseph (though this is debatable) and his foreign minister (Count Julius Andrássy), but it distorts the true nature of their policies. Closer to the mark would be to say that the policy of the Dual Monarchy during this period was revisionism impelled by "contingent necessity."[35] If the Ottoman grip on the Balkan Slavs remained firm, if the government in Constantinople remained stable, and if no other European power (namely Russia) sought to expand at Turkey's expense, Austria would be content to stay within its borders. But since it was unlikely that all three conditions would hold true, Austria was determined to secure Turkish territories through partition (particularly in Bosnia and Herzegovina), to crush any movements to form independent Slavic states near its borders, and to expand in response to any Russian encroachment in the Balkans. This was made abundantly clear in the 1876 Reichstadt convention between Austria and Russia, and in the following years Austria never wavered from that position.[36]

In addition to Francis Joseph, who "actively desired the aggrandizement" there were other powerful factions within the Austro-Hungarian government "eager to annex Bosnia and Herzegovina—military men who desired a more defensible frontier behind Austria's exposed Dalmatian coast, and Croats, who longed for a Southern Slav union that would lead the conversion of the Dual into a triple Monarchy."[37] Even Andrássy—a Hungarian who on principle was deeply opposed to absorbing more Slavs into the Monarchy—was by 1875 "committed to the idea of an Austrian secundogeniture in [Bosnia and Herzegovina], when and if Turkey could no longer carry on."[38] In short, if Vienna wished to preserve the status quo in the 1870s, the wish was predicated on tenuous, if not non-existent, conditions. Given the political realities of Ottoman decline in the Balkans, Russia's aspirations, and Austria's own problems with Slav minorities, Vienna's policy was de facto expansionist.

Russia's Expansionist Aims

Any measure of St. Petersburg's revisionist aims during this period must begin with Russian Pan-Slavism. This, in Langer's words, "went beyond the principle of purely Russian solidarity and preached the union of all Slavs under the aegis of Russia." Russia fostered Pan-Slavism in the Balkans, from the 1850s on, both as an ideological and political force.[39] The czar was certainly not above using the Slav insurrections to serve his larger aims in the region. The most expansive version of Russian Pan-Slavic ideology fingered the Dual Monarchy as the chief obstacle to Slavic unity. In this view, because Austria commanded access to Turkish territory in Europe, "the road to Constantinople lay through Vienna, and without the defeat of Austria all thought of Slav unification would be vain."[40] In this sense, Pan-Slavism potentially posed a direct threat to Vienna, and even if it never came to that, it was still "regarded with uneasiness and distrust by Austria as likely at any moment to embrace her own large and as yet unassimilated Slav population."[41]

Yet, for all of its patronage, St. Petersburg could not tightly control Balkan Pan-Slavism. The wellsprings for that movement were local, an indigenous response to Austrian and Ottoman domination.[42] And if Russian advocates of Pan-Slavism were influential in Moscow, they were less so in St. Petersburg, the seat of the Russian monarchy. Yes, there were important supporters in the czar's entourage, notably, his son Alexander III and Count Nicholas Ignatiev, his ambassador to Constantinople between 1864 and 1879.[43] Ignatyev, in fact, would play a key role in pushing Russia toward war with Turkey in the 1870s. However, it is going too far to say that the czar was too weak domestically "to stand out against Panslav sentiment," and was driven to support Pan-Slavism by the fear of the hangman.[44] Ultimately, the czar was the "real master and controlling factor in Russian foreign policy."[45] If he occasionally caved in to Pan-Slavic pressures, he more often tacked with them when they served Russia's interests and ignored them when they did not, as the Serbs, Montenegrins, and Romanians would learn at the Congress of Berlin.[46] So the important question is, what other expansionist interests did Russia have in the Balkans, and how could Pan-Slavism be harnessed to serve those ends?

One look at a map of the Near East will show that Constantinople commanded the Turkish Straits that gave Russia access to the Mediterranean from the Black Sea. In peacetime, this outlet was the conduit for Russia's primary exports, timber and wheat from the Ukraine. Since the 1833 Russo-Turk treaty of Unkiar Skelessi, and the multilateral Straits Conventions of 1841 that succeeded it, the Straits had been more or less closed to foreign warships during peacetime.[47] To the extent that this kept British and other European navies out of the Black Sea during peacetime, the convention served Russia well enough, especially since its own navy was so weak. But peacetime navigation was not Russia's preeminent concern—it was controlling the Straits when peace was in doubt. Russia learned all too well in the Crimean War—when the European "Concert" powers conquered the Black Sea port of Sevastopol and imposed a humiliating peace on Russia—that without control over the Straits, its underbelly would always be exposed to Europe's naval powers, most of all Britain. One of the onerous conditions imposed on Russia at war's end at the Congress of Paris was the "neutralization" of the Black Sea. For Russia, that meant naval disarmament there. Thus, since at least 1856, but in truth for much longer, Russia had a deep and abiding interest in controlling the Straits and the territory abutting the Black Sea.[48] A war against Turkey to liberate Balkan Slavs would provide the pretext for doing so.

Another consequence of the peace imposed at the Congress of Paris fueled Russia's revisionist aims in the 1870s. In 1854, under threat of war, Austria had compelled Russia to withdraw from the Danubian principalities. The Treaty of Paris baptized the loss, giving Turkey suzerainty over the Danubian outlet to the Black Sea, and erecting a semi-independent Rumania on what was formerly the Russian territory of Bessarabia. Since then, Rumania had served the thankless role of a buffer zone standing between Russian and Austrian ambitions in the Balkans.[49] If the political circles in St. Petersburg were divided over Pan-Slavism, they were united when it came to recovering Bessarabia. And since any move to rescue Balkan Slavs from Turkish oppression would require a Russian march through Rumania, even those with little sympathy for the Pan-Slav cause would find a reason to intervene under its banner in 1876. Last but not least, the czar had "fervent" personal reasons for wanting Bessarabia back: the "province had been wrested from his father on his deathbed."[50] Russia, in sum, had many strong impulses to expand in the direction of Bessarabia and beyond, where there lay dominions Vienna was loath to see fall under Russian sway.

Alignment Options

Alignment options were scarce during the Eastern Crisis. The only plausible alternative to Germany was Great Britain. Because London was a strong backer of Turkey, it naturally tilted toward Austria, which also opposed Russia's ambitions in the Balkans. So Britain was never an option for Russia. Far in the background were France and Italy. Italy had grievances against Austria that inclined it toward Russia, but it was much too weak for Russia to take it seriously as a hedge against Austria. Certainly Russia would not align with Italy *at the expense* of good relations with Germany. France during the 1870s was also weak and domestically unstable, and thus not a very attractive option. Making matters worse, its republican ideology was anathema to the eastern monarchs. This remained true well into the 1880s, even after the Dual Alliance and the pressure of the Bulgarian crisis had begun to drive Russia and France toward alignment. As late as 1888, the Russian foreign minister believed that "whatever may be the affinities which have grown up between ourselves and France, they cannot be of a practical nature in view of the chronic anarchy with which the French Republic is struggling." And the Russian press, too, despite its congenital antagonism toward Germany, showed a similar disposition: "an alliance with France at this moment" opined one Russian newspaper, "is a complete absurdity, not only for Russia, but for any other country."[51] Russia did not need an ally against Turkey alone, but it did need one if it were going to fight Turkey and Austria together. For that, Germany was Russia's only real option, and Germany would not commit.

Austria, on the other hand, wanted an ally *in addition* to Turkey if it were seriously going to challenge Russia. But Germany would not commit to Austria either. So Britain was the key alternative to Germany for Austria. But as we shall see, for both structural reasons (i.e., Britain was a distant sea power) and more transitory reasons (i.e., domestic outrage over Bulgarian atrocities and opposition to supporting Turkey), England was to prove a wavering and unreliable alignment option at critical junctures. London could not hold to a steady policy during the initial years of the crisis, could not contribute much militarily to a land battle between Russia and Austria in the Balkans, and could not even be counted on to remain engaged once its interests in the Straits were protected. Against this background, Germany's platonic but consistent and proximate friendship proved more attractive than Britain's fleeting overtures from afar.

PIVOTAL DETERRENCE IN THE EASTERN CRISIS, 1875–78

The South Slav Rebellion and the Budapest Conventions, 1875–77

The Eastern Crisis began in July 1875 when Slavs under Turkish rule, at least in part incited by Russian Pan-Slavs, revolted in Herzegovina and Bosnia.[52] They were soon joined by Serbs, Montenegrins, and Bulgarians. Pan-Slavic agitation so close to its borders did not bode well for Austria, which had significant Slav populations within its own borders that could be energized by the liberation movements.[53] For Austria, the emergence of new independent Slavic states in the Balkans could prove as dangerous as their outright annexation by Russia.

Clearly, Austria and Russia had conflicting interests in the Slav revolts. But the problem did not spring on them unawares, and in the three years prior to the outbreak, some diplomatic basis had been laid for cooperation. In Berlin in September 1872, Germany, Austria, and Russia began negotiations that led to the Three Emperors League (*Dreikaiserbund*). In May 1873, the agreement took a more concrete form in the Convention of Schönbrunn, where Austria and Russia "mutually promised, even though the interests of their States should present some divergences respecting special questions, to take counsel together in order that these divergences may not be able to prevail over the considerations of a higher order which preoccupy them." Furthermore, the two agreed to "come to a preliminary understanding between themselves" and to "agree to the line of conduct to be followed in common" should aggression from a third power threaten the peace.[54]

Thus, both Austria and Russia recognized that though their interests in the Balkans diverged on "special questions," there remained room for co-operation if Turkish control broke down. In this spirit, Czar Alexander II and Emperor Francis Joseph exchanged visits in 1873 and 1874, and "by 1875 relations between Russia and Austria, for the first time since 1854, had come to be on a good footing."[55]

Reichstadt Agreement

When the South Slav insurrection broke out, Serb and Montenegrin victories appeared to presage Ottoman collapse. Austria and Russia moved haltingly to coordinate a plan of action if Turkey in Europe disintegrated. Bismarck encouraged them in this direction, indicating to both sides that they should come to agreement because he would not "take action on the side of one against another."[56] The bargain that came out of these pourparlers was the Reichstadt agreement of July 1876, which established that if Turkey was defeated, Serb and Montenegrin aggrandizement in Bosnia and Herzegovina would be severely restricted, while "the rest of Bosnia and Herzegovina should be annexed to Austria-Hungary." In return, "Russia should resume her natural frontiers of before 1856 and might round herself off in the region of the Black Sea and in Turkey in Asia to the extent that this should be necessary for the establishment of better frontiers for herself in this direction and to serve as an equivalent for the slice of territory to be annexed to Austria-Hungary."[57] The reference to Russia's "natural frontiers" of 1856 clearly indicated that Russia meant to retake Bessarabia, and that Austria acceded to that end.

Bulgarian Atrocities, the Pan-Slavs' Defeat, and Russia's Call to Arms

In April and May of 1876, the Bulgarians joined the insurrection. The Porte's reaction was merciless: It unleashed on the Bulgarian rebels marauding militias of settlers who had been moved there after the Crimean War. This resulted in what became known as the "Bulgarian atrocities," which provoked outrage across Europe, even in Britain, which had a long-standing policy of unconditional support for Turkish rule. In London, the liberal party leader William Gladstone mobilized the opposition in a public campaign that condemned Turkish atrocities and called upon the Disraeli government to intervene against Turkey, or at least stop supporting it. Though Gladstone did not prevail, his campaign would hobble Disraeli's government throughout the rest of the year.

Beginning in July and continuing through October 1876, Turkey methodically crushed the uprisings and routed the Serbs. This allayed Austria's immediate fear that Serbian victories would result in an enlarged independent Slavic state near its borders. However, the Serb defeat was an affront to St. Petersburg, which had, if not incited the rebellion, at least given its nod to Russians Pan-Slavs who did. As an affront to Russia's prestige, Turkish atrocities provided a pretext for St. Petersburg to intervene in the Balkans and shape the future of the Eastern Question on its preferred terms. But the czar did not want to do this in the teeth of opposition from the other Great Powers. Rather, he wanted them to give him a "European" mandate and, if possible, military support.[58]

The prospect of Russia intervening directly in Turkey, however, did not sit well with Austria, and Austria was not alone. Russian advances toward the Turkish Straits were something Britain staunchly opposed. Since the Crimean War, Britain's policy had been rooted in the assumption that the passage to India lay through the Straits, and that Turkey in Europe must therefore be kept intact and friendly with England. Accordingly, throughout 1875, as the Slav rebellion flared up and was then smothered, Britain defended Constantinople diplomatically. It did so in December 1875, when Andrássy drew up a collective note from the Great Powers demanding the Porte enact internal reforms. Russia, France, and Italy immediately agreed to the identical action. Britain however, balked first, then adhered to the plan with reservations that neutralized Andrássy's initiative. Likewise, Britain put up resistance to Bismarck's Berlin Memorandum of May 1876, which had a similar aim.[59]

Bismarck did not share Britain's fears and saw in the prospect of Russian intervention a chance to solve the Eastern Question once and for all. He had no qualms about Turkey being dismantled. As he would put it to Disraeli at the Berlin Congress of 1878, Russia was stirred up for war by the unrest in the Balkans, and it "was better that she should go to war with Turkey rather than with Austria."[60] Thus, Bismarck looked favorably on the chance to vent Russian spleen, and settle the Eastern Question decisively, by dividing up Ottoman spoils, with Bosnia and Herzegovina going to Austria, Bessarabia and Bulgaria to Russia, and Egypt to England.

In September and October 1876, the Great Powers were scrambling to stop the complete rout of Serbia with an armistice agreement. At their behest, the Turks and Serbs had agreed to a ten-day cease-fire in mid-September. Three days after it expired, Serbia inexplicably resumed hostilities and paid dearly in a string of defeats that left its forces annihilated and the road to Belgrade defenseless. As the debacle transpired, Russia at first pressed for a six-month armistice—to give Serbian forces time to recover—while Turkey insisted on no more than four to six weeks. Then in early October, the positions reversed. Russia now was set on going to war and demanded an armistice of no more than six weeks—to allow time for its war preparations—while Turkey wanted no less than six months.[61] Turkey was supported by Austria, Britain, and France on this score. Fed up and fearing the complete ruination of Serbia, Russia rejected the six-month armistice and delivered an ultimatum to the Porte on 30 October. It demanded that Turkey agree to a two-month armistice within forty-eight hours or face a war with Russia.[62] Britain advised Turkey to comply, and it did so the next day.

While all of this maneuvering over armistice terms transpired, the powers were chewing on the more fundamental issues at stake. Russia was mobilizing for war with Turkey and trying to prepare the ground for it diplomatically.[63] Britain was trying to stop it and to achieve a united front with Austria on this score. France could do little or nothing to either impede or promote Russian aims, while Italy was far too weak for Russia to depend on in a confrontation with Austria and Britain. So in September 1876, Russia had found little choice but to seek its mandate for war with Turkey within the aegis of the *Dreikaiserbund*, where Germany, the closest thing Russia had to an ally, held the pivot.

Russia needed to get a fix on both Austrian and German positions. It was doubtful that Russia's war aims, especially if they included occupation of Bulgaria, would have Austria's blessing, or that Austria would acquiesce to Russian advances. Nor was it clear how Germany would react if the two went to war. Ideally, Austria would join Russia by immediately seizing Bosnia. Failing that, a pledge from Austria of benevolent neutrality would be desirable. But if Austria did not play along and joined instead with Britain to block Russia (something that looked increasingly likely), then a promise from Germany to keep Austria down and England out would be necessary. These were the main considerations of Russian diplomacy in the autumn of 1876. For all of these purposes, a firm German commitment would be beneficial. So that was where Prince Gorchakov, the czar's foreign minister, began.

Russia's Bid for German Alliance

In early September 1876, the first Russian feelers reached Germany. While the czar was in Warsaw observing maneuvers, Marshall Manteuffel (Prime Minister of Prussia, 1850–58) went there bearing a letter from Wilhelm assuring Alexander that the legacy of Russian support for Prussia during the wars of unification would "guide my policy toward Russia no matter what happens."[64] Warming to the theme, the czar replied with a note requesting payback from Germany against Austria. During the Franco-Prussian War, Alexander had promised to unleash an army of 300,000 against the Dual Monarchy if it marched against Prussia. Now, in return, he wanted Germany to "hold the ring" for Russia by forcing Austria to back down. The czar wished to preserve the *Dreikaiserbund*, but his efforts to come to terms with Vienna had so far not borne fruit. If, however, Germany came out and clearly supported Russia, Austrian resistance would surely melt.[65]

Bismarck did not respond to these soundings, on the pretense that German friendship with Russia was so well established that none were necessary. Unsatisfied, on 14 September Alexander demanded further clarification through Paul de Oubril, his ambassador to Berlin. What would Germany do if Russia went to war unilaterally? What diplomatic settlement to the war would it support?[66] Bismarck dodged again. His official reply on 22 September, through his envoy in St. Petersburg, General H. L. von Schweinitz, stated that the first question had already been answered in the earlier letters from Wilhelm to Alexander.[67]

In late September, a Russian envoy, General Sumarakov-Elston, carried a proposal to Vienna and London for combined military action against the Porte.[68] Russia would occupy Bulgaria, Austria would occupy Bosnia, while the European (British) fleet subdued Turkish resistance from the Bosphorus.[69] That Britain would reject the proposal was a foregone conclusion, so Russia's chief aim was to convince Vienna to agree to revise the Reichstadt agreement, so that Russia could occupy Bulgaria immediately and thereby hasten rather than await the collapse of Turkish control.

Andrássy refused. The proposal posited a false symmetry between Bosnia and Bulgaria. Russian occupation of Bulgaria would present a direct threat to Austria, while Austrian occupation of Bosnia would not do the same to Russia. Francis Joseph agreed. His rebuff of Sumarokov-Elston's plan on 3 October was cushioned by a disingenuous go-ahead to fleet action, a moot point in light of Britain's attitude. He also urged Russia to continue pressing for an armistice and to fully support British peace moves.[70] Vienna's apparent collusion with London in rejecting the plan—in conjunction with Anglo-Austrian opposition to Russia on the armistice question—signaled that Russia should expect more resistance from Austria in the future.

Alexander reacted to the rebuff by increasing the pressure on Germany to declare firm support for Russia. In early October, General von Werder, the German military attaché in St. Petersburg, notified Berlin that the czar was now seriously contemplating risking war with Austria and wanted to know how Germany would react if Russia did.[71] Alexander's decision to use the Werder channel was significant, for he had also been the one to convey the czar's promise of 300,000 troops in 1870.[72] Bismarck was alarmed. "The whole thing," he declared, "is an attempt to make us sign a blank check, which Russia will fill in, and cash for use against Austria and England."[73] He refused to make a formal engagement with Russia. After stalling for three weeks, he answered through Schweinitz on 23 October.

Bismarck's reply was fourfold: (1) In case of war between Russia and Turkey, Germany would endeavor to keep Austria neutral. (2) If war, nevertheless, broke out between Russia and Austria, Germany would not immediately take sides. (3) It would not serve German interests "if through a coalition of the rest of Europe, fate were unfavorable to Russian arms" and Russia's power position were "essentially and permanently impaired." (4) But "just as deeply" would it harm German interests if Austria "should be endangered in its position as a great European Power or in its independence, so that one of the factors with which we have had to reckon in the European equilibrium should disappear."[74]

What effect would Bismarck's response have had on Russia's calculations for going to war against Turkey without Austrian consent, and potentially, against active Austrian and British resistance? It must have been disheartening, for St. Petersburg was optimistic enough to hope for active German assistance against Austria as quid pro quo for previous favors to Germany.[75] Indeed, just five months earlier, Prince Gorchakov had boasted that in a war with Austria, Russia would "have a German Army at our disposal."[76] Now Germany had let Russia down. Said Gorchakov to Schweinitz, "We expected great things from you [and] you have brought us nothing."[77] That it could not count on German arms against Austria would have at least tempered Russia's estimates of fighting a successful war in the Balkans without Austrian consent.

Even more ominous, Bismarck had suggested that Germany could not brook a major defeat of Austria at Russian hands. Thus, Russia could not contemplate a strategy for winning the war against Turkey that included a stroke designed to knock out Austria in the Balkans. If Russia were to wage war in Turkey against Austrian resistance, and without incurring German wrath, then it would have to fight a strictly limited campaign, in a region where the defenders in combination had an advantage, and where the defeat of Austrian forces could not be more than local.

The only bright spot was that Bismarck had promised not to idle if Russia were laid low by a European coalition, as it had during the Crimean War. But again, in light of Germany's refusal to turn against Austria, the question of whether or not Vienna joined the anti-Russian coalition would be crucial. In short, if Russia were to have any confidence in Bismarck's promise to block a European coalition, Austria could not be part of that coalition. Therefore, Russia would first have to win over Austria to its war plans.

After delivering these points, Bismarck repeated his preferred solution to the Eastern Question—that Russia and Austria would come to an agreement on the amicable division of Ottoman spoils—and underscored his willingness to back any solution they both could agree to. Bismarck, in a dinner speech on 1 December 1876, that was published at his behest, elaborated on this theme. Russia's and Austria's relations with Germany could only be endangered "if one of our friends asked that we should treat the other friend as an enemy . . . and prove our stronger love to the one by hatred to the other." As R. W. Seton-Watson put it, "to the Tsar and Gorchakov this pronouncement, following so soon upon the Werder incident, was a very definite warning."[78]

Austria Bids for German Alliance

Meanwhile Vienna was seriously considering its military and diplomatic options against Russia. Austria's first preference at this stage was that Russia not go to war against Turkey at all. Rather, Andrássy wanted to keep Turkey in Europe intact, albeit weak and reformed. The Reichstadt agreement was premised on the internal collapse of Turkey—not its destruction by Russia or any other power. There were three potential threats to Austria embodied in Russia's war plans in the fall of 1876. First, a postwar expansion of Serbia and Montenegro would increase the strength of Austria's nearest Slavic neighbors and cut off its access to the Aegean port of Salonika. Second was the danger of Russian troops deploying on Serbian soil in support of Serb and Montenegrin forces. To Andrássy, that would make "out of the European action a Slav movement, out of the Christian humanitarian tendency a one-sided Orthodox movement, and out of war a revolution," a revolution liable to sunder the Dual Monarchy. Third, Austria feared a permanent Russian occupation of Bulgaria or, alternatively, its postwar reconstitution as an enlarged Slavic state subservient to Russia.[79] These Russian war aims formed the crux of the dispute between St. Petersburg and Vienna in September and October 1876.

After turning away Sumarakov-Elston on 3 October, Andrássy dispatched his envoy Baron Münch to Berlin to sound out Bismarck on an Austro-German alliance if Vienna and St. Petersburg came to blows.[80] The Bismarck-inspired press in Germany had already warned Austria that "Germany's armed support could not be counted upon in the Balkans."[81] Bismarck struck the same theme in his private consultations with Münch. First he tried to allay Austrian fears by suggesting that taking Bosnia would be advantageous and that any Russian occupation of Bulgaria would be short-lived and liable to weaken Russia through the likely resistance of Britain. Bismarck then spelled out to Münch why Germany would not take sides against Russia. If war broke out between Austria and Russia, and Russia suffered defeat, Germany would be placed in an untenable predicament, "between two states thirsting for revenge" (i.e., Russia and France).[82] Germany, therefore, would not make any commitment that encouraged Austria to war with Russia.

But, Münch queried, what if Austria did go to war with Russia single-handed? Then Italy might join up with Russia, hoping to reclaim territory in the Trentino. In that case, wouldn't Germany ally with Austria? At this point Bismarck revealed to Münch the czar's recent inquiries. Just as he had avoided the czar's questions because they implied hostility to Austria, he would reject any offer from Vienna that had an "anti-Russian focal point." If Germany allied with Austria now, said Bismarck, "this would amount to an alliance against Russia, because he could conduct an eventual war against Italy only by attacking Russia in order to make [Austrian] troops available against Italy."[83] Bismarck then invoked his famous mantra: It was "unwise to form an alliance for future eventualities"; any pact between Austria and Germany could "only be the result of a time of excitement" which the current situation, apparently, was not. Bismarck reiterated that the best solution to the problem was Austrian occupation of Bosnia and Herzegovina along the lines of the Reichstadt agreement, which he would certainly support, but beyond that he would make no commitments.[84] There is no doubt that Bismarck believed that a firm commitment to Austria would embolden it to war with Russia. As he noted in a memorandum, "a war between Russia and Austria is for us and our future an extraordinarily difficult and dangerous dilemma: and we cannot be expected to make it easier so long as it is not absolutely inevitable."[85]

Austria was as dissatisfied with Bismarck's evasion as Russia. On 24 November, Andrássy put it directly to the German ambassador in Vienna: He feared that in an Austro-Russian war, Germany would throw its weight behind Russia. Bismarck should make his position clear.[86] Bismarck's reply did little to calm Andrássy's fears. Germany had made no binding commitments to Russia, but Andrássy should not make too much of this, for it also refused to warn St. Petersburg against a clash with Austria. As Bismarck saw it: "Vienna must know as well as we do that Russia neither will nor can conduct war against both Turkey and Austria. Quite the contrary, Russia is on the verge of sticking its head in a noose that Austria is holding in its hand. *Therefore, it is Russia that has more of a right to ask of us a treaty guarantee and support against Austria.*"[87]

Now the critical choice for Austria was to either cooperate with Russia, under the aegis of the *Dreikaiserbund,* or to court an alliance with Britain against Russia. Rumania and Greece were at best insignificant and at worst total liabilities. Stronger, but still minor players in the overall equation, were Italy, which was patently hostile toward Austria, and France, which was amicable toward Russia. None of them amounted to a plausible alignment option.[88] In this context, Bismarck's pivotal deterrence policy worked at this time because conditional German friendship was more attractive to Austria than an alliance with an even less reliable Britain. Disraeli's government had, over the previous year, thrown up obstacles to every European effort at Turkish reform, including Andrássy's proposal of December 1875, and the Berlin Memorandum. Then, in late June, word reached London of the Bulgarian atrocities committed by Turkey the previous spring. Led by

Gladstone, the Liberal opposition was up in arms over the Disraeli government's downplaying of the atrocity reports and its firm support to Constantinople; public opinion echoed this sentiment. From late August on, dissension over that policy began to grow *within* the Cabinet—most notably, from the Earl of Derby, who was the foreign minister, and the Marquis of Salisbury, who was secretary for India.[89]

Historians agree that in the fall of 1876, European statesmen—Andrássy included—doubted the stability of Disraeli's government, and Derby's ability to formulate much less sustain a coherent policy on the Eastern Question.[90] Andrássy's doubts about Britain were increased in mid-October, when it became clear that Derby was reaching out to Russia to hash out an armistice agreement at an approaching conference in Constantinople, which Disraeli had proposed and which Andrássy opposed. To pressure St. Petersburg to come to terms at the Constantinople Conference, Disraeli had made a speech in November declaring a willingness to go to war to prevent Russian occupation of Turkey. In the aftermath of this fiery statement, Anglo-Russian pourparlers progressed rapidly. In December, at the Constantinople Conference, Russia agreed to a British-sponsored protocol for Ottoman reform, backed with guarantees of compliance. St. Petersburg was betting that the Porte would refuse to comply, and that its doing so would clear away British opposition to forceful Russian action.[91] The reform project had been hammered out by Ignatiev and Salisbury, who negotiated on Derby's behalf. But Derby and Salisbury were out of favor with Disraeli, and in this venture they failed to win over the prime minister, who cared little about Turkish reform. Disraeli's chief concern was to block Russian intervention regardless of Turkey's misdeeds. He thus refused to endorse the Salisbury-Ignatiev reform plan, and as a result, the demands placed on Turkey coming out of the conference were watered-down considerably. The Porte, in any case, rejected even those proposals and announced instead its own reform plan. This took matters back to square one because there was scant hope of the Porte implementing the reforms and no European unity to compel it to do so.[92]

Throughout all of this, Andrássy's suspicions regarding British reliability were justified, for in September 1876, London had sent an army officer to assess Austria's military and financial potential as an ally against Russia, and the prognosis reported back was not favorable.[93] So Austria's dubious opinion of Britain as a potential ally was reciprocated, and thus reinforced, throughout the last months of 1876. With the allure of an Anglo-Austrian alliance thus tarnished, the prospects for Bismarck's policy of pivotal deterrence between Austria and Russia were greatly improved.

Beyond the vagaries of domestic politics, there were deeper reasons why Britain was not a reliable and attractive ally to Austria. First, Britain had no army to speak of, and its navy could not sail in the Balkans and Carpathians. Second, Britain was most concerned about Constantinople and the Straits, not the disposition of Balkan territories. Once the Straits were secured, there would be little to keep London engaged. Andrássy well knew that Austria could end up Britain's cat's-paw on the Continent, discarded as soon as London's interests were served.

So, in 1876, nothing became of Russia's and Austria's attempts to lure Germany into a firm alliance. Neither side won Germany's firm backing. Both were made to understand that Germany could not tolerate the other side suffering a major defeat. Without Germany's firm allegiance, each faced great uncertainty over their prospects for success in a war against the other. The only thing they could be sure of was that Germany would not allow them to decisively defeat the other side. Russia and Austria decided to play it safe and to cooperate instead.

Austria and Russia thus returned with renewed vigor to negotiating an extension of the Reichstadt agreement. In mid-October, after his overtures to Germany were rebuffed, the czar sent Vienna another letter stating that he was determined to act against Turkey, but offering to work with Austria along the lines of the Reichstadt agreement. Francis Joseph responded a week later, stating that while he would not declare war on Turkey, he would promise Russia benevolent neutrality in exchange for the right to annex Bosnia and Herzegovina. Moreover, in the revived spirit of the *Dreikaiserbund,* he would be willing to seal the bargain in a secret convention.[94]

Gorchakov commenced negotiations with Vienna on 2 November, which continued in tandem with Anglo-Russian negotiations at the Constantinople Conference through December and into the next year. They centered on a number of issues arising from the poor fit between the Reichstadt agreement and current circumstances. There were disagreements over whether Austria's right of annexation included Herzegovina with Bosnia or not; over whether Russian forces could fight along side Serbs and Montenegrins in those territories; over the compensations to be granted Serbia and Montenegro; over the nature and duration of Russian presence in Bulgaria and its future independence; over the status of Albania, Rumelia, and Greece; and, more generally, over the need to preserve a buffer zone between Russian and Austrian forces. These were serious matters, but they were resolved by the two sides with an alacrity that had not characterized their recent relations. In the end, the general contours of the arrangement did not diverge greatly from the bargain laid out in Reichstadt: Austria would get Bosnia and Herzegovina; Russia would get Bessarabia and a green light to invade Turkey and aid the Balkan Slavs.

In January and March 1877, St. Petersburg and Vienna reached agreement on these terms in what are known as the Budapest Conventions.[95] Meanwhile, London's efforts to salvage a reform protocol agreement with

St. Petersburg that would entail Turkish disarmament and Russian demobilization came to naught. The Anglo-Russian protocol that was ultimately signed in London on 31 March had, as one historian put it, "no inherent value" save the signal it sent of British acquiescence to Russia's war.[96] On 12 April, the Porte rejected the protocol. Twelve days later Russia declared war on Turkey and commenced operations. Russia's conduct during the war, and its self-defeating attempt to settle it unilaterally at San Stefano a year later, would again raise the specter of Austro-Russian antagonism. But for the time being, the two were in accord.

From the Russo-Turkish War to the Congress of Berlin, 1877–78

The Budapest Conventions were proof that, without firm backing from Germany, Russia had few good alternatives to cooperating with Austria. In the Conventions, Russia agreed to submit for Austrian approval any territorial changes to Serbia and Montenegro; to refrain from sending Russian troops to support Slav forces in Serbia, Montenegro, and Herzegovina; to annex only Bessarabia; to promptly evacuate Bulgaria after the war; and to support Bulgarian independence only if there were a complete collapse of Ottoman rule in the region.[97] These agreements were put to the test in the spring and summer of 1877 when Russia scored a number of easy victories against Turkey in a campaign that threatened to spread far beyond the constraints of the Budapest accord.

In early July 1877, Andrássy considered intervening against Russia if it failed to conduct operations in a way that conformed to previous agreements, and he proposed the early mobilization of the army to make such intervention possible.[98] Salisbury later reported that when he raised the issue of Russia's overreaching at that time, Andrássy "replied by rising silently to his feet, walking to the map which hung on the wall, and laying his finger with a dramatic gesture upon the neck of land which separated Transylvania from the Black Sea."[99] The implication was clear; Andrássy envisioned an eastward thrust from the Carpathians into the flank of Russia's extended lines running down the Black Sea coast.

The British courted Vienna assiduously throughout this period, but Austria remained wary. London's policy in the coming year would justify this wariness.[100] As Salisbury himself had lamented in March, "English policy is to float lazily down stream occasionally putting out a diplomatic boat hook to avoid collisions."[101] In May, Andrássy had noted to his ambassador in London that "joint diplomatic action against Petersburg had been made impossible from the outset by England's attitude."[102] And with Britain unreliable, Austria would not tempt fate in a war against Russia without firm backing from Germany. As the British chargé d'affaires in Budapest reported to London, Andrássy's reluctance to undertake military action "was due mainly to his uncertainty regarding Germany's reaction to an Austro-Russian conflict."[103]

Austria's concerns about Russia receded after 30 July, when Russia suffered the first of three devastating defeats at Plevna. They would remain dormant until December, when Plevna finally fell and Russia began to march on Constantinople to deliver the coup de grace. During that five-month stalemate, British policy remained incoherent. In November, Britain's ambassador to the Porte wrote Disraeli: "I do not despair of holding my own and maintaining the honor and interests of England, if I could only know what the intentions and objects of my Government really were."[104] He was not the only one who wondered.

Austrian fears were aroused again in January 1878, when Russia circulated controversial if also vague drafts of the proposed armistice with Turkey, which spoke of a much enlarged Bulgaria "up to the Balkans." Andrássy denounced the aspirations of Russia's peace bid, charging that they left room for "nothing but ratification" by Austria, and he asked for German support in blocking it sans Europe-wide endorsement.[105] Bismarck would not agree to such joint action, and instead pressed for a meeting of the three powers in Vienna or Berlin. Russia rejected the offer to meet in Vienna but hinted that it was open to meeting in a less conspicuous German city. St. Petersburg also disclosed to Berlin in detail its settlement plans—which significantly overstepped the terms agreed to in the Budapest Conventions with Austria—hoping to secure Bismarck's backing before presenting them to Vienna.[106]

On 3 March 1878, Russia imposed on Turkey the Treaty of San Stefano, which, in defiance of the Budapest Conventions, provided for the creation of a greatly enlarged Bulgaria subject to a two-year Russian occupation. In the months leading up to San Stefano, Andrássy had worked to undermine these violations of the Budapest Conventions, and had even threatened to take military measures if Russia did not submit the terms of the settlement to European approval. In January, at Andrássy's request, the Austrian military had begun planning for such military measures.[107]

Yet, even as Russia's advance menaced Constantinople and the straits, British policy remained erratic. Disraeli had decided in mid-January to take a more vigorous military attitude and close ranks with Austria against Russia. But his Cabinet was divided on the issue. Derby and Salisbury, in particular, objected to Disraeli's program. And when he took the matter to Parliament he was, as Stojanovic records, "unable to propose any clear course of policy . . . all his efforts at asserting his determination for action afforded only new proofs of the weakness and irresolution of the British Government," which in turn, led Andrássy "to refuse [Disraeli's] invitation for cooperation." Still seeking to show a firmness that would cow Russia and entice Austria to ally with Britain, on 15 January Disraeli ordered the Navy to deploy in the Dardanelles without Turkey's consent, which would violate Ottoman territory rights as well as the tripartite treaty of April 1856, among Britain, France, and Austria. But when Foreign Minister Derby threatened to resign over the decision, the order was countermanded under public scrutiny. Ten days later the fleet was ordered back into the Dardanelles, then pulled back again. On 8 February, in response to rumors that the Porte would enter into a strictly bilateral accord with Russia on the Straits, the fleet returned to put down anchor near Constantinople, once again in defiance of the Porte's strenuous objections. The back and forth did much to undermine London's political position in Constantinople and elsewhere.[108] The sequence of fiascos meant that Britain's policy in the Eastern Crisis risked "becoming the laughing stock of Europe."[109]

It is not surprising, then, that the furthest Andrássy would go with Britain in the winter of 1878 was a confidential exchange of views. He would make no commitments to London, not even in secret.[110] Austria just could not pin its hopes on an alliance with Britain. Francis Joseph had little faith in the "vacillating policy of England." "For months England had been nowhere," griped Andrássy; "her policy seemed to be one of indecision, vacillation and tergiversation."[111] The German ambassador to London saw the British state of affairs similarly: "the political situation is so incomprehensible, and the position into which this Government has got the country and itself so peculiar and unaccountable, that the best informed and most conscientious report runs the risk of appearing obscure and confused."[112]

If Austria were going to challenge Russian pretensions with force in the winter of 1878, it would have to mobilize the support of a more dependable backer than Britain—that could only be Germany. So Andrássy began another campaign in February 1878 to enlist Germany as an ally, pulling out all the stops. He argued that without strong German backing, he would be removed from office and replaced with someone less Germanophile; that a big Bulgaria would threaten Germany directly; that the constitutional structure of the Dual Monarchy would crumble if Austria suffered a diplomatic setback in the Balkans; and on it went.[113] But again, Bismarck would not give Andrássy any firm commitment. As he put it to Bernard von Bülow, his foreign minister, there was nothing more "he could declare . . . in favor of Austria without coming under the suspicion of instigating war."[114]

When the Austro-Hungarian Crown Council met in February to decide whether to begin an immediate and full mobilization—a step that had already been endorsed by Count Kalman Tisza, the Hungarian prime minister—Francis Joseph balked. He feared that it would make war with Russia unavoidable at a time when it was not clear that Germany would back Austria, when British policy was in disarray, and when it was still possible that

Russia would return to the spirit of the *Dreikaiserbund*.[115] Thus, in February of 1878, Austria decided again not to go to war against Russia. Three months later Bismarck commended Count Peter Shuvalov, the Russian ambassador to Britain for Russia's decision in early 1878 to begin direct negotiations with Britain, for as he saw it, "Austria would only have made war if she had allies." In the first two months of 1878, thanks to Bismarck's policy, and Britain's fecklessness, Austria never found those allies. Consequently, in late March, Andrássy secretly agreed with Ignatiev that Austria would stand neutral if Britain and Russia went to war.[116]

When Salisbury took over as foreign minister in March 1878, British policy became more coherent and formidable, and Salisbury achieved surprising success negotiating with Russia directly. Gorchakov came around to the view that the Treaty of San Stefano was not set in stone but rather a provisional settlement that would be subject to revision at the forthcoming Congress of Berlin.[117] This fairly well insured that Austria's interests would be protected without it having to take up arms because, in Berlin, Britain would oppose the Bulgaria envisioned in San Stefano and most of the other provisions offensive to Austria. But even so, perhaps to strengthen its position at the Berlin Congress, Russia continued to advocate a much stronger line, arguing that since Russia had fought the war alone, it had the right to dictate the terms of settlement.

During the Anglo-Russian negotiations preceding the Congress of Berlin in June, Shuvalov took one last opportunity to sound Bismarck on a Russo-German alliance.[118] Such an alliance would have undoubtedly encouraged Russia to take a harder line at the Berlin Congress, which may very well have led to more hostilities. True to form, Bismarck demurred, reserving for himself at the Congress that attitude of an "honest-broker who gets the business done" for which he was to become so renowned.[119]

SUMMARY OF FINDINGS

Necessary Conditions

When it came to the Eastern Question, Bismarck was convinced that a prerequisite for changing the status quo was peace between Russia and Austria. Because a Russo-Austrian war involved danger for Germany, he had to do his "utmost first and foremost to stop it by one means or another."[120] So during the crisis Bismarck repeated to Russia and Austria that, in regard to their Balkan disputes, he "would support anything that they could agree on."[121] As he put it to his ambassador to St. Petersburg, "The basis of our policy remains our lively wish to preserve our two close friends Russia and Austria from differences."[122] In that same spirit, he explained to one of his subordinates in 1876 that "it little concerns German interests through what measures and in what form a regulation of Eastern affairs is concluded, but . . . we have a great interest that the agreement on this question should be achieved on a basis of the maintenance of good relations between the powers friendly to us."[123] Therefore, Germany supported Austria's moves to occupy Bosnia, so long as there was "no breach with Russia."[124] It also applauded Russia's war against Turkey, so long as Russia did not wage it in the teeth of Austrian opposition.[125]

Bismarck also was aware of the threats Russia and Austria posed to each other and understood that each would be more inclined to risk war with the other if it believed Germany would back it. As he noted in one memorandum, "a war between Russia and Austria is for us and our future an extraordinarily difficult and dangerous dilemma: and we cannot be expected to make it easier so long as it is not absolutely inevitable."[126] In October 1876 Russia asked for German backing in a war against Turkey and Austria. The bid was rebuffed with the polite response that in such a war, "Germany would have no reason to abandon her neutrality." Gorchakov was persistent. "I want more and I shall tell Prince Bismarck so!"[127] But he didn't get more for his efforts. So Russia had to sit down with Austria and agree on acceptable limits to a Russian war in the Balkans. The result was the Budapest Conventions of January 1877. Similarly, in January 1878, Austria asked for German support in a war that would cut off Russia's forces in Turkey. Bismarck declined. As he later told it to Shuvalov, Austria "would only have made war if she had allies," and "when Andrássy was in a warlike mood, I pacified him by proving that he could not fight you alone."[128]

It is clear that during the mid-1870s, Austria and Russia feared each other more than they feared Germany. Although Germany had defeated Austria in 1866 and had taken territory from it, the benign settlement afterward had reassured Vienna of Germany's intentions. On the other hand, besides Turkey itself, Austria was the only Continental power with much to lose if Russia had its way in the Balkans and much to gain by thwarting Russian advances. Accordingly, both Austria and Russia meditated going to war against each other between 1876 and 1878. Each time they did (that we know of), they came to Bismarck to ask for support. This behavior is consistent with the proposition that they perceived Germany to be less threatening than each other. Moreover, there is no record of either Austria or Russia seriously contemplating war against Germany during this period or of exploring between them an alliance for such a contingency.

Isolation Avoidance Effects

There is ample evidence of both the uncertainty and ingratiation effects at work in this case. During the crisis both Russia and Austria came hat in hand, seeking an alliance with Germany before running the risks of war with each other. Neither side was willing to take bold action in the face of uncertainty about Germany's allegiance. And neither side wanted to appear before Germany as obstreperous or indifferent to the other's vital interests. Because they left empty-handed each time they sought exclusive German backing, they were impelled to work out a mutually acceptable compromise that won Bismarck's endorsement. Thus, Austria and Russia were made to "come along" by Bismarck's pivoting between them. At his prodding, for example, Austria and Russia met for talks in Berlin in May 1876. When they came to loggerheads over Russia's ambitions, Bismarck insisted that neither side would be "swamped with a majority." He would only support what both sides agreed to. Consequently, Andrássy conceded that if Turkey collapsed, Russia could take back Bessarabia (but not create a new Slav state), while Gorchakov conceded that Austria could occupy Bosnia-Herzegovina.[129]

Nevertheless, there were also clear efforts by both sides to put the other in the wrong, further evidence of isolation avoidance pressures at work. Thus, when Austro-Russian talks over the fate of the Slav revolt deadlocked in 1876, Gorchakov asked Bismarck to corner Austria so that Russia could have a free hand against Turkey. He contended, not surprisingly, that while Russia was offering concessions in the spirit of the *Dreikaiserbund*, Austria spurned them. Since Austria would not cooperate, Russia would have no choice but to act unilaterally, and Germany, he argued, should screen out any interference from other powers—Austria chief among them.

We also find evidence of diversification efforts in this case. The most telling instance arose in Austria's courting of Britain. The expectation that Britain would support Turkey's (and thus Austria's) side in a war against Russia did, in some instances, encourage Austrian intransigence in negotiations with Russia. But the "Anglo card" did not make for a strong hand because Britain was too far away and too "perfidious" to be counted on in a land war with Russia. Moreover, Andrássy was unable to extract German allegiance by courting Britain because, to put it simply, Bismarck was the happy matchmaker. The abortive Anglo-Austrian alignment served German interests well enough; too flimsy for Austria to lean on, it nevertheless relieved pressure on Bismarck to take sides against Russia.

Alignment Options Effects

Germany was well positioned for pivotal deterrence between Austria and Russia. As I argued at the outset, although it was a peer pivot, Germany was centrally located between Russia and Austria, and it had an army that was better, that could mobilize sooner and move by rail faster, than either Austria or Russia. Thus, German military capabilities and geographic proximity would have permitted it to intervene between Russia and Austria in a timely and decisive manner. The immediacy with which its vital interests would be put in danger in a war between Austria and Russia also worked to Bismarck's advantage. Any war between Russia and Austria in the 1870s would have threatened both the territorial integrity and internal stability of Germany and would force it to intervene on one side or another.

Finally, and most important, alignment options were scarce for Austria and Russia. Throughout most of the crises of 1876–78, they did not have attractive alignment options that could substitute for German friendship or neutralize German opposition, and both desired German backing before going to war with their adversary. This allowed Bismarck to deter both Austria and Russia by refusing to support them in actions that risked war with the other side.

Accounting for Confounding Causes of Peace

Two other important conditions that favored success were at work in this case and should be taken into account. They are not captured in the theoretical framework that informs our research design, but they emerge in the historical analysis. First, Bismarck's efforts to keep Austria and Russia at peace had the advantage of building on a track record of relative détente between them, which was expressed in the spirit of the *Draikaiserbund*. In a sense, this was the default position, and Bismarck's prime task was to keep them engaged as they were before, working to minimize their emerging cross-purposes.

Second, although Austria and Russia had vital interests in the Eastern Crisis, and ultimately, as Stojanovic put it, "both of them aimed at completely dominating the Balkans, which neither could achieve except by the expelling of the other," the immediate conflicts between them were over control of what was essentially an "expanding pie"—the spoils of decaying Turkish rule.[130] It is a truism of politics that conflict over the distribution of increasing resources tends to be less intractable than conflict over the distribution of diminishing resources. Therefore, it was another point in favor of Bismarck's policy that the situation allowed him magnanimously to back solutions that aggrandized rather than subtracted from both sides.

There is no need to see either of these two factors as competitors to our main thesis. Indeed, the poverty of alignment options enhanced rather than detracted from them. The lack of attractive alternatives reinforced the relative value of the *Draikaiserbund*, where Bismarck's clout was greatest, and strengthened his ability to convince Vienna and St. Petersburg that it remained the best way to address their differences. There was another virtue to Austria's and Russia's inability to find other powers to support them directly in a fight over the Balkans: the appetite of no other Great Power needed to be sated in the carve-up of the Turkish lands between Austria and Russia.

Finally, we may ask whether the military balance between Austria and Russia at this time was sufficient in itself to deter the two sides from going to war. The problem with this query is that it presupposes a wildly unhistorical, counterfactual assumption—that Austria and Russia would tally the prospects for success in a war with each other, focusing only on the military challenge of fighting in an isolated contest. The truth is that the question of how the actions of outside powers would influence their military fortunes was a dominant consideration, not a footnote, in their calculations. Indeed, for that reason, the notion of a "dyadic" balance of military power between Austria and Russia determining the outcome of their political struggle in the Balkans is an abstract construct that, given the context, would not have made much sense to Austrian and Russian leaders. There was an appreciation on both sides that a war between them in the Balkans would scarcely be an isolated fight, that other great powers (namely Germany and Britain), would to one degree or another and in one manner or another, weigh in. Sometimes even with optimism, military planners and diplomats in Vienna and St. Petersburg would contemplate and prepare for hostilities involving the other side.[131] But the decisions of the supreme leaders in Vienna and St. Petersburg—Francis Joseph and Alexander—were shaped by the perilous uncertainties of the larger picture. Which is why they were reluctant to go to war with each other without the promise of German backing. That is what made Bismarck's efforts to deter them by withholding such support both possible and successful.

[4]

Pivotal Deterrence and the Chain Gang:

SIR EDWARD GREY'S AMBIGUOUS
POLICY AND THE JULY CRISIS, 1914

We can now snap our fingers both at the Triple Alliance and at France and Russia.
William Tyrell, Personal Secretary to Sir Edward Grey, April 1913

Our action is held in suspense, for if both sides do not know what we shall do, both will be less willing to run risks.
Herbert Samuel, British Cabinet member, July 1914

History looks unkindly upon British policy in July 1914. As the crisis in Europe escalated, Britain "muddied the European scene" by avoiding firm commitments to either fight with France and Russia or stand aside.[1] Instead it tried to play the pivot and broker a peace-saving compromise. British policy was roundly condemned at the time, and still is today. The policy of Sir Edward Grey, Britain's foreign minister, is seen as the archetype of waffling and reactive diplomacy. While Grey temporized, so the argument goes, the Continental powers careened headlong into war, both sides betting that in the end Britain would help rather than hurt them. Many of these criticisms came from statesmen at the time who were deeply implicated in the outbreak of war and eager to shift blame. German leaders argued that Britain caused the war by failing to declare that it would remain neutral. French and Russian leaders argued that Britain caused the war because it did not firmly commit to them at the outset of the crisis.[2] By their nature, such arguments attributed a great deal of causal significance to British policy; they had to if they were to exculpate those who made them.

[75]

But Britain probably could not have prevented the war, regardless of the policy it pursued in the crisis. So we must be more careful about how we draw conclusions from the failure of the policy it did pursue.

DID BRITAIN CAUSE WORLD WAR I?

In 1919, German Admiral Von Tirpitz put it succinctly: Britain "brought upon itself a large share of the responsibility for the outbreak of the war by uncertainty as to [its] attitude during the crisis."[3] If Britain's ambiguous attitude was a cause of the war, then Grey's policy is guilty on many counts. "If, early in the crisis," argues Glenn Snyder, [Grey] "had declared his firm support of Russia and France and warned Germany unequivocally, *or* if he had clearly declared to France and Russia that Britain would not fight, the war might have been averted."[4] Invoking Albertini, Trachtenberg takes the indictment a step further, arguing that "instead of trying to be friends with both sides, Grey should have taken a tough line with both Germany and Russia, warning each side that 'the political and moral strength of Britain would be thrown in against the aggressor and that, if war came, his decision would be influenced by the conduct, peaceful or aggressive, of the two sides.'" Indeed, argues Trachtenberg, "Britain's influence on each would have in itself increased her importance in the eyes of the other, and the British government would have been much better able to control the course of the crisis—that is, to maximize its ability to bring about a peaceful settlement."[5]

Though doing so casts Grey's policy in the most damning light, the various changes need not be joined together. Indeed, what rankles most critics is that Britain did not "put the fear of God into Germany" early in the crisis.[6] Others fault Grey's whole Entente policy prior to 1914. It was too late to deter Germany once the crisis began. Only a rock-solid alliance with France and Russia beforehand would have "permitted no confusion in Berlin about British intentions."[7] More subtly, some argue that because "Russia and France acted in part out of insecurity," they would have been less aggressive if they could have counted on Britain; or alternatively, that as a firmly committed ally, Britain would have had more control over Russia and France.[8] Which takes us to another indictment, that British policy caused war because it did not restrain Russia and France. This view—no surprise—was first advanced by German statesmen even before the war started.[9] Next to take it up were revisionist historians after the war who wanted to debunk the idea of German "war guilt."[10]

However, there are some that contend Grey's policy made little difference in the outbreak of the war. A. J. P. Taylor made the case boldly: Grey's policy had almost no influence over the decision making of either the Central

Powers or France and Russia. German military planners, Taylor argues, "always assumed that Great Britain would enter the war; they did not take her military weight seriously, and naval questions did not interest them. . . . On the other side, France and Russia decided on war without counting firmly on British support."[11]

That Germany would not have responded to stronger British warnings is an argument that has been made on a variety of grounds. Perhaps Germany was so eager for European—if not world—hegemony, that it simply could not have been deterred.[12] Or, more "tragically," Germany may have been so fixated on security against Russia that it ignored Britain or, as Dale Copeland argues, may have been so hell-bent on fighting a "preventive" world war with Austria in tow that it actively worked to subvert Grey's policy.[13] Some who are uncomfortable with the idea that Britain had no chance to deter Germany try, like Grey, to have it both ways. During the crisis "Grey's semi-detached position left doors open [that] may have encouraged [Germany] to gamble on his ultimate neutrality," writes Zara Steiner, "the absence of alliances provided the Germans with just that margin of doubt which encouraged illusions . . . [and] obscured Britain's strategic position." Nevertheless, "even if Grey had made it perfectly clear where Britain stood, the Germans would have moved. . . . [Germany] was too strong to accept a final check on her ambitions without at least trying to break out of her enclosed position unless that check was powerful enough to make all hope of success futile. Britain, even in alliance with France and Russia, could not pose that kind of threat."[14]

Finally, some dismiss the idea that a strong alliance with France and Russia would have given Britain more control over the Entente during the crisis. Political scientists who emphasize the importance of "chain-ganging" between France and Russia, for example, would conclude that even as a close ally, Britain would have had little influence over their decision making once the crisis erupted.[15] But others take the contrary view and argue, as Samuel Williamson does, that Britain's policy "by its very uncertainty exercised a greater restraint upon French policy than an alliance would have."[16] In short, far from making war more likely, Britain's ambiguous policy was a force for peace during the crisis, even if it did not prevail over stronger pressures for war. This argument expresses the logic of pivotal deterrence theory, and it is the driving thesis of this chapter.

OVERDETERMINATION AND THE MISMEASURE OF BRITISH POLICY

Any argument that Britain could have prevented war in 1914 if it had acted differently is difficult to sustain. The reasons for this are both simple and complicated. Put simply, World War I was probably overdetermined.

To argue that a different British policy would have prevented the war one must surmount a staggering panoply of other causes—multipolarity, offensive doctrines and strategic beliefs, arms races, imperial competition, domestic politics, psychological biases, social revolution, and even the "mood" of 1914 which made war more "thinkable" than before—that, taken together, would seem to swamp whatever difference that change might have made.[17] For this reason, it is well nigh impossible to infer from the outbreak of war that Grey's strategy failed *because it was ambiguous.*

Even Glenn Snyder, author of the most insightful theoretical treatment of Grey's diplomacy, succumbs to this problem. He argues that Grey's strategy "failed" because its ambiguity allowed both sides to draw "opposite conclusions from it," both of which were optimistic about Britain's attitude. "This is not to argue that Grey's ambiguity was a central cause of the outbreak of World War I," Snyder caveats, "but Britain was the only major power that still had both polar options available; in failing to exercise either one, she gave up *a chance* to prevent the war."[18] An alternative Snyder does not consider is that Grey's ambiguous strategy may have offered a better "chance" to prevent the war than the polar options, but that the war broke out anyway. There is some reason to doubt whether the polar options would have worked any better than Grey's strategy of pivotal deterrence. After all, both Continental alliances, amassing tremendous military resources, tried more forthright deterrence, brandishing the "big stick" against their adversaries, and failed.[19] Conversely, both France and Germany also tried to restrain their close allies between 29–30 July and could not pull it off. This is why it is hard to be both pessimistic about Britain's chances of preventing war and yet dismiss Grey's strategy as the worst of the available choices.

To properly evaluate the failure (and successes) of Grey's policy, we must begin by admitting that it was attempted under conditions that made Continental war likely regardless of what Britain did. We must also take into account the multiple purposes of Grey's strategy—conciliating and deterring Germany, while restraining France and Russia. It is easy, in hindsight, to condemn Grey's strategy as a half-hearted stab at deterrence or a wrong-headed way to restrain one's friends. But a public commitment to fight early in the crisis would have meant sacrificing the prospect of moderating France and Russia; and a clear declaration of neutrality would have eliminated any deterrent effect Britain might have had on Germany.[20] Therefore, for our purposes, the key question is why Britain's pivotal policy failed in 1914 when it had worked at other times in different situations.

Grey's policy of pivotal deterrence did not fail *because* it was ambiguous. It failed because the leverage that usually flows from such a policy was enfeebled by France's and Germany's strong alignment options (Russia and Austria) and by a host of other war-conducing conditions that put Britain in a position not unlike someone trying to steer a barge with a canoe paddle. Indeed, it is remarkable that British crisis diplomacy influenced the Continental powers as much as it did.

OVERVIEW OF THE CASE

In the July crisis, Britain's pivotal deterrence policy was undermined by the adversaries' strong alignment options. Nevertheless, the restraining influence of that policy increased as Britain's stakes increased. While its interests at stake were weak, the adversaries were unmoved by concerns about Britain's attitude because neither side thought it was likely to intervene. So long as the prospects for British intervention were weak, France hewed closely to Russia, and Germany backed Austria to the hilt. Austria and Russia never responded to Grey's strategy. But Britain's influence over France and Germany increased once war between them—which would directly impinge on Britain's vital interests—became more likely.

This turning point occurred with Russia's partial mobilization on 28 July, which destroyed any hopes of localizing the conflict. With the crisis now internationalized, Grey's strategy began to bear fruit in France and Germany. But at the same time, Paris and Berlin lost control over their allies. In this way, France's failure to stop general mobilization in Russia, and Germany's inability to deliver Austria to the bargaining table, combined to make general war in Europe almost inevitable on 31 July. Even after general war in Europe was imminent, Britain's pivotal policy continued to exert a gravitational pull on France and Germany. Both made costly adjustments in order to ingratiate themselves with Britain. That they were willing to make these so late in the game, after they were deeply committed to war, politically and psychologically, makes the adjustments all the more remarkable. These diplomatic maneuvers did not prevent the war, but they do show that Grey's pivotal policy continued to produce restraining effects into the first days of August.

DESCRIPTION OF SITUATIONAL VARIABLES

The Balance of Capabilities

By choosing to fight or remain neutral in July 1914, Britain could significantly improve the prospects for victory for one side in the long haul but would not seal the matter in the short run. Britain's greatest weakness was in the land forces it could deploy on the Continent at the outbreak of the war, which "could only marginally affect the overall military balance."[21] Britain planned to muster to the Continent on short notice no more than six divisions, and when the fighting started on the crucial left wing in August, a mere "four British divisions would face the might of two German armies."[22] The French chief of the General staff, Joseph Joffre, did not count on the British Expedition Force for the success of his offensive war plans. And while German Chief of Staff Helmuth Von Moltke assumed that he would have to "reckon on" British opposition if Germany attacked France through Belgium, he believed the outcome of such a war would "be decided on land," where British forces would have negligible effect.[23] Britain's rather skimpy military figure was seen through the lens of offensive strategic beliefs, and since both France and Germany planned for and expected a short war, it was discounted even further.[24] In all likelihood—so it was thought—the war would be over before British strengths would come to bear.

This does not mean Britain's attitude was irrelevant in the short term. It mattered to Germany for the deleterious effect it would have on Italy's already doubtful allegiance to the Triple Alliance (Germany, Austria, and Italy).[25] It mattered to France for the same reason, and for others. As Williamson put it, France considered a British commitment "a form of insurance, useful at a war's outbreak, imperative if the war prolonged."[26] If the war were not short, then Britain's greatest military capabilities, embodied in the navy, would become vastly more important, or so it was thought. The most powerful in the world, Her Majesty's fleet could neutralize the German fleet and then some and, over time, strangle the overseas commerce of the Central Powers, while keeping British trade and that of Russia and France flowing freely. Britain's economy was also formidable, and if the war was drawn out, it could float much of the war costs for the Triple Entente powers (France, Russia, and Britain). So Britain could not be ignored, neutral or not, its interests would have to be taken into account at the peace table, but then again, neither side saw it as the linchpin to success or failure in a short war.

The Distribution of Interests and Intentions

Britain in 1914, did not have vital interests at stake in the Balkans per se. Britain's traditional interests in the Turkish Straits—already weakened since acquisition of the Suez Canal—did not appear threatened in the dispute between Serbia and Austria-Hungary. Indeed, Grey made it clear at the beginning of the crisis that Britain would stand neutral so long as war remained localized. In other words, Britain's attitude would be determined by, rather than determine, whether the crisis was localized. However, Britain's vital interests would become engaged if the Austrian-Serb dispute turned into a war between France and Germany, and if Germany moved to establish control over channel ports. Then the British navy would have to focus on keeping the German navy bottled up and the channel open. And it could not police Britain's far-flung empire if it had to constantly stand ready to thwart a cross-channel invasion or German commerce raiding. Britain's vital interests would be harmed even in the less dire scenario of a humiliating diplomatic defeat that "broke" its ententes with France and Russia. In that case, things would go sour with France and Russia again overseas, and, more important, there would be no diplomatic ground to stand on for balancing against Germany in the future.

But to get from the Balkan's imbroglio to the latter contingencies, others would have to make a series of critical decisions about issues over which Britain had little influence. Only hindsight makes the sequence of events and decisions leading from Sarajevo to full-blown world war seem inevitable. For all of the actors at the time, there was considerable uncertainty at each link in the chain. Germany would have to decide to back Austria to the hilt rather than restrain it, all down the line. Austria would have to push Serbia to the wall and give it no quarter in its ultimatum. Russia would have to encourage Serbian resistance, rather than restrain it, or leave it to its fate. France would have to remain loyal to Russia. Germany would have to attack France and—what was far from given—achieve success.[27] And so on. In the early stages of the crisis, British interests were hardly salient.

Even if the two sides did chain-gang into a Continental war, Britain more than any other power had the freedom to cut itself loose, at least in the short term. Britain's vaunted strategic insularity meant that standing by while others fought out the first battles was a reasonable option, one that both sides took seriously, either as a threat (in the case of France) or an opportunity (in the case of Germany). Therefore, during the first crucial decisions of the crisis—those that dramatically narrowed the range of opportunities for peaceful solutions—neither side was very concerned about winning British support. Not because Germany assumed Britain would remain neutral in a long Continental war. Not because France was sure that Britain would support it in such a war. But instead, because both thought general war could be avoided by acting resolutely with their allies. And that greatly diminished Britain's influence. Only after Continental brinkmanship deadlocked, and the danger to Britain's vital interests became obvious, did the questions of what Britain would do, and how soon, press upon the adversaries. And then Britain's leverage over their policies increased.

But right up until it declared war, reasonable people could disagree about whether Britain should intervene immediately or wait for things to play out. There was no compelling need for it to intervene right away, even if it could have done so with great effect (which it could not). That is why in the last stages of the crisis, the French still struggled to prevent and the Germans still tried to secure British neutrality. It may, by that time, have become improbable, but the consequences for both sides were great enough to warrant the effort.

Alignment Options

Snyder argues that what made it "virtually inevitable" that Grey's strategy would fail was that "the continental powers were firmly locked into a collision course: Austria and Russia via their deep conflict of interests in the Balkans, Germany and France because of their high dependence upon and firm commitments to their allies." Scholars borrowing from Stanley Hoffmann, named the resulting dynamic "chain-ganging."[28] How these "tightly wound" Continental alliances frustrated Grey's pivotal deterrence strategy will be developed below, but I will make three points here.

First, and most important, alignment options were strong in this case: France and Germany both had *very attractive* allies, alternative to Britain. Indeed, Russia and Austria were much more valuable to them than was British allegiance or neutrality. Britain had neither the capabilities nor the motive to contribute to French or German security in the way their allies did. Its bargaining power as a pivot suffered accordingly. Second, and consequently, during the initial phase of the crisis, both pairs of Great Powers—France and Russia, Germany and Austria—focused on cohesion above all else. Grey would find it very difficult to move any of them toward moderation if that meant weakening the alliances, all the more so because both sides believed that "big stick" diplomacy would be the most likely way to preserve peace on favorable terms.[29] The final difficulty lay in the fact that even when Grey began to exercise greater influence over France and Germany, they were unable to control their allies. Although both threatened to do so, neither felt they could abandon their allies without writing their own death warrant in the long run. Thus they could not move far in the direction that Britain's pivotal policy pulled them or do what would have been necessary to prevent the war—leave their allies in the lurch.

BRITISH POLICY AND THE OUTBREAK OF THE JULY CRISIS

Origins of Grey's Pivotal Deterrence Policy

Grey's approach to the July crisis expressed a coherent strategic logic. It was not simply a policy of indecision, an artifact of domestic politics, or the product of a pattern of economic relationships with both Germany and France.[30] It was an extension of a set of policies begun a decade before that had worked in different ways in a variety of contexts. Grey took charge of the Foreign Office in 1906. Though a Liberal, he wanted to continue, rather

than overturn, the foreign policy of the departing Conservative government. A hallmark of that policy was the nascent *Entente Cordiale* with
France, a series of agreements designed to resolve or manage specific issues
in their colonial relationships.[31] But Grey used the Anglo-French entente to
improve imperial relations with other Great Powers too. Better relations
with France led to better relations with Russia, the one power that could
threaten British interests in India and Persia.[32] By reducing the colonial friction with France and Russia that gave Germany leverage over Britain, the
ententes also relieved Britain of having to endure what Grey called "the
rough side" of German friendship.[33]

But for both intended and unintended reasons, the ententes took on
larger political significance on the Continent where Britain had more vital
interests at stake.[34] Germany was not just a capricious friend. With its growing military and naval power it was fast becoming the most likely threat to
the balance of power in Europe, and a less significant if nevertheless spir-
ited challenger to Britain's mastery at sea. Thus, for Britain the ententes
were the rudiments of a balancing policy against Germany. But they were
not always or even mostly directed against Germany. Their very looseness
and ambiguity left more room for conciliating Germany—and for a way out
of the Anglo-German naval race—than firm alliances would have. As Grey
explained to parliament in 1909, "two things . . . would produce conflict.
One is an attempt by us to isolate Germany"; the other "would be the isolation of Britain . . . by any great Continental Power."[35] So, Britain's loose ententes with France and Russia were supposed to avoid isolating Germany
and, at the same time, encourage German moderation by posing the
prospect of *much tighter commitments* between Britain and France and Russia if Germany did not cooperate.[36] In April 1914, the British ambassador to
Petersburg used just this logic with Russian foreign minister, S. Sazanov,
when he argued that "it was doubtful" whether Britain could have successfully upheld Russian interests in previous Balkans crises if it had "approached [Vienna and Berlin] as the ally of Russia; whereas *the fact that we
were only a friend who might be turned into an ally* should Germany and Austria force a war on Russia made them much more ready to listen to us."[37]

Moreover, Germany was not the only restless power that threatened stability in Europe. Indeed, the ententes also restrained France and Russia by
leaving them in doubt about how far Britain would go in supporting
them.[38] This threat of abandonment was *more credible* because Britain did
not have firm alliance commitments with either France or Russia. As early
as 1907, Sir Francis Bertie, the British ambassador to Paris, would argue
that, while France should not be allowed to lose confidence in Britain
friendship, "at the same time we must not encourage [the French] to rely on
our . . . support to the extent of making them beard the Germans."[39] Four

years later, in the Agadir crisis, Bertie would report that the French government did "not feel sure how far they could rely on . . . the existing Entente between Britain and France" and admit that "this feeling is useful to us as a security against" French imprudence.[40]

Grey, too, worried about encouraging French recklessness by drawing too close to her. Britain, he argued in 1912, could "be no party to France precipitating a conflict for the revanche" and would have to restrain "as far as [possible] this aggressive spirit in France."[41] This purpose strongly informed British policy in the July crisis. As late as 30 July 1914, Bertie cautioned Grey that "if we gave an assurance of armed assistance to France and Russia now, Russia would become more exacting and France would follow in her wake."[42] Even Eyre Crowe, a tireless advocate in the foreign office of closer Entente relations, admitted the next day that "what must weigh with His Majesty's Government is the consideration that they should not by a decision of unconditional solidarity with France and Russia *induce* or determine these two power to choose the path of war."[43] Thus, in advancing British vital interests on the Continent, the ententes were much less and much more than means for deterring Germany: They left the door open for conciliating Germany and restraining France and Russia.

The entente policy yielded a track record of successes. In the Moroccan crises of 1905–6, the entente was used to give France diplomatic but not military support against Germany.[44] Similarly, in the 1911 Agadir crisis, Britain strengthened France diplomatically but pressured her to compromise, warning that it would not protect France if it adamantly opposed German access to Morocco.[45] In the 1908 Bosnia Annexation crisis, though Grey offered Russia diplomatic support, this did not stop him from deflating Russia's ambitions in the Straits with the warning "it must not be expected that we should push matters to the point of provoking conflict."[46] In 1912–13, Britain's ententes with France and Russia—much to their chagrin—did not preclude a warming of relations with Germany spanning imperial and naval concerns. Perhaps most important, they permitted a joint Anglo-German brokerage of the 1912–13 Balkan wars, in which Britain restrained Russia and Germany applied the brake in Vienna.[47] The legacy of this successful instance of Anglo-German cooperation would encourage both Grey's initial attempts to mediate in the July crisis and Germany's hopes that Britain would remain neutral.[48] So given the previous trajectory of its policy, what defined the feasible set of options for Britain in the July crisis was whether it would stand aside from the impending conflict or join with France and Russia against the Central Powers. The fulcrum in Grey's pivot strategy, therefore, would lay in the adversaries' concerns about how Britain would choose between these two options. We turn now to closer examination of British policy during the July crisis.

Before the Ultimatum: Localization and the Question of English Neutrality

In the first weeks after the assassination of the Austrian archduke Franz Ferdinand, Grey made it clear—both to Germany and to Russia and France—that Britain had few interests in the Austro-Serb dispute and would remain neutral so long as it remained localized. His initial approach to the crisis, as he described it to Prince Lichnowsky, the German ambassador to London, on 9 July, would be to "continue the same policy as I had pursued through the Balkan crisis, and do my utmost to prevent the outbreak of war between the Great Powers."[49] In practice this meant two things: (1) enlisting France in efforts "to encourage patience in St. Petersburg," and (2) pressuring Russia to "do all in their power to reassure Germany."[50] In short, Grey adhered closely to the view that the conflict should be localized, which for Britain meant restraining Russia and France.

Britain at Odds with the Entente

Between July 20 and 23, Raymond Poincaré, the president of the French Republic, and René Viviani, its prime minister and minister of foreign affairs, were on a state visit in St. Petersburg. During this visit there were many opportunities for Britain's ambassador to St. Petersburg, Sir George Buchanan, to advocate his government's views to both French and Russian leaders. The July 20–23 period is thus crucial. It was then that France and Russia laid down their initial approach to the crisis, and it sheds light on the influence of Grey's policy on Russian and French decision making.

A key aim of Grey's initial approach to the Austro-Serb difficulty was to promote direct consultations between Russia and Austria—*before* the Austrian ultimatum was delivered.[51] France and Russia immediately rejected that tack. Instead, Poincaré and Sazanov urged Britain to join them in warning Vienna directly not to take harsh measures against Serbia.[52] France and Russia acted in concert along these lines and did their best to present it as a Triple Entente approach.[53] But Grey did not authorize Sir Maurice de Bunsen, the British ambassador in Vienna, to participate in this approach, nor was there support for it in the Foreign Office, even among the partisans of Entente solidarity.[54]

Grey did not ignore the need to moderate Austria's demands. On July 23 he clearly indicated to Count Mensdorff, the Austrian ambassador to London, that his ability to restrain Russia would be determined by the character of Austria's ultimatum. But most of all Grey relied on Germany to rein in Vienna.[55] This, as we know, was a serious flaw in Grey's formula, for Germany was hardly counseling prudence in Vienna at this time. But even if Grey were fully aware of Berlin's duplicity, it is unlikely that he would have altered his position. That is because even without corresponding German restraint in Vienna, localization could have been achieved. Regardless of whether Austria crushed Serbia quickly while Germany stood guard or conceded to a compromise via Anglo-German mediation, the underlying premise still held: Britain did not wish to fight over Serbia. This is why one should not make too much of German Chancellor Theobald von Bethmann Hollweg's double game with Grey.[56] Grey would not have committed at this stage, even if he knew that Germany had given Austria a blank check and would back her to the hilt. So long as Russia and France had not become fully engaged to defend Serbia, he had no incentive to encourage them to become so.

In sum, at the beginning of the crisis, strong alliances on the Continent, and weak interests for Britain, stymied Grey's attempts to broker peace. In view of the low likelihood of British intervention, neither the Central Powers nor Russia and France showed much regard for Grey's peacemaking efforts. They focused more on securing their flanks than on winning British support. Both sides sought to achieve their goals through resolute coercive diplomacy, and regardless of Britain's attitude. The Central Powers believed "that vigorous action against Serbia and a promise of German support would deter Russia," while France and Russia held "that a show of strength against Austria would both check the Austrians and deter Germany."[57] Until these assumptions were proved wrong on July 28—when Austria declared war on Serbia, and Russia ordered partial mobilization—and a general war seemed likely, neither side significantly adjusted their policies in order to win British allegiance or neutrality.

From Austria's Ultimatum to Russia's Partial Mobilization

After Austria's ultimatum to Serbia on 23 July, Grey tried harder to restrain Russia and elicit German cooperation. But his initial optimism about the possibility of localizing the conflict faded as the severity of Austria's demands became clear, and Russia and France refused to remain passive toward Serbia's fate. On the heels of the ultimatum came a German démarche that raised the threat of a European war to enforce the goal of localization.[58] Over the next five days Grey tried to prolong the ultimatum deadline, promote Serbian compliance, propose mediation between Austria and Russia and Austria and Serbia, encourage Austria to accept Serbia's reply, and, before and after that failed, forestall Russian military preparations. The manner and extent to which the principal actors frustrated or supported these efforts is revealing.

While the French statesmen were at sea between July 23 and 29, policy making in Paris drifted too.[59] French policy did not become attuned to the problem of British allegiance until Poincaré and Viviani returned to Paris. It

[86]

was then that Russia's partial mobilization—and the resulting German counterthreat—made British allegiance a matter of vital importance to France. Russia only supported Grey's efforts when they coincided with Sazanov's goal of placing the dispute "on an international footing."[60] More important, British attempts to restrain Russian military preparations failed. Grey's attempts to moderate Vienna *through* German pressure also went nowhere, until indications that Britain was closing ranks with France and Russia began to produce slight adjustments in German policy after 26 July. But the dominant thrust in German policy remained fixed on localizing the conflict until Russia's partial mobilization on 28 July put that goal out of reach.

The Failure of Grey's Attempts to Restrain Russia

Between 23 July, when the French statesmen left St. Petersburg, and 29 July, when they reached Paris, the bulk of Grey's efforts went to restraining Russia. After the Austrian ultimatum, he tried to do two things: promote Serbian compliance and moderate Russia. Both efforts were set back on the evening of 24 July, when the Russian Council of Ministers made two critical decisions.[61] First, it seems likely that the Council decided to encourage Serbia to adopt a more defiant response to the ultimatum than it otherwise would have.[62] It is certain that, although the Council advised Serbia to "show a desire for conciliation," it also advised Belgrade to only "fulfill the Austrian Government's requirements in so far as they did not jeopardize the independence of the Serbian state."[63] This was a far more conservative view of acceptable Serbian compliance than Britain took. Grey would not quibble over a reduction in Serbia's political independence if that were the price for peace in Europe.

Second, the Council decided to begin preparatory military measures. Well before the Austrian ultimatum (18 July), Sazanov had meditated a partial mobilization in response to such a move by Vienna.[64] Before the Council meeting, he stressed to Buchanan that Britain should join France and Russia in warning Austria not to meddle in Serbia's internal affairs, because if Austria took military action "Russia would at any rate have to mobilize." Buchanan tried to ward off such a move. Grey was unlikely to make a "declaration of solidarity that would entail engagement to support France and Russia by force of arms. [Britain] had no direct interests in Serbia, and public opinion in Britain would never sanction a war on her behalf."[65] This had no effect on the Council's decision. Sazanov warned the Council that if war came "it was not known what attitude Great Britain would take in the matter."[66] Despite this uncertainty, the Council resolved upon preparatory military measures and the next day, the czar ratified its decision. The Russians were willing to gamble on not having British support because they thought that Austria could still be deterred without it, that a firm Russian response (backed by France) would secure the peace.[67]

The Fate of Grey's Four-Power Mediation Proposals

On 25 July, anticipating that both Austria and Russia would soon be mobilizing, Grey tried to rally the four powers in a combined effort to "interpose" a pause between mobilization and operations that would allow them to "arrange matters" between Russia and Austria.[68] Bethmann correctly saw this as a proposal for localization, and so accepted it promptly.[69] For much the same reason, however, it ran into immediate resistance from both the French and Russian ambassadors in London.[70] Officially, neither rejected the proposal, but nor did they embrace it. French acceptance came obliquely on the 28th, too late to matter.[71] Sazanov evaded the issue by indicating a willingness to support four-power mediation *between Austria and Serbia,* on the condition that Serbia requested it. France and Russia, in other words, would not follow Grey's lead if that meant deviating from a policy of firmness and alliance solidarity.

Germany's commitment to mediation was limited to a formula that would "hold the ring" for Austria while it punished Serbia.[72] On the day that Germany endorsed his proposal, Grey also pressed Berlin to urge Vienna to accept what he expected to be a compliant Serbian response.[73] This suggestion went nowhere. German Secretary of State Gottlieb von Jagow passed Grey's request to Vienna without endorsement, indicating that it was sent merely to placate London and should be disregarded.[74] The limits to Germany's enthusiasm for mediation were also displayed in its reaction to Grey's 26 July proposal for a four-power conference in London. The proposal, inspired by Sazanov, called for mediation between Austria and Serbia.[75] This one was warmly received by Russia and France, for it envisioned internationalization of the affair.[76] But in Berlin, it was rebuffed, for the same reason that France and Russia embraced it.[77] The four-power conference proposal represented a dramatic shift from Grey's previous line: It implied that "the localization of the conflict . . . was wholly impossible, and must be dropped from the calculations of practical politics."[78] This Berlin was not ready to concede.[79]

Germany Rejects Grey's 27 July Proposals

Grey's four-power conference proposal sent an important message to Berlin: He had lost faith in localization and was drifting closer to France and Russia. So now Bethmann worked harder to deflect Grey from the Triple Entente. He was not willing to cede substantive ground, but he did begin to make cosmetic adjustments. On 27 July, Grey tried again to get

Germany to pressure Vienna into accepting the Serbian reply, at least as a satisfactory basis for negotiations. In his cables to Berlin relaying the proposal, Lichnowsky warned that Germany "should no longer be able to count on British sympathy" if Austria were bent on "crushing" Serbia. Britain "would place herself unconditionally by the side of France and Russia [and] if it comes to war under these circumstances we shall have Britain against us."[80] That evening, Bethmann sent instructions to Vienna asking Austrian Foreign Minister Leopold Berchtold to consider the English proposal, then cabled back to London that he had "at once inaugurated a move for mediation at Vienna along the lines desired."[81] This latter message was, according to Fritz Fischer, "completely untruthful."[82] Laslo von Szögyeny, Austria's ambassador to Berlin, cabled Berchtold the same day to say that Jagow "in strictest privacy" had revealed that Grey's mediation proposals would be forwarded only to appease Britain, and that Germany "does *not identify itself* with these propositions . . . on the contrary it advises to disregard them."[83] The next day, Austria declared war on Serbia and rejected Grey's proposal.[84]

Bethmann's duplicity on the 27th is interesting for what it reveals about German perceptions of Britain's attitude. Bethmann clearly saw in Grey's recent proposals a shift toward the Entente. Kurt Riezler records Bethmann saying on the 27th that "Britain's language has changed—apparently London finally realized that the Entente will be torn asunder if Whitehall is too lukewarm towards Russia."[85] At this point in the crisis, Bethmann began to have serious doubts about British neutrality. It was beginning to slip away and therefore demanded at least surface compromises to keep the breach from widening.

Russia Escalates to General Mobilization

Meanwhile, in St. Petersburg, Buchanan hammered on two themes: Russia should avoid taking provocative military action, and Britain would not commit to taking Russia's side.[86] Under no circumstances did Grey think Russian general mobilization—against both Austria and Germany—was necessary or desirable. When Vienna declared war on Serbia on 28 July, Sazanov began to push for an immediate partial mobilization against Austria.[87] On hearing that, Buchanan urged Sazanov not to take "any military measures which might be considered as a challenge by Germany"—a clear warning against general mobilization.[88] The next day Berlin decided that even partial mobilization by Russia was intolerable. Bethmann sent a warning to St. Petersburg to demobilize or "a European war could scarcely be prevented."[89]

Russia's 28 July decision to partially mobilize might suggest that Grey's admonitions hit home. But Sazanov's brief success in convincing the czar to opt for general mobilization the next day, and the final decision for general mobilization on 30 July weigh against this conclusion. It is certain that on the night of the 28th—in spite of Buchanan's counsel—Sazanov lobbied hard for general mobilization, and the next day the czar signed two orders, one for partial and one for general mobilization.[90] Both were held pending further developments. But, in any event, the Russian military took steps toward general mobilization that were transparent to Germany. News on the afternoon of 29 July that the Austrians had shelled Belgrade was followed by something more ominous—the warning from Berlin to stop partial mobilization. This, after Jagow had said that Germany could tolerate partial mobilization, sealed it for Sazanov.[91] He redoubled his efforts to secure full mobilization, with some success that evening. The czar ordered full mobilization, but then countermanded it when Wilhelm sent assurances that he continued to urge compromise in Vienna. Britain's attitude played no role at all in the czar's reversal. On the 30th, Sazanov convinced the czar to reorder general mobilization, making German countermobilization, and a general war in Europe, all but inevitable.[92]

INTERNATIONALIZATION OF THE CRISIS

Russia's mobilization and Germany's threat of countermeasures transformed the crisis. If the prospect of localizing it had put Britain at odds with France and Russia, the internationalization of the crisis sped a convergence between them. The shift in Britain's attitude mirrored a dramatic increase in the intensity of its stakes. Through the interaction of alliance commitments, the prospect of a Balkan war had morphed into the prospect of a Great Power war in Western Europe that directly threatened Britain. Thus, it was the hardening of the conflict between Austria and Russia, and the implications this had on relations between France and Germany, that made British intervention more likely.

This increased British leverage over *both* sides. Britain's allegiance became a more salient issue for the antagonists. Even as it became less likely, British neutrality became much more valuable to Germany—something to be courted aggressively rather than assumed. And it became much more dangerous to France—something to be avoided at all cost and not merely the subject of more diplomatic pleading. Because Britain's position still remained ambiguous, French and German policies began to move in directions meant to curry its favor. Thus, on 29 July, and in the days that followed, their policies were cast with an eye toward, in the French case, securing full British support at the outset of the war and, in the German case, seducing its neutrality or at least delaying its entry.

France Reacts to Doubtful British Allegiance

When Poincaré returned to Paris on the 29th he met with bad news: Russia had begun partial mobilization, and Britain remained elusive.[93] There was great concern that Russia might appear to be the instigator of war and that, if so, Britain would not fight. Paris now had to do more than call for British support—it needed to restrain Russia. On 29–30 July, just before Russia ordered general mobilization, Viviani heard from Sazanov that Russia had decided to ignore the German warning and "speed up" military measures. Sazanov added that he was confident Russia could "entirely count upon the allied support of France."[94] Viviani fired off a response strongly urging St. Petersburg not to proceed with "any measure which might offer Germany a pretext for total or partial mobilization of her forces."[95] A similar message went to Alexander Isvolsky, the Russian ambassador in Paris.[96] Poincaré wrote in his diary that day: *"Because of Britain's ambiguous attitude,* we have told St. Petersburg that we shall naturally fulfill our obligations as allies, but that we recommend that in its defense preparations the imperial government should not take any steps which could be regarded by Germany as a pretext for aggression."[97] Viviani's warning reached St. Petersburg on the 30th, but, in the czar's words, it had "come too late." The order for general mobilization had already been given.[98]

Signals coming from Britain did not reassure France. On 31 July the British Cabinet decided to probe both French and German intentions regarding Belgian neutrality—a potential avenue by which it might become engaged—but it would not, said Grey to the French ambassador, Paul Cambon, "undertake a definite pledge to intervene in a war." Yes, Grey had warned Berlin "that if France and Germany became involved in war, we should be drawn in," but he was vague about *when* Britain would be drawn in, and it was not something France should bank on.[99] Worse, Grey told Cambon that he thought Russian mobilization would "precipitate a crisis" making "it appear that German mobilization was . . . forced by Russia."[100] All the more imperative then that France not credit this view in Britain by its own military preparations.

France began precautionary military steps on 26 July, after Germany did the same in Alsace.[101] By the 30th, Germany's military preparations were raising great alarm. When the French Cabinet met that morning to decide on countermeasures, there was concern that, in Poincaré's words, "our initiative may be held up against us by the German Empire in Britain and Italy and . . . [France] should be made to appear the aggressors."[102] So the French Cabinet adopted a plan for military preparations with an eye to winning British favor. They would not order general mobilization and instead merely deploy covering forces between Luxembourg and the Vosges Mountains. This *couverture* was to come no closer than ten kilometers to the Franco-German border, in order to avoid any contact between French and German forces that might give Berlin a pretext to declare war and to make patently clear in Britain that French intentions were defensive.[103] These two objectives served the same end—to induce British loyalty. London was immediately notified of the French Cabinet's decision.[104]

Germany's ultimatum to France came on 31 July.[105] France had eighteen hours to declare itself neutral or face war with Germany. The risks of delaying military preparations out of deference to Britain were mounting. To be caught flat-footed now could spell disaster. That night, Joffre threatened to step down if the government did not order full-fledged mobilization. But again, they did not. They authorized further covering operations, but no call-up of reserves. The ten-kilometer buffer still remained in force, a fact that was impressed on London repeatedly throughout the day.[106] On 1 August, Joffre threatened again to resign if general mobilization was not ordered. This time the Cabinet agreed to start mobilizing the next day (2 August), but it continued to insist on maintaining the buffer zone.[107]

That day, the German ambassador in Paris called on Viviani to receive France's answer to the ultimatum. France, Viviani replied, would do what was in her interest. The Russian envoy Isvolsky also probed Poincaré that day, with essentially the same question: Now that Germany had declared war on Russia, "what is France going to do?" Poincaré assured him that France would do its duty as an ally, but "for considerations mainly touching Britain it would be better if the declaration of war were to come not from France but from Germany."[108] The Cabinet revoked the buffer zone on 2 August, but still, it sharply curtailed the activities of French forces despite the offensive character of its plan against Germany.[109] These restraints remained in force until 3 August, when Germany gave France the dismal prize it waited for: a declaration of war.

Germany Reacts to Doubtful British Neutrality

Before Russia mobilized, German leaders had reason to believe British neutrality was not just possible but probable. For all intents and purposes, it would be the upshot of localization, which Grey strove for until 26 July. After Russia mobilized, British neutrality became less likely but not impossible, especially if Russia could be made to seem the aggressor. German leaders were not wildly naive to think this way. After all, what they hoped for was identical to what the French feared.[110] Berlin's subsequent reactions to British policy are best understood as evidence, in Marc Trachtenberg's words, of Germany doing "what it could to maximize the probability that Britain would stay out of the war" rather than evidence of any conviction that Britain was *likely* to stay out of the war.[111] Because the benefits to Germany of British neutrality were considerable, its efforts to improve the chance of that occurring make sense. Due diligence is not wishful thinking.[112] By 28 July, Bethmann saw clearly that Britain was moving closer to France and Russia, and he tried to reel Grey back in two ways. First, he tried to deliver Austria to the negotiating table. Second, he tried to cast blame on Russia for starting the war, if it did break out. The two were obviously interrelated.[113] If Austria would not compromise, it would be difficult to make Russia appear the aggressor, which, in turn, would make it that much harder to keep Britain out of the war.

The Halt in Belgrade Proposals and Austria's General Mobilization

Kaiser Wilhelm provided a way to bring about a volte-face in Vienna. On the 27th, Wilhelm read the Serbian reply and was convinced that it went so far that "every cause for war falls to the ground." He ordered Jagow to prepare a plan for mediation in Vienna that would let Austria occupy Belgrade as a hostage, while negotiations proceeded and its demands were implemented.[114] Well into the next night, Bethmann cabled a proposal to Vienna that was fairly consistent with Wilhelm's plan, and a departure from Berlin's previous line.[115] This "Halt in Belgrade" proposal was delivered to Berchtold on the morning of the 29th. That night Bethmann began to pressure Vienna to either endorse the kaiser's proposal or a very similar one advanced by Grey. Most historians agree that an important cause of this change in Berlin's attitude was Grey's warnings to Lichnowsky that day that Britain would be "drawn into" a European war if Vienna did not renounce war against Serbia and make real efforts to negotiate a solution to the dispute.[116]

At a Crown Council early on 29 July—before Grey's warnings arrived—Bethmann argued that Britain should be offered guarantees of French territorial integrity and a naval agreement like that considered in 1912, in return for neutrality. The kaiser quashed the naval idea, but Bethmann left the meeting determined to seek a neutrality agreement with Britain.[117] In other words, Bethmann was feeling his way toward a neutrality deal with Britain *before* he learned of Russia's partial mobilization and *before* he received Grey's strongest warnings later that evening. He wanted British neutrality, and he did not think it could be gotten for free.[118]

After the Crown Council Bethmann met with Chief of the General Staff von Moltke and Minister of War Falkenhayn, to discuss the fresh news of Russia's partial mobilization. Bethmann convinced the military leaders to delay countermobilization. Such drastic measures should wait until his mediation efforts in Vienna, St. Petersburg, and London had time to bear fruit. Or at least until Russia could be put squarely in the wrong, since "England would not be able to side with Russia if Russia unleashed a general war by an attack on Austria."[119]

Bethmann then held an interview with Lord Goschen, the British ambassador to Berlin, in which he made a formal pitch for British neutrality.[120] Goschen did not respond warmly.

Next Bethmann read the report of Lichnowsky's first interview with Grey that day, which indicated that Vienna had rebuffed direct negotiations in St. Petersburg.[121] Between 10 and 10:30 P.M., Bethmann cabled Vienna twice, seeking Austria's response to his proposals of the night before. He followed up with two more two hours later that ordered his ambassador, Heinrich von Tschirschky to inform Berchtold "at once" that Berlin considered the Halt in Belgrade formula "an appropriate basis for negotiations."[122]

Any lingering hopes in Bethmann's mind about British neutrality were then dashed by another report from Lichnowsky. Grey had said bluntly that Britain would immediately join the fight on the side of France: a more explicit threat could not have been given without a public declaration and Cabinet approval, which Grey still lacked. On the brighter side, Grey tendered a mediation proposal almost identical to the kaiser's, which still remained secret. The basis for an Anglo-German bargain was within reach. If Austria could be persuaded to stop in Belgrade and begin negotiations, then Britain would remain on the sidelines.

Just after midnight on the morning of 30 July, Bethmann set to work. Over the next three hours he sent two sternly worded telegrams to Vienna, insisting that it accept the kaiser's Halt in Belgrade proposal or Grey's similar plan and begin bilateral negotiations with St. Petersburg, or risk losing German support. Writes Luigi Albertini: "This meant that either Vienna must be reasonable and agree to yield, or Germany would leave her to her fate."[123] Throughout most of that day, Bethmann received no word of the breakthrough in Vienna that he badly needed. That night the kaiser and Bethmann both applied more pressure.[124] But the news, when it came, was not good. Any decision would wait until noon of the 31st, and, whatever the case, compromise along the lines of Grey's last proposal was unlikely.[125] At 9:00 P.M., Bethmann wrote back commanding Tschirschky to "urgently advise that Austria accept the Grey proposal."[126] But Vienna did not deliver. Indeed, that night, at a conference with the emperor in which Bethmann's warnings and the kaiser's letter to Francis Joseph were discussed, the Austrians decided to reject Grey's proposal and begin full mobilization the next day.[127]

After that, Bethmann moved closely into step with military counsels. At about 11:30 P.M., 30 July, he cabled Tschirschky again, rescinding his previous instructions.[128] The next morning Goschen relayed to Bethmann Grey's official rejection of the neutrality proposal.[129] Just before noon, Russia's general mobilization was confirmed. A state of impending danger of war was ordered, and the ultimatum was given to St. Petersburg. When Grey made his last bid to bring Austria to the table in the afternoon of 31 July, it fell on deaf ears.[130] Jagow shrugged it off: Now it was "impossible for [Germany] to consider any proposal until they received an answer from Russia."[131] The Wilhelmstrasse assumed that the ultimatum to Russia would be rejected, and thus, by the 31st, the end had come to peacemaking in Berlin.[132] Goschen queried whether Germany intended to respect Belgian neutrality. Jagow would not answer officially but opined that no response could be given because any answer would reveal German campaign plans. He set fire to one of the last bridges between London and Berlin.

Between the evening of 28 July and late in the night of 30 July, Grey's strategy had begun to bite. Britain's increasing tilt toward the Entente extracted from Berlin concessions meant to lure it back toward neutrality. The efforts began with, but were not limited to, Bethmann's formal neutrality bargain. There were also serious attempts to secure Austrian acceptance of compromise proposals, including the one advanced by Grey on the 29th. If Bethmann's efforts were also bent toward "putting Russia in the wrong" a very important reason for doing so was to make it hard for Britain to side with Russia. But, in the crunch, Bethmann could not control Austria, just as Paris could not derail Russia's full mobilization. And that stopped Bethmann's efforts cold.

By 31 July Germany had resolved for war against Russia and France, and German leaders had little doubt that Britain would fight with France. But Britain had not yet publicly declared its allegiance, and so long as it did not, the lure of British neutrality exerted a gravitational pull on German policy. It was much too weak to melt Germany's resolve for war, but it was strong enough to evoke costly adjustments in Berlin.

The "Misunderstanding" of 1 August[133]

On the night of 31 July, London knew that Germany had declared an imminent danger of war, given Russia twelve hours to demobilize, and sent a similar ultimatum to France.[134] By daybreak, Grey was in a frenzy to create more options. Sometime in the morning of 1 August, Grey's secretary William Tyrell telephoned Lichnowsky indicating that Grey wished to discuss the possibility that "in the event of [Germany] not attacking France, Britain too, would remain neutral and would guarantee France's passivity."[135] Without waiting to meet Grey, Lichnowsky quickly relayed the news to Berlin.

Berlin quickly sent a favorable response to the proposition—which arrived in London at 8:00 P.M., in a cable from the kaiser to King George. Thus put on the spot to formulate a response, Grey disowned the trial balloon: It had arisen from a "misunderstanding as to a suggestion that passed in" conversation between he and Lichnowsky "when they were discussing how actual fighting between German and French armies might be avoided while there is still chance of some agreement between Austria and Russia."[136] Debate still rages over how the misunderstanding came about, and if there was a misunderstanding at all.[137]

The Germans, in any case, were outraged by the reversal when they learned of it around 11 P.M.. With good reason, for they had already taken practical measures to facilitate British acceptance of the kaiser's response. These actions show the lengths to which German authorities would go on 1 August to secure British neutrality. Lichnowsky's first cable of that day arrived in Berlin twenty-three minutes after 4 P.M., when the full mobilization order Moltke had clamored for since 29 July had been given. This meant going full-steam ahead to war on both fronts—starting in the west—with no turning back. There was a great incentive to do this because the first moves in the German campaign were to seize crucial transportation points in Luxembourg and Belgium. Any delay might result in the destruction of these facilities before German forces could take them, with crucial consequences for the success of the German war plan. Nevertheless, when Lichnowsky's cable arrived, the kaiser halted the penetration of Luxembourg just getting underway. Moltke was apoplectic, but his violent objections went unheeded. When he insisted that the invasion of Luxembourg must proceed so that the rail hubs could be seized, the kaiser brushed him off with a curt "use other railroads instead."[138] In this instance at least, civilian authority called the shots. Until word came back from Britain, the armies in the west would only be allowed to continue concentrating behind German borders.

The lure of British neutrality was, at this late date, enough to stall the German war machine, even after it had begun to roll and despite the severe dislocations delay would cause. This, in itself, is no mean feat. But even more startling are the long-term strategic implications of the decision, if it had stuck. The political authorities in Germany were apparently willing to risk a war against Russia with an armed France—albeit neutral—at their back, against every premise of the Schlieffen-Moltke War plan, which ruled out the possibility of a single-front war. The risks of such a move—even if it came with full British assurances of French neutrality and with French border forts as down payment—would be extraordinary. That German authorities would countenance this, and even undertake initial steps to bring it about, demonstrates the continuing influence of the prospect of British neutrality.

Late in the night of 1 August, after he dispatched the "misunderstanding" letter to Berlin, Grey cabled Paris a copy of the German refusal to guarantee Belgian neutrality. It had sat in the Foreign Office since 3:30 A.M. that morning.[139] This was the first clear signal to France that Britain would fight with the Entente. The next day the Cabinet decided that the British navy would protect French channel ports. On 3 August, Grey called on Parliament to authorize intervention. After the speech, the Cabinet decided to make an ultimatum to Germany the next day that it respect Belgian neutrality. When it expired at midnight on 4 August, the German invasion of Belgium had already begun. Britain's ambassador to Berlin packed his bags, and the two were at war.

Summary of Findings

Necessary Conditions

At the outset of the July crisis, Grey's focus was on preventing war among the major powers by working out Serbia's fate among them. Through France and Germany, he tried to apply pressure on Russia and Austria to "discuss things together" and come to an understanding on Serbia "so as not to involve Europe in the consequences."[140] Once this tack floundered and Britain took a more vigorous approach to the crisis, the particulars of Grey's numerous settlement and conference proposals may have changed, but they were all cast with an eye toward one goal: keeping the Continental powers at peace.

Grey was not ignorant of the difficulty of this task. Britain had ample reason to suspect that both France and Germany (and their allies) harbored revisionist aims and, given the opportunity, would pursue them aggressively. Before the crisis, Britain refused on several occasions to give Germany a neutrality agreement; similar refusals to commit to neutrality, as well as warnings not to attack France, occurred during the crisis. There is no doubt that London feared that Germany would act aggressively if it were not deterred. But just as important was the fear that by aligning with France, Britain would become "party to France precipitating a conflict for the revanche."[141] For that reason, it was seen as a good thing that France did "not feel sure how far they could rely on" Britain, and British policy, both before and during the July crisis, actively sowed that uncertainty.[142]

By the same token, in July 1914, both Germany and France believed that there was a reasonable possibility that Britain would remain neutral in a war between them. That both sides seriously entertained this notion is powerful evidence that they perceived each other as greater threats than Britain. France and Germany had no illusions about their enmity, which is why their uncertainty about what Britain would do mattered, and why they both made concessions to Britain in order to enlist its support (in the case of France) or its neutrality (in the case of Germany).

[97]

Isolation Avoidance Effects

Grey's position at the beginning of the crisis made it clear that Britain would remain neutral so long as the dispute remained localized—Britain's attitude would flow from, rather than determine, localization. Therefore, during this period, neither side made adjustments with an eye to winning British support. Not because Germany assumed Britain would remain neutral in a general war, or because France assumed Britain would support her, but rather because both thought general war could be prevented by acting resolutely with their allies, in which case Britain's vital interest would not become engaged. It was not until these efforts failed and the danger of general war increased that Britain's vital interests became definitely engaged and the question of its attitude became more salient to the adversaries.

Thus, early in the crisis, when the Continental powers focused on locking in their key allies not on courting Britain, there is little evidence for a caution-inducing effect of Britain's pivotal policy. Uncertainty in Berlin and Paris about Britain's attitude did not exert a real tug on their policy until the end of July. Then two patterns emerged. First, the pivot's most likely ally, France, worked hard to avoid losing its support. Second, the pivot's most likely adversary, Germany, undertook efforts to draw it toward neutrality. As the cataclysm loomed, and indications from London suggesting that Britain would stand aside did not abate, France showed signs of real caution. Namely, in its genuine if unsuccessful attempt to block Russia's full mobilization. France's decisions to delay mobilization—even as German mobilization lurched forward—were also clearly intended to curry British favor. Germany showed fewer signs of caution, but its last minute efforts to restrain Austria do indicate that it was keen to find a way to keep Britain neutral. Likewise the kaiser's countermand to German forces advancing into Luxembourg on 1 August was a concession made by Berlin to purchase British (and it was hoped French) neutrality.

A less felicitous feature of isolation avoidance also arose: that tendency for adversaries who are vying for pivotal support to work toward the goal of putting the other side "in the wrong." As Albertini, Fischer, and Copeland have stressed, Bethmann tried to ensure that Russia mobilized first so that it would look like the aggressor. Not only because he wanted to unify Germany domestically but also because he believed that putting Russia in the wrong might determine England's attitude. Britain, it was hoped, would not go wholeheartedly to war in support of Russian aggression, and if Britain would not commit then France might delay too. Similarly, France's decision to deploy its screening forces well back from the German border was also intended to signal to Britain that German forces were the aggressors. If Britain were not still in play at this time, there would have been no justification for this sort of action. Russia, after all, was not about to bolt, regardless of whether France acted more aggressively or not.

Alignment Options Effects

Britain was poorly positioned to play the pivot in the July crisis because of its weakness in land power, especially in terms of what it could bring to bear in a short war on the Western front. If Britain's army cut a meager figure on the Western front, it cut no figure at all in the East: Russia would not gain any immediate benefits from British allegiance in a short war, and Austria would not suffer any immediate costs. It is not at all surprising therefore that British pivotal policy had no discernible effect on the behavior of those powers in the July crisis. But besides helping to "swamp" Britain's relative military power, the strong Continental alliances undermined pivotal deterrence in other ways too. First, they gave France and Germany other, more attractive options than winning British support early in the crisis; namely, that of presenting a solid front with their allies in an attempt to intimidate the opponents into backing down. Alignment options also diminished Britain's influence through imperfections in intra-alliance control, which meant that the restraining effects of its policy on France and Germany did not translate into similar restraints on Russia and Austria. Consequently France and Germany were unable to impel their allies to moderate their policies and, once a general war seemed imminent, could not abandon them without writing their own death warrants. Thus, once the likelihood of war in the West became a focal point of the diplomatic contest, British influence over France and Germany increased, but not enough to prevent the war.

[5]

Hurting the One Who Loves You Most:

THE UNITED STATES AND THE
CYPRUS CRISES, 1963–67

The worst rat-race I've ever been in—trying to deny Greeks and Turks their historic recreation of killing one another.

Dean Acheson, August 1964

Anything we do gives the appearance of our working for the other side . . . if we described the terrible consequences of a Greek-Turk war, the Greeks would simply ask why, then, would we refuse to stop a Turk invasion. . . . [T]he average Greek thinks that we're holding the gun of a Turkish invasion at Greek heads to force a deal. The Turks feel that, because we restrained their invasion, we're pro-Greek.

George Ball, July 1964

In 1964 and 1967, Turkey and Greece almost fought over Cyprus.[1] The overriding U.S. interest in both crises was to prevent war between its two key allies in NATO's southern flank. Because they were both allies, the United States could not align with one in order to deter the other. The chief reason to keep the peace between them—to contain the USSR—limited U.S. options to pivotal deterrence.

Though its approach to these crises was, at bottom, pragmatic, many observers whose views are inscribed by the subsequent and more traumatic 1974 crisis, do not see it that way. In July 1974, a military regime in Athens staged a coup in Cyprus to replace the leftist president, Archbishop Makarios, with a right-wing stooge who would allow Greece to quickly annex the island. Greece was isolated internationally even before the coup; afterward, it was downright beleaguered. Turkey decided to intervene, and for all intents and purposes, both Washington and Moscow gave a green light.[2] When Turkey invaded on 20 July, the discredited regimes in Athens and Nicosia collapsed. As Turkish forces established and expanded a bridgehead, the United States became engaged, urging Ankara to cease fire and begin negotiating a settlement.[3] At the first round of negotiations, held in Geneva 25–30 July, Greece was desperate to halt Turkey's advance. So it agreed, in principle, to most of Turkey's demands. Another round of negotiations began on 8 August. Betting then that Turkey was immobilized by international pressure, Athens renounced the idea of a separate Cypriot Turk community and rejected every Turkish proposal for "federation." U.S. Secretary of State Henry Kissinger warned, through indirect channels, that if Greece rebuffed even Turkey's most moderate federation scheme, the United States would not punish a further Turkish advance.[4] On 15 August, as Greece stalled for time, Turkey launched a second offensive, rolling up 37 percent of the island.

In 1974, the United States did little to forestall a forcible solution to the Cyprus conflict. In light of this episode many observers (especially Greek) see "continuity" in the U.S. approach to Cyprus during the previous decade, a consistent bent toward Turkey's preferred solution—partition.[5] But this is misleading, for in the 1960s the United States made preventing war between Greece and Turkey a top priority, not partitioning Cyprus. Turks, similarly, tend to see a consistent anti-Turkey tilt in U.S. policy, for more than once in the 1960s, it prevented Turkey from intervening. Of course, there are those (typically American) who see more impartiality in U.S. policy. Washington, in their view, was an "honest broker" that assumed the role of "heavily involved neutral," playing it "almost entirely by ear" or, put less charitably, wobbling "incontinently back and forth."[6] Though each of these perspectives contains some truth, they all fail to capture the essential pattern of U.S. policy.

Overview of the Case

In the 1960s crises, the United States used the threat of abandonment to force both Greece and Turkey, at different times, to moderate policies likely to spark war. What was consistent about U.S. diplomacy in these crises was that it leaned against the side most dependent on U.S. support and least likely to draw succor from Moscow. This explains why the United States was able to prevent war in those crises and why both sides, with some cause, felt betrayed by it.

Before the 1964 crisis, Ankara assumed that its support for U.S. policy in Korea, its steadfastness in the Cuban Missile Crisis, and its spurning of Soviet blandishments insured U.S. backing when Turkey's vital interests were at stake. Exuberantly pro-western, Turkey dug a moat between itself and Moscow. Greece, by contrast, was ruled by a leftist government that vilified U.S. "imperialism" and publicly supported Makarios, the "Castro" of the Mediterranean. By no means was Greece a direct ally of the USSR. But in a war with Turkey over Cyprus, Moscow could offer Greece an indirect axis of support.

In June 1964 Greece was sponsoring a campaign to weaken the Turkish minority on Cyprus and pave the way for annexation. Turkey, in response, was about to invade and partition the island. With war imminent, the United States did not join Turkey to oppose a putative Athens-Nicosia-Moscow alignment. Instead, it threatened to abandon Turkey if the Soviets intervened, which caused Ankara to back off. War was thus averted, and the gravest threat to the Cyprus status quo deflected.

Imagine a similar scenario, but with one big difference: it is clear beforehand that Moscow will have no truck with the Greeks. Here the U.S. threat to stand aside would fall heavy on Greece because it could not hold its own in a war with Turkey. Athens would have to scale back its creeping policy to annex Cyprus. This situation actually happened in 1967. After it was burned by the United States in 1964, Turkey became more friendly toward the USSR, and relations quickly improved. On the Cyprus question, the Kremlin reversed course and adopted Ankara's line. When the 1967 crisis erupted, the rapprochement paid off. The Cypriot National Guard was, by then, a proxy of the right-wing military dictatorship in Athens. Manned by Greek army "volunteers" and commanded by a Greek general, the Guard launched major operations against Turkish Cypriot enclaves. Turkey poised for full-scale war, demanding that Greece not only end the attacks but also immediately withdraw its forces from Cyprus. Did the United States close ranks with the anticommunist colonels in Athens? Did it align against Turkey, which had embarrassingly warm relations with Moscow? No. The United States wanted to end the crisis peacefully, but in a way that would not drive Turkey closer to the USSR. It did not have to worry about *that* with Greece. By its animus toward Moscow, the military junta in Athens had painted itself into a corner. Under a veneer of "honest brokerage" the United States forced Greece to comply with the substance of Turkey's demands by threatening to leave Greece to Turkey's tender mercies if it did not.

DESCRIPTION OF SITUATIONAL VARIABLES

The Balance of Capabilities

In June 1964, U.S. President Lyndon Johnson imparted to the Greek ambassador, Alexander Matsas, a Texas take on the Melian Dialogue: "America is an elephant. Cyprus is a flea. Greece is a flea. If these two fellows continue itching the elephant, they may just get whacked by the elephant's trunk, whacked good."[7] Four months earlier, Johnson expressed a similar view of America's power over Turkey. If Turkey made a grab for Cyprus, he said, "we might have to tell the Turks 'It's good night nurse' . . . We were in a position to force them to settle peacefully. If we told [İsmet] İnönü [Turkey's prime minister] we'd cut off aid, he'd have to back down."[8] Johnson's remarks underscore a basic truth: The United States was preponderant over Greece and Turkey. The most obvious military indices make the point. Average annual defense expenditures for the United States (1960 dollars) were $55 billion, for Turkey $324 million, and for Greece $220 million. Strictly in terms of *their own* outlays, Greek and Turkish defense spending combined barely amounted to 1 percent of the U.S. budget in those years.[9] The United States was also the chief military aid patron to both sides and the gatekeeper for what they additionally received from the United Kingdom and Germany. Again, rough figures give a clear indication of Greek and Turkish exposure to U.S. pressure. Between 1950 and 1967, military aid from the United States, United Kingdom, and Germany accounted for 36 percent of Greece's, and 38 percent of Turkey's, overall defense budget.[10]

Head-to-head, Turkey was mightier than Greece. Between 1960 and 1967, Greece spent 61 percent as much on defense as Turkey.[11] U.S. military patronage during the same period also favored Turkey by a similar ratio.[12] Turkey's military responsibilities in the region, however, were also more taxing than Greece's. The important point here is that with relatively little effort, the United States could radically alter the Greco-Turk balance by cutting aid to Greece or by cutting aid to Turkey and upping Greece's share. The United States could also manipulate the balance qualitatively, as in the late 1950s when it gave Turkey more advanced fighter aircraft than it gave Greece.[13] In short, the United States could largely determine who won a war between Greece and Turkey without actively fighting in it.

The Distribution of Interests and Intentions

The stakes in the Cyprus dispute were vital to Greece and Turkey (and also to the Cyprus Republic, whose survival was threatened by both sides). For Greece, absorbing Cyprus was central to the national purpose. The goal of *enosis*—the union of Cyprus with mainland Greece—dated back to the origins of modern Greek nationalism and was declaimed by governments in Athens and Nicosia. In that spirit, Athens backed Nicosia's efforts to crater the Cypriot constitution and suborn the Turkish minority. Though Athens would not relish going to war for enosis, it armed the Greek Cypriot government, underwrote its program to crush the Turkish minority, and promised to defend it against Turkey's reaction. Thus, Greece's aims in Cyprus were revisionist, and it was willing to use force to advance them.

The stakes were vital for Turkey too. The threat to ethnic Turks on Cyprus was obvious, but kinship aside, history had shown that when the opportunity arose, Greece would not hesitate to take its pound of flesh from the "sick man of Europe."[14] Thus enosis would not merely imperil the Cypriot Turk minority on the island, it would give Greece a strategic fighting platform on Turkey's southern flank. As Turkey would demonstrate, it was easy to project force from mainland Anatolia to the island. That same short distance would make Turkey vulnerable to Greece were Cyprus in Athens' hands. Then Greece could strike Turkey from north and south and force it to fight on two fronts. Ankara, therefore, would not for long be content merely to uphold Turkish-Cypriot minority rights on the island. It wanted *taksim*, the partition of the island into ethnic entities, with each part joined to and ruled by their respective motherland.

The substance of the Cyprus dispute was not vital to the United States. The most important U.S. interest was NATO cohesion. With Greece and Turkey circling over Cyprus, that cohesion would be compromised, and with it, deterrence of the Soviets. On the island itself, U.S. interests were appreciable but not compelling.[15] The United States wanted access to Cyprus bases and to continue operating on the island "strategically important" Voice of America transmitters.[16] These issues were largely covered by the 1959 London-Zurich treaties, which preserved two British bases on Cyprus after it became independent. More troubling was Cyprus' Communist party (AKEL), which had strong ties to Moscow. A significant base of support for the Greek Cypriot regime, AKEL followers accounted for 35 percent of the Greek Cypriot electorate.[17] If the Communists were allowed to dominate the politics of Cyprus it could become the Cuba of the Mediterranean. Accordingly, the United States took an interest in, and measures to influence, the political complexion of the Nicosia government.

Washington did not oppose change in the Cyprus status quo if it could be achieved peacefully. It would support whatever changes Greece and Turkey could agree to.[18] But it would oppose forceful moves by either side to change the status quo because such moves were liable to trigger a general war between them.[19] That, as Secretary of State Dean Rusk put it, would "afford opportunities for expansion of communist power in Cyprus, endanger Greek and Turkish Governments and seriously weaken NATO."[20] Which leads to an interesting dimension of the situation: alignment options.

Alignment Options

The Cold War gave the United States a reason to pursue pivotal deterrence between Greece and Turkey. By the same token, it made Moscow a potential—if indirect—alignment option. Consequently, Soviet conduct influenced the way America's pivotal deterrence policy played out. Still, the Soviets were *never* a strong alignment option for Greece and Turkey in this case. There are a few important reasons for this. First, the shadow of the Soviet threat made Moscow a far from plausible general ally. Neither Greece nor Turkey could seriously contemplate *trading* American security commitments for Soviet tutelage. Second, despite Krushchev's occasional grandstanding, Moscow was unlikely to fight directly for Cyprus. The most Athens and Nicosia could count on from Moscow was support in the UN and arms aid to Cyprus. Third, and most important, Moscow opposed both enosis and partition. Both would spell the end of Cyprus' independence and its prized Communist party and put it under NATO's thumb. Moscow, therefore, did not encourage Greece and Turkey to pursue their revisionist aims the way a strong alignment option might have. The Kremlin did not undermine U.S. pivotal deterrence efforts because it simply did not want to. That, in the end, made it a weak alignment option for Greece and Turkey.

BACKGROUND TO THE CYPRUS CRISES

When Turkey ceded de facto control of Cyprus to Britain in 1878, Greek and Turkish communities were already rooted there. Ancient Greeks colonized Cyprus around 1.5 B.C. Ottoman Turks did likewise three thousand years later (1571). Britain formally annexed Cyprus in 1914, after Turkey entered World War I on the side of the Central Powers. In 1923, under the Treaty of Lausanne, Turkey endorsed the transfer and Cyprus then became an official British mandate. Under British rule, the ratio of Greek (80 percent) to Turk (20 percent) Cypriots remained stable, and the ethnonationalist themes of enosis and taksim flowered.[21]

In the 1950s, Cyprus became a focal point and catalyst of Greek-Turkish rivalry and a serious concern to the United States and NATO. Between 1955 and 1959 Greek Cypriots waged guerilla war to force out the British and bring about enosis. The political mastermind of the movement was Makarios, archbishop of the Orthodox Church in Cyprus. His dirty work was done by an underground militia—the EOKA (National Organization of Cypriot Fighters)—led by a retired Greek General named George Grivas. Makarios, Grivas, and their goal of enosis were fully backed by Athens. As the revolt gathered momentum, Turks on Cyprus and the mainland rallied to the banner of taksim and violence between the Cypriot communities intermingled with anticolonial rebellion.[22] With order breaking down, Britain's international position deteriorated too. Between 1954 and 1958, Greece excoriated Britain before the UN, demanding that London bend to the "repeatedly and solemnly expressed will of the overwhelming majority of the people of Cyprus for union with Greece."[23] The Soviet bloc and most of the developing world sided with Greece, an embarrassment, to say the least, for NATO.

In 1959 Britain, Greece, and Turkey began to negotiate an end to the British colony and the terms for Cyprus independence. The results were the London-Zurich treaties. The Treaty of Establishment gave Britain continued sovereignty over two key bases on the island. The Treaty of Alliance allowed Greece and Turkey to deploy small contingents on the island (of 950 and 650 troops respectively), ostensibly to defend against outside threats. In the Treaty of Guarantee, the new Cyprus republic promised to defend its independence and territorial integrity and to oppose any attempts to partition or annex it. Britain, Greece, and Turkey guaranteed this pledge, which meant, on paper at least, that the latter two renounced enosis and taksim. The guarantors pledged "in the event of a breach" to "consult together with respect to the representations or measures necessary to ensure" observance of the treaty. If concerted action were not possible, each reserved the right "to take action with the sole aim of re-establishing the state of affairs created by the present treaty."[24]

For Turkey, the linchpin of the deal was an agreement on the republic's basic structure of government, written into its constitution with the three treaties. Cyprus would be a sui generis state of two distinct communities, governed on the principle of communal dualism. In the executive branch, there would be a Greek Cypriot president, a Turkish Cypriot vice president, and a Council of ministers, seven Greek and three Turkish. Council decisions relating to foreign policy, defense, and security could be vetoed by either or both the president and vice president. There would also be a House of Representatives, divided thirty-five to fifteen along ethnic lines, and two Communal Chambers, each representing and regulating the different ethnic groups on a host of matters within each community. The judicial branch was similarly divided. On the Supreme Court would sit three judges, an ethnic Greek, an ethnic Turk, and a neutral foreigner. Public service and police posts would be allocated 70/30 along ethnic lines, military posts 60/40. These safeguards were enshrined in the constitution to protect the Turkish minority, and according to the constitution (which also included the Treaties of Alliance and Guarantee), they could not "be amended, whether by way of variation, addition, or repeal."[25]

The London-Zurich Bargain Breaks Down

At the London-Zurich negotiations, Greek Cypriots were represented by Greece, a weaker and less critical NATO ally than Britain and Turkey. Athens therefore had a weaker hand. For the sake of Cyprus independence, Greeks agreed grudgingly to Britain's demands for bases and to Turkey's demands for a bicommunal government that favored ethnic Turks. Makarios and his Cypriot backers did not intend to abide by the agreements, and neither, ultimately, did Athens.

The Cyprus Republic was officially founded on 16 August 1960. On 4 January 1962, President Makarios announced that he would seek to revise the constitution. His target, at this stage, was the veto powers of the Turkish minority. Cypriot Turks in the House were using their veto to pressure Makarios to implement the 70/30 civil-service provisions, which he had failed to do. In December that year, Makarios went further, announcing that the constitutional provisions for dual Greek and Turk municipality structures were unworkable and that his government would take over all their governing functions. Cypriot Turks appealed to the Constitutional Court of Cyprus to contest these moves. In January 1963, Turkey's foreign minister, Feridun Erkin, stepped into the fray, declaring that Turkey could not "accept what amounts to a practical violation of the Cyprus agreements." In February, the Cyprus Court upheld the Turkish representatives' use of the veto. In March, before the Court could render a decision on the municipalities question, Makarios stated that he would disregard an unfavorable decision, and he did so in April. Three months later, Makarios revealed the details of his program to overhaul the constitution's "utopian" and "inapplicable" provisions, which he insisted was "a strictly internal Cypriot affair."[26]

The scramble for U.S. support was already in full swing. In January 1962, Spyros Kyprianou, Makarios' foreign minister, asked the United States to support his bid to revise the constitution. The United States refused. Similarly, after Makarios' December 1962 decision to challenge the dual municipalities, Fazil Küchük, the vice president of Cyprus, asked the United States to "support Turkish Cypriot views." He too was rebuffed.[27] Turkey and Greece likewise jockeyed for position. In February 1963, Erkin warned Raymond Hare, U.S. ambassador in Ankara, that Turkey would react strongly to the "possible termination of Turkish municipalities." This "would lead to *enosis*" and the consequences "could be disastrous not only for Cyprus but for Turk-Greek relations and NATO solidarity."[28] In autumn of that year, Turkey labored to convince Washington that Makarios' program was not about minor revisions but a "broad attack on the constitution" sponsored by Greece.[29] On 20 October in Ankara, Turkish officials presented Assistant Secretary of State Phillips Talbot with a démarche. "If the London-Zurich agreements and Constitution were not upheld, the only alternative would be partition." Since that would create "unfortunate . . . strain on the NATO alliance both in the region and generally," Ankara urged the United States to play a role in "influencing Cypriots and guarantor powers."[30] The latter phrase could only mean the *Greek* Cypriots and Athens because Cypriot Turks and Britain opposed revising the London-Zurich agreements.

At the same time, Athens and Nicosia were pressing their case. On 26 November 1963, Makarios told Fraser Wilkins, the U.S. envoy to Cyprus, that "he was convinced that amendments or improvements in [the] Constitution were required and that if Turkish Cypriots, with backing of Ankara refused, it would be necessary to seek changes in other ways." In Washington the next day, Greece's deputy prime minister stated to Rusk that Athens believed "it was essential [to] make some amendments to [the] Cyprus constitution," and asked the United States to "contribute [to] finding a solution." Greece, in other words, wanted the United States to pressure Ankara to acquiesce to revisions. For Rusk, Athens' position was a "cause [of] concern."[31] If he had any doubts about what was afoot, they were soon dispelled. On 30 November, Makarios sprung his "Thirteen Point Proposal to Amend the Constitution," which were measures, in his words, "to facilitate the smooth functioning of the State and remove certain causes of intercommunal friction."[32] If implemented, they would gut the constitutional mechanisms that empowered the Turkish minority.

The U.S. government understood that Athens wanted enosis more than Makarios, who espoused it expediently, to mobilize Greek support for his domestic power-grab. "Makarios' long-term objective," noted Undersecretary of State George Ball, was "not union with Greece" but to eliminate "those provisions [in the] London-Zurich agreements and constitution which . . . circumscribe [the] sovereignty of [the] Republic." The danger was that Makarios would wreck NATO by taking "a hard or defiant line with island Turks and Ankara," while relying on the United States and United Kingdom to keep Turkey "off his neck for the sake of peace and quiet."[33] Thus, Makarios' motives added an explosive layer of complexity to the pivotal deterrence problem. To advance his parochial agenda, he stoked nationalist sentiment in mainland Greece and took steps certain to provoke Turkey, while banking on the United States to keep Greece and Turkey apart.

Initial U.S. Strategy

U.S. policy, nevertheless, targeted Greece and Turkey and the key political movers in Cyprus. "Athens and Ankara . . . know best how to influence their communities here," advised Wilkins, the United States should press them to "coordinate their efforts . . . to encourage agreement on reasonable compromise solution."[34] The goal, as the White House put it, was to push Greece and Turkey "to take a more forthcoming approach" without, as Lucius Battle noted, "forfeiting our freedom of action."[35] The danger of moral hazard and the belief that a detached U.S. attitude would encourage moderation informed the U.S. approach. In January 1963 Rusk instructed his ambassadors to "politely but firmly reject" attempts "by either party to

[108]

draw [the] U.S. into [the] dispute . . . [B]elief on the part of either community that it has solid foreign backing will discourage compromise and encourage extremism."[36]

The London Conference and Lemnitzer's Plan, January–February 1964

When communal fighting erupted in December 1963, the United States
thus remained aloof, sticking to a policy that encouraged Britain to lead the
way in bringing Greece and Turkey together in a "coordinated 3-power"
solution."[37] Britain, however, was hard-pressed to conjure such a solution.
On 24 December, as fighting worsened, the United Kingdom, Greece, and
Turkey issued a joint cease-fire appeal to the Cyprus factions. This was to
be the three guarantors' last concerted action. The next day, the violence escalated. Turkey deployed its Cyprus contingent in defensive positions
around Nicosia and mobilized its land, sea, and air forces. At this stage,
Turkey's military threats were still seen, and rightly so, as bluffs aimed to
energize U.S. and U.K. diplomatic efforts.[38] The saber-rattling produced decidedly mixed results. Though the United Kingdom mobilized its forces on
the island to support "tripartite action" against the violence, Greek and
Turkish contingents deployed to support their ethnic brethren, not to enforce a truce between them.

Still, a fragile truce took hold on 26 December. In the UN Security Council, Cyprus accused Turkey of intervening in its "internal affairs . . . by the
threat and use of force against its territorial integrity and political independence." Makarios invoked the specter of Soviet involvement: "We are not
alone in this struggle," he declared, "there are other nations standing with
us." He also announced that if Turkey intervened, Cyprus would unilaterally terminate the London-Zurich treaties. The Soviet Ambassador to
Cyprus followed up, delivering a message from Moscow on 1 January supporting "the Greek Cypriots and the independence, sovereignty, and territorial integrity of Cyprus."[39]

In a desperate maneuver, Britain invited all the parties to London on 15
January to hash out a long-term settlement. Scant progress was made. The
Turks and Turkish Cypriots sought to strengthen the constitution's minority provisions and to concentrate ethnic Turks in enclaves that Turkish
forces could better protect. Greek Cypriots wanted to dispose of the constitution's minority safeguards and to nullify Turkey's rights as a guarantor.
Athens was passive, awaiting the results of its own general elections. The
talks deadlocked. On 22 January, Britain informed the United States that it
"could no longer assume responsibility for the maintenance of law and
order on Cyprus without outside assistance" and proposed a peacekeeping
force composed of NATO troops.[40]

İnönü recalled his delegation to the London conference on 28 January, called on the United States to intervene on behalf of Turkish Cypriots, and warned that Turkey would act unilaterally if violence resumed. Turkey stepped up military activities suggesting that an invasion was in the offing. Athens responded by alerting airborne commandos and naval squadrons and beginning military exercises in the Aegean. Washington, now alive to the danger of war within NATO, conceded that it must become more involved in Cyprus. NATO's supreme allied commander, U.S. General Lyman Lemnitzer, was sent to Athens, Ankara, and then London, to propose a three-month deployment of a 10,000-strong NATO peacekeeping force. Athens gave Makarios an early version of the plan, and he immediately countered with a proposal for a UN rather than NATO force that essentially doomed Lemnitzer's. The London conference ground to a halt, and the diplomatic focus shifted to the UN.[41]

Makarios' moves were strengthened by Moscow, which denounced the NATO plan as an attempt "to turn Cyprus into a military bridgehead."[42] In a 7 February letter to heads of state of the United States, United Kingdom, France, Greece, and Turkey, Krushchev wrote that the "dispatch to Cyprus of NATO troops" meant a "crude encroachment on [its] sovereignty, independence, and freedom," which in essence had one aim: "to place this small neutral state under the military control of NATO."[43] Moscow, he declared, could not "remain indifferent" to such a development—Cyprus was a matter for the UN Security Council. A UN force would serve Makarios' purposes well. Unlike a NATO force, it would be a weak impediment to Greek Cypriot operations on the island; and it would bring the Soviets into play in the Security Council, which might neutralize the Turkish threat to intervene.

Ball's Mission and the Origins of UNFICYP, February–March 1964

Seeking to keep the dispute within the NATO "family," Ball went to the region with a brief to humble Makarios, bring Greece and Turkey together, and keep the Soviets and the UN out. First off, Ball tried to increase Makarios' fear of unilateral Turkish intervention. On his first day in Cyprus, Ball warned Makarios that "if he continued to block a solution that would eliminate Turkey's reason for intervening" the United States would "not protect him from a Turkish move." On the next day, Ball was blunter: The Turks would "inevitably invade," he said, "and neither the U.S. nor any other Western power would raise a finger to stop them."[44] Still the crisis escalated. In Turkey on 14 February, İnönü warned Ball privately that if the UN failed to stanch the violence, he would intervene. That day Turkey began military exercises off the coast of Cyprus. Three days later, Greece re-alerted its forces. On 18 February, Ankara announced publicly that if the

UN failed to produce an effective peace plan that stopped communal fighting, it would be compelled to intervene.

Makarios did not bend to Ball's threats, or Turkey's, because the United States had not squared Greece or the Soviet Union. Athens refused to support a NATO force; it would only support what Makarios endorsed. Because Athens let Nicosia call the tune, the United States bid to impose a solution "over the head" of Cyprus foundered, as did its attempt to marginalize the Soviets. The dispute could not be kept within NATO if Greece would only parrot Cyprus, and Cyprus insisted on the UN. Ball's mission failed. The only option left was a UN operation. On 17 February, Britain resolved to "bring the matter without further delay to the Security Council." A UN force would take time—and haggling with Moscow—to produce. Meanwhile, Turkey and Greece were coming closer to war.

On 18 February, the UN Security Council began debate over how to respond. Greece, Turkey, and Cyprus were all in attendance. The new government in Greece (elected two days earlier), led by George Papandreou, came out strong, calling for abrogation of the London-Zurich agreements that Athens had signed five years before.[45] With Makarios trumpeting enosis, Papandreou committed Greece to defending Cyprus if Turkey intervened. "A war clash between Greece and Turkey would be madness," he said on 25 February, "but if Turkey decides to enter the insane asylum, we shall not hesitate to follow her."[46] The Soviets closed ranks with Athens and Nicosia. Moscow's ambassador to the UN decried a NATO conspiracy against Cyprus and called on the Security Council to "protect Cyprus from aggression and halt and prevent any form of intervention in her domestic affairs."[47] Turkey, on the other hand, was supported by the United States and United Kingdom, who insisted that the London-Zurich treaties must remain in force.

A compromise resolution on 4 March authorized the deployment of a peacekeeping operation, the United Nations Force in Cyprus(UNFICYP). For ten days, UN Secretary General U Thant scrambled to find funding and men, while violence on Cyprus escalated. London notified U Thant on 11 March that it could no longer "carry . . . this burden alone." The next day Turkey warned Nicosia that it would "use its unilateral right to intervene" unless there were an immediate cease-fire.[48] Nicosia remained defiant, and Turkey mobilized an army division based at Iskenderun. In Athens, Makarios accused Cypriot Turks of provoking violence in order "to give the Turkish Government a pretext for intervention" and warned: "We will fight back any unprovoked attack with all the means at our disposal." Papandreou, the newly elected Greek premier, promised support, put Greek armed forces on "advanced alert," and deployed warships near Cyprus.[49] Finally, on 13 March, after the United States had cajoled enough contributors, U

Thant announced UNFICYP would deploy immediately. Turkey stepped back from its ultimatum.

When the peacekeepers arrived, the violence tapered off, but not for long. Full-scale fighting began again in mid-April, dragging UNFICYP into the fray. Now Makarios repudiated the Treaty of Alliance and demanded that Turkey's contingent withdraw. Ankara warned Athens that it would consider any attack on its contingent by Greek Cypriots an "act of aggression against Turkey and act accordingly." Makarios went back to Athens, where Papandreou announced a "campaign for self-determination" for Cyprus and declared the Cyprus agreements untenable; the UN deployment demonstrated the need for "a new political formula for the island."[50]

Papandreou and Makarios agreed to insert clandestine Greek forces into Cyprus to increase its strength. These Hellenic Army "volunteers" would fill out the ranks of a conscript Cypriot National Guard, an organization that violated the 1960 constitution. Papandreou would later maintain that these volunteers were merely meant to deter Turkey. But they also "gave Greece a large measure of control over events in Cyprus" and vastly strengthened Makarios' hand against the Cypriot Turks.[51]

THE FIRST CYPRUS CRISIS, JUNE–AUGUST 1964

On 27 May, Cyprus' House of Representatives—now composed exclusively of Cypriot Greeks—floated a bill to create the National Guard, the vehicle for Papandreou's and Makarios' infiltration scheme. Nicosia also announced that it was purchasing arms from abroad to equip the Guard. Turkey and Britain denounced both moves as violations of the constitution, since they would require—and certainly not receive—the consent of Cypriot Turk Vice President Küçhük. When the House passed the bill on 1 June, Küçhük vetoed it in abstentia. To Turkey's note of protest against the bill, Nicosia retorted that it had "an inalienable right to take all measures for the defense of the island."[52]

On the night of 2 June, U.S. ambassador to Turkey, Raymond Hare, informed Washington that Turkey was planning to invade, and this time, it was not bluffing.[53] Two days later the National Guard draft began. That day Hare met with İnönü, and relayed to Washington İnönü's "strong conviction that, unless [Turkish] military force [were] put in Cyprus, no one would take Turkey seriously. . . . All [the Government of Turkey] has in mind is [to] occupy part of island and stop there."[54] The Johnson administration now acted with alacrity to stave off war.

Though Turkey had a decisive military advantage over Cyprus and Greece, it was in a poor diplomatic position to act unilaterally: It needed the United States to run interference with Moscow while it invaded Cyprus and fought Greece. Turkish diplomacy had long labored to ensure U.S. allegiance for just such an occasion. As İnönü said to Hare on 5 June, "Since the beginning of crisis [Turkey] had told [the United States] everything, has always taken U.S. advice, and has subordinated interests of Turkey to advice given by [the] U.S."[55] Now, in order to defend forcefully its Cyprus interests, Turkey needed U.S. fidelity. But a forceful Turkish stand was the last thing the United States wanted, for that would mean war within NATO. So the United States tilted against Turkey, the side that needed it the most.

Johnson's Letter

İnönü informed Hare on 4 June that Turkey would invade Cyprus the next day. Hare asked for and received a twenty-four–hour delay so that he could report to Washington and receive instructions.[56] The next day a U.S. aircraft carrier was stationed eight hours from Cyprus in case there was need for emergency evacuations or some "show of force."[57] Johnson sent İnönü a letter that, in Ball's words, was the "diplomatic equivalent of an atomic bomb."[58] First, Johnson upbraided Turkey for failing to "fully consult" with the United States, a disingenuous point since Johnson had the opportunity to send the letter precisely because İnönü had consulted the United States. Second, Johnson quibbled with Turkey's reading of its rights under the Treaty of Guarantee. This too was problematic, for the United States had long backed Ankara's claim that the Treaty was valid and gave Turkey the right to intervene unilaterally. Perhaps more germane was Johnson's warning that intervention could "lead to the slaughter of tens of thousands of Turkish Cypriots" which Turkish and UN forces "could not prevent," but that was surely a risk Ankara had considered and decided to accept. Johnson raised two prospects, however, that Turkey had probably not considered. One, he threatened to abandon Turkey: "I hope you will understand that your NATO allies have not had a chance to consider whether they have an obligation to protect Turkey against the Soviet Union if Turkey takes a step which results in Soviet intervention without the full consent and understanding of its NATO allies." Two, he insisted that Turkey could not use U.S.–supplied arms against Cyprus and implied that such aid would be terminated if they were.[59]

Johnson's threats worked. In his response, İnönü stated "upon your request [we] postponed our decision to exercise our right of unilateral action in Cyprus." İnönü also noted that the letter had revealed "substantial divergences of opinion in various fundamental matters."[60] In the next few years, these "divergences" would indeed become sore points in U.S.–Turkey relations. In any case, at the risk of embittering relations with both sides, the United States had now stepped up its pivotal role in the management of the crisis.

In the wake of Johnson's letter, Ball returned to the region. He met with Papandreou, who insisted that "Greece . . . needed a Cyprus solution based on *enosis*" and who seemed convinced "that the U.S. would always stand ready to thwart the Turks."[61] Ball tried to bring home to Papandreou that it was "only by President Johnson's forceful intervention," that Turkey had not invaded, and Johnson was not "in a position to do so" again.[62] Greece and Turkey had to come to terms over Cyprus, and Johnson wanted Papandreou to go to Washington to meet with him and İnönü. Papandreou accepted the invitation but insisted that he would *not* meet with Inönü and that talks in Washington could not supplant the UN approach.[63] Ball shuttled next to Ankara to assure Inönü that the United States did not wish to cut Turkey loose or to take Greece's side, but only to prevent NATO fratricide. The key was to get U.S.–Turkish relations back on track, and for that, Johnson needed İnönü to come to Washington to talk directly.

İnönü and Papandreou in Washington, June 1964

İnönü came to Washington on 22–23 June. The talks went well, given the circumstances. Most important for Turkey, the United States publicly affirmed the "present binding effects of existing treaties"—that is, the London-Zurich agreements. Most important for the United States, Turkey agreed to negotiate with Greece through the auspices of an American mediator—in parallel with the UN track.[64]

Papandreou's visit to Washington on 23–24 June was less salutary. In an attempt to pressure Greece to compete with Turkey for U.S. favor, Johnson pointed out that he had "made a positive request of the Turks and even though they didn't agree they would comply. I now make a positive request to you to talk. If you comply, we will then make some suggestions to the Turks. That's better than fighting." Dangling this carrot, the administration hammered away with the stick—if Greece would not cooperate, it could not count on the United States restraining Turkey again.[65] Andreas Papandreou, the prime minister's son, and a far-left member of his government called it "a brainwashing operation." Over dinner with Papandreou's entourage, Defense Secretary Robert McNamara opined that if Greece and Turkey went to war, "Turkish planes would literally burn up the Greek countryside." Papandreou, as recorded by his son, replied: "We thank you, Mr. Secretary, for having given Turkey such a powerful Air Force. Allow me to remind you, however, that Turkey neighbors on a country [i.e., the USSR] that has a much more powerful Air Force. It is more than likely that this Air Force would be drawn into the conflict were the Turks to attack."[66] Many appetites were no doubt ruined by the sordid truths beneath the bravado.

On 25 June Papandreou told the press that he was against direct negotiations with Turkey: "[N]o one is more competent than the UN mediator . . .

[114]

so long as there is a mediator I do not see what services other people could offer." But secretly, Papandreou agreed to consult with a "shadow" mediator, an unofficial U.S. diplomat who would also maintain contact with Turkey.[67] This was as good as it was going to get, so Ball went to seek U Thant's approval of a U.S. mediator working in tandem with the UN's official Cyprus mediator in Geneva, Sakari Tuomioja. Whatever goodwill between the United States and Greece that may have been wrought by this minor breakthrough was tainted by Papandreou's parting announcement. For Greece the London-Zurich agreements were no longer binding, and it was committed to "full independence" and "self-determination" for Cyprus. Full independence meant the departure of Turkey's contingent on the island, and self-determination meant majority rule, which it turn, meant enosis.[68]

Acheson's Plans, July–August 1964

The UN mediator set up shop in Geneva with official representatives of Cyprus, Greece, and Turkey. The "shadow" U.S. mediator was Dean Acheson, drafted out of retirement for the job. His diplomatic talent was renown, and his reputation among Greeks and Turks as the father of the Truman doctrine gave him a modicum of goodwill to work with. His primary goal was to carve out a bargain for Greece and Turkey to impose on Cyprus. Makarios, accordingly, was not invited to the talks. As the two sides met with Acheson out of the public eye, Papandreou and Grivas conspired (with U.S. backing) to arrange an "instant enosis" option that would dispense with Makarios and forgo any interim of "full" independence and would instead immediately dispose of Cyprus according to a secret agreement between Athens and Turkey.[69]

During July there was a promising lull in the communal fighting. Tuomioja's effort, slow to get off the ground, collapsed when he suffered a stroke. But Acheson charged ahead. For months, the State Department had toyed with enosis as an ultimate political solution. By June this had gelled into support for a "compensated" enosis that traded Greek annexation for Turkish gains elsewhere and minority guarantees on the island.[70] As Acheson's first plan shaped up in July, it built on that basic formula: Greece would get enosis, but Turkey would get a permanent base and Greek territorial concession elsewhere. Cypriot Turks would have autonomous enclaves under Greek rule and compensation if they wished to immigrate.[71] Turkey was apparently ready to make a deal if the base area were under its sovereignty and would encompass the Karpas peninsula. Greece countered with the offer to lease a smaller base area on the peninsula for twenty-five years, and there appeared to be upward flexibility on that time frame. At this point, Makarios stepped into the fray. Acheson's first effort to close the gap between Greece and Turkey would not survive the archbishop's intervention.[72]

Acheson's formula would end Makarios' tenure in Cyprus—and he was not about to let that happen. This is why Soviet support and nonaligned backing in the UN were crucial to his delicately balanced position. Moscow did not want Cyprus divided up between Greece and Turkey, both members of NATO. It wanted Cyprus to remain an independent "non-aligned" Republic, with a thriving Communist party. Thus, when Makarios called for "unity with Greece" but "not unity with NATO" he revealed the hitch in his commitment to "Hellenism," and invoked Moscow as a counterweight against enosis.[73] When Robert Komer and McGeorge Bundy later discussed with Johnson the prospects for "instant *enosis*" they correctly predicted that "if Makarios smells a rat he'll appeal to the UN and to Moscow." Makarios did exactly that. When he got wind of an early version of Acheson's plan, he denounced it publicly and then went to Athens and forced Papandreou to disown it.[74]

As Talbot, now the U.S. ambassador to Greece, summed up the situation on the Cyprus question, "the capital of Hellenism is in Nicosia."[75] Makarios was not content merely to wreck Acheson's plan; he wanted to eliminate any chance of a Greek-Turkish bargain at his expense. So, at the end of July, he decided to escalate.[76] Claiming that his security forces had been subjected to "unprovoked attack," Makarios unleashed his militias on the Turkish communities of Kokkina and Mansoura on the northwest coast of Cyprus, key focal points of supply and support from the Turkish mainland. Such tactical concerns were secondary, however, to the key political aim—to discompose relations between Athens and Ankara.

Within days the enclaves had been emptied of Turks, who fled to UN zones for protection. After an initial delay—to allow the United States to deliver on its assurances that Makarios would halt the attacks—İnönü's government firmly decided to bomb Greek positions on Cyprus.[77] Turkey had informed the United States that it would respond to renewed violence on the island with air strikes and stated that such warnings should be considered due "consultation."[78] This time the United States did little to interfere. On 7 August, Turkish jets strafed the Greek Cypriot coastal town of Polis. The next day they conducted intimidating overflights near Greek Cypriot villages in the northwest. The day after that, sixty-four Turkish jets used rockets, cannons, 750–pound bombs, and napalm, while offshore, Turkish warships shelled Greek positions near Mansoura.[79]

In addition to hundreds of Greek Cypriot casualties, the bombing provoked bloodcurdling rhetoric from Athens and Nicosia. In the Security Council on 9 August, Greece threatened to support Cyprus "with its air force and every military means at its disposal" if Turkey did not stop bombing. In London, the Cypriot High Commissioner warned that Cyprus would defy Turkish demands "even if it means a third world war."[80] Through back channels, Makarios threatened to attack every Cypriot Turk village on the island if Turkey did not stop, and he openly called on the Soviets and Egypt to intervene.[81] Nevertheless, the bombing put a quick stop to the anti-Turk violence. Makarios had overplayed his hand. Greece simply could not defend Cyprus from the air.[82] If the United States would not call off the Turkish air force, Greek positions in Cyprus were utterly vulnerable. As for the prospects of Soviet rescue, Moscow's response, much as U.S. officials expected, was less than resounding.[83] Krushchev wrote İnönü warning of "the responsibility" Turkey assumed by attacking Cyprus, a member of the UN, and assured Makarios that Soviet "sympathies" were on his side. Sympathy was a paltry substitute for Soviet air-cover, or at least the threat of it. Egypt's leader, Gamal Abdul Nasser, was simply silent until 11 August, when he stated that, while he fully supported the Cypriot people's fight against aggression, he hoped "that wisdom will prevail."[84] In Nicosia's hour of need, these flaccid warnings and assurances did not inspire confidence.

Neither did Johnson's identical letter to Turkey, Greece, and Cyprus, which urged "all possible restraint" on all sides because "no statesman would wish to bear responsibility" for the costs of a Greco-Turkish war. The question of responsibility aside, there was no doubt which side in a Greco-Turkish war would bear the larger share of pain and suffering. The "deassuring" message to Greece was reinforced by a private one to Papandreou demanding that he rein in Makarios, who had now gone so far as to invite Soviet forces into the Cyprus conflict. That was not something that Athens would wish for; it certainly would not bode well for enosis. Athens, shocked by its apparent loss of control over Makarios and Grivas, heaped pressure on Nicosia to stand down. At the same time, the United States privately implored the Turks to cease bombing: They now had "made their point emphatically by military action," further air strikes risked provoking an island-wide massacre of Cypriot Turks. Turkey agreed to call off the next day's sorties, provided Makarios had halted all attacks on Turkish enclaves.[85]

Late on 9 August, Greece and Cyprus accepted the U.S.–U.K. cease-fire resolution in the Security Council. The next day, Makarios reined in the Guard and militias. İnönü, against resistance from his military, halted the air strikes. Now the key, as Rusk saw it, was to "put [a] leash on [the] ebullient Turk military while at the same time to push a thoroughly scared Papandreou into serious negotiations."[86] Thus, in the days that followed, the United States pressured both Athens and Ankara to resume serious negotiations on the Geneva track. Acheson proposed another scheme for "instant" and "compensated" enosis: Turkey could lease a large base on the Karpas peninsula for fifty rather than twenty-five years, but there would be no autonomous communal areas in Greek-controlled Cyprus.

The two sides would not, however, close the gap. Greece would not agree to a base area large enough to win Turkey's approval. After the debacle of early August, Papandreou was desperate to separate himself from Makarios in American eyes, but he simply could not challenge Makarios' appeal to Greek public opinion. When Makarios declared that he aspired "to unite with Greece the *entirety* of Cyprus, not part of her," Papandreou's hands were tied.[87] Turkey, for its part, objected to the "precarious foundation of a lease arrangement" and would take nothing less than full sovereignty over the base area.[88] After weeks of pushing the boulder uphill, Acheson still came up empty-handed and departed Geneva on 4 September. Although it was not obvious at the time, a three-year period of relative calm ensued; the lessons taught Athens and Nicosia by the diplomacy surrounding the air strikes were an important cause of the lull.

Making Sense of the Soviet Response

Once the cease-fire was in place, Krushchev became more strident. On 15 August, the Kremlin announced that "if a foreign armed invasion of the Republic takes place" it would "help Cyprus to defend her freedom and independence" and was prepared "to begin negotiations on this matter immediately." Krushchev, the next day, declared that the Soviet Union "cannot and will not remain indifferent to the threat of an armed conflict near our southern borders . . . [Turkey] cannot drop bombs on Cyprus and destroy old people, women, and children with impunity."[89] A master of political theater, Krushchev's most colorful rhetoric on Cyprus was also the least substantial.

Indeed, the Soviet response to the 1964 Cyprus crisis was two-faced. At bottom, Moscow wanted to support Makarios and promote an *independent* Cyprus. The anticommunist Grivas had now assumed a large role in Cyprus politics. In June 1964, the Greek General Staff sent him back to Cyprus to organize the strengthening of the National Guard with mainland troops and material. On 28 June, his first public appearance, Grivas thrilled a throng of ten thousand with the parting words "long live tomorrow's Greek Cyprus!" Before another crowd a few days later, he declared himself "the apostle of union with mother Greece." The next day, in the House of Representatives, he called on all Greek Cypriots to "march hand-in-hand for the realization of enosis."[90] On 13 August, Grivas was officially dubbed the commander of the Cypriot National Guard. The Kremlin was not blind to these events. The Soviets knew that Grivas had conspired with the United States to achieve "instant" enosis and get rid of Makarios, and they did not want to arm the National Guard if that meant strengthening the pro-enosis right wing.[91]

Thus, over the summer, the Soviets became strong advocates of UNFI-CYP, not only because it obstructed NATO solutions but also because it reinforced the political independence of Cyprus, which was more important to Moscow than fomenting a war between NATO allies.[92] That explains the otherwise curious fact that Krushchev did not encourage Makarios to stand firm during the Turkish bombing campaign. Any Greco-Turkish war over Cyprus would end badly for the Soviet Union and the Cypriot Communist party. So, as Adams and Cotrell put it, "Soviet equivocation" during the crisis "strengthened the U.S. position."[93] Most important, Moscow did not directly threaten Turkey to make it stop bombing Cyprus. Soon after the August bombings, Moscow began to distance itself from Cyprus and assure Turkey that it was neutral toward the dispute.[94] Moscow's lack of ardor gave Greece and Cyprus pause. If the Soviet air force could not be counted on, then U.S. warnings that it would not restrain Turkey had to be taken much more seriously.

In September, with the crisis safely past, the Security Council took up the matter again. Here, Krushchev embraced the opportunity to score propaganda points: He excoriated the United States and NATO for masterminding the Turkish bombing, and invited the Cypriots to Moscow to plan a program of military aid. The Cypriots went on 1 October and were duly promised increased trade and generous military aid.[95] But the Kremlin's promises would prove hollow, especially after Krushchev was ousted from power on 15 October.[96] Moscow's public overtures to Nicosia were little more than a smoke screen for a reversal of Soviet policy toward the dispute—in favor of Turkey.

THE TURKISH-SOVIET RAPPROCHEMENT

Until 1964, Turkey essentially "followed a policy of blindfolded dependencies on the West" and "unswerving hostility" toward the USSR.[97] The Johnson letter changed all that. The key driver of this change in Turkish policy toward the USSR was the Cyprus problem.[98] The Soviets were more than happy to capitalize on Turkey's new mood. The first ripples of shifting alignment appeared on 15 August when the Soviet ambassador to Nicosia visited Küchük, the sidelined Cypriot Turk vice president. Coming less than a week after Turkey's air strikes, and on the same day that TASS, the Soviet press organ, trumpeted Moscow's fealty to Nicosia, this was the first such visit since violence began in December 1963.[99] From there, Turkish-Soviet relations just got better.[100]

At the end of October, Erkin went to Moscow on official business. No

Turkish foreign minister had done so since 1939. He parted with a joint communiqué that declared support "for the legal rights of the two national communities" on Cyprus, which moved Moscow far toward Turkey's position in the dispute. So much, in fact, that Rusk worried that the Soviets had "gone further in supporting the Turkish position on the inviolability of treaties than [the United States] had in the joint communiqué issued after the İnönü visit to Washington."[101] In January, Soviet Foreign Minister Andrei Gromyko floated a proposal for a "federal" solution to governing Cyprus and praised the "warmer wind" that had "begun to blow" in Soviet-Turkish relations. The same month, Soviet President Nikolai Podgorny regaled the Turkish Parliament with platitudes about improving relations and repeated the Kremlin's new stance on Cyprus, drawing fire from Makarios and Papandreou.[102] After Podgorny's visit, the United States announced that Turkey would withdraw from NATO's nuclear multilateral force (MLF). Moscow applauded.[103]

İnönü's government fell in February to a no-confidence vote led by Süleyman Demirel's Justice Party (JP). The JP had long opposed better relations with Moscow. But the new coalition government made Hayri Ürgüplü, who favored the rapprochement, prime minister, and he made Turkey's ambassador to Moscow his foreign minister. Gromyko visited Turkey in May, after it had been revealed earlier that month that Soviet surface-to-air missiles (SAMs) were being delivered to Cyprus through Egypt.[104] Gromyko publicly reinforced Moscow's pro-Turkish position on Cyprus and, off the record, promised to stop shipping "heavy arms" to Cyprus.[105]

In August, Ürgüplü visited the Soviet Union, the first Turkish prime minister to do so since 1932. Moscow endorsed another joint communiqué that voiced Turkey's position on Cyprus, and Ürgüplü pocketed a proposal for Soviet financing for a massive dam project and generous offers of credits for nine major industrial development projects.[106] Overall, Turkish-Soviet commerce was improving dramatically; Turkey's trade with the USSR in 1965 doubled that of 1964. A cap to this remarkable upturn in Turkish-Soviet relations occurred in October, when a shipment of Soviet SAMs destined for Cyprus was reversed *en route* and returned to Egypt.

Later that month the JP formed a new government, with Demirel as prime minister. Though ultimately Demirel was committed to NATO, his "government . . . expanded relations [with the Soviet Union] faster and more profoundly than its predecessors." In December 1965, he put a stop to U.S. U-2 flights originating in Turkey. In July 1966, he withdrew Turkey's contingent from UN forces in Korea and signed civil air and bilateral trade agreements with all the Eastern Bloc countries.[107] Turkey also clamped down on host-country sovereignty and the scope of U.S. activities on Turkish bases, putting pressure on the United States to clarify its defense commitments to Turkey under NATO and to take positions in the Cyprus dispute more favorable to Turkey.[108] Thus, improved relations with Moscow gave Turkey more bargaining power, and Demirel tried to use it to eliminate the ambiguity in U.S. commitments that had let Johnson threaten to abandon Turkey. But more than a change in treaty language could, Turkey's improved relations with Moscow ensured that Johnson's ploy was not again used against Turkey.

In December 1966, Soviet Premier Aleksei Kosygin visited Turkey. In what was now a familiar tableau Kosygin endorsed Turkey's position on Cyprus, provoking outcry in Nicosia.[109] When Turkish officials voiced concerns about recent (November 1966) sales of Czech weapons to Makarios (which he apparently intended to use against a Grivas-led coup), Kosygin condemned the Warsaw Pact ally. To top it off, in March 1967, Moscow agreed to a $200 million economic aid package for Turkey, "the most far reaching industrial assistance agreement it had ever concluded with any country."[110]

GREEK INGRATIATION AND BILATERAL TALKS, 1965–67

After the crises of 1964, the basic assumptions of U.S. policy toward Cyprus changed little. The key interlocutors were still Ankara and Athens. And as Parker Hart, the new U.S. ambassador to Turkey, put it, Washington would "support whatever the two could agree on."[111] After the August 1964 crisis, the Acheson negotiations had deadlocked. "The horses," wrote the U.S. ambassador to Greece, "have been led to water but have refused to drink."[112] With the fighting on Cyprus in a lull, Washington wanted out of the exposed role of middleman. Nicosia could plead its case with Galo Plaza, the new UN mediator, and the United States would press its allies to negotiate directly in secret. Athens sensed the dangerous thaw in Soviet-Turk relations and moved to avoid isolation by ingratiating Washington. Papandreou, heeding U.S. suggestions to begin bilateral talks, stressed that it was now "essential to have harmonization" of U.S. and Greek views on Cyprus, and he tried repeatedly to put Turkey in the wrong.[113] Although the talks yielded little progress in the years ahead, they served Washington well enough. In order to facilitate negotiations, Athens and Ankara both worked to enforce calm on the island. The bilateral talks also undermined the UN negotiating track, where Makarios had an independent voice.[114] As long as Athens and Ankara were engaged bilaterally, America's clout as a pivotal ally was maximized, and Cyprus was subdued.

Recall that the key problem for the United States in the 1964 crises was that Athens could not be counted on to deliver or dispose of Makarios when a Greece-Turkey deal was within reach. For all of its evils, when the right-wing junta took over Greece in April 1967, after an increasing polarization of party politics and a procession of ever-less-stable caretaker governments, this situation changed for the better.[115] Even before the junta took over, the Greek government was working hard to secure firm U.S. backing against Turkey.[116] But the colonels, led by George Papadopolous, turned Athens' policies upside-down: They were, in the U.S. ambassador's words, "a thousand percent pro-American . . . pro-NATO, [and] rigorously if not fanatically anti-Communist."[117] While Ankara made trouble with the United States over basing rights, and forged diplomatic and economic ties with Moscow, Athens "continued, if not intensified, single source military purchases from the United States," and Papadopolous "went out of [his] way to offer privileges and facilities to the United States, the one country the brusque dictator considered as a viable outside protector."[118] The junta was openly disdainful of Makarios, and it needed a foreign policy success. Papadopolous wanted to cut an enosis deal with Turkey, and be rid of the "Red Bishop," Makarios.

In May and June 1967, Papadopolous engaged in low-level bilateral negotiations with Turkey. Then, in August, he invited Turkey to take negotiations to the prime ministerial level in a two-day September conference. The Turks were skeptical about the prospects for progress but, not wanting to appear intransigent, accepted the offer.[119] Demirel and the junta's puppet prime minister, Constantine Kollias, met in Keshan on 9 September and in Alexandroupolis the day after. Kollias opened with a strong pitch for "compensated" enosis. Greece would absorb the island entirely—including the British base at Dhekelia—and then give Turkey de facto control over the base under the aegis of NATO or, if necessary, full sovereignty over it. Demirel threw cold water on the proposals. Cantonment or federation of Cyprus, under some mutually agreed alteration of the London-Zurich agreements, might be conceivable. But not a deal that, at the outset, gave Greece full sovereignty over Cyprus. Unable to reach agreement, the two sides barely managed to produce a joint communiqué pledging to "safeguard and ease efforts being exerted for a peaceful and agreed solution."[120]

The Turks left convinced that Athens would lunge for a fait accompli on Cyprus in the very near future.[121] Nine days later, Demirel was party to another set of high-level talks—this time in the Soviet Union. At a Kremlin dinner in Demirel's honor, Kosygin denounced the Cyprus "intrigues" of "certain circles", a thinly veiled attack on Athens' bid for enosis. Back at home, Demirel pronounced the "mistrust, doubt, and prejudice which for many years marred and damaged Turkish-Soviet relations" a thing of the past, and Turkey's NATO membership would not be allowed to impede this progress.[122]

THE NOVEMBER 1967 CRISIS

After the Keshan-Alexandroupolis talks, relations between Turkey and Greece deteriorated quickly. In mid-November, communal violence on Cyprus broke out again, provoked by the aggressive patrolling of Grivas' Guard. The escalation may not have been authorized by the junta, but Athens did not move quickly to suppress the patrols once they began, probably on the assumption that the United States would give diplomatic cover to Athens, its firmly committed ally.[123] If so, Athens made the same miscalculation that Ankara did three years before.

Since 1964, Turkey and Greece had been feeding material, manpower, and leadership to the contending forces on Cyprus. Under Grivas, Athens maintained an army of "twelve to fourteen thousand," or more, far in excess of the London-Zurich allotment of 750.[124] Likewise, although on a lesser scale, Ankara moved personnel from its treaty contingent forces into the ranks of the Cypriot Turk militia, the Turkish Fighters Organization (TMT), which increased the TMT's capacity to fight, and Ankara's control over it. Thus, Grivas, who answered to Athens, had his evil twin, a Turkish officer with the nom de guerre "Mehmet," who commanded the TMT.[125]

The November surge in fighting began around the town of Ayios Theodoros. During the previous summer, the TMT had begun to impede biweekly patrols by the Cyprus police (CYPOL) in that predominantly Turkish enclave. UNFICYP had negotiated a temporary halt to the patrols, but Grivas persevered. On 15 November, he led a CYPOL patrol into Ayios Theodoros, bristling with a platoon of infantry and artillery. The TMT took the bait and opened fire. Grivas retaliated with machine guns, cannon, and mortars, killing nine and wounding nine others, and then overran three UNFICYP posts. After securing Ayios, he moved on to TMT strongholds near Kophinou, which neighbored a National Guard base. Grivas shelled Kophinou, killing another twenty-two and wounding nine more.[126] A flimsy UN cease-fire took hold late on 15 November. That night Demirel's cabinet decided to retaliate with air strikes if Grivas did not immediately restore the status quo ante.[127] At the UN, Turkey decried the provocations, and the Secretary General took the unusual step of agreeing with a strongly worded condemnation.[128]

Initial Efforts to Calm the Crisis

When the fighting broke out, Washington urged restraint in Turkey and implored Greece to restore the status quo. Athens responded with a formal request to Nicosia to call off the Guard. Just in time, Hart relayed the news to Ankara, which decided to cancel impending air strikes. The crisis, it seemed, had been defused. Yet Grivas remained in Cyprus, and he did not let up. By 17 November, he had launched two new patrols in Ayios Theodoros. To Ambassador Talbot, King Constantine maintained Athens' innocence in these matters, claiming that Grivas answered to Nicosia, not the junta.[129] Talbot, however, insisted that Greece could not wash its hands of the crisis: Grivas was a general in the Greek army who took orders from Athens. The king yielded the point. He instructed the junta on the 17th to *order* Grivas to cease fire, restore the status quo ante, and return to Athens.

But now Ankara had moved into a hard-line position. That day, the Turkish Grand National Assembly authorized an invasion. Afterward, Demirel declared that Turkey "would do everything possible and necessary to stop Greek aggression."[130] Ankara decided to exploit Athens' diplomatic blunder by demanding much more than Grivas' recall. Demirel sent a letter to Greece on 17 November that blamed the crisis on "the presence of a part of the Greek army on the island, and the irresponsible action by General Grivas, who is appointed by Greece," and insisted that Athens must "find a solution to the real source of this crisis, which is the situation of the Greek National Guard." Turkey, meanwhile, would "take all necessary measures" to respond to the deteriorating situation.[131] The letter produced no immediate response from Greece, convincing Ankara that Athens was stalling, betting the United States would intervene on its behalf.

On 18 November, Johnson sent similar messages to Nicosia, Athens, and Ankara, calling for restraint on all sides.[132] In reply to the U.S. démarche, Turkey declared its "fundamental demand for a withdrawal of Greek forces from Cyprus," and began mobilizing for war. It was "reasonably clear," according to a State Department report, that the Turkish military had "been given the authority to act without further consultation if they decide the situation required it." In Athens, the king pledged to do his utmost for peace, while the colonels debated whether to launch a preemptive "surprise attack" (an option Papadopolous reportedly favored). "The prospects for maintaining peace between Greece and Turkey," the State Department report concluded, "are poor."[133]

On the night of 19 November, Hart met with Turkey's Foreign Minister İhsan Çağlayangil to develop political alternatives to military intervention. They produced a five-point plan: (1) Turkey would pledge to respect the territorial integrity of Cyprus; (2) both sides would remove their forces from Cyprus exceeding the London-Zurich limitations; (3) UNFICYP would be given a key role in monitoring the drawdown; (4) Greece and/or the Cyprus Republic would pay an indemnity to the Turkish victims of the recent violence; and (5) some "special kind" of security measures—not dependent on Greek Cypriot police or military—would be created to protect Turkish Cypriots. The hitch was that Turkey would not engage on any of these issues until Greece began to withdraw its forces from Cyprus. This was Turkey's minimum demand: Athens would not be permitted to continue reinforcing Cyprus under the cover of continued talks.[134]

The United States passed the proposal to Athens and aired it with Makarios. Makarios, whose rule was now threatened as much by Grivas' pretensions as Ankara's, endorsed the first three points but bridled at the "special security" provisions and compensation for Cypriot Turks.[135] On 22 November, Athens responded negatively on the most important points: it would not agree to a rapid withdrawal of Greek forces over treaty limits, and it would only agree to a dialogue conducted "in an atmosphere free of threats."[136] Turkey responded with blunter threats: The Greek ambassador in Ankara was told "unless those extra Greek forces were withdrawn, the Turkish Army would go in and create a balance. If this were opposed, Turkey would fight its way in."[137]

The United States tried to reframe the situation by having U Thant propose the essentials of the five-point plan. U Thant, however, would not put forth the plan without guarantees that all sides—including Nicosia—would accept and that the Security Council would fund the increased UNFICYP mandate. On 24 November, U Thant dispatched Jose Rolz-Bennett, his "personal high level representative," to mediate, but he refused to be the first to publicly advance a proposal that looked to be a loser. The Johnson administration now had to either embrace the unhappy task of deterrence among friends or watch NATO's southern flank internally combust.

Cyrus Vance's Mission

By 22 November Turkey was within forty-eight hours of invading Cyprus.[138] Johnson sent former Deputy Defense Secretary Cyrus Vance to the region, with "full discretion to . . . exert pressure on either side to ensure peace."[139] "You will have to play this by a sensitive ear," instructed the State Department, "but don't hesitate to push in our stack to get results."[140] Before departing late on 22 November, Vance met in Kennedy Airport with Assistant Secretary of State Lucius Battle, to flesh out a negotiating strategy. Vance would avoid intermeddling in the particulars of the Cyprus dispute and focus instead on the current military confrontation.[141] He was to impress on Ankara that Greece had genuinely tried to defuse the situation, with some results, and that Turkey should avoid doing anything now to "stir up" the situation. In a dire emergency, and as a last resort, Vance was to inform Ankara: (1) "military action by Turkey would horrify" Americans; (2) that if such action involved U.S. equipment, it would lead Congress to terminate any further military or economic aid; and (3) that such action would signal "a fundamental change in relations between the two countries."[142] In Athens, Vance was to start off by preaching the gravity of the situation and warning of Greece's exposure. If Greece did not remove its troops on Cyprus, Turkey was "mobilized and ready to go to war," and Vance should "say there is no give in this position." To both sides, he would affirm that "any settlement . . . agreeable to the parties is acceptable to us."[143]

When Ankara was informed that Vance was en route, the response was not encouraging. Vance was denounced as a "living Johnson letter" in the Turkish Cabinet, and there was a movement to refuse to receive him.[144] Word leaked out to the public, and rioting accompanied Vance's arrival. Into this heated atmosphere, Vance trod gingerly. In his first meetings with Demirel and Çağlayangil, he pressed for time, urging that the Greek response of 22 November should not be taken as final until he had the chance to talk with Athens. His first proposal to Turkey, a simultaneous Turkish demobilization and Greek withdrawal from Cyprus, was promptly rejected. Turkey would not stand down until all Greek forces were out of Cyprus.[145] Vance then met with Turkey's president, General Cevdet Sunay, who wished him luck in Greece and warned him that "time was of the essence."[146]

On the evening of 23 November, Vance shuttled to Greece, spurred on by what he sensed was "a Turkish hope that we can pull a rabbit out of the essentially ultimative hat they have presented to us."[147] His aim: to obtain a Greek commitment to withdraw forces from Cyprus and to get Athens to "take [this] first step" before Turkey stood down.[148] That day, the Soviet ambassador to Turkey delivered to Demirel a "very courteous" letter from Kosygin. It restated Moscow's view of the Athens junta as "fascist," but cautioned that the costs of using force should be "carefully considered" by Turkey. In no way did it suggest that Moscow would oppose Turkish intervention.[149]

On 24 November, Vance met with the junta's newly appointed foreign minister, Panayiotis Pipinelis, and Prime Minister Kollias. The Greeks were at first uncooperative; they could not make compromises "under the threat of war."[150] But after day-long negotiations, Pipinelis agreed to a modified version of Turkey's proposal, a six-point plan that differed in both substance and tone. First, in order to save face for Greece, it would be pitched as an opportunity for both to "respond favorably" to an urgent appeal by the UN Secretary General. It called for a *phased* withdrawal of *all* non-Cypriot forces (with an immediate token withdrawal of five hundred Greek troops), not just those exceeding the Treaty of Alliance limits. This would proceed in tandem with a phased buildup of stronger means for safeguarding the internal security of Cyprus, protecting minorities, and defending against external threats. The phased withdrawal of all national contingents—which was to result in a "complete demilitarization" of Cyprus—

would nullify the London-Zurich agreements. On top of that, Pipinelis insisted that Greek withdrawal be keyed to "immediate" *simultaneous* steps by Turkey to demobilize to pre–November 14 levels.[151] Vance told Pipinelis bluntly "the chances of a peaceful settlement [were] slight unless Greece move[d] first."[152] If Athens insisted on simultaneity, it would probably have war with Turkey on its hands, and the United States could not stop it. So Athens reconsidered and devised a plan that maintained a facade of simultaneity on paper but allowed Vance to convey verbally that Greece would begin withdrawing troops first, if Turkey would agree to begin demobilizing soon after.

While Vance persevered in Greece, Turkey turned up the heat. In the afternoon of 24 November, Hart was informed that Turkey would begin military operations immediately unless Vance produced a favorable Greek response to the original five-point plan. That day President Sunay wrote heads of state in the United States, France, United Kingdom, USSR, and elsewhere, notifying them that Turkey had "decided to solve the Cyprus problem once and for all." The United States and United Kingdom evacuated their citizens from Cyprus. Turkey stepped up reconnaissance missions over the island. The ports of Mersin and Iskenderun bustled with mobilization for an invasion. Time was running out. That night, Vance authorized Hart to convey to the Turkish foreign minister the State Department's stern "last-ditch" warnings and his concern that Turkey's ultimatum would scuttle his efforts in Greece to devise a peaceful settlement.[153]

The next morning, Vance flew to Turkey to deliver Athen's "phased withdrawal" proposal. Turkey's response was hard-nosed. The foreign minister indicated right off that he was unmoved by the previous night's warning that if Turkey rejected Greece's conditions and went to war using U.S. equipment, U.S.–Turkey relations would be seriously damaged. Vance, for his part, countered that Turkey should not "turn down" his proposals, for Washington would "conclude it had been tricked by [Ankara] and [that the] entire exercise has been a Turkish charade."[154] For this, Vance managed to extract from Sunay a "flat assurance" that Cyprus would not be attacked while his parleys were still underway.[155] Ankara, in any case, objected to a number of elements of the new proposal. First, it rejected the phased withdrawal from Cyprus as an invitation to Greek foot-dragging and mischief.[156] Second, it could not agree to a total demilitarization of the island because this would gut the Treaty of Alliance. Finally, Turkey objected to the simultaneity in Athens' offer; it "refused to stand down until all Greek [forces were] out."[157]

Turkey's counterproposal—after massaging by Vance—invited both sides to reaffirm the "independence and territorial integrity" of Cyprus, and required an "expeditious" withdrawal of all non-Cypriot forces over

the limits "specified in the treaties signed in Nicosia on August 16, 1960."
"Following this" the Turks would take "all the necessary measures for re-
moving the crisis."[158] After much cajoling by Vance, Turkey agreed to
change the phrase *following this* to *accompanying this.*[159] With that official
Turkish rejoinder, Vance would also deliver a confidential letter to Pipinelis
confirming that Turkey would stand down the forces it had mobilized after
15 November "in parallel" with the expeditious Greek withdrawal. Against
Vance's protests, Demirel refused to disclose the letter publicly.[160]

Back in Athens on 26 November, the Greeks vetted the new Turkish proposal. Their reply again excluded reference to the London-Zurich agreements, "which Greece considered dead," and the national contingents man-
dated by them, and called for the "ultimate complete demilitarization" of
Cyprus.[161] To sweeten the deal, Athens promised off the record to withdraw
all Greek forces from Cyprus in three months. Vance warned Pipinelis that
Turkey would probably reject the rejoinder, despite the concession, and it
did the next day. Predictably, Turkish leaders objected to the failure of the
Greek proposal to refer to the London-Zurich agreements, which they
deemed a ploy "to show the public that [Turkey] has renounced the Lon-
don/Zurich accords, thus prejudging the Cyprus question."[162] They also refused to countenance a three-month withdrawal period.

After this cycle of proposals and counterproposals deadlocked on 27 November, Vance introduced his own four-point plan, which he had aired in
Athens the night before, as a fallback to Turkey's rejection of Athen's latest
bid.[163] In it, the Greeks would agree to begin an expeditious withdrawal
from Cyprus to be completed in three months, "accompanied" by the demobilization of Turkish forces. Treaty limits would not be referred to explicitly, but the Greek and Turkish forces to be withdrawn "expeditiously"
would be those that exceeded those "present in 1963."[164] The troop withdrawals would be counterbalanced with an enhanced UNFICYP given a
more vigorous security role. The actual deployment and operation of the
robust UNFICYP would not, as Athens wished, be a *precondition* for remov-
ing Greek forces. The withdrawals would begin once the political "arrangements"—not the capabilities—for UNFICYP's new mission were in place.

Turkey immediately undertook to revise Vance's proposal. At first, it insisted on a withdrawal period of no more than thirty days. Vance argued
that Greece would need at least two months to complete such an extensive
drawdown. Turkey grudgingly agreed to a complete withdrawal in forty-
five days. This was their final offer: Greece had to "accept it or accept war."
Vance was to convey this to Athens and not to return in official capacity.[165]

Vance headed to Greece on the morning of 28 November with Turkey's
final offer and their 6:00 P.M. deadline for a response. If Greece did not answer favorably, Turkey would go to war the next day.[166] Vance told Pipinelis "time is very short and [the] Turks will not accept any change in the

draft. This is [a] fact of life."[167] If Greece walked away from the deal, war would come, and the United States would not stop it. Athens agreed just before the six o'clock deadline, with one caveat: that Greece could not speak for Makarios, especially in relation to the UN's "increased pacification role," which would challenge the Cypriot National Guard.[168]

With Greece and Turkey in tune, Vance went to Nicosia on 1 December to press for Makarios' assent. Officials in Washington, Athens, and Ankara were all expecting Vance to have trouble bringing "aboard" Makarios.[169] Turkey made it clear that it would not allow Vance to return to Ankara with new demands for "further modifications" from Makarios.[170] Vance thought Makarios did "not believe that he [was] about to be invaded" and that he failed to understand that he must "pay for his folly of November 15–16." So in Nicosia, Vance warned the archbishop that "if Greece had not accepted the proposals, the Turkish units would have been on shores of Cyprus this morning." If Makarios did not approve the proposal in full, "carnage would result." Turkey "could and would put fifty thousand men on the island within forty-eight hours, along with heavy equipment and complete mastery of the air." According to "best estimates," warned Vance, the result would be "100s of thousands dead." Makarios should not assume "that a Turkish invasion resulting from a Cypriot effort to torpedo the accord would cause the United States to intervene militarily." When Makarios pressed for a U.S. guarantee against Turkish attack as the price for his assent, Vance suggested that he instead "look to" the UN Security Council for such a guarantee.[171]

Makarios remained dissatisfied with troop reductions to 1963 levels and with the prospect of a UN force increasing its role at the expense of CYPOL and the National Guard. He therefore would agree to "acknowledge" the plan as the first step "toward the ultimate withdrawal of all Greek and Turkish troops," but repeatedly, over the next few days, raised objections meant to deter U Thant's endorsement or to invite Turkey's rejection, and thereby to wreck it.[172] But the premise of U.S. pivotal strategy—that Greece and Turkey were the key interlocutors when it came to imposing peace— proved out. After U.S. calls for more Greek pressure on Makarios, Athens pulled the rug out from under the archbishop, announcing on 1 December that its troops over treaty limits would be removed in forty-five days.[173] The Secretary General pitched his appeal on 3 December, and Greece immediately endorsed it and notified Turkey that it would begin withdrawing troops from Cyprus as soon as Turkey embraced it, which Ankara promptly did. The momentum was now ineluctable; Makarios' spoiler tactics went nowhere.

Greece had seen that unless it abandoned Nicosia—and took a U.S.–brokered deal—it would be left alone to face Turkey. Having no alignment options, Athens had to choose between putting down Cyprus or being put down by Washington. So it caved. Greece could not save itself or Cyprus from a determined Turkish attack—only the United States could do that. Athens did what was necessary to avert isolation: It isolated Cyprus and left Makarios to push his cause in the UN.

The Soviet Role in the Crisis

The Soviets kept a low profile in the crisis and did little to exploit the opportunity to sow dissent within NATO.[174] Soviet passivity resulted from two contradictory impulses. On the one hand, Moscow did not want to jeopardize its vastly improved relations with Turkey by trying to restrain it the way the United States had in 1964. In purely practical terms, good relations with Turkey counted for much more in the Soviet calculus than Cyprus. On the other hand, the Soviets did not want Turkey to invade Cyprus, and they did not want to do anything unwittingly to encourage it in that direction. As Ambassador Hart put it, the Soviet Union feared "either a partition of Cyprus between Greece and Turkey or an outright conquest of the island by Turkey. In either case, Cyprus would be the potential site for NATO bases[,] and the strongest Communist party in the Middle East . . . would go down the drain."[175] So Moscow did the sensible thing: It laid low and let the United States put NATO's house in order. As Vance put it:

The Russians did not play an important part. They only appeared at one time on the scene. They made a statement to the effect that should war come about that they would give support, and by that I believe they meant logistical support, to the Turks. But other than one meeting which took place in Ankara between the Russian Ambassador and the Turkish Government, they did not appear to be playing an important role in the controversy.[176]

Of course, the United States did not want to end the crisis in a way that would drive Turkey even closer to the USSR. This was not something it had to worry about with Greece. Just as Turkey had a few years before, the colonels in Athens made themselves ripe targets for the threat of abandonment by burning their bridges to Moscow.

SUMMARY OF FINDINGS

Necessary Conditions

In the 1960s Cyprus crises, the United States preferred the status quo to a Greco-Turkish war brought on by one or the other side's efforts to change it forcibly. As Rusk put it, "Our great interest was in good relations between

Greece and Turkey and in a stable situation in Cyprus."[177] Accordingly, Washington would "have no trouble with whatever was worked out by negotiation and agreement."[178] While it is true that the United States encouraged its NATO allies to cut a Cyprus deal, at the expense of Makarios' regime, it is also true that when the price for getting rid of Makarios looked to be a war between Greece and Turkey, the United States preferred the status quo.

The United States harbored no illusions about its allies' aims in Cyprus. Both sides had publicly and privately expressed their desire to either annex the whole island (Greece) or at least part of it (Turkey). The United States would only encourage Greece in its schemes for enosis if Athens squared Ankara first. Otherwise, Turkey would intervene in force, and it said as much to Washington on many occasions. And there could be no question, as Johnson put it, that "a Turkish intervention in Cyprus would lead to a military engagement between Turkish and Greek forces." If Greece, as Prime Minister Papandreou boasted, was mad enough to blindly follow Turkey into the "insane asylum" of a war, the United States did not want to encourage that madness by promising to save Greece. As Secretary Rusk put it in January of 1963, "belief on the part of either [side] that it has solid backing will . . . encourage extremism."[179]

Likewise, during the 1960s, Turkey was convinced (correctly) that Greece was orchestrating much of the violence on the island and that Athens sought to annex it as another step in the "encirclement" of Turkey. As the crisis brewed in 1964, the Turkish president admitted that "Turkish-Greek Friendship is dead."[180] The feeling was mutual. As early as 1958, Greek statesmen warned the United States of Turkey's "unfriendly attitude towards Greece and the centuries of Greco-Turkish conflict that lay behind it."[181] By 1964, Greece saw Turkey as more threatening than Moscow, which is to say, much more threatening than the United States.[182]

Isolation Avoidance Effects

In both 1960s crises, Turkey showed caution. In 1964 Johnson had the chance to apply the brake because Ankara informed him of its intentions to invade Cyprus beforehand, and when the U.S. ambassador asked for a twenty-four–hour pause so that Washington could respond, the request was granted. Similarly, in 1967 Ankara warned the United States of its plans to invade if Greece did not withdraw troops from the island, and it agreed to let the United States try pressuring Athens into acquiescence before it went to war. Turkey, in other words, would not use force against Greece until the United States was implicated in a failure to bring Athens to terms peacefully and thus likely to support Turkey's use of force.

The crises also illustrate interesting instances of the "concession producing" dynamic, although no long-term settlement resulted. In August 1964, Greece learned the hard way how dangerous it could be to disregard U.S. concerns. After Athens repeatedly undercut U.S. efforts to foster a bilateral Greco-Turkish solution to the Cyprus conflict, Washington indulged Turkish air strikes against Greek Cypriot positions in August 1964, which Greece was helpless to prevent. After that bracing chill of isolation, Greece quickly endorsed the bilateral formula that it had spurned just months before. Similarly, although they "were very much against holding them," the Turks agreed to attend the September 1967 bilateral talks with Greece because they did not want to appear "intransigent" before the United States, which was quietly urging the talks in the background.[183] In the November 1967 crisis, Vance was able on numerous occasions to extract concessions from the adversaries by warning them that to appear intransigent while the other side cooperated could cost them U.S. support.

Alignment Options Effects

Because its leaders believed they could draw on the indirect support of Moscow, Greece ran high risks in 1964. Papandreou's scheme to arm and man the National Guard with mainland forces was a bold one. The Guard would not stand a chance in a real slugging match with Turkey. But odds were against such a fight ever happening. The United States could be counted on to stop Turkey from invading precisely *because* there was some danger of escalation involving Moscow. Which is exactly what the United States did in June 1964. Because the Soviet Union was a brace for Greece that Turkey did not have, the United States leaned heavily on Turkey when war threatened to break out. However, the United States understood that by sheltering Greece from Turkey, it had emboldened Athens to act more aggressively. Thus, in August, when Turkey began air strikes against Cyprus, the United States adopted a palpable attitude of greater detachment. And when the Soviets did not come to the rescue, Athens and Nicosia—despite their bloodcurdling theatrics—backed down with alacrity.

Nevertheless, Turkey had felt the rough side of American friendship in June 1964, and soon after, it began to seek better relations with Moscow, which would give it more freedom to maneuver over Cyprus. Moscow was glad to reciprocate. The Soviet Union did not become Turkey's ally, but it did cease to be a source of indirect support to Greece, especially once the right-wing junta took over. By thus diversifying its relations, Turkey insured itself against questionable U.S. support in another Cyprus crisis. Now Turkey could trump Greece if (1) the United States sided with Turkey, or (2) the United States stood aside. The only scenario in which Turkey would lose was if the United States sided firmly with Greece. But by improving relations with the USSR, Turkey vastly reduced the chance that this would happen. Now the United States had a tremendous incentive to avoid tilting hard against Turkey, for by doing so, it would drive Turkey further into the Soviet embrace and thus sacrifice NATO's strong southern anchor. In short, Turkey solved the problem of bidding against Greece for U.S. sympathy on Cyprus by forcing Washington to compete with Moscow for Turkish friendship.

Conversely, the Turkish air strikes of August 1964 taught Athens that it had better close ranks with the United States because it could not rely on Moscow to underwrite the risks of an aggressive policy. Indeed, Moscow's equivocation in August presaged a warming in Soviet-Turk relations. Papandreou's approach to the Cyprus dispute did a U-turn, moving toward the bilateral talks the United States preferred—which excluded Nicosia and Moscow—and away from the UN track, which did not. By the time of the 1967 crisis, the separation between Greece and the USSR was complete, and the right-wing regime in Athens had put itself in a position of great dependence on U.S. support.

Accordingly, when the 1967 crisis broke out, the weight of U.S. pressure fell more heavily on Greece. Behind the veneer of Vance's honest brokerage lay a brutal threat: if Greece did not significantly roll back its deployments on Cyprus, the United States would leave Greece to face the full brunt of a war with Turkey. Because Greece had no alignment option to hedge against U.S. abandonment, it moved to ingratiate the United States by making the concessions it insisted were necessary to defuse the Turkish threat. War was averted, but not without a price. And because Greece was more dependent on the United States, it had to pay the lion's share.

Accounting for Confounding Causes of Peace

It may be argued that U.S. efforts to keep the peace were destined to succeed because of the powerful pacifying effects of Greece and Turkey's common membership in the NATO alliance. But while it is true that, in both 1964 and 1967, NATO fora and officials came into play during the crises, we should not exaggerate their independent impact. The United States kept a strong hand over the nature and scope of NATO engagement, and in the heat of the crises, NATO was an instrument of, rather than a complement to, the dominant thrust of U.S. initiatives.

More broadly, we should avoid the simplistic inference that membership in NATO was a stabilizing factor in Greco-Turkish relations during this period. The contrary is more likely the case. As Ronald Krebs has forcefully demonstrated elsewhere, the "perverse" consequence of Greece and Turkey sharing a NATO umbrella—hoisted by the United States—was that the intense and inherent antagonisms of their relationship would often prevail over their common interest in balancing against the USSR.[184]

Finally, the evidence in the case study helps us to gauge whether the military balance between Greece and Turkey was sufficient in itself to cause peace. Given Turkey's dominant advantage in that balance, we can say quite confidently that it was not deterred by the military posture of Greece. In the 1964 crisis in particular, what stopped Turkey was not the prospect of Greek and Cypriot resistance but, rather, the threat of abandonment by the United States combined with the prospect of Soviet intervention. In the 1967 crisis, we saw that the Greek Cypriot forces were willing to risk provoking an all-out war with Turkey, *despite* Turkey's overall military advantage. We also saw that the military leaders in Athens were initially inclined to gamble on a war rather than to back down in the face of Turkey's escalating pressure. Behind these attitudes there lay an assumption that the United States would check or cushion the blow from Turkey. The United States had to disabuse the Greek leaders of this assumption before the coercive weight of Turkey's military might would begin to shape Greek behavior in ways that Ankara and Washington desired.

[6]

Playing the Pivot in a Crowded Market:

THE UNITED STATES AND THE

KASHMIR CONFLICT, 1962–65

Pakistan-Indian bitterness makes it extraordinarily difficult to keep good relations with both . . . we could never fully support the policy goals of either India or Pakistan.

> Dean Rusk, U.S. Secretary of State, September 1965

Our policy in regard to India and Pakistan is leading us up a dead end street in both countries.

> Chester Bowles, U.S. ambassador to India, May 1965

When India and Pakistan went to war over Kashmir in the summer of 1965, an ailing U.S. policy of pivotal deterrence went up in smoke. The war began quietly on 5 August, as a few thousand Pakistani guerillas crossed the 1948 cease-fire line (CFL) into Indian controlled Kashmir, in a fruitless attempt to incite a Muslim uprising. On August 15 and 24, India struck back across the CFL, cutting off the infiltration routes. With its guerillas trapped in Kashmir, Pakistan escalated. On 1 September, Pakistani armor drove into Kashmir through the seam joining the CFL and the international boundary between India and Pakistan and threatened to cut communications between Kashmir and India. India counterattacked across the international border in Punjab, forcing Pakistan to draw back in Kashmir. Once the war bogged down, India accepted a UN–backed cease-fire on 21 September, as did Pakistan the next day.[1]

The conflict almost triggered a wider war in South Asia. On 27 August,

Beijing accused India of border violations in Sikkim. A week later, as Pakistani armor plunged into Kashmir, Zulfikar Ali Bhutto, Pakistan's foreign minister, hosted his Chinese counterpart, Chen Yi, who announced that Beijing supported Pakistan's efforts to repulse Indian attacks across the CFL.[2] When India counterattacked, China condemned it as "naked aggression," promised "firm support to Pakistan in its just struggle," and alerted its forces on the Indian border, demanding that India demobilize in Sikkim.[3] Premier Zhou En-lai assured Pakistan's president, Mohammed Ayub Khan, that China would crush any Indian moves against vulnerable East Pakistan. The same message was passed to U.S. diplomats in Warsaw.[4] On 16 September China gave India three days to dismantle all military positions in Sikkim or face "grave consequences."[5] Behind the scenes, the United States and Soviet Union warned China against intervening. On 19 September, with the fighting deadlocked, China extended the ultimatum three more days. President Ayub went to Beijing for counsel, and returned to accept the UN cease-fire.[6]

China was the only power to openly take sides in the conflict. There is debate over how serious it was about intervening, but the threat to block an Indian attack against East Pakistan was credible and taken seriously by the United States.[7] Certainly China's maneuvers tied down Indian forces on its border.[8]

Moscow was more ambivalent. If China had intervened, and the West responded, it would have to choose between siding with the West or sacrificing relations with India.[9] But Moscow also worried about Pakistan, with which it had worked to improve relations in order to offset China's influence. Thus, Moscow struck an impartial pose and strongly backed the UN cease-fire.

The war was a huge fiasco for the United States. In 1962 it had become enmeshed in Indo-Pakistani relations, arming both sides while pressuring them to negotiate a Kashmir settlement. When the war ignited, the United States was in a bind. It could not, as Robert Komer of the National Security Council (NSC) noted, move "beyond even handed grave concern without goring someone's ox."[10] On 8 September, the United States cut economic and military aid to both sides, throwing its full weight behind a UN cease-fire. It faced an ugly conundrum: It had promised to defend Pakistan against Indian attacks, and to help India defend against China. It could finesse the issue with Pakistan if the war remained localized. But if China intervened against India, what then would the United States do? Fortunately, China did not, and this, combined with the arms embargo, meant Pakistan could not endure a long unlimited war. Pakistan had no choice then but to accept the UN cease-fire.

When the shooting stopped, Moscow took the lead, sponsoring the Tashkent peace talks and agreement. U.S. influence and prestige in the region was spent. That nadir is puzzling in light of its central role over the preceding three years. In 1962, after the Sino-Indian border war, the United States seemed well positioned to play the pivot. India needed its help against China; Pakistan needed its help against India. Washington held a strong hand. Why then did its efforts to produce a Kashmir settlement, and prevent war, fail?

Overview of the Case

U.S. policy expected that India's and Pakistan's need for its support would lead to an "ingratiation contest" in which both tried to win U.S. favor by compromising on Kashmir and avoiding action that could provoke war. However, each side reduced its exposure to U.S. pressure by cultivating support from others. As a hedge against doubtful U.S. defense commitments, Pakistan struck a tacit alliance with China, which had plenty reason to stop India from conquering Pakistan. If the United States abandoned Pakistan, China would seize the opportunity to isolate India by making Pakistan a close ally. This prospect encouraged U.S. fidelity to Pakistan. Thus, U.S. arms and assurances would work together with the China entente to shield Pakistan from India.

India, by contrast, did not need U.S. defense commitments against Pakistan, and it had in Moscow an enthusiastic alternative source of arms. That was unfortunate for the United States, which tried to use military aid to influence India's Kashmir policy. Moscow did not attach such strings to its military patronage. In the UN, it backed India's Kashmir position. So rather than luring India into a competition with Pakistan for its support, the United States got into a bidding war with Moscow over who could give India more, and India gave up any pretense of compromising on Kashmir.

In sum, by tapping the Sino-Soviet split, India and Pakistan cultivated Beijing and Moscow as alignment options; and by making the United States compete with their Communist patrons, they drove down the political price of its military patronage. This helps to explain how and why the United States, despite its pivotal position, failed to prevent war or produce a Kashmir compromise.

Description of Situational Variables

The Balance of Capabilities

The United States was preponderant over India and Pakistan. Between 1960 and 1965, the United States spent (in 1960 dollars) almost $292 billion on defense, while Pakistan spent $1.4 billion, and India $4.8 billion.[11] That works out to 1.6 percent of U.S. spending for India, and 0.4 percent of U.S. spending for Pakistan. Arms transfers and, less so, security guarantees, were the coin of U.S. power over the India-Pakistan rivalry. Because they were poor and unable to produce sophisticated modern weapons, the United States could significantly sway the military balance between them. Since the early 1950s the United States had indirectly subsidized the military of both countries through nonmilitary economic aid. More important, the United States could directly augment the arsenal of either side so that it had an edge against the other; or it could deny either side such an advantage.

The size of India's army made it impossible for the United States to give Pakistan *numerical* parity. Between 1960 and 1965, India outspent Pakistan on defense by roughly a 3:1 ratio.[12] The United States could not make Pakistan invulnerable or able to conquer India. But the United States could and did add much to Pakistan's strength. Between 1954 (the first year of U.S.–Pakistan military cooperation) and 1965, Pakistan's overall military effort cost $4 billion, of which about $1.5 billion (37 percent) was covered by U.S. military assistance.[13] During that twelve-year period, U.S. military aid to Pakistan was about twenty times larger than that to India.[14] The United States also gave Pakistan's military a *qualitative* edge—particularly in armor and aircraft—that diminished India's quantitative strengths.[15] By the same token, the United States could dramatically increase Pakistan's vulnerability to India by cutting aid to Pakistan, giving India arms that matched Pakistan's in quality, and underwriting an expansion of India's military.

The Distribution of Interests and Intentions

For India and Pakistan, Kashmir was a vital interest.[16] Their stakes involved an explosive mix of strategic interests and contradictory ideological commitments. From Kashmir, India can strike into the heart of Pakistan, well behind the official border running from the Indian Ocean to Punjab. For this reason alone, Pakistan would want to control it.[17] Indians likewise saw Kashmir as vital to their territorial integrity. As an Indian official once put it: "for nearly eight centuries . . . India had been subject to periodical invasions from the north-west . . . within less than ten weeks of the establishment of Pakistan, its very first act was to let loose a tribal invasion through the north-west. Srinagar today, Delhi tomorrow."[18]

Kashmir also crystallized their fundamental ideological conflict. As a part of India, Kashmir proved Delhi's claim that "Muslims could live without fear of discrimination of harassment in a predominantly Hindu state built upon secular principles."[19] But for Pakistan, such an outcome challenged its raison d'être—that Muslims could only find security in a Muslim state. As Bhutto put it in 1963: "Kashmir is to Pakistan what Berlin is to the

West, and . . . without a fair and proper settlement of this issue the people of Pakistan will not consider the crusade for Pakistan as complete."[20] In this view, India's refusal to give up Kashmir after partition was tantamount to denying Pakistan's right to exist.[21]

The United States had relatively weak interests at stake in the Indo-Pakistan conflict, and South Asia remained a low priority region in U.S. grand strategy. The United States had no compelling interest in a particular solution to the Kashmir conflict. It had a general interest in there being *a* solution, arrived at peacefully. That interest flowed from a desire to keep Communism out of South Asia.[22]

From the outset, some in Washington saw Pakistan as an attractive political and strategic Cold War asset.[23] Momentum for arming Pakistan increased as Indian Prime Minister Jawaharlal Nehru's policy of nonalignment came to be seen as neutrality favoring the Communists, while Pakistan's firm support for U.S. policy in Korea put it in a much better light. With India, the USSR, and China all opposing U.S. arms for Pakistan, a deal was almost inevitable. President Dwight Eisenhower agreed in February 1954.[24] Pakistan's U.S. ties were cemented when it joined the Southeast Asian Treaty Organization (SEATO) in September 1954 and the Baghdad Pact in February 1955, which soon became the Central Treaty Organization (CENTO). Pakistani statesmen strove to focus U.S. commitments on defending Pakistan against India. The United States tried to avoid naming India publicly, but that contingency was covered under the general commitment because it was never explicitly *excluded*.[25] U.S. intelligence facilities at Peshawar, which permitted U.S. spy planes to fly deep into Soviet territory, tangibly expressed Pakistan's value to the United States as a strategic asset and convinced most U.S. policy makers of the need for strong ties to Pakistan.

Early in the Cold War, U.S. policy makers recognized that India would dominate the subcontinent, play an important role in the developing world, and perhaps become the "chief stabilizing influence in Asia." India could not contribute to U.S. military strategy against the Soviet Union the way Pakistan did, but as a long-run bulwark against the spread of Communism in Asia, it was seen as vastly more important.[26] India's poverty invited Communist subversion; the United States had an obvious incentive to support it with famine relief and developmental aid. Beyond that, the United States sought to enlist India as an ally against the Eastern Bloc. Nehru's policy of nonalignment stood in the way. He saw no need for India "to appear as supplicants before any country" and he bristled at political strings attached to U.S. aid.[27]

The Korean War led to a downturn in U.S.–India relations. At first India supported UN action against North Korean aggression but as the war escalated, Nehru turned against the United States. Though India remain non-aligned, its relations with Moscow and Beijing improved as it fell out with Washington over admitting China to the UN, the French Indochina war, the U.S.–Japan treaty, and, most of all, the U.S. pact with Pakistan. Eisenhower assured Nehru that U.S. arms to Pakistan would not be used against India.[28] But these assurances were dismissed, and U.S. support in the UN for Pakistan's position on Kashmir made matters worse. Still, if Nehru tilted toward Communists internationally, he had no truck with them domestically. That the United States could strengthen Indian democracy and insulate it from Communism through economic aid was something Nehru and the U.S. leaders could agree on.

These were the basic contours of Indo–U.S. relations in the early Cold War. They would not change markedly until China menaced India in 1962. Only then would Nehru recant his repugnance for Western military ties and the United States be willing to arm India on a scale that risked alienating Pakistan. Finding a solution to the Indo-Pakistan rivalry and the Kashmir dispute then became an increasingly important U.S. goal.

Alignment Options

Both Pakistan and India had strong alignment options: China and the Soviet Union. From Sino-Indian antagonism there flowed a de facto Chinese interest in defending Pakistan and curtailing India's writ on the subcontinent. Pakistan could thus hedge against the uncertainty of U.S. allegiance with a reliable tacit ally that would close ranks with Pakistan if the United States abandoned it. On the other hand, the Soviets were eager to patronize India, even if that meant sharing the role with the United States. Moscow wanted to keep India a strong balancing force against China, and it did not want the United States to corner the market for arms to India.

It was precisely to check the influence of the USSR and China that the United States armed Pakistan and India, and sought to defuse their rivalry by brokering a Kashmir settlement. In this sense, China and the Soviet Union play two roles in our explanation of events. First, they are what motivated the United States to attempt pivotal deterrence. Second, they are an important reason why the U.S. policy failed.

Kennedy's Pivotal Policy

President John F. Kennedy aimed to improve relations with India. There were important obstacles, however, especially warm U.S.–Pakistan ties.[29] When President Ayub visited Washington in July 1961, Kennedy promised long-term military aid, including highly advanced F-104 jets, and the continuation of economic aid. Kennedy also assured Ayub that he did not intend to arm India, and would not do so without consulting Ayub first.[30] In January 1962 Pakistan called on the United States to deter India "from aggressiveness" by publicly declaring that it would defend Pakistan against Indian attack and by increasing military aid to Pakistan.[31] Kennedy demurred. "As a firm ally," he wrote Ayub, "Pakistan is entitled to the reaffirmation you requested of the prior assurances given by the United States to Pakistan. My Government certainly stands by those assurances. I trust that you will agree, however, that a public statement to this effect would not be fruitful at this juncture."[32] The letter was a model of artful evasion.

The 1962 Sino-Indian War and the Window of Opportunity

On 22 October 1962, a festering border dispute between India and China erupted into open warfare.[33] China scored overwhelming offensive victories, shocking India and the world. Tentative feelers for U.S. military aid came from India in early October, while the United States was fixated on the Cuban Missile Crisis. Kennedy waited for Nehru to jettison the "nonalignment" pose and openly plead for support.[34] On 25 October, Moscow shifted to supporting China in the war. India, humbled by China, was now also isolated. The next day, India's ambassador gave Kennedy a letter from Nehru asking for "sympathy and support." Kennedy was forthcoming, urging Nehru to meet promptly with U.S. Ambassador John Kenneth Galbraith to "translate our support into terms that are practically most useful."[35] Kennedy then notified Ayub that the United States would lend India immediate military assistance against China. Within six days, it began airlifting arms that, through an exchange of notes, were strictly limited to the purpose of Indian defense against "outright Chinese aggression."[36] They proved insufficient. On 16 November, China struck again, routing Indian forces and capturing all the disputed territory and more. Five days later China halted and announced a unilateral twenty-kilometer withdrawal.

Kennedy's peremptory notice to Ayub that the United States would arm India was a far cry from the promised "prior consultation." Kennedy went further, asking Ayub to assure India that Pakistan would not move on Kashmir. This would allow India to deploy forces against China that it otherwise kept poised against Pakistan.[37] Pakistan's leaders reacted bitterly to this request.[38] In an effort to assuage them, Walter McConaughy, the U.S. ambassador to Pakistan, gave Ayub an aide-mémoire that, according to Ayub, promised the United States would "come to Pakistan's assistance in the event of aggression from India against Pakistan." In a letter to Kennedy, Ayub expressed doubts about the U.S. assurance, questioning India's reliability as well as Kennedy's.[39] Ayub insisted that Washington publicize the aide-mémoire, which it did.[40]

Pakistan did not give India the no-war pledge that Kennedy requested.

Such assurance was impossible, wrote Ayub, without "a settlement of the question of Kashmir."[41] Still, Pakistan did not move on Kashmir while China was mauling India.[42] Ayub decided that "it would not be common sense for Pakistan to precipitate military action against India" and informed McConaughy of this, if not Nehru.[43] Ayub's reasoning is not hard to infer. The United States would now have considerable leverage over Delhi, which could be used to produce results in Kashmir. Better that Pakistan get what it wanted in Kashmir through the auspices of U.S. friendship than at the expense of it. Ayub's hopes were matched in Washington. Secretary of State Dean Rusk wrote in late November, "the Sino-Indian confrontation has given us what may be a one-time opportunity to bring about a Pak-Indian reconciliation." To Kennedy, Komer marveled at the "sheer magnitude of the opportunity handed us by [Beijing]" which could "not only bring about a Kashmir settlement and Pak-Indian reconciliation, but induce an aroused and strengthened India to join us in the containment of Red China."[44]

The Harriman-Sandys Mission

Assistant Secretary of State Averell Harriman was to usher in the breakthrough. Officials were already meeting in London to hammer out an initial $50–60 million military aid package for India. After the second wave of Indian defeats, Harriman, his British counterpart Duncan Sandys, and their retinues descended on India and Pakistan.[45] Harriman and Sandys proposed direct bilateral negotiations on Kashmir and secured a public commitment from both sides to begin them.[46] Two key premises informed these efforts. First, that both sides could agree that China was a serious common threat, which provided a "basis for the resolution of Pak-Indian differences [that] did not previously exist."[47] Second, that the United States could drive them to compromise because it was a key source of arms that both sides dearly needed.

For India, the fulcrum of U.S. leverage lay between limited emergency military aid and a larger long-term commitment. The trick was to convince India that a Kashmir settlement was a necessary condition for the latter. In India, Galbraith "campaigned in depth," to convince "political leaders below Nehru" of the "relationship between U.S. capacity to aid India and resolution [of the] Kashmir dispute." In Washington, Kennedy lectured the Indian ambassador, "the question of Kashmir is inescapably linked to what [the United States] can do to assist India militarily." The message was tangibly expressed in the emergency military aid package, which was contrived to make India "capable of holding the Chinese where they are now" but not to "re-conquer the Chinese-occupied area." To do the latter, India "would have to use half to two-thirds of the forces they now have on their border with Pakistan." Thus the aim was to give "a respectable amount of aid" to the Indians while putting "pressure on them to improve their relations with Pakistan."[48] The pristine logic masked a gnawing contradiction: How could the United States hold up the China threat and yet hold back on arms?[49]

As for Pakistan, it had aligned with the West chiefly to balance against India. U.S. officials could see that "the value of this alliance" might shrink "in the face of U.S. military assistance to India." To compensate, U.S. policy makers assumed they would have to generate progress in Kashmir.[50] They also assumed, however, that they could pressure Pakistan to make Kashmir concessions without driving it "off the reservation."[51] They had to make Ayub see that it was time to make painful compromises toward a Kashmir solution.[52] Ayub sensed the urgency, but he doubted that Nehru's willingness to compromise would last once India secured U.S. military assistance. Thus, Ayub wanted the United States to explicitly link any further military aid to India to a settlement. Kennedy would not do that, but he insisted to Ayub that long-term aid to India would be conditioned by its willingness to make a deal.[53]

Ayub's doubts were justified. The day after he and Nehru jointly pledged to "resolve the outstanding differences between the two countries on Kashmir" and begin bilateral talks, Nehru ran roughshod over Harriman and Sandys' handiwork.[54] "Anything that involved the upset of the present arrangement [in Kashmir]," he declared to the Lok Sabha, India's lower house of parliament, "would be very harmful to the people of Kashmir as well as to the future relations of India and Pakistan."[55] To repair the damage, Harriman and Sandys pressed Nehru to make a conciliatory statement. Thus, on 1 December, he conceded that there were no "pre-conditions or . . . restrictions on the scope of the [bilateral] talks."[56]

Nehru collected his reward on 20 December, when Kennedy and British prime minister Harold Macmillan agreed in Nassau to a combined $120 million in additional emergency military aid for India. Pakistan was quick to respond. Just before the talks began, it announced that it had agreed with China "in principle" to demarcate their common border and thus remove what had been a sore point in their relations. The timing of the announcement sent a blunt warning: The United States had better pressure India on Kashmir, or else Pakistan would close ranks with China.[57]

Round One: December 27–29 (Rawalpindi)

India and Pakistan aired their long-standing positions on Kashmir in the first round. Zulfikar Bhutto, Pakistan's lead negotiator, proposed moving forward on the basis of previous UN resolutions that called for a cease-fire, the withdrawal of Indian troops from Kashmir, and the determination of the status of Jammu and Kashmir "through the democratic method of a free and impartial plebiscite."[58] Nehru had long since dismissed that formula as inapplicable.[59] India's negotiator, Swaran Singh, thus opened with India's boilerplate positions: By conventional standards of international law, Kashmir was an integral part of India, and as a secular democracy, India could not allow a plebiscite along religious lines. No agreement issued from this round, and nobody expected one to, so it ended on an empty but upbeat note.[60]

Washington prepared for progress in the talks, while moving ahead with emergency military aid to India. Galbraith was ordered to redouble his efforts to persuade Indian leaders to give ground in Kashmir in order to get a long-term U.S. deal.[61] Galbraith balked, worried that pressing on Kashmir would make India mend fences with China.[62] There were already signs of a receding Chinese threat, which would affect the urgency of Delhi's approach to talks.[63] An important step in that direction occurred on 15 January, when India accepted the Colombo peace proposals, which solidified the Sino-Indian cease-fire.[64]

India had another reason to resist U.S. pressure. An initial shipment of Soviet MIG-21s, first approved in October 1962, was slated to begin arriving in February. The deal had been waylaid in November after Moscow took sides with China. Once hostilities abated, Moscow publicly reaffirmed it on 16 January, the first day of the second round of talks.[65] The Soviets were back in play as India's alignment option, and the United States and United Kingdom hustled to develop programs to meet Nehru's ballooning requests for defense support.

Another "clear danger" to the talks, as Undersecretary of State George Ball put it, was Pakistan's "philandering" with China. On 4 January, Pakistan signed its first trade agreement ever with Beijing.[66] In response, Ball argued, Washington needed to increase military and nonmilitary aid to Pakistan and to reaffirm "US determination to push for [a] Kashmir settlement."[67] Showing such a determination, however, would not be easy because Washington would not take sides or advance its own Kashmir proposal. It still hoped that momentum for compromise would build from a common perception of the China threat and both sides' efforts to lock in long-term U.S. support.

Round Two: January 16–19 (New Delhi)

The second round focused on a Kashmir plebiscite. Delhi contended that after fifteen years of Indian supervision, democracy in Kashmir was a reality on the ground. A plebiscite would ignite communal violence and imperil minorities in both countries. Instead, India proposed partition (along the lines of the status quo), disengagement of forces, and a no-war pledge. After much haggling, the two sides appeared to converge on partition and agreed that next round they would "examine proposals for honorable, equitable and final boundary settlement" in Kashmir.[68]

Washington began mulling over a partition plan "to throw into the breach" if the third round faltered. But the first priority was to get Nehru to offer "more than just a minor adjustment of the cease-fire line." If India made a real move toward compromise, the United States could pressure Ayub "to make reciprocal noises."[69] This approach capsized when Ayub tendered a partition proposal before the United States could wrench one from Nehru. Pakistan offered to partition areas in the north and south of Kashmir, but demanded the whole Valley, to be transferred after a year of international supervision and a plebiscite. Pakistan also urged the United States to become more proactive by submitting a bridging proposal between the two sides' positions.[70]

Given India's refusal to consider a plebiscite, Kennedy saw Pakistan's proposal as a nonstarter. And he did not want to intervene directly in the talks and "be left holding the bag" if they failed. Kennedy's response touched on familiar themes. Ayub needed to make "substantial compromises to [his] present positions" and to consider the possibility of partition through Kashmir. There was not likely to "ever be a better opportunity than this one . . . Pakistan should make every possible effort to achieve a compromise settlement now." As for a U.S. partition plan, Kennedy warned, "you overstate my influence if you think that it alone can be decisive. The United States . . . cannot force a solution on either India or Pakistan."[71]

Kennedy did not let Nehru off the hook. He advised him to make "concrete" proposals that went far enough toward Pakistan's position "to be proof positive" that India was "genuinely seeking a settlement." Kennedy closed with a tactful warning: "If only this issue could be settled [it would eliminate] a painful diversion which . . . inevitably complicates U.S.-Indian relations in ways disadvantageous to both." Meeting with Nehru and Singh, Galbraith spelled out the implication of Kennedy's note: India should offer a partition proposal that transferred to Pakistan some portion of the Kashmir Valley.[72]

Round Three: February 8–10 (Karachi)

In round three Singh offered to write off all Pakistan-controlled territory in Kashmir, plus small parts that India controlled north and west of the Valley, but nothing in the Valley itself. Bhutto, having been promoted to foreign minister, recycled Ayub's 4 February proposal. The talks nearly blew up, but at the last minute, Bhutto and Singh agreed to another round.[73]

Washington decided on a tactical change. Nehru still had to give up a tangible portion of the Valley, but next time Ayub had to make a forthcoming offer. This made sense: last round India had shown a bit more willingness to compromise than Pakistan. If India could be held to its previous offer the onus would be on Pakistan to soften its position. This scheme depended on two things: that Pakistan could be pressured without causing it to bolt, and that Nehru would not backtrack once the U.S. commitment to arm India solidified. Both would be undermined before the fourth round began.

U.S. leverage over India eroded as China's menace faded and Washington charged ahead with military support to Delhi. On 31 January and 1 February, Western defense experts arrived in India to develop military modernization plans. Two weeks later, Komer noted to Kennedy that "we see little evidence that [Beijing] is planning any spring attack; indeed the pace of Indian preparations suggests that they don't really expect one either." And yet, on 21 February, Kennedy announced the concept of a U.S./U.K./India joint air defense program.[74] The United States still tried to convince Nehru that long-term military aid depended on success—or at least India's good faith—in the Kashmir talks.[75] But the burden was on Pakistan to make the first "business offer." Kennedy suspected that Pakistan would try instead to "blackmail us into holding off on aid to India." Pakistan's extortion came as feared. On 22 February, the United States learned that Bhutto would soon visit Beijing to sign the China boundary agreement. Rusk put the screws on Pakistan's ambassador. The timing and venue had been contrived by China to "wreck the Kashmir talks," which would seriously damage Pakistan's interests. "If Kashmir was not settled now," Rusk warned, "the situation would become more serious all around." China would continue meddling in South Asia, and the United States would be "compelled to provide India with further military assistance." And if Pakistan obstructed the talks, "the sympathy" that it enjoyed in the UN "from other governments on Kashmir" would be replaced with "indifference."[76]

Nevertheless, on 3 March, Bhutto endorsed the Sino-Pak boundary accord in Beijing. Pakistan ceded to Beijing some 2,000 square miles of territory in Kashmir that it controlled, and it acquired, in return, 750 square miles of new land. Indian policy makers were apoplectic, for Ayub had traded away Kashmir territory that India still had claims to. What added to India's outrage was the broader political symbolism of the accord. China encouraged this reaction, using the occasion to declare, for the first time, that India-occupied Kashmir was disputed territory, thus rejecting India's claims to sovereignty over it.[77]

Afterward, Kennedy wrote Ayub that "there is no blinking how adversely [the boundary accord] has affected the Kashmir negotiations" and urged him to make ammends with "far more forthcoming and realistic" proposals. "There will probably never be a better opportunity for an honorable settlement." At the same time, Kennedy could not allow India to lapse into intransigence. So he pressed Nehru to make proposals in the next round that signaled a willingness to "compromise the central issue of the dispute" and "give Pakistan a *substantial* position in the Vale." Alluding to the potential for India's stonewalling to jeopardize U.S. military aid, he warned Nehru not to wait "too long to take this step."[78] Above all, the United States sought to avert a breakdown of the talks. But "at the minimum," wrote Komer, "we must get the Indians to be sufficiently forthcoming that the failure can be attributed to Pakistan . . . [which would] ease our problem on going ahead with [military] aid to India." Less cynically, State Department officials were drafting a proposal giving India and Pakistan a dual presence in the Valley and dividing up the rest of Kashmir. They hoped to avoid presenting it, but if the talks verged on collapse, they wanted an option ready.[79]

Round Four: March 12–15 (Calcutta)

The Sino-Pak border agreement doomed the fourth round—at least according to India. India gave no ground on partition, and Pakistan demanded the whole of Kashmir. With this deadlock, the two sides agreed—without the United States advancing its own proposal—to have another go in April.[80] Kennedy concluded that India had "lost [its] sense of urgency over settlement" and had taken its objections to the Sino-Pak accord too far. "We can't let them hide behind this issue any longer." He also worried that Delhi had concluded "that we've already decided to go ahead on longer term military aid, so they can relax on Kashmir." He commanded Galbraith to impress on Delhi "that a Kashmir settlement or at least an all out effort to get one" was key to his "ability to secure them the massive aid they want" from Congress. The President saw his options for influencing India diminishing: "We'll have to move fairly soon on [more aid to India], so we don't have too much time before this leverage on the Indians will no longer be as useful."[81]

Galbraith had had enough of the "campaign in depth." Taking Kennedy's cue, he wanted to get down to a "crude bazaar level" and offer Nehru a "plain political bargain." "We will give the Indians substantial [defense] support . . . [and] a sizeable program of longer-term aid," and in return, India must give "a clear indication that they will make a substantial concession, not a sliver, in the [Kashmir] valley." If this bid could produce a plausible Indian proposal, the United States could then "put the arm on Pakistan in equally serious way," and if Ayub did not reply with a reasonable offer, it would "of course go ahead with military aid."[82]

The State Department and NSC advocated a different approach. They wanted to introduce a vaguely worded "elements of a settlement" that would help to flush out the parties' redlines; the fifth round would then become a "key test of the seriousness with which both sides seek compromise." Thus, before round five, the United States would not give Delhi any more defense commitments and would tell it to quit harping on the Sino-Pak border agreement.[83]

Although initially inclined toward Galbraith's approach, Kennedy decided to hold back the hard sell until the State Department's plan had a run in round five.[84] It all backfired in mid-April when Galbraith soft-pedaled the "elements" and instead (with what he thought was Kennedy's mandate) pitched the "bazaar level" deal in Delhi.[85] His meetings with Nehru on April 15 and 20 "repeatedly reached the bare knuckles stage." The United States and India, Galbraith declared, "had important tasks ahead and Kashmir stood in the way of completing them." There had to be "a prompt move toward a settlement," and that could only be achieved "by dividing the Valley." Galbraith stressed that a Kashmir settlement and U.S. military aid "were inextricably involved by nature" because of the need for congressional approval. Did India have "nothing to offer"? As Galbraith would later put it, Nehru "turned me down flat, then he turned me down flatter." Nehru wrote Kennedy directly, refusing to consider a partition through the Valley.[86] He had good reason to stand firm, for already in Washington, State, Defense, and the White House were hosting a delegation of Indian officials to plan a long-term military aid program and procure material for the Indian army overhaul already underway.[87]

Rusk still hoped that neither side was "ready to accept the onus for causing a breakdown." If the talks were to fail outright, the U.S. response should "depend upon our appraisal of the cause and responsibilities for the failure. Strategically, we would still need to be in a position to give India some assistance against Chinese Communist pressure, tailoring this as best we possibly can to maintain our security interests in Pakistan." Yet, if it was true, as Komer noted, that Nehru was "personally . . . the chief roadblock to a forthcoming Indian position on Kashmir," how could he be impelled to budge when the flow of U.S. arms to India would continue despite his intransigence?[88]

In mid-April this contradiction surfaced in an unfortunate diplomatic gaffe. In his "bare knuckles" talks with Nehru, Galbraith had not fully aired the State Department's "elements" plan, but on 18 April, Nehru was briefed on the plan by his envoy in Karachi, who got a copy from McConaughy. Nehru denounced it as a U.S.–Pakistan conspiracy. The unorthodox way in which he received the proposal, however, did not cause him to rule out partition. Nehru had turned Galbraith down "flatly" before learning of the "elements." But he seized on them, as Komer noted, "to cover his tracks."[89]

In round five Washington wanted Delhi to concede a part of the Kashmir Valley large enough to justify U.S. pressure on Pakistan to reciprocate. If Pakistan played along, the talks could be taken to a more productive stage. If Pakistan did not, then Kennedy could go ahead with military aid to India armed with evidence of Delhi's good faith, which would smooth the way in Congress. But Nehru saw no need to do Kennedy this favor. On 17 April, in an interview with the *New York Times,* Nehru asserted that the Kashmir Valley was an "economically and psychologically" indivisible unit that could never be partitioned."[90]

Round Five: April 22–25 (Karachi)

Bhutto's fifth round proposal was designed to be rejected by India. If India would give up all of the Kashmir and Chenab Valleys, Pakistan would promise to grant the Indian military "temporary transit" through them to respond to a Chinese threat. India scoffed at the indecent offer. Nevertheless, the two sides agreed to continue the talks in May.[91] Bhutto announced that the next round would be Pakistan's "last go."[92]

As the fifth round stalled, Pakistan's ambassador to the U.S., Ghulam Ahmed, informed Rusk that the "elements" plan was a dead end because Pakistan could never agree to partition the Valley. He also confronted Rusk with the growing evidence that the United States would give long-term military aid to India, regardless of whether a Kashmir solution was reached. Rusk beat a retreat from earlier U.S. assurances. The "initial arms aid may have had something to do with [the] Chicom [Chinese communist] cease-fire and . . . future arms aid might act as [a] deterrent to possible future Chinese aggression directed at the subcontinent." It was therefore in the U.S. national interest to "get a clear signal to the Chinese about the consequences of further aggression," a signal that might be muddied by cutting off arms to India.[93]

A more pointed argument for giving long-term military aid to India resurfaced at this time. Chester Bowles, the former and soon-to-be U.S. ambassador to India, warned that Washington should not assume "that the Indians don't have other options; they are perfectly capable of patching up their differences with China and of getting more Soviet help as an alternative to . . . US/UK support." Kennedy agreed and decided to "tell Ayub we've got to go ahead with Nehru, while telling Nehru that military aid to him without a settlement will cause us all sorts of trouble with the Paks and our own Congress." Thus, on 26 April Kennedy decided to give India long-term military aid, deal or no deal on Kashmir.[94]

Rusk labored to prepare India and Pakistan for a more productive round six. To Kennedy and his advisers, he laid out the problem:

Our overriding purpose is some accommodation between Pakistan and India. The question is how to achieve it. If we back India against the Chinese, we may drive the Paks off the deep end; if we abandon the Indians, they might move toward the USSR and China again. On the merits of Kashmir . . . the shape of the settlement [is] irrelevant to us. We could buy anything they could agree on. The trouble [is] that any settlement would be more favorable to Pakistan than the status quo; it [is] precisely that which created the problem with India.[95]

Rusk shuttled first to Karachi. There, Ayub convinced him that Pakistan would never concede the need to increase India's military strength to deter China, and that additional U.S. promises to defend Pakistan would not suffice to ease its security concerns.[96] Rusk's mission to Delhi was barely more productive. Nehru did float the idea of appointing a mediator "in lieu of further rounds" if the sixth one failed. Rusk promised to explore it with Ayub and offer it up as a U.S. proposal, if necessary.[97] Despite Nehru's overture, Rusk returned convinced that he was the chief stumbling block, that there was "somewhat more readiness in Karachi than in New Delhi to make substantial moves away from starting positions."[98]

On 8 May, Rusk advised Kennedy to proceed with the plan for a U.S./U.K. air-umbrella for India. "If we do nothing [on air defense] in the near future, our capacity to push the Indians into a reasonable posture on Kashmir may actually diminish."[99] Thus, the tactical logic of U.S. military aid to India had changed. The United States would now extend the long-term military aid without conditions and hope to extract concessions down the road. There was a real credibility problem in this formula. It would require the United States to convincingly threaten to sever military aid to Delhi, even though Washington thought doing so was out of the question. The next day, Kennedy approved the air-defense program. How would he sell it to Congress? Since "it would be unwise to make it appear that the failure of the Kashmir negotiations was Nehru's fault," he decided to "point to the unreasonable demands made by the Pakistanis."[100] On the eve of round six, Kennedy asked Macmillan to support the joint air-defense program.

With a Kashmir settlement now a long way off, and Nehru in an unyielding mood, I believe it would be a mistake to let the Indians conclude there is little prospect of any further military help in the absence of a Kashmir settlement. . . . They still think they have other options, and if we push Nehru too hard it is by no means inconceivable that he would harden his attitude toward Pakistan rather than the reverse. Indeed he might transfer to us some of his current animosity toward [Beijing], attempt to disengage from his confrontation with the Chinese, and rely primarily on the hope, however illusory, of substantial Soviet military help.[101]

Round Six: May 14–16 (New Delhi)

Round six began with Ayub sounding a warning: if the United States continued to arm India without a Kashmir agreement, "the smaller nations of the region would be forced to look elsewhere." Bhutto reverted to the prior proposal for international supervision of Kashmir and a plebiscite in six months. India countered with its standard "no-war pact" proposal— tantamount to asking Pakistan to accept the status quo. The bilateral talks broke down for good.[102] "It is now," mused Galbraith, "only a maneuver for position to see who will be blamed or not blamed for the breakup of the talks."[103] Washington then put forward the Nehru-inspired mediation plan. Pakistan accepted subject "to conditions which can never be mediated," wrote Galbraith. The conditions: (1) a three-month deadline for mediation; (2) a freeze on U.S. military aid to India during the process; and (3) a strict focus on Kashmir.[104]

Birch Grove and the Rise of Sino-Pak Relations

"We must go ahead with help to India but do so in a way which [will] not drive the Paks off the reservation." Rusk thus posed the problem to Kennedy and the NSC on 17 May. India's minister of defense and secretary of the foreign ministry had come to Washington to meet with Kennedy about long-term military aid and were greeted with the fleshed-out U.S./U.K. air-defense plan. The Indians did not object to the scheme per se, but they found it insufficient. They wanted the United States to round it out with three squadrons of F-104 supersonic fighters—like it gave Pakistan.[105]

India's request provoked renewed debate in Washington. Bowles argued that the United States should make India "de facto allies instead of de facto associates" by giving Delhi a firm five-year commitment and supersonic jets. Rusk hedged: Washington should indicate to India that it "was prepared to 'go big' in principle." Kennedy was also cautious. Yes, "at the minimum some sort of substantial response to India was required." But the United States should do "the least [it] could get away with politically." Harriman fought to keep Kashmir strings attached: "Let's not give the Indians an idea that mediation was just an exercise, let's press on Kashmir. Let's not forget our Pakistan interests."[106]

In his meetings with Indian officials in the coming weeks, Kennedy did stress the need for a Kashmir solution.[107] But the fiction that long-term aid depended on one had worn thin. On 16 June, after three successive Indian delegations returned with assurance of extended military aid, Nehru announced that "Kashmir was, is and will continue to be an integral part of India."[108] Somehow, fumed Rusk, the Indians had gotten the "impression most of [the] heat from U.S. on Kashmir is off." He gave fresh instructions to Galbraith to "make it clear we continue to attach great importance to resolution [of the] Kashmir problem and to getting mediation started." But Galbraith could only muster flimsy arguments to support that contention, and they were surely overshadowed by the rather more encouraging news he was to convey confidentially—that Washington had decided to allocate another $30 million for India's air-transport, communications and radar, and ordnance production facilities.[109]

Finally, on 30 June, Kennedy and Macmillan released a joint communiqué at Birch Grove (U.K.) disclosing their plans to give India $100 million in military aid, over and above the Nassau agreement, despite the lack of progress on Kashmir, and announcing three-way air defense exercises for November 1963. India had asked for an astronomical three-year $1.6 billion military aid program. Washington was working toward a more "realistic" program closer to $300 million over three years, and as Defense Secretary McNamara saw it, "perhaps only half that."[110]

In July, Bowles replaced Galbraith and at once became the strongest advocate for "going big" with India. Bowles thought little of the U.S.–Pakistan alliance and derided the "inept" strategy of using U.S. aid to pressure India on Kashmir. In Washington he had lobbied hard for a $500 million five-year military aid program. "If we were not prepared to help India to this extent," he later wrote, "India would . . . go to the Soviet Union for the military equipment [and] almost certainly the Soviets would grasp the opportunity to establish a closer relationship with this major strategically placed nation."[111] Initially, Bowles was against the Nehru-inspired mediator proposal. Now, so was Nehru. Feeling no need to appear conciliatory on Kashmir after the Birch Grove decisions, he dismissed mediation as no longer "practical politics in the context of Pakistan's current attitudes." Then Bowles, realizing that there had to be a veneer of progress on Kashmir to sustain congressional support for a major military commitment, struggled to keep the mediator option afloat in Delhi.[112]

Meanwhile, signs of a major shift in Pakistan's foreign policy were afoot. "By not tying [Birch Grove] aid to resolution [of] Kashmir," said Pakistan's galled ambassador to Kennedy, "the U.S. has in effect written off a Kashmir settlement."[113] Before Pakistan's National Assembly, Bhutto raised the prospect of a Sino-Pakistan defense pact: "any attack by India on Pakistan would no longer confine the stakes to the independence and territorial integrity of Pakistan . . . it would also involve the security and territorial integrity of the largest state in Asia." Ayub later denied any secret defense agreements with China, but when asked about the potential for one in the future, said: "The answer to that lies with the U.S. . . . If India grows menacingly strong, we shall be in a great predicament and shall have to look around for someone to help us. And if we are attacked by India then that means that India is on the move and wants to expand. We assume that other Asiatic powers especially China would take notice of that."[114]

Ball met with the NSC to chart a damage control mission to Pakistan. As he saw it, the primary problem was that "Ayub can't defend himself against India so [he] has to rely on us." The United States had to find a way to make its defense assurances credible. Similarly, Harriman saw the crisis rooted in Ayub's determination to "take care of the Indian threat himself." Washington needed to convince Ayub that he "must rely on us" and that "we mean what we say." If the United States demanded that Ayub "stop his flirtation with China" it had to "give him confidence we will protect him." For Ball and Harriman, Pakistan's chief motivation was fear of India. Less generous was Kennedy, who saw more greed than fear in Pakistan's policy. Ayub was not "worried militarily about the Indians," he wanted to "use us against the Indians on Kashmir and we couldn't give this to him." Kennedy was at wit's end: "The best we can do is remind them we don't like the Chicoms" and "if they don't play ball, we will give our aid to someone else." Capturing the prevailing attitude in the administration, Ball concluded the "Paks need us more than we need them. Ayub [will] pull back from his China gambit if we press him hard enough."[115]

In the last weeks of August the situation deteriorated. Pakistan affirmed that it would not be the one to reject mediation outright, but neither would it soften its preconditions.[116] Then Nehru declared that he would refuse mediation unless Pakistan adopted a neutral or, better yet, pro-Indian attitude toward the conflict with China. This doomed the mediation proposal, for on 29 August, Ayub dropped another political bombshell, announcing a Sino-Pak Civil Air agreement. China touted the agreement as a defeat for "those who tried to isolate and blockade China." It was perceived similarly in the United States, where it was condemned as a "breach of free world solidarity." Washington retaliated by holding up a loan for the construction of a new airport in Dacca, where Chinese planes would presumably land. In turn, Pakistan elevated its Cuban legation to an embassy, and, on the eve of Ball's arrival, rolled out the red carpet for a Chinese Communist trade delegation. Nehru delivered the coup de grace. On 4 September, the day after Ball arrived in Karachi, Nehru declared before India's Upper House that any change in the status of Kashmir would have "disastrous consequences."[117]

Ayub told Ball there was no hope for mediation because Nehru now had no "compulsion to move on Kashmir." Ball, in return, warned Ayub not to be duped by "Chinese overtures," for if he got "too close" to Beijing "it would nullify" the U.S.–Pakistan alliance. Unshaken, Ayub assured him Pakistan would not do anything "stupid." Its overtures to China were driven by U.S. military aid to India, which made it "imperative for Pakistan to bring down its political and military liabilities . . . and normalize our relations with as many of our neighbors as possible."[118] As for Ball's contention that the United States had given "straightforward assurances on coming to [Pakistan's] aid if it should be attacked from any source," Ayub was unimpressed. A conflict with India would likely start in Kashmir, where it would be hard to identify an "aggressor." Even if India were clearly at fault, the United States could not be expected to fight against the recipient of so much of its military and economic aid, and a likely Soviet counterthreat would reinforce that reluctance. In any case, with its increasing military might, India could subjugate Pakistan before the United States could prevent the fait accompli.[119] If Washington genuinely wished to guarantee Pakistan's security, then it should send more arms so that Pakistan could do the job itself.[120] Ball came home determined to allay Ayub's skepticism, but Washington's vague public assurance a week later that "there would be an American response" in the "highly unlikely event that either country should attack the other" would have been anything but reassuring.[121]

During the last days of the Kennedy administration, Delhi took an increasingly hard line on Kashmir, moving overtly to integrate it into India proper.[122] This provoked a barrage of Pakistani complaints in the UN Security Council and Washington. The State Department took up the matter with India in late October, stressing that in view of "Pak flirtation with [the] Chicoms" India should avoid actions that would "aggravate rather than lessen our mutual problems with Pakistan." India's ambassador assured Rusk that Kashmir integration could occur only through a change in article 370 of the Indian constitution, which his government had "no intention or desire to change." The ambassador was ill-informed. On 27 November, Prime Minister Nehru announced before the Lok Sabha that integration would continue: Article 370 "would be eroded gradually . . . until Kashmir was fully integrated."[123]

The Kennedy administration spent its last days trying to keep India enthusiastic about planning a long-term military aid program, while deflating its requests to levels that would not alienate Pakistan. By mid-November, Kennedy had resolved not to send India supersonic jets. But he was "favorably impressed" by Bowles revised five-year, $65–75 million per year plan and, according to Bowles, would have endorsed it had he not been assassinated.[124] Thus matters stood when Kennedy was shot. India had been brought closer to the West through military aid. But it had not given up Soviet patronage. Nor had it made the compromises needed for a Kashmir settlement—something that had been considered necessary for defending South Asia against Chinese expansion and a sine qua non for long-term military aid. Instead, the U.S. buildup underwrote a more aggressive Indian policy in Kashmir and unwittingly helped to expand Chinese influence in the region. It increased Pakistan's alienation from the United States and fueled the growing collaboration between Pakistan and China.

JOHNSON'S PIVOTAL POLICY

When Johnson took over, the chairman of the joint chiefs, General Maxwell Taylor, was slated to go to South Asia to gauge the military aid requirements of both India and Pakistan. Johnson froze any further commitments until Taylor reported back.[125] Johnson thought well of Pakistan, and of Ayub in particular. But he detested China, and that animus was fully displayed when he met Bhutto on 29 November. Johnson first assured Bhutto that the United States would "not let India attack Pakistan" and then dressed him down about the dangers of consorting with China. Johnson warned Bhutto that congressional support for aid to Pakistan would erode if he hosted Chinese state visits as planned. Talbot continued the scolding. "When Pakistan got itself mixed up with Communist China" said he, "this tied our hands domestically and . . . removed any leverage we might have had to influence India in the direction of accommodation with Pakistan."[126]

Meanwhile, momentum built for a "major initiative toward India" and a balancing program for Pakistan. State, Defense, and Bowles all supported a five-year package for India. Bowles, with NSC backing, was also pushing to give India supersonic jets. Backlash from Pakistan was inevitable, but Bundy and Komer could not see letting Pakistan "veto" U.S. policy, "especially when we have a major opportunity to move India closer to us." "To mollify" Ayub, they suggested offering Pakistanis "a similar long-term commitment . . . if they . . . behaved themselves vis-à-vis [Beijing]." Rusk and McNamara, by contrast, recommended offering two squadrons of supersonic jets to Pakistan and not offering any to India. When Washington announced India's five-year package, argued Rusk and McNamara, it should simultaneously offer Pakistan the jets and a three- to five-year military aid plan. On the condition, of course, that Pakistan would "place acceptable limits" on its relations with China and "fulfill the basic requirements of its alliance relationship."[127]

Johnson wanted to ensnare India in a prolonged planning process before disclosing the full commitment he was willing to make. This would encourage Indian moderation, dampen its planned buildup, limit damage to U.S.–Pakistan relations, and avert a South Asian arms spiral fueled by U.S. dollars. The problem was that Moscow was not standing still. Ball put it to India's ambassador that the United States wanted a "fairly exclusive" relationship; it "could not work out longer-run aid for India if [Delhi] would go around shopping in [the] USSR." Nehru had other ideas. India would orchestrate the buildup, with the United States and USSR each giving major components and funding. Moscow would play along. So the United States was under pressure to reveal its long-term commitments and forfeit leverage over Indian policy.[128]

Taylor's brief was to shore up relations with both sides by plying them with reassurances and "dangling the carrot of long-term military assistance." He had a tough time in Pakistan. Why, he asked Ayub, did Pakistan have such "strong reservations about U.S. assurances . . . covering the contingency of Indian aggression?" At first, Ayub was polite. He didn't doubt America's intentions, but the United States "might not be able to come to Pakistan's assistance promptly. . . . the world situation and U.S. global responsibilities might make it difficult *even if the case were clear*" (italics added). Properly equipped by the United States, Pakistan "could do the defense job for herself."[129] But when Taylor suggested a joint Indian Ocean Task Force and military exercises as ways to strengthen the U.S. defense commitment, Ayub scoffed at such "gimmicks." The only joint maneuvers that made sense—based on defending Pakistan against India—were impossible politics.[130]

Taylor's conclusions favored Rusk and McNamara's approach: The United States should offer Pakistan a long-term package, including supersonics, in tandem with the its five-year offer to India. His recommendations stymied those who wanted to give India immediately a five-year commitment. He argued that India should develop its own plan first, so the United States could "verify their intentions as to force goals, Soviet procurement and the diversion of foreign exchange from economic development." Doing this raised "an undesirable time factor" in light of the Soviet's willingness to deal quickly with India, so he also recommended an immediate "interim one-year" commitment of "about $50 million" over the levels already agreed.[131]

Johnson backed Taylor's plan, with a few important caveats. Both countries should be encouraged to develop "austere" five-year plans that the United States could support, but given no firm estimates to count on. And the political price had to be clear. India had to stop diverting development aid to cover defense spending; Pakistan had to embrace its "alliance obligations." Accordingly, Ayub would not be offered Taylor's program before the results of Chinese Premier Zhou En-lai's March visit to Pakistan were evident.[132] What is surprising here is that Johnson's and Taylor's formula ignored Kashmir, even though serious unrest had broken out there in December 1963.[133] A key postulate of U.S. strategy, that deterring China required rapprochement in South Asia, had disappeared.

In 1964, U.S. relations with India and Pakistan went into a tailspin. In January, Ayub lamented in *Foreign Affairs* that "the distinction in American eyes between an ally and a neutral had become . . . blurred to a vanishing point." In February, during a state visit to Pakistan, Chinese officials announced unqualified support for Pakistan's position on a Kashmir plebiscite—a diplomatic coup for Ayub. After Kashmir unrest began in December, Pakistan had escalated its call for UN action on a plebiscite. The call was ignored by the United States and languished under the threat of a Soviet veto.[134] After Talbot warned Ayub in late March that future military aid hinged on Pakistan's attitude toward China, and its observance of alliance obligations, he concluded that Pakistan would probably still seek "a strengthened entente with China." In April the United States offered Pakistan two new squadrons of F-104s in the coming fiscal year "if the political climate was right at the time."[135] Pakistan seemed to ignore the carrot. That month, new signs of a Sino-Indonesian-Pak triangle emerged as the three convened in Jakarta for the prefatory meeting for the second Afro-Asian Conference. This was a direct snub to the United States, for Bhutto skipped the annual SEATO meeting in Manila to go to Jakarta.[136]

Meanwhile, India became impatient with U.S. stalling on long-term military aid. Delhi had expected a commitment right after Taylor's mission—it did not get one. Then, in May, India's defense minister came to Washington with a five-year plan, ready for U.S. backing. Instead, he got $50 million for one year (1965), plus $50 million in credit for purchases of U.S. equipment. Coming the day after Nehru's death, the U.S. offer struck a sour note. Meanwhile, the Soviets were, as Komer complained, "doing more than we to woo the Indian military establishment." In August, India began courting Soviet assistance for an indigenous program to build SAM missiles, which it previously had bought off the shelf. The next month, India sealed a deal with Moscow for $400 million in military aid and a promise of three squadrons of MIG-21 supersonic jets.[137]

While India's arsenal grew, Johnson stalled Pakistan's arms package to punish it for warming up to China. Ayub sneered that "now Americans do not hesitate to let down their friends" and wrote Johnson to say that Pakistan would have to undertake an agonizing reappraisal of its SEATO and CENTO commitments. Johnson retorted that if Pakistan reconsidered its alliance commitments, the United States would too. He ordered McConaughy to tell Ayub that Pakistan must at least "show the flag" in the "free-world" fight in Vietnam. Undeterred, Ayub announced that if China and the United States came to blows over Vietnam, Pakistan would not participate in a SEATO response. In July, with exquisite political timing, the Chinese produced a $60 million interest-free loan to Pakistan, which Ayub accepted. Fed up, Johnson put U.S.–Pakistan relations on ice.[138]

In January 1965, Johnson eased off, inviting Ayub to Washington in April so that they could revive U.S.–Pakistan relations.[139] But Pakistan was incensed over U.S. acquiescence to India's moves in Kashmir.[140] While India was destroying "even the fiction" of a separate Kashmir government, the

United States shipped arms to India and failed to press for a plebiscite in the UN.[141] A major shift in Pakistan's foreign policy was underway.[142] Much to Washington's chagrin, Bhutto declared in the UN General Assembly that "Taiwan is an integral part of China" and signed an economic and technical cooperation pact with China. In Beijing in March, Ayub pledged "lasting friendship and fruitful cooperation." Zhou En-lai reciprocated with the promise "if India commits aggression into Pakistan territory, China would definitely support Pakistan." Mao Tse-tung said "China and Pakistan can trust each other." Gone were the days when Ayub would say, as he had in 1961, that he "wanted nothing of China; he'd like to see it go to hell."[143]

The White House geared up for a "showdown" with Ayub in April. Johnson would really "blow the whistle" on Pakistan and shake its "confidence that continued full U.S. support can be taken for granted, irrespective of [its] international posturing."[144] But on 3 April, Ayub went too far, meeting with Soviet Premier Alexei Kosygin in Moscow. The White House decided to give Ayub the "shock treatment." Johnson revoked Ayub's invitation, claiming that his visit to the United States would "seriously jeopardize" Pakistan's share of the administration's foreign aid bill by focusing Congress' "attention on [his] Peiping and Moscow trips and recent unfortunate statements."[145] In order to appear even-handed, the invitation to India's new premier, Lal Bahadur Shastri, to visit Washington in June was also retracted. Indians were galled by the "equal treatment" with Pakistan.[146]

The Rann of Kutch Crisis

It was a bad time for Johnson to push U.S. relations with India and Pakistan to a low point, for in April a small-scale war brewed up in the Rann of Kutch, a desolate stretch of marshland on the northwest border between India and Pakistan. The hottest battles were fought in the last week of April, but sporadic fighting continued through May, and it was not until 29 June that an agreement was reached to resolve the dispute through arbitration. Tensions had been rising in the area since January 1965, with minor provocations from both sides, but Pakistan struck the first serious blow in early April.[147] Pakistan's move was a probe of India's military responsiveness and resolve, and of the diplomatic reactions of others to Indo-Pakistani warfare.[148]

Pakistan outfought India in the Kutch, and India's agreement to arbitrate—after it had refused to accept anything but a return to the status quo ante—suggested to Pakistanis that India lacked the will to stand firm and fight. It also seemed to set a precedent for the resolution of Kashmir. Just as important, China came out firmly in support of Pakistan, while the Soviets did not offer similar bracing for India.[149] Washington's response was tepid. Behind the scenes, the United States told both sides that it felt "neither side was justified" in using force; it demanded that they not use U.S.–supplied weapons, and it refused to pass judgment on the "fuzzed over" Kutch situation.

Both sides reproached Washington for letting the other use U.S. weapons.[150] Pakistan was the worst offender, since most of its arsenal was American made. When faced with U.S. censure, Bhutto urged Washington to recognize "that [an] attack on Pakistani territory [was] involved" and therefore Pakistan's right to use the arms in self-defense. The State Department suspected that Pakistan had escalated the conflict to force this issue. Washington's insistence that both sides not use U.S.-supplied weapons stood in contrast to the USSR: as a State Department analysis noted, "the Soviets have imposed no conditions whatsoever on . . . military equipment they have supplied to India."[151] The United States also pressured both sides to accept the U.K.-sponsored cease-fire and arbitration scheme, warning that "if one side agrees to cease-fire" and the other did not, "such action . . . would have to be construed as [an] aggressive position." Presciently, Bowles argued that Washington should tell "both sides we will cut off military aid unless they accept the . . . cease-fire proposals."[152]

"This Rann of Kutch business could build up to a real mess," Komer wrote Bundy on 26 April. India was "building up to a binge" and might retaliate "elsewhere, where the odds favor them more."[153] Three days later, Shastri announced that India reserved the right to fight Pakistan on the battleground of its choosing. Here was the old bind: how to deter an Indian escalation without encouraging Pakistan? On 30 April, Bhutto recalled for McConaughy the many U.S. promises to defend Pakistan: What would the United States do if this "unmistakable Indian threat" to attack across international borders materialized?[154] McConaughy replied that "in principle" the United States "always stood and would stand solidly behind its commitments, agreements, and formal statements." Then he "shifted ground" to the "confusing" present situation where "belligerence is not justified on either side."[155] McConaughy advised Washington against any quick official response: "a little uncertainty on [Pakistan's] part for the next few days could provide the additional leverage needed to achieve a cease-fire." On the other hand, there was an increasingly warlike India to worry about, and for that, he urged Washington to immediately remind India "of the *standing explicit assurances to Pakistan* as a . . . deterrent against an Indian . . . retaliatory action . . . in another area, such as East Pakistan."[156]

Next, Ayub wrote Johnson directly. "Time and again" the United States had assured him that it would defend Pakistan. Now he wanted the United States to "remind Mr. Shastri of the existence of American assurances in the event of aggression against Pakistan."[157] Pakistan's ambassador in Washington called particular attention to India's military provocations near East Pakistan, and asked the United States to bear down on Delhi. Ball, who received him, was suspicious. Pakistan seemed determined to "turn tables" by shifting "our attention from Kutch . . . to the broader question of . . . Indian action elsewhere and our assurances relating thereto."[158] Pakistan did not let up. In mid-June, Ayub told McConaughy that recent Indian incursions across the Kashmir CFL were probably "implementation of the Indian threat to respond to [the] Rann of Kutch incident at an unrelated place" and called for an immediate increase in military aid to Pakistan.[159] But Washington evaded Pakistan's attempts to pin down American allegiance, just as it rebuffed Delhi's call for it to "exert maximum possible pressure on Pakistan."

Why did this strategy of evasion fail to restrain Pakistan? Because Pakistan had reason to believe that support against India would also come from China, *especially* if the United States vacillated. Indeed, precisely because China was likely to help Pakistan in the lurch, it was reasonable to think that the United States would intervene to stop Indian aggression before China became involved. So Washington's response to the Rann of Kutch affair probably left Pakistan with two unfortunate views: (1) The United States would not take sides in low-level fighting over disputed territory and would instead press both sides toward a negotiated solution that would yield gains for Pakistan. (2) If the United States would not intervene directly to stop an Indian attack against Pakistan across international borders, it would probably work hard to prevent such a move in the first place. Yet, the truth was, America's ability to broker relations between India and Pakistan was fading fast.[160] While India and Pakistan gunned it out in Kutch, Talbot had posed a riddle to Rusk: What should the United States do "if one or both sides should venture into territory beyond dispute?" Other than cutting off military aid to both sides, Talbot was at a loss.[161]

The Kashmir War

After an agreement to arbitrate the Kutch dispute was sealed in June, Johnson decided to delay the Aid to Pakistan consortium, which was about to release $500 million in nonmilitary aid over the next three years. He meant to "soften up" Pakistan and India "to the point where they want to come for help." Johnson was through with Shastri "telling us how to solve Vietnam" and with Ayub "off receiving Zhou Enlai." Ayub had to learn that "he can't play China's game while being banked by the U.S."[162] "Let these people know," said Johnson, "we have pulled up business for a while." India's requests for F-5 jets were stalled, as were Pakistan's requests for more F-104s, ammunition, and tanks.[163]

Embittered, Ayub complained that "anyone can see that this amounts to more than a mere delay." He would have to "look elsewhere." Pakistan announced that it was reviewing concrete proposals with Moscow for "economic and other assistance . . . following the [U.S.] aid freeze."[164] This was the first leg of Pakistan's attempt to close the gap between it and the United States—by making it compete with the Communist powers. The second leg was to convince the United States that Pakistan had not entered into any compromising secret treaties with China, but that Pakistan could "not afford to incur the avoidable enmity of large Communist neighbors."[165] These half-hearted pledges of fidelity elicited their corollary: fake assurances from Rusk that the aid delay was about U.S. domestic politics, not pressuring Pakistan.[166] After these two approaches failed, Ayub tried the silent treatment. He refused to meet with McConaughy and empowered Bhutto to represent him in all matters relating to U.S. relations. McConaughy warned Bhutto in early August that Pakistan's unwillingness to get "a meaningful dialogue started" was likely to make the United States tie "very clear and explicit" strings to Pakistan's aid. Bhutto bristled at this "threat to take a hard line" and warned that if the United States did so, "Pakistan would immediately take a harder line."[167]

Three days later Pakistan began infiltrating guerillas into Kashmir, and after it backed them up with regular forces, India retaliated across the Punjabi border. Many of the dynamics presaged in the Rann of Kutch crisis would play out again in August and September. These patterns help to explain why Pakistan undertook the provocative moves that it then did, and why U.S. policy failed to stop the escalation to war.

In one of the best analyses of the outbreak of war in August 1965, Sumit Ganguly argued that Pakistan's provocation in Kashmir, in defiance of India's military might and threats to retaliate elsewhere, are a puzzling instance of deterrence failure.[168] "Why was the Indian deterrent called into question?" His answer is that Pakistan's policy "stemmed from fundamentally flawed...estimates of the likelihood of military success" caused by psychological biases that "skewed estimates of the prevailing military balance."[169] Ganguly's explanation is incomplete and probably exaggerates the role of irrationality in Pakistani decision making. It mistakenly poses the problem as an isolated duel between two unequal adversaries, India and Pakistan.

It is reasonable to assume that the decisions by Pakistan's leaders to begin and escalate the war were strongly informed by estimates of what outside powers would do. Their country's survival had always depended on international support. Ayub and Bhutto undoubtedly knew that they could not beat India in an unlimited one-on-one fight. There is no reason to believe that they thought it possible, much less desirable, to fight in a passive international environment. Supporting this view was "most reliable" intelligence received by the White House on 26 August reporting that the guerilla infiltration was part of a "well organized" plan to force a Kashmir settlement, worked out in combination with China and Indonesia.[170] The beauty of such a plan—if it existed—was that it would be likely to stimulate renewed efforts by the United States to settle the dispute. Indeed Ayub admitted as much on 8 September to the British and Canadian High Commissioners. "I never wanted *all out* war with India" he exclaimed, "we want Kashmir, but we know we can't get it by military action. If only some of you people would show some guts, we would have it!"[171]

Thus, there were probably two key planks in Pakistan's theory of victory. One was a bet that outside powers would intervene to keep the war limited or, failing that, intervene on Pakistan's side if the war escalated. This was not wildly misconceived. In fact, the United States did try to stop India from attacking across international boundaries, after Pakistan moved into Kashmir with regular forces.[172] The second bet was that, in *a war limited* to Kashmir, Pakistan could win or at least fight to a stalemate. Either way, the result would be better than the status quo. An outright military victory could give Pakistan all of Kashmir, and a stalemate would bring in the United States, more determined than ever, to impose a settlement that gave Pakistan more than it currently had.

What else may have led Pakistan to believe that outside powers would keep the war limited? First, there was China, which did in fact take an active diplomatic role on behalf of Pakistan. It mobilized forces on the Sino-Indian border near East Pakistan and delivered an explicit back-channel threat against an Indian move against it. When India struck in Punjab on 6 September, it was also concentrating forces on the border with East Pakistan.[173] The Chinese threat to intervene two days later checked this danger. The likelihood that China would do this was surely part of Pakistan's political strategy for winning a limited war.[174]

After India crossed the international border, Pakistan came to collect on U.S. promises to defend it against Indian "aggression." Ayub's other CENTO allies—Iran and Turkey—put the United States on notice that they were watching to see "how in a pinch the United States meets its assurances."[175] When McConaughy met with Ayub and Bhutto on 6 September, Bhutto opened by urging the United States to use "the realities of the situation to press for an honorable settlement" to Kashmir. Ayub came straight to the point: The United States had "a bilateral obligation" to defend Pakistan and "we . . . demand fulfillment."[176] True to form, the U.S. ambassador waffled: The "case was hardly clear, certainly not black and white." Ayub conceded that it had started in Kashmir, but that was "disputed territory, and [Pakistan] has not aggressed across any international boundary against Indian territory."[177] Washington's response was a blow. It refused to see India's attack as "aggression."

We must view India's attacks across Pak border in [the] over-all context [of] events [of the] past few weeks. It [is] clear . . . that the immediate crisis began with substantial infiltration of armed men from the Pakistan side. We [are] aware that India first put regular forces across [the] CFL but Pak responses thereto . . . struck at points India considered vital, and Indians have long asserted (a) they could not tolerate continued Pak offensive, and (b) if Pakistan should strike India's vital interests, India would have no choice but to respond in an area of its own choosing. Government of Pakistan must have been well aware of [the] risk involved in its own actions in Jammu and Kashmir.[178]

So how would the United States fulfill its Pakistan commitments? By "acting urgently" to support "immediate UN action to end the hostilities." The United States urged Pakistan and India to immediately, and fully, accept the UN cease-fire. This had to be done before there could be any move to settle Kashmir. "Subsequent" U.S. actions would depend "on the response of both countries to UN efforts."[179]

Neither side wanted to quit yet. India had backed down too soon in the Rann of Kutch crisis and would not do so again. Pakistan was still "hell bent on forcing a Kashmir negotiation—whatever the cost" and jockeying for U.S. support.[180] Ayub and Bhutto insisted the United States "fulfill" its bilateral commitment first; then Pakistan would accept a UN cease-fire, but only if it meant "settlement, plebiscite." McConaughy replied that the United States was fulfilling its bilateral obligations through the UN effort "as a first step."[181] Yes, U.S. obligations to Pakistan went beyond "appeal to the UN," and if that avenue failed after "Pakistan had cooperated with it in good faith and clarity," then the United States could do more. Bhutto burst out:

[Secretary of state John Foster] Dulles promised immediate U.S. action in the event of Indian aggression . . . Ball became irritated when [I] pointed out the U.S. would not intervene promptly enough. President Kennedy [said] the U.S. would break relations with India in [the] event of aggression. Ambassador Harriman had asserted [the] U.S. simply would not permit Indian attack.[182]

McConaughy stuck to his lines. First Pakistan should accept the UN initiative. That would "buy time" to work for a Kashmir agreement, and if India did not endorse the UN plan while Pakistan did, the United States then would be in a better position to go further in its bilateral obligations.[183]

For the United States, the UN cease-fire initiative was the best thing going. As Rusk advised Johnson, it "could get us back to the disagreeably bumpy, but relatively safe, verbal hassling over Kashmir with each country still seeking maximum United States support for its position." But the strategy of inducing restraint by dangling the prospect of U.S. support was not cutting it. And waiting for the belligerents to become bloodied enough to accept a cease-fire looked untenable. If Pakistan "played the Chinese communist card" the war could turn into a "Free World–Communist confrontation." If the conflict just ran its present course, Pakistan would still "wind up deeply committed to the Chinese Communist[s,] while India, feeling let down by the West and its national prestige at stake, would almost certainly go for the nuclear bomb."[184]

Bowles proposed cutting off military aid to both sides on 6 September.[185] Johnson seized on it. Two days later, Rusk informed Congress, and the next day, McConaughy and Bowles imparted the news to Karachi and Delhi. Bhutto was aghast at the "deplorable" U.S. decision. Pakistanis would "fight with hands if necessary but never surrender." Nothing, he declared, could more frustrate the UN peace efforts than this.

Pakistan's arms come almost exclusively from [the] U.S. while India has other suppliers . . . plus [a] substantial internal war production capacity. U.S. action actually constitutes assistance to [an] aggressor . . . Pakistan, cornered, deserted, bitched, has no alternative but to interpret U.S. action as [a] punitive one assisting India, a non-aligned and treacherous country aggressing against [a] U.S. ally.

Bhutto punctuated the tirade with a plea: if the United States must cut off aid, it should at least agree to *sell* arms to Pakistan.[186] McConaughy turned him down.

Without U.S. resupply Pakistan would soon wither in the high-intensity war that it was fighting. For this reason, India quietly applauded the U.S. decision, even if it denounced the affront in public. More worrying to India were China's moves, which intensified as the U.S. arms cutoff was announced. Beijing delivered its first ultimatum on 8 September and began concentrating forces on India's eastern border near Assam.[187] India notified the United States that it had no designs on East Pakistan, but that Pakistan was trying to provoke an incident in that area to trigger a Chinese counterstroke.[188] India's President Sarvepalli Radhakrishnan met with Bowles to convey that India would begin moving to accept the UN cease-fire and asked what Delhi "could expect from the U.S." if China in the meantime attacked. Bowles replied that the U.S. response would "no doubt depend on conditions existing at that time," that the United States had no desire to see China "overrun" any part of India, but by the same token, it had "no desire to underwrite total war on the subcontinent." The best way for India to guard against China would be to make a genuine effort for peace with Pakistan, so that the "bulk of her resources could be used against China."[189]

The UN Security Council's 10 September resolution called for a cease-fire and return to the status quo ante, within twelve days. Pakistan continued to press the United States to support its own cease-fire formula, wherein both sides would immediately withdraw from undisputed territory and then withdraw from Kashmir as a UN force went in to supervise a plebiscite.[190] Pakistan was trying to harness the international concern caused by China's brinkmanship, to push the United States and Soviet Union into backing a UN plan that delivered a political victory in Kashmir.

India accepted the UN's plan on 14 September, on the condition that Pakistan's guerillas as well as regular forces must be withdrawn from Kashmir. These and Pakistan's conditions doomed U Thant's efforts to seal a cease-fire on 16 September. After he announced no progress, China sent a three-day ultimatum to India to dismantle its positions in Sikkim and began mobilizing on that border too. A U.S. national intelligence estimate that day predicted China would avoid "direct, large scale, military involvement" short of an "impending Pakistani defeat." But the United States was not taking chances. The day before, the U.S. ambassador to Warsaw had passed his Chinese counterpart a warning not to intervene.[191]

India's ambassador implored Rusk to deliver a "formal" U.S. warning to China and an explicit promise to intervene if China attacked. Rusk divulged the Warsaw exchange, but was otherwise noncommittal.[192] Johnson decided not to send any messages to India or Pakistan "for the time being" or to make any military moves in the region. As for India's request, Delhi got gobbledygook instead of a guarantee. Johnson would only confirm publicly that India had discussed its concerns about the "Chinese development" with the United States, that the United States had discussed its concerns with India, and that it would take note of them as it pursued its policy within the Security Council.[193] The next day India tried again. The Foreign Ministry reported to Bowles menacing Chinese movements that "indicated Peking is getting ready for military action." India wanted Washington "on a strictly covert basis" to authorize its military personnel to "consult" with India's military on contingency plans. The response: Washington was "not prepared to initiate contingency planning." Johnson stuck to his decision to "avoid commitment of any sort" till the UN cease-fire bid played out.[194]

On 17 September Moscow stepped forward as the honest broker. It sent conciliatory identical letters to both sides, urging them to accept the UN cease-fire, and offered its good offices to host a meeting to negotiate a peace agreement.[195] Ayub tried one last time to enlist the United States. All he asked was that Washington "blame India" for aggression on 6 September and work for a Kashmir solution consistent with America's previous pro-Pakistan attitude on the question.[196] Johnson gave no quarter. China's ultimatum and troop movements had compromised Pakistan. If China intervened, Johnson would blame Ayub for failing to agree to a cease-fire. He was "not the sort of man who will ever give his approval to one thin dime for a country which supports or encourages the aggressive pressures of Red China."[197]

The next day China added three more days to its ultimatum. Now, as the

American consul in Dacca wrote, "the Chinese immediate military threat to India turned out to be a bluff," and "the game was up" for Pakistan.[198] Two days later, both sides agreed to cease-fire and acknowledged Moscow's invitation to peace talks in Tashkent. China's propaganda organs declared that its ultimatum had succeeded, and its army on India's border stood down. The Tashkent Conference was held in January 1966. Pakistan and India signed an agreement that was unpopular on both sides and went largely unimplemented. Nevertheless, it was the capstone to Moscow's policy of establishing a central position in South Asian affairs. In the aftermath of the Kashmir war, China became Pakistan's most reliable ally and chief arms patron, as did the USSR for India.

SUMMARY OF FINDINGS

Necessary Conditions

In this case, the United States sought to prevent war between India and Pakistan and to impel them to negotiate a peaceful Kashmir settlement. In relation to the Kashmir dispute, the United States would try, through the aegis of bilateral negotiations, to prod India into making "more than just a minor adjustment of the cease fire line."[199] Just as it would try to push Pakistan to make a "real business offer" in the talks. But, in Kennedy's words, there was no question of the United States "forc[ing] a solution on either India or Pakistan."[200] The "main business" was for both sides to compromise, for "each side [to] accord [the] other a substantial position" in Kashmir.[201] In Rusk's words, America's "overriding purpose is *some* accommodation between Pakistan and India, the question is how to achieve it . . . the shape of the settlement [is] irrelevant to us. We could buy anything they could agree on."[202]

Washington understood that both India and Pakistan wanted to force the issue of Kashmir and that each side sought "maximum United States support for its position." This was why, as Rusk put it, the United States could "never fully support the goals of either India or Pakistan."[203] Kennedy was convinced that Pakistan was not "worried militarily" about India but instead wanted to "use us against the Indians on Kashmir."[204] Similarly, Komer spoke of Pakistan's "cherished ambitions of using the U.S. as a lever against India."[205] Kennedy also suspected that India "was not serious about negotiating an acceptable compromise settlement," and he blamed Nehru's "unyielding mood" for the failure of the talks.[206] In any case there was plenty of evidence in the public declarations that came out of both Nehru's and Shastri's governments to support the view. Indeed, Delhi hardly swerved from its determination to move forward with the project of integrating Kashmir into India, in defiance of its earlier UN commitments and despite U.S. blandishments for it to do otherwise.

India and Pakistan saw each other as more threatening than the United States—they were each other's worst enemy. Karachi was convinced that India's refusal to give up Kashmir was also a refusal to accept Pakistan's right to exist. Ayub warned Kennedy in 1962 that "the arms now being obtained by India from you for use against China will undoubtedly be used against us at the very first opportunity," for India "regarded Pakistan as enemy number one."[207] Even during the 1962 war, when Indian forces were reeling from Chinese attacks on all fronts, India kept the bulk of its forces deployed against Pakistan.

Isolation Avoidance Effects

In this case, there is little evidence of caution in the sense of trying to enlist U.S. support or acquiescence before acting. Pakistan was the initiator of both the Rann of Kutch fighting and the Kashmir war. In the declassified documents available, it does not appear that Pakistan consulted with the United States before making these moves.[208] Indeed, it appears that in both cases Pakistan acted first, hoping to entrap the United States into coming to its aid if things got out of control. Pakistan's leaders in 1965 (Bhutto especially) tend to be seen as risk-prone decision makers. This might suggest why the caution-inducing effects of a pivotal deterrence policy did not appear to operate on their decision making. As I pointed out in Chapter 1, the theory of pivotal deterrence is based on an assumption of risk-averse actors. But the problem with this easy explanation is that the risk-propensity of the statesmen in question has not been measured independently of their disastrous foreign policies. Moreover, in this case the adversaries had powerful and attractive alignment options. This suggests that it may not just have been the leaders' personalities but also the larger strategic situation that encouraged them to run risks. We will say more about this below.

Alignment Options Effects

U.S. policy confronted an unfavorable motivational asymmetry. The security competition between India and Pakistan was intense, and their stakes in Kashmir dwarfed U.S. interests in the region. But the United States was a preponderant pivot. If it were to tilt decisively toward one, it could mean a bitter defeat for the other. Yet, despite that preponderance, the United States was unable to use its pivotal position to orchestrate a political solution to Kashmir or to stop the outbreak of war.

America's leverage over India and Pakistan was undermined by their alignment options. Mutual enmity toward India made Pakistan and China "natural" allies. Though there was no formal alliance between them, there was no need for one. China had a vital interest in preventing Indian dominance on the subcontinent. This geopolitical reality was an important reason why the United States was unable to restrain Pakistan. However, U.S. policy after 1962 contributed to rather than muted warming Sino-Pak relations. If China and Pakistan did not want India to become mightier, U.S. policy magnified the threat. As common interests between Pakistan and China grew, Pakistan's dependence on the United States decreased. In result, the United States found it harder to pressure Pakistan to compromise on Kashmir. It could not credibly threaten to punish Pakistan for intransigence on Kashmir if doing so would drive Pakistan headlong into the arms of China.

U.S. influence over India was similarly diminished by the Soviet Union. As early as the summer of 1961, India was negotiating to purchase Soviet MIG-21 aircraft, and jet engines to outfit an indigenously produced supersonic fighter.[209] After the Sino-Indian war, these deals came through. India still needed U.S. weapons because the Soviets could not support the scale of buildup and modernization necessary to equip India against a major Chinese threat. But Moscow remained an enthusiastic purveyor of arms to India, even if that meant sharing the role with the United States. Moscow wanted to strengthen India as a balance to China and it did not want to allow the United States to monopolize military aid to India. Just the same, the United States was eager to arm India, not only to balance against China but also to limit Soviet influence in Delhi.[210] Since Moscow was willing to share the stage, Washington had little grounds for demanding an exclusive relationship with India. Consequently, the United States had to worry that if it asked India to pay a steep political price for military aid, India would go to the Soviets for a better offer. So, despite India's need for U.S. arms after 1962, the United States could not translate its military aid into influence over India's Kashmir policy. The Moscow option allowed India to defy U.S. pressure, and the China option undermined U.S. influence over Pakistan, which meant that Kashmir would not be settled, and India and Pakistan would remain on a collision course.

[7]

U.S. Pivotal Deterrence in the Unipolar Era, 1990–2002

International stability is never a given. It is never the norm. When achieved, it is the product of self-conscious action by the great powers, and most particularly of the greatest power, which now and for the foreseeable future is the United States. If America wants stability, it will have to create it.

Charles Krauthammer, *Foreign Affairs*, 1990/91

When the Eastern Bloc dissolved and the Soviet Union broke up, the United States became a unipolar power. No combination of other great powers could contest its military might in areas beyond their vital interests, where the logic of basic nuclear deterrence would not operate. The resulting power vacuum, predictably, invited greater U.S. activism. The United States found new freedom of action, and more reasons to use it. Expanding conceptions of its national interests encouraged the United States to become deeply engaged in disputes, such as that in Kosovo, which in the past it might have ignored. Also competing for attention were conflicts—such as those between Greece and Turkey, India and Pakistan, and in the Taiwan Strait—that endured after the Cold War's end.

In these situations, and many others, the United States was called on to deter two sides from provoking or escalating fighting. Although this was an important subtext to U.S. policy even during the Cold War, it was largely overshadowed by the strategic problems of basic and extended deterrence against a clearly defined, and formidably armed, adversary and its allies. As this most salient strategic challenge faded, however, U.S. policy makers waded into a raft of messier conflict scenarios saddled with a corpus of deterrence theory that was not always relevant. That the field of security studies had not come fully to grips with the new challenge was at least partly due to the inertia of thinking about deterrence in terms of the basic and extended models inscribed by the Cold War.[1]

The tenacity of Cold War thinking about deterrence should not be underestimated. In a recent piece on the "changing role" of alliances and alignment in a "globalizing world," for example, Lawrence Martin asserts that "shifting, limited, and uncertain alignments lack the great value of more established relationships [such as] standing, formal, and stable alliances . . . in deterrence of hostile tendencies."[2] The inertia is also expressed in *Post Cold War Conflict Deterrence,* a volume of papers by many scions of Cold War strategy. The introduction states that the authors set out to rethink deterrence theory because the "context for deterrence has changed dramatically since the end of the Cold War." But what follows is a reprise rather than rethinking of the "enduring" postulates of the old model. Credibility, demonstrating political will, integrating nuclear and conventional forces, nuclear targeting, and no-first-use doctrine, all these and more, are the key focal points. The problems of more fluid and "less than vital" national interests, on the one hand, and of extended deterrence, on the other, are flagged by the writers. But the connection between conflicts involving less pressing national interests and the need for more flexible and subtle forms of deterrence is not probed and, indeed, barely noted.[3]

In the most careful analysis of the problem of "extending deterrence" to "weak or medium strength states" beyond the ambit of vital U.S. interests, the chief prescription is, predictably, to "recognize and express interests, including less-than-vital interests, explicitly and credibly."[4] Pat prescriptions like these may make sense in clearly drawn extended deterrence contexts, but for the United States such contexts became less prevalent after the Cold War.[5] Indeed, the utility of strong signals and hard commitment techniques was not obvious in many of the deterrence scenarios facing U.S. policy makers in the 1990s.

In this chapter, we shall review four cases to illustrate the variety of contexts in which the United States dealt with the problem of pivotal deterrence in the 1990s and to highlight the relevance of alignment options (or the lack of them) in these circumstances. Our purpose here is not to test hypotheses, but rather, to apply insights gained from the preceding chapters to illuminate recent pivotal deterrence challenges in U.S. foreign policy.

THE 1990 KASHMIR CRISIS

In early 1990, Washington came alive to the danger of a new war in South Asia. In late 1989, widespread civil unrest had broken out in Kashmir, largely due to local discontent with India's neglectful rule. But given its long-standing opposition to Indian claims in Kashmir, Pakistan could hardly stand aloof once the revolt began.[6] By May 1990, the Kashmir conflict was developing into a crisis that threatened to ignite a wider Indo-Pakistan war. With nuclear fears never far in the background, both sides conducted military exercises and counterexercises. For Washington, these summer maneuvers coupled with growing concerns about Pakistan's covert nuclear program raised the specter of an uncontrolled escalation in the fall when better weather would make fighting more feasible and therefore exacerbate mutual fears of a surprise attack.

We should not exaggerate the intensity of this crisis. From Delhi's perspective, and that of the U.S. ambassador there, the danger was not acute. Pakistan, however, was more worried, particularly by India's military exercises. And Washington, which was taking a longer view of things, was perhaps most anxious of all.[7] This may, therefore, have been an "easy case" in that neither side was bent on going to war. Indeed, it appears that by the time the United States took a hand, both were probing for outside assurances that would allow them to de-escalate. Nevertheless, important strands of pivotal logic are at work in the play of events. The fear of being isolated by the United States appears to have encouraged restraint, most notably in Pakistan but also in India, and the reluctance of the Soviet Union and China to become involved magnified U.S. influence over the two sides.

Gates's Mission

In mid-May 1990, the Bush administration decided to send deputy National Security Advisor Robert Gates to South Asia. Gates was joined by two other senior NSC officials, John Kelly and Richard Haass. The chief aim was to stabilize the situation, by reinforcing both sides' awareness of the extreme danger of a new war and convincing each side that the other was not looking to start one. There was no intention to orchestrate a political solution to the Kashmir problem, although Gates would encourage both sides to negotiate bilaterally "or through other peaceful means."

Gates, who was on official business in Moscow, went directly to Pakistan first, where concerns that, as the then foreign minister of Pakistan put it, "worst case analysis" would trigger escalation were most pressing.[8] Pakistan had by this time taken a barely disguised role in stoking the Kashmir uprising. Now Pakistan feared that India would retaliate massively, and it was Pakistan's requests for assurances regarding Indian intentions that had triggered Washington's intervention. Pakistan's prime minister, Benazir Bhutto, did not receive Gates in Islamabad. She was in the Middle East lobbying for support on Kashmir. So Gates, joined by Robert Oakley, the U.S. ambassador to Pakistan, met with Pakistan's president, Ghulam Ishaq Khan, and its army chief, General Aslam Beg.

Gates imparted a gloomy message to Pakistan. The United States "had war-gamed every possible scenario for Indo-Pakistani conflict" writes Gates, and "there was not a single scenario in which Pakistan won."[9] Oakley recalls Gates presenting "a very sober assessment . . . in the event of war . . . it [would] not be a guerilla warfare in Kashmir. It [would] be conventional warfare the length of the border." Pakistan might very well "find the Indian Navy in Karachi . . . the Indian Air Force deep into Pakistan territory." The U.S. envoy urged Islamabad to shut down the training camps supporting Kashmiri insurgents and to avoid provocative military exercises, and he cautioned Pakistan's leaders not to gamble on the prospect of U.S. support.[10] In Oakley's account, Gates warned, "we will have to stop providing military support or any kind of support to whichever side might initiate things. . . . and this, of course, will impact upon [Pakistan] more than it will upon the Indians." Gates, according to Oakley, was at least partly successful in these efforts because he played on Pakistan's fears that the United States was "beginning to tilt toward India, and if there were a crunch, the United States would let Pakistan down once again."[11]

In Delhi, Gates met with Indian Prime Minister V. P. Singh and other senior government and military officials. The gist of Gates's message concerned "the consequences for [India] of a war, including that it might go nuclear."[12] It was important to stress this latter element of danger because in a conventional war, India could count on military if not political victory. The envoy also informed Delhi that he had extracted an agreement from Pakistan (which Pakistan latter denied) not to support the Kashmir insurrection. According to Singh's principal secretary, who was a party to the talks, Gates said that he had told the Pakistanis "not to expect any help from the Americans if they started a war," and he conveyed with "quiet firmness" a similar message to India.[13] In both capitals, Gates forwarded proposals for confidence-building measures and offered to share intelligence on the force dispositions of both sides, but on this latter score, it appears that his mission produced no response from India or Pakistan. Nevertheless, after the mission, the situation soon mellowed, with both sides taking steps to restrain military activities that might be perceived by the other as provocative.[14]

Alignment Options

The circumstances surrounding this largely successful foray into pivotal diplomacy by the United States support the alignment options thesis. As Stephen Cohen and his associates noted, "the initiatives of other countries . . . were notable perhaps by their limited and tentative quality."[15] The only one-sided encouragement that Pakistan received in the crisis came from Iran, which, according to Oakley, "had assured Pakistan at the military level of strong support in the event that hostilities broke out between India and Pakistan over Kashmir."[16] Alone, this would hardly be a reliable insurance policy against the risks of a full-blown war with India. More important, during the Gates mission, Islamabad and Delhi received signals from both Moscow and Beijing saying, in Oakley's words, "both of you back off, because you're not going to get any of us to take sides in this operation."[17] William Clark, the U.S. ambassador to Delhi, supports this view, suggesting that Gates brought an "oral message" from Moscow indicating that "they supported the [U.S.] position that there should not be a war between them."[18]

The historical context is important. Moscow had just made an ignominious retreat from Afghanistan, and it was in no position to resume an activist foreign policy in South Asia. Similarly, China was at this time mired in its own problems surrounding the democracy movement in Tiananmen Square and elsewhere. Neither could summon the wherewithal to broker relations between India and Pakistan. George Sherman, a U.S. defense attaché in Delhi at the time, put it this way: "As far as the superpowers were concerned, there was absolutely no doubt that the United States was taking the lead, was the only one actively involved in trying to restrain both parties."[19]

THE 1996 GREEK-TURKISH "WAR OF FLAGS"

On 25 December 1995, a Turkish cargo ship ran aground on a tiny uninhabited islet in the Aegean Sea, four miles off Turkey's western coast. The Greeks call the islet Imia; the Turks call it Kardak. It is part of an archipelago around the larger Greek island of Kalimnos, which in turn is a part of the Dodecanese chain that rims Turkey's Aegean shoreline. Populated almost wholly by Greeks, the Dodecanese were transferred from Italy to Greece in the 1947 Treaty of Paris, to compensate for Greek losses under Axis occupation. Turkey was not a party to the treaty and has argued that these islands are part of a "gray area" that remains to be negotiated between Greece and Turkey.[20] When the Greek coast guard came to help the Turkish ship, the captain refused assistance, insisting that Kardak was a part of Turkish territory. Ankara backed him up.

The Turkish captain could not have had worse timing. Throughout the 1990s, Turkey had been pressuring Greece to agree to a deal expanding Turkish control over resources and territory in the Aegean, while Greece had been seeking from the United States, and the European Union (EU), guarantees of the Aegean status quo. In 1995, Ankara escalated its long-standing demand for the demilitarization of Greek islands in the eastern Aegean. After the 1974 Cyprus conflict, Athens had built up militia forces on these islands, in palpable violation of the 1947 Paris treaty, among others.[21] Making matters even more complex, while Turkey's insists that Greece must demilitarize the Dodecanese in keeping with it obligations in the Paris treaty, Ankara also denies the validity of the treaty in respect to Greek sovereignty over those same islands.

To understand how a dispute over a few "rocks" in the Aegean could bring Greece and Turkey to the brink of war, one must take into account the broader bargaining context behind it.[22] For many years Turkey has pressed Greece to negotiate bilaterally the whole range of disagreements between them in a package deal. Turkey is obviously the stronger party, and therefore bound to get the better of any package deal worked out in a bilateral context. Greece, therefore, has rebuffed Turkey's overtures for linked negotiations and, indeed, even refuses to acknowledge Ankara's enumeration of the issues "in dispute" between them. For Athens, many of these so-called disputes are part and parcel of the status quo, which Turkey is trying to undo by threats of force. Accordingly, Athens will not enter into bilateral negotiations where all such issues are on the table. Instead, it insists that Turkey must take its claims individually to the Hague, where Greece's strong legal claims are likely to win out. This Turkey refuses to do.

Thus, Athens believed that Ankara, by calling into question Greek sovereignty over tiny Imia, which for many years had gone unchallenged, had taken a dramatic new step in its program to force Greece to negotiate a package deal. However, what made Athens' reaction to Turkey's Imia challenge so explosive was its landing of marines on the islet. This Ankara saw as the thin edge of a renewed Greek intransigence on the demilitarization issue. Athens had now upped the ante, by deploying regular armed forces to a part of the Dodecanese where it had not before.

Meantime, domestic politics in Greece and Turkey were in tumult. On the day the Turkish boat ran aground, Turkish Prime Minister Tansu Ciller resigned, her True Path party having lost its majority in the legislature. In the aftermath, President Süleyman Demirel asked Ciller to run a caretaker government until a new one could be formed, and now she was bargaining with the nationalist Motherland Party to form a winning coalition against the Islamist opposition party of Necmettin Erbakan. There was a sudden spike in demand for the rocket fuel of Turkish politics, nationalism. On the other side of the Aegean, a new Greek prime minister, Costas Simitis, had just taken over two weeks earlier, and he was under great pressure to establish his leadership credentials.

In late January the situation quickly escalated. On 25 January, the Greek mayor of Kalimnos raised the Greek flag on Imia. Two days later, two journalists from Turkey's national newspaper, *Hurriyet,* replaced the Greek flag with a Turkish one and filed a story claiming that Greek officials were disputing "Turkey's sovereignty over the island." The next day Athens ordered

Greek marines to deploy on the islet and replace the Greek flag, and then raised the matter with U.S., Russian, and EU diplomats in Athens. The Greek foreign minister, Theodore Pangalos, rebuffed Ankara's call for a "negotiated solution" as well as U.S. urgings that Greece and Turkey consult on "confidence measures" in the Aegean. To do that under the circumstances, declared Athens, would be to appease Turkish aggression.[23]

Turkey denounced Athens for turning the affair into an "official" issue by deploying Greek forces. Turkey, announced Ciller, would take "every necessary" step to reverse Athens' "fait accompli." Ankara sent a note to the Greek ambassador protesting Athens' move, and Foreign Minister Baykal demanded that Greece "pull back" its forces from the islet and "remove all signs indicating Greek sovereignty there." "Turkey is determined to protect its rights," said Baykal, "we won't yield to Greek pressures on the issue."[24]

The next day, matters boiled over with nationalist outbidding in Ankara. Bulent Ecevit, the architect of the Turkish invasion of Cyprus in 1974, and now the leader of the nationalist Party of the Democratic Left, called for Turkey to "finish matters off without waiting for another Greek fait accompli." A spokesman for Erbakan's Islamic party likewise declared that if Greece did not back down, Turkey "should once more prove its capabilities, as it did in 1974." Ciller added to the belligerent drumbeat: "Turkey does not authorize another flag on its territory, [it] will not sacrifice even one pebble." The Greek flag "will be lowered and Greek soldiers will leave."[25] Greece, in turn, alerted its forces facing Turkey in the Aegean and sent a formal note to Ankara protesting the violation of Greek territory by Turkish forces.

As naval forces from both sides converged on the area, the international community began to react. That evening UN Secretary General Boutros Boutros-Ghali and NATO Secretary General Javier Solana called both sides, asking for restraint. And the Russian Foreign Ministry declared itself "opposed to the upgrading of tensions" and called for "the utmost tolerance, for settling conflicts peacefully on the basis of UN principles and international law in the interests of peace, security, and stability in this region."[26] Nevertheless, the escalation continued. At about 4:00 A.M., 31 January (9:00 P.M. 30 January in Washington) Turkey deployed commandos to an islet adjacent to the one occupied by Greek marines and notified Athens of the deployment. In those early morning hours, the Greek Government Council for Foreign Affairs and Defense met. Pangalos informed Greece's chief of general staff that Turkish commandos had landed and asked for options. The chief offered two: (1) "recapture the rock within five hours" by sending commandos from the nearby island of Kos, "who will either exterminate or arrest" the Turkish troops; or (2) "immediate bombing, we will burn all of them up in a few minutes." The Greek civilian authorities recoiled from these extreme options and decided to chart a middle course between "war" and a "disengagement of forces." Greece would play for time. While the risks mounted, it would strive to marshal international pressures on Turkey to back down and to establish Greek rights through a diplomatic victory.[27]

Athens' bid ultimately failed. For while it was playing to prolong the crisis, the White House began to take active steps to defuse it. According to Richard Holbrooke, a key player in the U.S. intercession, by the morning of 30 January, the United States had received "clear warnings that the Turks were going to retake [Imia] by force."[28] Thus, in Washington, there was the perception of a "serious possibility of use of force." That afternoon President Clinton had made phone calls to Simitis in Athens, and Demirel and Ciller in Ankara, urging both sides to "move their forces away from that little island and to find a diplomatic solution to the issue."[29] These phone calls established U.S. engagement, but did not, as Holbrooke put it, "remotely resolve the crisis." Over the next eight hours, Secretary of State Warren Christopher, Secretary of Defense William Perry, Chairman of the Joint Chiefs John Shalikashvili, and National Security Advisor Anthony Lake, all contacted political leaders in Athens and Ankara. Holbrooke coordinated these calls and orchestrated the negotiations, through the U.S. ambassadors in the respective capitals and with the governments directly. Although the details of the negotiations still remain murky, the basic dynamics can be traced.

As Holbrooke put it, the nub of the problem was that neither side would promise to the other that they would not escalate further. But, ultimately, each side "was willing to say to the U.S." confidentially that they would not do so. The United States, therefore, held this pair of commitments "in escrow" and conveyed to each side that it was confident in the other's assurance. The end result was a brokered agreement "to go back to the status quo ante." What remains unexplained, therefore, is how the United States got the two sides *to undo* steps they had already taken.

We do know that at about 11:00 P.M. Washington time (8:00 A.M. Aegean time), Pangalos agreed in a phone call with Holbrooke, Christopher, and Shalikashvili to proceed with a mutual withdrawal monitored by U.S. overflights.[30] By the end of the day, the Greek and Turkish flags had been lowered, and their forces had begun to withdraw. We can reasonably infer from this outcome the two key pressure points in U.S. diplomacy. First, the United States probably warned Greece that it would not intercede to stop the Turks from ousting the Greek forces from Imia, which as Holbrooke said, "would have been easy." Second, and this was clearly demonstrated at the time, Washington refused to support Greek claims in the dispute.[31] The weight of this position would have been reinforced by the reticence of other international players. Boutros-Ghali, NATO secretary general Javier Solana, and Britain's Foreign Secretary Malcolm Rivkin each called on both sides to de-escalate, but did not take up Greece's position. Indeed, at the weekly meeting of NATO ambassadors that day, there was no mention of the dispute. Likewise, the EU remained silent during the heat of events on 31 January and, other than Moscow's carefully balanced plea for "utmost tolerance" the day before, so did Russia.

It seems likely, therefore, that Athens was not willing to risk war with Turkey without outside allies and was frustrated in its diplomatic strategy to enlist international support for its position. In fact, that day, Pangalos denounced NATO as "incapable" of resolving Greek-Turkey conflicts. And as Simitis later complained, "our EU and NATO partners maintained an equal distance policy, and hesitated to recognize our rights or to support us decisively."[32] In short, the United States was positioned to play the pivot. And by refusing to tilt toward Athens, it forced Greece to agree to a "mutual withdrawal" under conditions that it had previously ruled out, thus averting a war that would almost certainly have followed Turkey's impending move to dislodge the Greek forces from Imia.[33]

THE KOSOVO CRISIS, 1997–99

NATO's air war against Serbia in 1999 stemmed from the failure of NATO's Kosovo policy in the preceding years, which sought, above all else, to maintain regional stability.[34] Keeping the peace, or at least keeping the violence to low levels so that it would not spread to neighboring states, was the main goal. NATO also had humanitarian aims in Kosovo, but stability was seen as an important condition for achieving them.[35] Restoring Kosovo's lost autonomy, which Belgrade revoked in 1989, was also a consideration, but it was low on NATO's list of priorities, and Kosovo independence was anathema to NATO. Belgrade, on the other hand, wanted to maintain maximum political control over the province. Given Yugoslav president Slobodan Milosevic's record, there was reason to believe that he might try something drastic, like ethnic cleansing, if it would advance that goal. By contrast, the agenda of Ibrahim Rugova's unofficial "shadow" government of Kosovo was mostly benign. It called for the restoration of autonomy and then for eventual independence, but only through nonviolent resistance and negotiations.

Thus, from the early 1990s to late 1997, the only pressing threat to stability in Kosovo came from Belgrade. So between 1992 and January 1998, NATO policy toward Kosovo was straightforward extended deterrence. In December 1992 the Bush administration leveled a stiff threat: "in the event of conflict in Kosovo caused by Serbian action, the U.S. will be prepared to employ military force against Serbians in Kosovo and in Serbia proper."[36] In February and July 1993 the Clinton administration repeated the threat. Then political meltdown in Albania in spring 1997 sent a flood of small arms into Kosovo, and the Kosovo Liberation Army (KLA) began a bona fide insurgency, vowing to liberate ethnic Albanians in Kosovo and Macedonia and unite them in a "Greater Albania."[37] Now NATO had to contend with the aggressive and destabilizing efforts of both sides.

NATO's problem in Kosovo thus called for a straddle strategy. Belgrade would have to be deterred from further depredations in Kosovo by the threat that NATO would firmly oppose him. The KLA, on the other hand, was gambling on outside intervention and would have to be deterred from provocative escalation by the threat that NATO would abandon and isolate it. Thus, in trying to prevent the war from spiraling in 1998, NATO threatened to intervene if Belgrade escalated the repression in Kosovo, and to abandon the KLA if it continued to provoke retaliation and block a negotiated political solution. At different times, both threats failed, and insight on the role of moral hazard and alignment options in pivotal deterrence helps to explain why.

The first clear indication that NATO, with the United States in the vanguard, was shifting toward pivotal deterrence appeared on 23 February 1998, when the U.S. special envoy to the Balkans, Robert Gelbard, stated in Pristina that the KLA was "without any question a terrorist group" and that the United States "very strongly" condemned terrorism in Kosovo.[38] The Clinton administration saw that the KLA threatened Balkan stability and was sending it a warning.

Escalation nevertheless followed, with KLA assassinations of Serb police in Kosovo and heavy Serb reprisals against KLA strongholds. The reprisals aroused massive protests in Pristina, which Serb police, in turn, brutally suppressed. That month, the Kosovo shadow government held elections, and Rugova's moderate Democratic Alliance of Kosovo (LDK) took more than 90 percent of the vote. But ominously, the KLA boycotted the election and condemned Rugova's nonviolent stance.

The Contact Group, comprising Britain, France, Germany, Italy, Russia, and the United States, set out to "isolate the terrorists" and edge the LDK and Belgrade into negotiations, vowing to use "all appropriate elements of pressure and influence with both sides" to achieve this end.[39] The UN Security Council passed Chapter VII resolution (1160), which condemned the Serbian repression and "all acts of terrorism," embargoed arms to both sides, and demanded a political solution "based on the territorial integrity" of the Federal Republic of Yugoslavia (FRY), and "a substantially greater degree of autonomy and meaningful self-administration" for Kosovo.[40]

With the LDK fragmenting over the issue of nonviolence, Rugova put forth a "Group of 15" to partake in the Contact Group's negotiations. NATO scrambled to shore him up. On 30 April, it condemned "the excessive use of force by the Yugoslav army" but also reiterated that it was "firmly opposed to independence for Kosovo" and to "all use of violence . . . by terrorist groups."⁴¹ President Clinton's personal envoy, Richard Holbrooke, orchestrated a 15 May meeting in Belgrade between Rugova and Milosevic to jump start negotiations. It backfired. Nothing was accomplished, and just a few days later Serbia launched a new campaign against the KLA. On 29 May Rugova met with Clinton in Washington, and then with UN Secretary General Kofi Annan in New York.⁴² Rugova's team informed Clinton that they were through negotiating with Belgrade. After the recent offensive nothing less than a quick transition to full independence was acceptable.

In June, the Contact Group ratcheted-up the economic pressure on Serbia. It had already frozen Serbia's international assets, now it banned foreign investment and demanded an immediate cease-fire and withdrawal of Serb forces from Kosovo. Meantime, as Kofi Annan reported, the KLA had "increased its attacks . . . [on] government security forces" and "Kosovo Albanians who allegedly cooperate with [them]."⁴³ NATO began military exercises over Macedonia and Albania on 13 June, calling for a settlement that gave "enhanced status" to Kosovo while "preserving the territorial integrity" of the FRY.⁴⁴ On 16 June, Moscow delivered what appeared to be important concessions from Belgrade. Milosevic agreed to begin negotiating with Rugova on "forms of autonomy"; to stop repressing civilians; to permit access to Kosovo for diplomats, international organizations, and humanitarian nongovernmental organizations (NGOs); and to return Serb forces to their barracks if the "terrorist activities are halted."⁴⁵ Holbrooke moved to exploit the opening. Between July 4 and 6, he and Russia's deputy foreign minister shuttled between Milosevic and the LDK, pushing for an agreement. They failed, according to Holbrooke, because the Kosovars did not "get their act together."⁴⁶ Rugova's spokesman blamed their disunity on the lack of a coherent Contact Group strategy, saying that the "biggest problem for us is that there's no international agenda."⁴⁷ There was, however, a clear international agenda. Kosovo could not, as Christopher Hill, the Contact Group's chief negotiator, put it, "shoot its way out of Serbia."⁴⁸ The Kosovo factions could not agree to a "negotiating position" because the most powerful among them opposed negotiations *period*. By midsummer 1998 the KLA controlled much of Kosovo. With NATO on the verge of intervening, which would mean a KLA victory and open the way to independence, why would they want to negotiate for something less? The moral hazard problem was thus debilitating NATO's strategy for producing a settlement.

Nevertheless, NATO did not take action at this time to stop the Serb's summer offensive, and by late July, that offensive was taking a real toll. KLA fighters and thousands of civilians were forced into the hills. The FRY was back in control of most of Kosovo. The KLA was chastened. This seemed a good time for NATO to push again for the settlement that it wanted—one that kept Serbia intact. In that spirit, Hill made the first official contact with the KLA leadership on 29 July and showed them an early draft of the Contact Group's initial settlement proposal.[49] Bringing the KLA into negotiations now would force their leadership into the open and expose them to international pressure. For that reason, Hill's attempt to draw them out failed. On 9 August, the Contact Group floated the plan, calling for an autonomous Kosovo that remained a "special part" of Serbia. The KLA condemned it, insisting that they would settle for nothing less than independence. Accordingly, when Rugova fielded another negotiating team to take up the Contact Group proposal, the KLA was not included. Milosevic, in any case, refused to negotiate with the KLA. But now NATO also "warmly welcomed" the new team sans KLA.[50] If NATO wanted a compromise, and the KLA refused, then it was better sidelined.

In mid-August NATO staged a new round of Partnership for Peace exercises in Albania to pressure Milosevic, and on 24 August, the Security Council called again for a cease-fire. Belgrade still did not relent. As the KLA crumbled in the field, the LDK became more flexible at the negotiating table. First they set aside their demand for immediate independence and agreed to work toward a cease-fire based on a three-year "interim" political solution. Then, on 20 September, as Serb forces rolled up KLA strongholds around Prizren and Pec, the LDK endorsed an interim plan to make Kosovo "temporarily part of Yugoslavia as an independent entity, equal to the other two republics in the federation."[51] Milosevic was sure to oppose any scheme that gave Kosovo status in the FRY equal to Serbia and Montenegro, for such a scheme would guarantee his ouster by constitutional means. So with the KLA in tatters, the LDK were now maneuvering to ingratiate NATO, and put Belgrade in the wrong, by moving toward the settlement formula NATO preferred, but in a way that was likely to be spurned by Belgrade.

Resolution 1199 and the Holbrooke Agreement

On 23 September the UN Security Council passed resolution 1199 (UNSCR 1199), which condemned "all acts" of violence in Kosovo, especially the "indiscriminate use of force by Serb security forces," and commanded the two sides to cease fire and seek a political solution.[52] Significantly, Russia did not veto this Chapter VII resolution. The North Atlantic Council (NAC) then authorized General Wesley Clark, the supreme allied commander (SACEUR), to seek forces from alliance members for use in Kosovo.[53] On 31 September, Hill pitched a revised settlement plan. The next day, U.S. Secretary of Defense William Cohen announced that forces were ready to begin air strikes in two weeks. Three days later, Milosevic cracked and announced that Serb forces would be pulled back.[54] On 5 October, Holbrooke went to Belgrade to pin him down.

Russia expressed "deep disquiet" over NATO's threats, but in the end, its objections were half-hearted. Behind the scenes at a secret 8 October meeting of the Contact Group in London, Russian Foreign Minister Igor Ivanov gave Russia's tacit assent to NATO taking forceful action without Security Council approval.[55] The next day, Ivanov predicted publicly that "Milosevic ultimately will knuckle under" to NATO demand for a withdrawal.[56] Milosevic could have no confidence in Russian backing at this time.

On 13 October, NATO ordered air strikes in ninety-six hours if Belgrade did not comply with UNSCR 1199.[57] That day Milosevic and Holbrooke announced what is known as the "Holbrooke Agreement." It affirmed that any Kosovo settlement must respect the territorial integrity and sovereignty of the FRY, and it unilaterally committed Serbia to completing by 2 November an agreement on the "core elements" of a settlement based on Hill's 2 October proposal.[58] Most important, Milosevic agreed to withdraw Serb forces deployed in Kosovo after February 1998. The Yugoslav army (VJ) elements that remained would return to their barracks, except for limited numbers that were to defend the Serb-Albanian border. The activities of the police forces would also be scaled back, their chief task to maintain twenty-seven "observation points" along critical lines of communication. Milosevic also agreed to NATO overflights to verify the withdrawal of Serb forces, and to the deployment of two thousand unarmed Organization for Security Cooperation in Europe (OSCE) verifiers who would then monitor both sides' compliance with UNSCR 1199.[59]

It was now up to NATO officials—namely SACEUR Clark and Klaus Naumann, chairman of NATO's military committee—to meet with Milosevic and turn the broad language of UNSCR 1199 into fine print with specific benchmarks.[60] Belgrade began haltingly to meet NATO's demands on 16 October, prompting a new ten-day window for compliance. Clark and Naumann pressured Milosevic to commit to real numbers and comply with them. If he did not comply, they warned, NATO would bomb; if he did comply, he could "turn the table so that the KLA [were] seen as the bad guys."[61] By the 27 October deadline, Milosevic had complied, at least enough to escape the ultimatum, and Naumann and Clark had assured him that NATO would try to control the KLA.[62]

The KLA denounced the Holbrooke Agreement, but they were unwilling to be put in the wrong by Milosevic, so they declared a "unilateral" ceasefire and agreed informally to comply with UNSCR 1199. NATO wanted the LDK to seize this opening to make real progress in negotiations with Belgrade, so it amplified its threats to abandon the KLA if it tried to spoil the breakthrough. What it failed to do, however, was take active measures to squeeze the KLA's sources of material support.[63] Consequently, its efforts to control the KLA failed. As the VJ pulled back, the KLA came down from the hills and resumed the campaign of provocations—ambushing Serb police patrols, even firing on diplomatic observers who accompanied them, and occupying and fortifying key positions vacated by Serb forces. The cease-fire allowed the KLA to reconstitute quickly as a political and fighting force, and it is clear that the KLA bore a large measure of the blame for the renewed escalation after the Holbrooke Agreement. NATO leaders, however, were now more inclined than ever to publicly blame Belgrade for the conflict and for the collapse of the cease-fire. Nevertheless, stability harmed the KLA's goals more than Serbia's, and stability is what NATO tried to create in October. Success in the Contact Group negotiation process led by Hill depended on it, and for that reason, the KLA worked hard to upend it.[64]

Between the Holbrooke Agreement and the Rambouillet conference in February 1999, the Kosovars' intransigence was as big an impediment to the achievement of a political settlement consistent with NATO's goals as Belgrade's. The Contact Group's goals certainly came closer to what Belgrade wanted than what the LDK wanted. The Contact Group sought a political autonomy solution that would obviate the need for NATO peace enforcers and would keep the FRY intact. Rugova, by contrast, was now demanding independence and NATO ground troops deployed in Kosovo.[65] As the KLA recovered, the LDK became more obdurate.[66] While NATO and the Contact Group were pushing an interim solution that did not give Kosovo independence, and that would not establish an international protectorate there, the LDK and the KLA converged in demanding both.

On December 24–27, the VJ launched the "Christmas Offensive" in northern Kosovo in response to a string of KLA provocations. In early January, tensions mounted further in southern Kosovo. There was a rash of KLA ambushes and kidnappings and increasingly aggressive KLA patrolling on major roads in the area. As KLA men and material poured in from Albania, Serb forces ambushed the infiltrating columns and retaliated in a number of surrounding communities. Most notoriously, on 15 January, they killed forty-five ethnic Albanian civilians in Racak. The Racak massacre prompted international outrage against Belgrade, diverting attention from the LDK's intransigence and the KLA's provocations. The Contact Group met throughout the rest of January, and at the end of the month, called for a settlement conference at Rambouillet. Threatening to hold "both sides accountable," the Contact Group demanded that they attend— and seal a political deal. NATO was now "ready to act and rule[d] out no option to insure full respect by both sides of the demands of the international community."[67]

Rambouillet End Game

For the KLA, the Rambouillet conference carried with it, for once, a powerful threat of abandonment. If the KLA refused to participate the prospect of international backing would evaporate. Moreover, while the Contact Group was demanding that the two sides reach a political settlement, NATO was demanding on a separate track that the *implementation* of the settlement include the deployment of NATO peacekeepers. This then was the political bargain: if the Kosovars would agree to the Contact Group's plan, they would get at least half a loaf, an international protectorate for the length of the interim period. And that breathing space might well provide the launching pad for independence. By the same token, this gave the Contact Group new leverage over the Kosovars, for it meant that *any* interim political settlement the Contact Group could extract from Serbia the Kosovars would have to accept—or else Milosevic would "put them in the wrong" and they would be isolated.

There were few surprises during the first two weeks of negotiation. The Serbian delegation temporized. The Kosovo delegation worked hard to ingratiate themselves with the Contact Group through serious negotiations. Three days before the deadline, Hill went to Belgrade to engage Milosevic directly and returned with a new proposal, one that still held that Kosovo would remain part of the sovereign territory of the FRY. The Kosovo delegation rejected Hill's new proposal. They objected to the lack of (1) an independence referendum at the end of the interim period and (2) measures to transition the KLA into a peacetime existence. Three days followed of cajoling and courting the Kosovars by Secretary of State Madeleine Albright, her staff, military representatives of NATO, and other members of the Contact Group. On 23 February, the plan still referred to FRY sovereignty and territorial integrity. But without clearing the change with the Contact Group, the United States had inserted an oblique reference to a referendum at the end of the interim period and assured the Kosovars that KLA would be aided in the transition to a civil political force. The rest of the Contact Group, however, refused to endorse the wording change. And thus matters stood when the deadline expired.[68]

Hashim Thaci, the political spokesman for the KLA and the head of the Kosovo delegation, was forced by KLA hard-liners to refuse to endorse the plan on 23 February. But the Kosovars could not flat-out refuse, or Milosevic would accept the plan, and they would be cornered. So the Kosovo delegation tentatively accepted the agreement, on the condition that it would sign in two weeks, after "consultations" back at home.[69] The U.S. government launched a public relations blitz in Kosovo in favor of the plan. Former U.S. Senator Bob Dole, a longtime supporter of Kosovo, toured the region warning Kosovars "We'll abandon you if you don't sign."[70] The KLA hard-liners stepped down, which gave Thaci the leeway to sign the deal.

On 23 February, Milosevic had waited for the Kosovars to reject the plan, so that he could take a more conciliatory tack. When the Kosovars tentatively endorsed it, Belgrade mimicked the position. Serbia would not sign yet; clarifications were still needed on "the scope and character" of the "international presence" that would implement the agreement.[71] The Contact Group announced that a "signing" conference would be held in Paris on 15 March. When that day came, the Kosovars were fully on board with the existing plan, so the Serbs refused to sign anything but their own "revised" plan, which gutted everything important from the 23 February document. When NATO denounced the move, Milosevic seized on the wording of the Status of Forces (SOF) agreement in the implementation annex of the Rambouillet plan, as a pretext for rejecting in toto.[72] Now the Kosovars had put Belgrade in the wrong, and it was cornered by NATO. The air war began four days later.

Why did Milosevic, for all intents and purposes, give up the game at Paris? Rather than string out negotiations, he refused to sign anything. If he had wanted to keep NATO at bay, he could have agreed to sign the interim political agreement and then used the signing conference as an opportunity to prolong negotiations on the particulars of "implementation" and thereby dilute NATO's peace-enforcement plan.[73] Instead, he gave up the pretense of negotiation and abandoned any effort to avoid isolation. Why would a pragmatist like Milosevic choose to do this and to brave NATO's bombs?

Russia: The Illusory Alignment Option

Some argue that Milosevic believed that the NATO campaign would be a short series of pin-prick air strikes, like the "Desert Fox" campaign against Iraq four months earlier.[74] Others argue that Milosevic planned to hunker down and ride out an extended air campaign, betting that a defensive operational strategy in Kosovo could deter a NATO ground invasion, while political tensions within NATO would lead it to cave in before he did.[75] Behind both of these plausible explanations there stands a more fundamental one: that Belgrade's expectations of *Russian support* are what probably led it to gamble that NATO would strike weakly, and that internal tensions within the alliance would then soon cause it to relent.

In March 1999 Belgrade overestimated Russia's influence on the United States and Russia's ability to cushion Belgrade from NATO's wrath. Unlike the previous October, in February and March 1999 Russia stridently opposed NATO threats and the deployment of NATO peacekeepers in Kosovo without Belgrade's consent. In October 1998 Moscow did not present itself to Belgrade as a potential alternative to coming to terms with NATO. In March it did. When Belgrade quit negotiating after Rambouillet and went full steam ahead with a new assault on Kosovo, it gambled—with some justification—that Russia would derail NATO's military response or at least significantly blunt it.[76]

In February and March there were many opportunities for Belgrade to infer that Russia would do this. Most notoriously, on 17 February, with the Rambouillet talks under way, Russian President Boris Yeltsin shattered the fiction of a unified Contact Group, claiming publicly to have warned Clinton over the phone "we will not allow you to touch" Serbia. Though the Clinton administration denied it (and still does), the technical point was moot since Yeltsin made the claim publicly, reiterating that "the bombing will not happen."[77] At Rambouillet, the Russian Ambassador Boris Mayorskii said that Yeltsin's statement was being "taken very seriously," and it probably was by the Serbs, if not the others. Aggravating matters, Russian Prime Minister Yevgeny Primakov, whose star appeared to ascend as Yeltsin's physical and political grip declined, was quoted as saying that Russia would give Belgrade "whatever they ask for" if NATO used force against it.[78]

In the weeks after the Rambouillet conference, Russia tried hard to eviscerate NATO threats. The most important sources of Russian leverage were not military. Rather, the leverage lay in the prospect that it would disrupt important U.S.–Russia and NATO–Russia relationships that Washington and other NATO capitals might think twice about losing as the price for bombing Serbia. In hindsight, it is clear that Russian policy was mostly political theater. But to assume that this was apparent at the time ignores many factors, most of all the considerable uncertainty in Russian politics in early 1999. Yeltsin was ailing and fading fast on the political scene, and it was not clear what sort of transition there would be. This was itself an incentive for NATO to conciliate Moscow, in order to strengthen the moderate factions within Russia that had staked their political fortunes on cooperation with the West. Moreover, Milosevic had good reason to believe that his position would improve in either of the two likely scenarios for a sudden collapse of Yeltsin's government: the takeover by a communist/nationalist coalition with Primakov in charge, or by an interim regime led by the military and national security apparatus.[79] But even with Yeltsin in power, there were enough signs of Russia's growing discontent with the West that Belgrade might plausibly see benefiting from either a true breach between Russia and NATO or, more likely, from NATO efforts to avoid one.

The backdrop for Moscow's "diplomacy of disaffection" was the serious clash between the United States and Russia over the arms control issues that were the keystone of their strategic partnership. On 16 March, the day after the Paris conference convened, Primakov warned that if the United States abandoned the Antiballistic Missile (ABM) treaty—which it then appeared likely to do—then Russia would "have to think about a completely new military situation that would require an arms race."[80] The next day, the Russian Foreign Ministry released a statement calling the U.S. Senate's passage of a bill favoring ABM deployment a "serious threat to the whole process of nuclear arms reduction as well as strategic stability."[81] The Speaker of the Duma announced on 23 March that NATO bombing would put Russian ratification of the Strategic Arms Reduction Treaty (START-II) in jeopardy. The next day, Vladimir Lukin, a former ambassador to the United States and the chair of the Duma's Foreign Relations Committee lamented publicly that the "US has clearly shown that it does not care one whit about relations with Russia or about the START-II treaty."[82] On 27 March the Duma voted 366–4 in favor of a resolution condemning the impending NATO bombing, and more important, postponing START-II ratification. On the same day, a Pentagon delegation sent to Russia to consult on the Nunn-Lugar program for preventing loose nukes was turned away. Thus, just as Belgrade was considering its options vis-à-vis NATO, U.S.–Russian relations on a set of key security issues went south. It was reasonable for Milosevic to believe (because many in the United States also believed) that the United States should find it prudent to make concessions in one area of its security policy in exchange for getting its way in another, and that strategic arms control would trump Kosovo in this context.

Russia magnified this trade-off by putting its relations with NATO on the chopping block too. On the third day of the Paris conference, the NATO–Russia Permanent Joint Council (PJC) met in Brussels, and Russia threatened to pull out of Partnership for Peace if its wishes were ignored.[83] On 18 March, in a startling gesture of disassociation, the Russian delegation to the Contact Group simply refused to witness the Kosovo delegation's signature of the Rambouillet plan. Four days later Holbrooke went to Belgrade for one last-ditch attempt at diplomacy, warning Milosevic that NATO's response would be "swift, sustained, and severe." At the same moment, Moscow publicly warned that Primakov's visit to the United States— slated to begin on the 23rd and to cover major aspects of U.S.–Russian relations, from arms control to International Monetary Fund funding—would be canceled if NATO used force against Serbia.[84] On 24 March, just after the bombings began, Russia made good and quit NATO's Partnership for Peace and military cooperation programs. The next day Yeltsin's deputy chief of staff warned that U.S.-Russian relations were damaged "in a most serious way."[85]

Most of Russia's campaign to "hold the ring" for Belgrade turned out to be posturing. But only in hindsight is it obvious that Russia would abandon Serbia before NATO abandoned the Kosovars. Russia did not divert NATO. But its efforts, more than anything else, probably caused Belgrade to gamble on the chances that Russian intercession would dilute the air strikes to symbolic gestures, if not prevent them altogether, and that Russian pressure would soon drive a wedge in NATO cohesion. A strong indication that Russia had emboldened Belgrade to stonewall at Paris appeared in late May, when Belgrade surrendered after Moscow publicly withdrew its support.[86]

STRATEGIC AMBIGUITY AND THE TAIWAN STRAIT

America's security policy toward Taiwan and China, known as "strategic ambiguity," is another incarnation of the straddle strategy of pivotal deterrence. Its reigning characteristic is a waffling and hedged U.S. commitment to defend Taiwan against China. The reason: The United States wants to deter both China and Taiwan from provoking war. Today, that means the United States must mount threats to deter China from attacking Taiwan or otherwise coercing reunification, and, at the same time, it must leave open the option to abandon Taiwan in order to deflect it from declaring independence.

The pragmatic basis of this pivotal deterrence policy flows from the tension between the two main thrusts of U.S. policy in Asia, between the need to cooperate with the People's Republic of China (PRC) and to shield Taiwan from mainland coercion. The tension between the two has not been resolved, and that sends a basic message: What the United States will do in a Taiwan Strait crisis depends on the circumstances and context.

Cold War Precursors

When the Chinese Communist Party (CCP) took control of the mainland in October 1949, President Harry Truman's Secretary of State, Dean Acheson, was aiming to cut U.S. ties with Chiang Kai-shek's ailing Koumintang (KMT) regime, which had retreated to Formosa (Taiwan), and was seeking a modus vivendi with the CCP.[87] But this vision met with opposition at home. At Foggy Bottom, figures such as Dean Rusk and John Foster Dulles lobbied for increasing U.S. commitments to the KMT. NSC-68—a combined effort by rollback enthusiasts in State, Defense, and the National Security Council—put forth a powerful vision for aggressive resistance to Communist expansion in which Taiwan figured as an important strategic outpost. When the Korean War began in June 1950, this approach won out.

The day Truman decided U.S. forces would fight in Korea, he sent the Seventh Fleet to the Taiwan Strait to block a possible invasion from the mainland. In tandem with the naval deployment to the Strait, Truman also called on the KMT "to cease all air and sea operations against the mainland . . . the future status of Formosa must await the restoration of security in the Pacific." In February 1951, five months after the Chinese intervened directly in Korea, the United States announced a Mutual Defense Assistance (MDA) agreement, providing arms to Taiwan. The use of these arms was limited to maintaining "internal security" or "legitimate self-defense."[88] Thus, even in the heat of the Korean War, the United States would not agree to underwrite a KMT attack on the mainland. From the outset, U.S. security policy toward Taiwan involved measures not only to deter China but also to restrain Taiwan.

When Dwight D. Eisenhower assumed the presidency in January 1953, the United States was still mired in the last year of the Korean War. To pressure China to make peace, Eisenhower "unleashed" Taiwan. In his first State of the Union address, he announced that the U.S. Navy would no longer "shield Communist China" from a Nationalist invasion of the mainland.[89] Taipei began immediately to press hard for a stronger U.S. pact and stepped up preparations for a mainland invasion. Taiwan courted the United States with such urgency because the United States had overlooked Taiwan when it formed the nascent Southeast Asia Treaty Organization (SEATO). That was not a mere oversight. As strong a supporter of Taiwan as he was, Secretary of State Dulles wanted to avoid the inflexibility of a firm U.S. commitment to Taiwan. His State Department reasoned "that ambiguity in America's ties to Taiwan would have the benefit of making Peking uneasy" without tying U.S. hands.[90]

As a substitute for SEATO, Chiang wanted a U.S.–Republic of China (ROC) bilateral defense pact. The PRC, in a clumsy attempt to derail such a development, began shelling KMT forces on the offshore islands of Quemoy and Matsu in September of 1954.[91] The Eisenhower administration reacted by signing the Mutual Defense Treaty between the United States and ROC in December 1954. Now the United States was formally engaged to use its forces to defend Taiwan. Given Chiang's appetite for control over the mainland, the U.S. pact carried with it a considerable moral hazard. This was dealt with in an exchange of letters between the Secretary of State and Taiwan's Minister of Foreign Affairs, in which it was agreed that any use of force by either the United States or Taiwan from the treaty area would "be a matter of joint agreement."[92] In short, when Eisenhower enhanced the U.S. commitment to defend Taiwan, he also imposed a safeguard for checking Taiwan's ambitions.

This was all the more important because the Eisenhower administration was now entertaining the prospect of a "two-China" solution to the Taiwan problem.[93] Beijing, of course, opposed such a division, but so did Chiang, who still aimed to unify China under KMT rule. A contingent U.S. commitment to defend Taiwan against mainland attack, but not to support a KMT offensive, was the logical tool of Eisenhower's two-China vision. The U.S. veto over offensive military action by Taiwan put the "leash" back on Taipei. That leash would be used in the August 1958 Quemoy and Matsu crises, when Eisenhower pressured the KMT to withdraw its built-up forces from the islands in the wake of mainland artillery attacks upon them.[94] It would be wielded again by President Kennedy in the spring and summer of 1962, when, through temporizing and "polite postponement," the United States quashed Chiang Kai-shek's wildly optimistic plans to in-

[188]

vade the mainland and topple Beijing.[95] Thereafter, Taipei would be constrained to focus on the more limited goal of promoting its international status as the legitimate government of China, in a de facto world of two China's, where Beijing, thanks to the Communist block, had ever more clout.

Normalization and the Advent of Strategic Ambiguity

In the early 1970s, President Richard Nixon and Henry Kissinger, his national security adviser, laid down the groundwork for "normalizing" U.S.–China relations. The now famous idea was to corner Moscow in the strategic triangle.[96] Yet, in order to really improve relations with the PRC, the United States would have to recognize the PRC and downgrade the U.S.–Taiwan alliance. As the PRC's vice premier, Deng Xioping, put it to Kissinger in 1974, "the treaty you have with Taiwan must be done away with."[97] The result of this process of normalization was the U.S. policy of strategic ambiguity that we know today.

The transition to strategic ambiguity was achieved through the "constructive ambiguity" of the "One China" concept. For this reason, constructive ambiguity and strategic ambiguity are closely intertwined, but they should not be conflated. The purpose of *strategic ambiguity* is competitive, to make it harder for China and Taiwan to do what they want. *Constructive ambiguity*, on the other hand, conduces cooperation; in this instance, its aim is to make it easier for the United States and China to do what they want.[98] This has always been the leading purpose of the "One China" concept in U.S. policy. The secondary effect has been to pose an implicit warning to Taiwan of the limits of U.S. support should it move toward independence. This deterrent threat, it should be noted, would remain dormant as long as Taipei was wedded to the idea of one China (under KMT rule) and therefore also opposed to separate independence.

In the first open move toward normalization, the 1972 Shanghai Communiqué, the Nixon administration "acknowledged" that "all Chinese on either side of the Taiwan Strait maintain" that "there is one China and that Taiwan is part of China. The U.S. government does not challenge that position. It reaffirms its interest in a peaceful settlement of the Taiwan question by the Chinese themselves."[99] Nixon also assured China's leaders that the United States would "support any peaceful resolution of the Taiwan issue that can be worked out" and would reduce its military presence in Taiwan "as progress is made on the peaceful resolution of the problem."[100] A similar formula was announced in conjunction with President Jimmy Carter's January 1979 communiqué, in which the United States formally recognized the PRC and withdrew recognition of the ROC, and "acknowledge[d] the

Chinese position that there is but one China and Taiwan is a part of China."[101]

Coupled with the cooperative thrust of the One China principle, there has always been in the policy of strategic ambiguity a deterrent threat pointed at Beijing. That is the repeated assertion of U.S. interest in the Taiwan question being resolved peacefully. With the 1972, 1978, and 1982 communiqués, and every other time the United States officially acknowledged the One China principle, it also affirmed the proviso of peaceful resolution. Kissinger, for one, worried that this would not be enough. If the United States recognized Taiwan as part of China, "our saying we want a peaceful solution has no force. It is Chinese territory. What are we going to do about it . . . For us to go to war with a recognized country . . . over a part of what we would recognize as their country would be preposterous."[102]

What compensated for this weakness was the 1979 Taiwan Relations Act (TRA). The TRA was passed by Congress after Carter normalized relations with China in 1978. The TRA said explicitly that the normalization of relations with the PRC was contingent on the "expectation that the future of Taiwan will be determined by peaceful means," and it established an informal U.S. diplomatic presence in Taiwan and vice versa. Additionally, the TRA went against the grain of the executive agreements by mandating a continuing U.S. commitment to sell arms of a "defensive character" to Taiwan and to maintain a posture "to resist any forms of coercion" that would threaten Taiwan's security. Although it fell well short of firmly committing the United States to defend Taiwan, it did declare that any attack on Taiwan would be seen as "a threat to the peace and security of the Western Pacific area and of grave concern to the U.S."[103]

During his first two years in office, President Ronald Reagan was forced to grapple with the contradictions inherent in the policy of strategic ambiguity.[104] The United States was eager to cultivate good relations with China in order to reinforce its renewed Cold War diplomacy against the USSR. China seized the leverage, and as the ten-year anniversary of the Shanghai communiqué approached, Beijing threatened to weaken cooperation with the United States if it did not take concrete steps to end military support for Taiwan. Reagan refused to set a date to cut off arms to Taiwan, but he did sign off on a joint communiqué in which the United States applauded China's fundamental policy to "striv[e] for a peaceful resolution of the Taiwan question" and pledged that it would not "seek to carry out a long term policy of arms sales to Taiwan," that its future sales would "not exceed" either in quality or quantity "the level of those supplied" since 1979, and, indeed, that the United States intended to "gradually reduce" those sales "over time."[105]

However, Reagan later qualified the agreement to mean that U.S. arms would be limited to what was needed to maintain the cross-Strait balance of military power. In tandem with the 1982 agreement, Reagan assured Tai-wan's President Chiang Ching-kuo (Chiang Kai-shek's son), that the United States would not consult with Beijing on U.S. arms to Taiwan, would not try to mediate between Beijing and Taipei, and would not press Taipei into negotiations with Beijing. Consequently, there was no real impact on the level of U.S. military aid to Taiwan. This did not go unnoticed in Beijing, but the outpouring of U.S. efforts to conciliate China in the 1980s (Most Favored Nation trading status, technology transfers, and security cooperation vis-à-vis Moscow) counterbalanced the negative repercussions, and the U.S.–Taiwan arms issue faded in political significance.[106]

In the early 1990s, however, U.S.–China relations took a downturn: The USSR had collapsed and thus reduced the incentive for Sino–U.S. cooperation, the Tiannanmen Square massacre had soured public support for China, and democratization in Taiwan spurred renewed U.S. favor toward Taipei. It was then that Taiwan began to move into the opportunity, undertaking serious efforts to undermine the One China policy, establish a Taiwan presence in the UN, and proceed toward independence. China reacted to these efforts with increasing belligerence and accused the United States of abetting Taiwan with military support and a de facto two-China policy. As the confrontation spiraled, the pivotal deterrence problem, always latent in U.S. China–Taiwan policy, would become immediate and pressing.[107]

Strategic Ambiguity after the Cold War

The crux of the pivotal deterrence problem in the 1990s was to deter China from attacking Taiwan and trying to force reunification, while preventing Taiwan from doing what was certain to trigger such an attack: declaring independence.[108] Much of the instability in cross-Strait relations during that decade was caused by (1) democratization in Taiwan that fueled a challenge to the One China principle and (2) a growing sense of U.S. support that undoubtedly encouraged this trend. When, in 1992, the Bush administration decided to sell F-16s to Taiwan, which were much superior to aircraft in its existing arsenal, this almost certainly spurred Taipei to reject the PRC's diplomatic efforts to begin reunification talks.[109] More broadly, throughout the early 1990s, both the Clinton administration and an increasingly pro-Taiwan Congress took steps to upgrade diplomatic and security ties between the United States and Taiwan, and it stands to reason that these, too, encouraged Taiwan's independence movement.[110]

But just as important as external forces was the domestic dynamic of "nationalist outbidding" between the ruling KMT and the Democratic Progressive Party (DPP) during the democratic transition.[111] In 1991, during the early phases of the transition to democracy, the DPP opposition called for independence and made that demand a part of its platform. As the DPP's domestic clout increased, the KMT moved toward independence rhetoric to avoid being outflanked. Although Lee Teng-hui, the KMT leader, had previously paid lip service to One China and reunification, he turned increasingly to the rhetoric of independence and launched a campaign of "pragmatic diplomacy" that sought to counteract China's efforts to undermine Taiwan's bilateral relations with other states and to gain a seat for Taiwan in the UN.[112] This domestic political dynamic became increasingly salient in the run up to legislative elections in December 1995 and, after that, in the campaigning for the first fully free presidential elections in March 1996.

Against this backdrop, missteps in U.S. policy fueled PRC fears that Taiwan, under U.S. cover, would lunge for independence. In January 1995, Beijing put forward an eight-point proposal for cross-Strait negotiations; President Lee replied in April with a six-point counterproposal, and the prospects looked good for momentum in "unofficial" cross-Strait negotiations.[113] Then, in May 1995, under pressure from Congress, Clinton reneged on earlier assurances to Beijing and gave Lee permission to visit the United States, a major victory in Lee's head-of-state "vacation" diplomacy.[114] This was the impetus behind China's decision to scuttle the unofficial negotiations, and, in July and August 1995, to conduct missile tests and military exercises in the Strait.[115] The purpose was to send a strong signal to both Taiwan and the United States that it would not tolerate Taiwan's bid for independence or a U.S. policy that underwrote it.[116]

In high-level contacts between the United States and China over the winter of 1995, the United States assured Beijing that it still embraced the One China principle and did not support Taiwan independence or UN membership. These assurances did not convince Beijing; there was little evidence that the United States was acting to curtail the momentum toward independence in Taiwan's approaching December elections. Beijing wanted concrete public commitments from the United States, not cheap talk. It did not get them. So in mid-November, just weeks before the elections, it staged large-scale military exercises in the Strait, with the declared purpose of thwarting Taiwan independence. The United States did not move to counteract Beijing's coercive diplomacy and, in fact, played down its significance. One reason for this passivity was the hope that it would focus minds in Taiwan on the dangers of flirting with independence.[117]

Between December 1995 and March 1996, the Clinton administration permitted a variety of high-level officials from Taiwan to enter the United States, which China interpreted as further evidence of U.S. collusion with Lee's agenda. Beijing then commenced its most provocative military exercises to date, which culminated in the March 8–18 series of missile tests in the Strait.[118] U.S. officials did not perceive this to be a mobilization for imminent war, but rather as a clear attempt to cow Taiwan voters in the midst of elections and to challenge the credibility of the U.S. position to ensure a peaceful resolution of the conflict.[119]

The United States answered the Chinese provocations with the deployment of two carrier battle groups to waters near the Taiwan Strait. Administration officials invoked the TRA, but were careful to avoid specifics relating to U.S. military responses to a Chinese move and to reassert the preeminent goal of a "peaceful resolution" to the problem.[120] On 23 March, Lee was elected with flying colors, but he did not follow up with a declaration of independence, and tensions began to wind down. Robert Ross argues that after the U.S. show of force in 1996, Beijing had to assume "that regardless of the source of a future crisis, including a formal Taiwan declaration of sovereign independence, the United States will almost certainly intervene militarily against Chinese use of force."[121] This may be an exaggeration, but even if true, it does not mean that the United States gave up on pivotal deterrence in 1996. For what is crucial is that Taiwan was not *also* encouraged to infer from U.S. actions an unconditional commitment. On that score, the Clinton administration was alive to the moral hazard problem and took steps within the traditional parameters of strategic ambiguity to restrike a balance between the ambitions of the two sides.

Indeed, on 18 March 1996, Assistant Secretary of Defense Joseph Nye observed that the United States did not want "to give Taiwan a 100 percent guarantee that no matter what Taiwan does, the Americans will come to their defense, because that would encourage Taiwan to take actions that would be risky."[122] At the end of March, with the annual decision on arms sales to Taiwan upon him, Clinton turned down much of what Taiwan had asked for. Next, Clinton curtailed the visits to the United States of Taiwan officials.[123] To the point, in May 1996, Secretary of State Warren Christopher stated, "[W]e have made clear our view that as Taiwan seeks an international role, it should [do so] in a way that is consistent with One China policy."[124] Thus, after the 1996 crisis, the Clinton administration moved to counteract the risks of moral hazard with Taiwan resulting from its forceful intervention in the Strait.

The administration had long been pushing a conciliatory policy of "engagement" toward China, and in the wake of the 1995–96 crises, it initiated a string of initiatives to improve relations with China. It also began to quietly edge Taiwan toward talks on an "interim" agreement with China, which Taiwan correctly perceived as a departure from Reagan's promise not to press Taiwan into negotiations with China.[125] Clinton's efforts came to full blossom in his first state visit to China in June 1998. In Shanghai, Clinton declared publicly that the United States did not "support independence for Taiwan; or Two Chinas; or one Taiwan and one China. And we don't believe Taiwan should be a member in any organization for which statehood is a requirement."[126] Many supporters of Taiwan argued that Clinton had thus thrown away strategic ambiguity to cultivate the "strategic partnership" with China. But this argument erroneously conflates constructive ambiguity with strategic ambiguity. There was nothing in Clinton's 1998 statement, or in the high-level U.S.–China summitry that followed, that shelved America's option to intervene militarily to ensure that the Taiwan question was resolved peacefully.

In the summer of 1999, with U.S.–China relations at a low ebb after the U.S. bombing of the Chinese embassy in Belgrade, Lee decided "to gamble" on the U.S. commitment and launched a new campaign for international recognition and to establish the principle that Taiwan and China are "two equal political entities."[127] A lame duck, Lee's sights were on positioning the KMT for victory in the 2000 elections. He publicly touted the "state-to-state" concept of China–Taiwan relations, and argued that Taiwan's constitution should be amended to reflect it.[128] This was followed by other indications that Taiwan had it in for the One China policy.[129] The PRC barked blistering new denunciations and threats, backed by the mobilization and exercise of forces on the Strait. Lee's new bid backfired. While the United States quietly warned China not to escalate, it strongly reaffirmed its support for One China.[130] This, coupled with Clinton's decisions to deny Taiwan's 1999 request for Aegis-equipped destroyers to counter China's growing missile threat and to approve, instead, a decidedly skimpy arms package, sent a tangible signal of restraint.[131] The public in Taiwan lost confidence in the KMT's diplomacy, and Lee quieted down as campaigning got underway for the election of his replacement.

China saw in Taiwan's March 2000 elections another dangerous opening for a sudden lurch toward independence. The KMT had gone far to establish its independence credentials, and its primary opponent, the DPP, had long called for independence in its platform. China again reverted to coercive diplomacy, aiming to frighten Taiwan voters into backing a candidate who did not espouse independence. The White House showed some appreciation of these fears when, in February, the President threatened to veto legislation passed by the House for a dramatic upgrade of U.S.–Taiwan security ties, warning that it would "create dangerous, false, and inaccurate expectations on both sides of the Taiwan Straits."[132] Later that month, Beijing released a "white paper" that threatened to use force against Taiwan if it "indefinitely delayed" on reunification through negotiations.[133]

This tough talk suggested that there was a growing willingness to take risks to compel unification. Traditionally, U.S. observers believed that while China would be cautious about trying to conquer Taiwan or otherwise compel unification, it would be bolder, and more willing to run high risks, to avoid losing ground on the issue; in other words, to preserve the status quo.[134] Now it seemed that China's leaders were reframing the issue, that *progress toward reunification* was the status quo that must be defended, even at high risk. If it was serious—not just bluster gauged to rise above Beijing's usual threats—then it warned of a dangerous evolution in China's strategic calculus.[135]

In March 2000, the DPP candidate, Chen Shui-bian, was elected President. His government reverted to a more cautious approach to cross-Strait relations, closer to the "median voter" position in Taiwan favoring cooperation with the mainland and the status quo over bold moves for independence.[136] Chen pledged: "I will not declare independence, I will not change the national title, I will not push forth the inclusion of the so-called 'state-to-state' description in the Constitution, and I will not promote a referendum to change the status quo in regards to the question of independence or unification."[137] He also tried to downplay the importance of the difference of views about the meaning of the One China principle, suggesting that the two sides "agreed to disagree" on the question.[138] Chen's reversion to a more low-key and moderate stance garnered a significantly more generous U.S. arms package for 2000 (~1.8 billion) compared to the year before (~$637 million).[139]

Scarce Alignment Options and Strategic Ambiguity in the 1990s

One of the things that allowed the United States to play the pivot successfully in the Taiwan Strait in the 1990s is that China and Taiwan did not have alignment options. To hedge against the United States intervening against a campaign to coerce unification, Beijing needed an alignment option that could block or sway the United States. This was simply not possible. As Ross noted in 1997, China had no "global superpower" ally "that can shield it in a conflict with the United States over Taiwan."[140] Likewise, Gerald Segal noted that China "is an ally to no one. No other supposedly great power is as bereft of friends."[141] The fact that such an ally was out of China's reach did much to enable U.S. pivotal deterrence in the Strait.[142] China, of course, did not stand still. Indeed, it tried to cultivate Russia as a "strategic partner" to balance against U.S. meddling in the Taiwan dispute.[143] But so far as the 1990s go, the Sino–Russian strategic partnership was tenuous at best.[144] Even if it were a more reliable option for China, Russia simply does not have—and for a long time to come, will not have—the military wherewithal to contest America's role of "king maker" in the Strait. In a Taiwan crisis involving U.S. military intervention, Russian support for China would not carry weight beyond the UN Security Council, where any action supporting a U.S. military response would be nullified by the PRC in any case.

For Taiwan to hedge against the risk of declaring independence and then being abandoned by the United States, it needed a potential ally strong enough to help it block a Chinese invasion or break a Chinese blockade. Given a regional inclination to balance against China, it would not be inconceivable for Taiwan to have cleared this hurdle. But in the 1990s there was no such inclination to be found. In particular, during the 1995–96 crises, when one would have most expected to see such tendencies, "Taiwan received no support from anyone in the region."[145] Japan's lethargy during the crises not only exposed glimmers of divergence between Washington and Tokyo, but more important, suggested that Japan could not be counted on to pick up slack dropped by the United States.[146] Another key regional player that was surprisingly idle during the crises was India, a state that, like Taiwan, feels considerably threatened by China.[147] This lack of support for Taiwan from the two key regional counterweights to China was another external pressure pushing Taiwan back toward a status quo policy at the end of the decade. The threat of military punishment by China was surely the most important cause of caution in Taipei. But the prospect of abandonment by United States added to this pressure, and the lack of regional powers to back up Taiwan if U.S. allegiance failed reinforced it.

Another way to think about Taiwan's dependence on the United States is to look at its external sources of arms. Here, as one analyst put it, "The U.S. is essentially the sole source of imported arms for Taiwan's military."[148] China's efforts to isolate Taiwan from other sources of Western military support took a real toll—eliminating Israel, Germany, and France as key suppliers. The effect was to put the United States "firmly in the middle" and further reinforce its leverage in the Strait.[149] If Taiwan could meet its most pressing defense needs indigenously, or if it could easily buy elsewhere the arms the United States refused to sell, Washington would get less influence from its sole source position. But Taiwan cannot for long fend for itself, and it cannot easily substitute for U.S. military aid. This too has given Washington leverage over Taipei in the context of crisis management.

To stress the importance of weak alignment options in supporting pivotal deterrence is not to deny the importance of military factors in the China–Taiwan balance that may also have favored peace. China was likely to be deterred from invading Taiwan by Taiwan's air superiority over the Strait and the difficulty of a cross-channel assault.[150] Taiwan was likely to be deterred from declaring independence by the fearsome consequences of a Chinese missile barrage on Taipei.[151] But neither side would be assessing these options in a vacuum: The question of what the United States would do in a crisis inevitably would intrude on both sides' calculations. For China, the utility of a whole array of military options, from "shows of force" to blockade to missile salvos to full-scale invasion, would differ vastly depending on the U.S. reaction. Whether, for example, the PRC would punish a move toward independence by Taiwan with conventional missile strikes, and the magnitude of damage it would dare to inflict, could be influenced by the quality of the U.S. commitment to defend Taiwan. And, whether or not a missile barrage would be too high a price for Taiwan to pay for provoking China would depend on whether the end result in political terms was utter isolation or U.S. recognition of Taiwan's independence and an airtight alliance. Thus U.S. policy could promote pivotal deterrence, in part, by reinforcing rather than occluding the dimensions of the regional balance that favored deterrence of both sides. And, the fact that there was no significant outside interference from countries other than the United States facilitated this outcome.

The Bush Administration and the Persistence of Strategic Ambiguity

When the Bush administration took over in January 2001, there was reason to believe that the U.S. policy of strategic ambiguity would be replaced by a much firmer security tie to Taiwan. Many who became senior foreign policy officials in the new administration—e.g., Paul Wolfowitz, who would become undersecretary of defense, and Richard Armitage, who would become undersecretary of state—had in the 1990s railed against strategic ambiguity and called for an "unequivocal" tight alliance with Taiwan. In their view, strategic ambiguity encouraged China, the aggressor, and discouraged Taiwan, the victim, and was therefore doubly destabilizing.[152] Their argument carried implications not just for avoiding Strait crises but also for *improving* China–Taiwan relations. China and Taiwan, they argued, *both* became more intransigent when they sensed weakness in America's Taiwan commitment, and, as Wolfowitz put it, "Taiwan-PRC relations improve when Taiwan . . . feels secure in its reliance on America."[153]

Moreover, Bush indicated early on that he was through "engaging" China as a "strategic partner"; now the United States would approach China as a "strategic competitor." Two issues quickly threw the question of future U.S.–China relations in stark relief. The first was anticipated: the annual decision in April 2001 on Taiwan's arms package. Taiwan was lobbying hard for a deal that included, among other things, Aegis-equipped destroyers and a corresponding commitment to include Taiwan in a U.S. Theater Missile Defense system. Any U.S. decision to provide more arms to Taiwan would call forth the usual denunciations from China, but if the United States signed off on all of Taiwan's requests, then it would be certain to signal a dramatic new tilt toward Taipei. What was unexpected was the crisis with China in early April over the downed U.S. spy plane. The unfortunate concatenation of these two things forced the issue of whether Bush would now depart from strategic ambiguity and the underlying premise of pivotal deterrence.

Bush's 25 April decision on arms to Taiwan seemed to signal a continuation more than a reversal of the balanced approach of strategic ambiguity.

The United States agreed to sell Taiwan four decommissioned "Kidd Class" destroyers rather than the more advanced Aegis-equipped destroyers, twelve P-3 antisubmarine aircraft, eight diesel submarines, and a variety of other systems and to increase cooperation in defense planning.[154] In addition to turning down Taiwan's request for Aegis ships, Washington also nixed the sale of JDAM (air-to-air), HARM (air-to-ground), and PAC-3 (ground-to-air) missile systems.[155] Bush also announced that he would end the annual review cycle of Taiwan's defense requirements that became institutionalized in the early 1980s in the wake of the TRA and would instead make decisions to sell arms to Taiwan on a routine "as-needed basis." Because the annual controversy surrounding the reviews allowed Taiwan's formidable lobbying apparatus to bring great congressional pressure to bear on the President, doing away with the annual review would give him more flexibility to work around the TRA. In other words, it would enhance the executive freedom of action that makes pivotal deterrence through strategic ambiguity possible.[156]

But if the message was that the United States would continue with a policy of strategic ambiguity, the message was contradicted in a televised Bush statement on 25 April. China, he said, "needs to understand" that the United States would do "whatever it took . . . to help Taiwan defend itself" against attack by China.[157] This seemed to presage a decisive departure from strategic ambiguity. In the wake of this statement, therefore, what was truly surprising was the rapidity with which the Bush administration backtracked. Just a few hours after Bush's televised comments, the State Department announced that the United States would continue to adhere to the One China policy of the previous five administrations.

In the coming year, nevertheless, the United States moved fast to improve Taiwan's defense capabilities, through new arms sales and stronger U.S.–Taiwan military-to-military contacts. In late April 2002, in the flush of these improving ties, an unnamed State Department official said, "Taiwan is not looked at as a problem anymore," while another senior administration official (again, anonymous) asserted, "our ambiguity on Taiwan has become less ambiguous."[158] Then, on 23 May, President Chen stated on CNN that "Taiwan is an independent sovereign state . . . and my country is not a part of the People's Republic of China" and declared his intention to visit Washington in the future—something the PRC has said would be an extreme provocation.[159] One week later, the Bush administration came out fully on the record. Confessing that he did not wish to make U.S. policy "any muddier," Wolfowitz stated before a press conference: "We're opposed to Taiwan independence . . . we support a 'one China' policy; that means we do not support independence for Taiwan." Wolfowitz carefully coupled this statement with the warning to China that "we oppose strongly any attempt to settle the issue by force." But the language directed at Tai-

wan ("the U.S. is opposed to") was even tougher than the Clinton administration's Shanghai formulation, which was that it did "not support" independence for Taiwan. Ironically, when Clinton used the "do not support"
language, conservatives rushed to condemn the administration for under-
cutting Taiwan. Now in office, they had taken U.S. opposition to Taiwan independence to a new level.[160]

Thus, in the Bush administration's first two years in office, the tension in
U.S. policy between maintaining good relations with the PRC and support
for One China, on the one hand, and fidelity to Taiwan on the other, was reinforced not abolished. At bottom there remained an obstinate truth—because the United States does not support Taiwan's most ambitious aims, it
is not fully committed to defending Taiwan against China. It needed to
deter both sides from provoking a war that, regardless of who started it,
would gravely damage U.S. interests.

The Future of Pivotal Deterrence in the Taiwan Strait: Ambiguity or Clarity?

Is pivotal deterrence through strategic ambiguity still viable, and, if so,
how long can it last? Both detractors and supporters of strategic ambiguity
hold out hope that more peaceful relations between China and Taiwan, and
perhaps even reunification, will follow from democratization in China.[161]
The problem is that in the *process* of liberalization and the *transition* to democracy, states usually veer toward nationalism and risk taking in foreign
policy.[162] This is a particularly nasty problem with states that are "late de-
velopers" with weak civil societies—like China.[163] Thus between now and
the long-term promise of peace between mature democracies in Beijing and
Taipei there stands an enormous problem—that of getting there from here.
When China begins to democratize, it will in all likelihood become much
less patient and prudent about Taiwan, and the United States will have to
take much stronger measures—both politically and militarily—to deter it.
This, in turn, will require stronger offsetting measures to restrain Taiwan,
where the ruling DPP still maintains that Taiwan is "already a sovereign
and independent country" and will not renounce the option to formally
declare itself as such, if only to maintain its bargaining power in cross-
Strait negotiations.[164] Which raises a crucial question about the future of
U.S. China–Taiwan policy: Is pivotal deterrence through strategic clarity
possible?

What is at issue here is not a departure from pivotal deterrence. The
question is whether it is possible, or desirable, to unambiguously deter
both sides. After the crises of 1996, calls for "strategic" or "diplomatic" clarity became more frequent. The United States, it was argued, was in danger
of encouraging adventurism from both sides and should therefore declare
its political aims more crisply.[165] Nye, for example, proposed that the

United States "state plainly that our policy is 'one China' and 'no use of force' . . . that if Taiwan were to declare independence, we would not recognize or defend it . . . [and] that we would not accept the use of force [by China]."[166] In a more pointed and cogent formula, Thomas Christensen urges the United States to make a "clear but conditional commitment to Taiwan's security," to tell it "in no uncertain terms that Americans will not fight and die to defend a Taiwan that declares constitutional independence from the Chinese nation. At the same time, America should warn the mainland that a military attack on a Taiwan that is still legally Chinese will meet with a U.S. military response."[167]

As sensible—and simple—as these proposals for clarity sound, they have their weaknesses. One of their key assumptions is that strategic ambiguity is dangerous because it will encourage the two sides to take risks and "inadvertently" blunder into war.[168] Accordingly, the way to make sure that China and Taiwan do not do this is to declare unequivocally the redlines that will trigger a punishing U.S. response. A rebuttal to this view is that if China and Taiwan cannot pin down those lines in advance, but know that crossing them could mean catastrophe, they will be cautious about approaching them at all. If policy follows the prescription of strategic clarity, and clearly sets forth the redlines, it will invite from both sides the maximum degree of pressure and political maneuvering possible, within those thresholds.[169] This two-way brinkmanship is likely to trigger an accidental war.

On this central point, however, both the advocates and opponents of strategic clarity overlook a basic truth. Not even a clearly stated conditional policy will resolve the ambiguity that stems from the tension between the two vectors of U.S. interests that motivate pivotal deterrence in the first place, nor will it dispense with questions about how those interests will be prioritized in a given situation. Key here is the question: What will the United States do in a "fuzzy" crisis, where both sides transgress essentially in tandem, where both sides, with some justice, can be blamed for drawing first blood? What costs will it impose then, and how will it distribute them? Because even a policy of strategic clarity must be silent about this probable crisis scenario, the deeper cause of strategic ambiguity is not merely vaguely articulated policy goals but the tension between them, and this will not go away. The advocates of strategic clarity exaggerate the problem of dual "misperception," suggesting that both China and Taiwan fail to understand what are the two key aims of U.S. policy.[170] The critics of strategic clarity, on the other hand, who worry that both sides will rush to the redlines, exaggerate the degree to which concise declarations can dispense with the ambiguity that inheres in any pivotal deterrence policy.

Nevertheless, setting forth explicitly that the United States will not fight for Taiwan if, free of military coercion by China, it formally declares independence, may, as Christensen argues, ease Beijing's fears "of a closing window of vulnerability on Taiwan independence" that might push it to aggress unnecessarily.[171] The critical assumption here is that China's intentions to attack Taiwan are motivated less by greed than by "Beijing's fear of eventual Taiwanese independence with U.S. backing." Hence, allaying those fears would dampen what "seems the most likely cause of war across the Taiwan Strait."[172] Although it is likely that both greed and fear coexist in China's designs on Taiwan, Christensen is right to stress that a properly conceived policy of strategic clarity could help to assuage China's fears, without weakening deterrence.[173]

Which raises the fundamental question, whether the structural conditions exist to make feasible a shift from strategic ambiguity to pivotal deterrence based on clarity. Here alignment options matter. It is safe to assume that after the United States clearly sets forth the conditions of its commitment to defend Taiwan, both China and Taiwan will begin to work harder to diversify, to reduce U.S. leverage by cultivating alignment options to hedge against U.S. action under those conditions. On this score, there is reason to be cautiously optimistic about the prospects for strategic clarity. The last decade has shown that both sides confront a dearth of options, and it is hard to see any real competitors to U.S. preponderance in the region in the coming decades. Assuming that a domestic consensus on the postulates of strategic clarity can be formed in the United States, admittedly a big assumption, it could very well work in the Taiwan Strait in the years ahead.

Conclusion:

THE PROSPECTS FOR PIVOTAL
DETERRENCE IN U.S. FOREIGN
POLICY

Wafting from isolation to world supremacy, the United States has never comfortably occupied the intermediate ground of international relations, in which there is no white or black, only many different shades of gray.
              Robert Skidelsky, *Foreign Policy,* March/April 2002

Pivotal deterrence is one of many security policies available to states that occupy a pivotal position. Saying that a state is in a pivotal position does not reveal the goals that it will pursue. Rather, it describes a structure of power among three actors or groups of actors, a three-way bargaining situation with two key features. First, the actor playing the pivot has some flexibility to align with either of the other two, or stand aloof, if they go to war. Second, by choosing one of those options, the pivot can significantly influence the outcome. The pivot's relative capabilities are obviously important here, but to a large degree they are *subsumed* in the definition of the situation as a pivotal one. So the key insight of this heuristic goes beyond static "hard power" relationships, directing our attention to the degree and exercise of influence over others that flows from unique features of the bargaining context.

A policy of pivotal deterrence aims to harness the power of a pivotal position for a particular purpose—to prevent war between adversaries whose animosity makes playing the pivot possible. All of the major and minor cases in this book demonstrate that pivotal states—with widely different shares of relative power—have used their pivotal position to serve that end. In the 1870s, for example, Bismarck, who did not shy away from aggression in other circumstances, played the pivot to promote peace rather than war between Austria and Russia. During the Cold War, and after, the United States struggled to achieve similar ends among its friends and allies, Greece, Turkey, India, and Pakistan. It has also worked to maintain a similar equipoise between China and Taiwan.

For defensive realists, who maintain that states usually have status quo inclinations, this sounds like par for the course. Conversely, this may appear to pose a problem for offensive realists, who hold that states are not merely content to uphold the status quo, but rather seek to increase their power position whenever possible.[1] This contradiction between our findings and offensive realism is more apparent than real. Pivotal deterrence can be a useful policy for even the most aggressive states. For it is often the case that in order to marshal their forces to pursue gains in one area, states strive to promote stability in others.[2] Although the affinities between pivotal deterrence and defensive realism are obvious, that states sometimes pursue it neither strikes a blow for defensive over offensive realism nor exposes a significant point of controversy between them. Pivotal deterrence may figure in a revisionist or status quo grand strategy, depending on circumstances that are extraneous, and irrelevant, to the model. The thrust of this research abrades the simplistic assumptions on both sides of the debate. Most states have a mixed bag of preferences: They play defense and offense at the same time, seeking to preserve the status quo in some situations and to upend it in others.[3]

ISOLATION AVOIDANCE BEHAVIOR

A basic axiom of diplomacy is that one should strive to increase the number of one's friends and to decrease the number of one's enemies. In pivotal deterrence, the aim is to prevent war between adversaries by creating a situation in which that rule alone will lead them to be more cautious and make compromises that they otherwise would not. Isolation avoidance is thus the mainspring of our explanation for how pivotal deterrence policies prevent war. Two peace-causing mechanisms flow from it.

The first is caution induced by fears of losing the pivot's support or provoking its opposition; that is, the uncertainty effect. The various contours of this dynamic were crystallized in the three models presented in Chapter 1 and demonstrated in many of our cases. Austria and Russia, for example, showed such caution in the Eastern Crisis when (to no avail) they appealed to Germany for support before taking steps that would result in a war between them. In the 1964 Cyprus crisis, Turkey showed similar caution, deciding not to invade without strong U.S. backing. Similarly, in the 1990s Taiwan was at least partly deterred from more strident moves toward independence by its doubts about U.S. support in the face of China's reaction.

[203]

The second is the ingratiation effect, which turns the adversaries' efforts to win the pivot's support or neutrality into concessions. Because Austria's and Russia's appeals for German allegiance in the 1870s were not granted, they were impelled to work out a series of mutually acceptable compromises that kept them from fighting in the Eastern Crisis. In its efforts to secure British allegiance in the July 1914 crisis, France tried (but failed) to restrain Russia's full mobilization. Germany, in order to improve the fading chance of British neutrality, took steps at the end of July to pressure Austria into making concessions acceptable to London. In the November 1967 Cyprus crisis, the United States extracted concessions from both sides—albeit the most far-reaching ones from Greece—by warning them that to appear uncooperative while the other made compromises could cost them U.S. support. Similarly, in the 1996 Imia crisis, braced by the cold chill of potential isolation, Greece and Turkey recoiled from their mutual determination to forcefully assert sovereignty over the island. A number of times in the last decade, Pakistan scaled back its support for insurgency in Kashmir when confronted with the prospect that failing to do so risked damaging relations with the United States and driving it fully into India's quarter. Taiwan, in a similar fashion, has toned down its provocative independence agenda at a number of points in recent years (especially in 2000), owing partly to fears that not doing so would jeopardize U.S. support.

While concessions like these are often tactical and mercurial—that is, they do not indicate a willingness to concede the core issues in conflict—such concessions, nevertheless, can mean the difference between war and peace when tensions run high. From the perspective of a pivotal deterrer, frustrating the ambitions of the adversaries will often suffice to meet its main goals, which may have little to do with the substance of the dispute and much to do with whether it is manifest in hot war or cold peace.

Nevertheless, pressuring adversaries to avoid isolation can have its drawbacks, most notably in the "blame game." As the saying goes, "if you can't make yourself look good, make the other guy look bad." This less salutary aspect of isolation avoidance emerged in the case studies. It is likely to arise when one or both sides believe that they can determine the pivot's attitude, not by showing moderation and willingness to compromise but instead by manipulating aspects of the situation in ways that cast the other side in a bad light.

In the more benign forms, this involves what Galbraith called "a maneuver for position to see who will be blamed or not blamed" for the breakdown of negotiations. When Austro-Russian talks over a response to the Slav revolt foundered in 1876, Gorchakov asked Bismarck to corner Austria, so that Russia could have a free hand against Turkey. His main contention was that Russia, in the spirit of the *Dreikaiserbund*, was offering concessions, while Austria spurned them.

[204]

The stakes get much higher when one adversary tries to bait the other side into escalating in a way that triggers punishment from the pivot. In the July crisis, German leaders strove to ensure that Russia mobilized first and thus looked like the aggressor, not only to ensure domestic unity but also in the belief that putting Russia in the wrong might lead Britain to abandon the ententes. Similarly, in the 1965 Kashmir war it appears that Pakistan tailored its escalation in a way that tempted India to commit "aggression" across international boundaries so that Pakistan could cash in on the U.S. alliance or, failing that, induce the United States to sever military support to India.

It is worth stressing that such efforts to put the other side in the wrong are a *normal* consequence of a pivotal deterrence policy, not an anomaly. Indeed, blame-game behavior in a pivotal deterrence scenario gives added support for the inner logic of our theory. If the adversaries harbored no doubts about the pivot's attitude, or if its attitude were irrelevant to the outcome of their conflict, we would be less likely to see such behavior. Indeed, it would be puzzling if in the presence of a powerful pivot, this sort of behavior *did not* appear. Common sense suggests an important extension of the logic: The more powerful a pivotal deterrer is, the more compelling will be the adversaries' incentives to put each other in the wrong. Beyond this, however, we would like to know whether there are other general conditions that influence the extent to which blame-game tactics prevail over more beneficial aspects of isolation avoidance. The research embodied in this book does not offer answers. That question thus represents an important line of further inquiry.

ALIGNMENT OPTIONS

Pivotal deterrence is a power play on the rampant ambiguity and complexity of international politics. For that reason, no master key can explain the outcomes of such policies, all in the same way. That said, each of the four major cases (Chapters 3 through 6) evinced the necessary conditions and essential bargaining relationship of pivotal deterrence. Bargaining is what makes the alignment options hypothesis such a natural and powerful explanation for why some pivotal deterrence policies fail. The hypothesis makes the model both *strategic* and *contingent*. It helps to explain why adversaries sometimes respond to a pivotal deterrence policy in ways that make it work, and other times respond in ways that make it fail.

The connection between one's leverage over others and their access to alternatives shapes international politics (and many other areas of life). Alignment options cause pivotal deterrence to fail in ways that directly negate the conditions that make it work when the adversaries do not have them. Just as making sacrifices to sustain relations with a key supplier makes good sense when reliable alternatives are scarce, hedging across options, and playing them off each other, makes sense when suppliers are plentiful. We should not be surprised to find that when their dependence on a pivot exposes them to unwanted pressure, adversaries diversify if they can.

This was an important reason that Britain first pursued the ententes with France and Russia. The goal was to reduce its dependence on German support in colonial disputes with those powers. This was also the spirit behind Turkey's decision to improve relations with Moscow after the 1964 "Johnson letter." Better relations with the Soviets garnered Turkey more, rather than less, support from the United States on Cyprus. With Moscow angling for détente with Turkey, the United States did not want to give Ankara more reasons to wander in its loyalties. And that is why, in the 1967 crisis, the United States leaned harder on Greece than Turkey.

The damaging affects of alignment options on pivotal deterrence were most starkly displayed in the case of India and Pakistan in the 1960s. That case showed how bidding wars can arise when adversaries have attractive alignment options. This dynamic occurs when the adversaries turn the tables on the pivot and make it compete with others who also offer support. With its leverage thus diminished, the pivot cannot extract from the adversaries concessions that will reduce the likelihood of war, and, in the midst of a crisis, its threats to withhold benefits will carry much less weight. Both India and Pakistan had attractive alignment options in the 1960s, which nullified America's pivotal deterrence strategy. The extraordinary leverage that seemed to follow from Washington's central position as a purveyor of arms and security guarantees to both sides proved illusory. Once Soviet largesse came through for Delhi, the United States had to ante up just to stay in the game, and its efforts to extract Kashmir concessions from India were thwarted. By the same token, Pakistan's warming relations with China (catalyzed by U.S. arming of India) meant that the United States was caught in a bidding war on that front as well. Hence, the United States could not extract Kashmir concessions from either side, and, ultimately, the prospect of losing U.S. support was not enough to deter Pakistan from going to war or India from retaliating across international borders.

The two major cases in which the negative effects of alignment options were most pronounced—the July crisis and India-Pakistan in the 1960s—occurred in conditions of rough multipolarity. The power structure in Europe before World War I is a paradigm of multipolarity. But even within the overarching bipolarity of the Cold War, the United States shared the stage in South Asia not just with Moscow but with Beijing as well. A reasonable extension of both the core theory and the alignment options hypothesis would be that pivotal deterrence by a great power is more likely to fail in multipolar systems than in more concentrated constellations of power. Put differently, it would appear that pivotal deterrence is most likely to succeed when the pivot is preponderant not just over the adversaries but over the international system writ large.

This would suggest that today the prospects for U.S. pivotal deterrence have improved with its ascent to unipolar preponderance. The Kosovo crisis (see Chapter 7), in which Russia's role as an alignment option to Serbia frustrated NATO's pivotal policy, should at least cause us to be cautious about taking this line of argument too far. But it still stands to reason that if other great powers are unable to compete with the United States for influence in regional disputes, there will be little to insulate local adversaries from the pressures to avoid being cornered or abandoned by the United States. This should bode well for U.S. pivotal deterrence in a unipolar world. We will expand on this line of argument, and a battery of objections to it, more fully below.

UNIPOLAR PREPONDERANCE AND U.S. PIVOTAL DETERRENCE

Public debates over U.S. policy toward regional conflicts in the Balkans, South Asia, the Middle East, and elsewhere do not always elucidate the pivotal deterrence problems involved. From an "objective" standpoint, the United States may have an interest in preventing war in a given conflict, without firmly choosing sides. But the scrutiny given to such conflicts in the public sphere will be dominated by those who do not see it that way, vocal advocates who strongly favor one side or the other. There is a great deal of difference between the ambiguity and tactical shiftiness of pivotal deterrence, and the clarity (moral and otherwise) of the policies they propound and crave. Compounding the problem of portraying such conflicts in Manichean terms is the tendency to frame the options for responding to them in "in-or-out" terms. In this way of thinking, the United States must either step "in" to deter or suppress a conflict or stay "out," which is tantamount to abdicating any peace-promoting role. It is not easy to shake free of such sterile categories and think through the implications of pivotal deterrence theory for current U.S. foreign policy. But doing so yields fresh insights into the challenges of managing conflicts that today confront us.

The United States today is a preponderant power, not merely in any conceivable triad but also in a systemic sense.[4] In 1944, William Fox defined the "super-powers" (the United States, Britain, and the Soviet Union) as the most important allies in the system, the ones that no one else could afford to ignore.[5] Today this description holds only for the United States. On the most critical dimensions of "hard" (material) and "soft" (ideological) power, the United States overshadows all others. In many respects, this suggests promising prospects for U.S. pivotal deterrence in the coming years. Because of its strength in many dimensions of power, the United States should have many points of leverage and be better able to offset pressures against one side in a conflict with restraints on the other. Furthermore, in many conflicts, other bystanders may simply lack the wherewithal to influence events without enlisting U.S. support or coordinating their efforts with it. Thus, pivotal deterrence may be easier for the United States both because it commands many sources of leverage and because alignment options for the adversaries will be hard to come by.

Nevertheless, powers that are unable to compete with the United States globally will still contest it in areas that are vital to them, when the thrust of U.S. policy disregards their interests.[6] China, for example, cannot remain indifferent to the character of U.S. involvement in Indo-Pak relations or to the security competition between North and South Korea. Preponderance, as Fox noted, does not "provide an escape from power politics," and it will not, therefore, mean an open field in most regional conflicts of concern to the United States.[7] Yet, if it does not banish the alignment options problem, it may still be true that preponderance will allow the United States to artificially "induce" the isolation of the adversaries in a given conflict. In blunt terms, Washington may be better able to "buy off" the adversaries' alignment options by promising to reward them for noninterference or to "blackmail" them with threats to punish them if they do interfere. If the situation is such that the threat of direct U.S. opposition is needed to keep the adversaries at peace, then forcing their alignment options out of the equation will increase their exposure and attentiveness to the threat of U.S. punishment. If the situation is less dire and the adversaries are unwilling to risk war *without* outside backers, the United States may also deter them by freezing out their alignment options, even it is itself unlikely to intervene directly.

Thus, to play the pivot in a unipolar world will, almost inevitably, require a multilateral approach. The ability to "go it alone" may or may not be useful for prodding other interested powers to go along or get out of the way. But as a formula for pivotal deterrence in today's world, it cannot but fail. Executing pivotal deterrence in a unipolar world will require considerable diplomatic acumen and entanglement, and that is even before one gets to dealing with the internal dynamics of the conflict itself.

It is illusory to think that the United States can achieve the detachment of a "regulator" of international security—objectively imparting stability— free of its own parochial stakes and prejudices. However preponderant, it shall not remain aloof from the jostling of others for international influence and advantage. Although this could change sooner than we think, the main lines of that competition do not yet involve a well organized and mobilized effort to balance against the United States. Rather, the struggle is over who will benefit from and who will suffer by its power.[8] Particularly when it comes to the antagonists in a regional conflict, much of this involves maneuvering to garner U.S. support or to deflect its anger. Why they want to woo America cannot be divorced from what they want to take from, or fear losing to, each other.

Forward Engagement, Global Leadership, and U.S. Pivotal Deterrence

As the preponderant power in a globalized and interdependent world, the United States—so we are told—must embrace "forward engagement" and "global leadership." Depending on one's preferred partisan formula, it must either "address problems early before they become crises," or "shape circumstances before crises emerge."[9] In these slogans there is a strong whiff of an enduring nostrum. As an early twentieth century writer put it, "the secret of foreign policy" is that "a nation cannot be merely passive . . . a nation should in every line take the most vigorous initiative."[10] Or, as President George W. Bush put it in September 2002, "In the world that we have entered, the only path to peace and security is the path of action."[11]

Those who trumpet such an activist posture tend only to see peaceful consequences resulting from forward engagement. For them "American power is now the linchpin of stability in every region, from Europe to Asia to the Persian Gulf to Latin America."[12] They rarely concede that the strong prospect of U.S. involvement in regional conflicts may not always cause stability but instead cause instability. But the incentives (if not the underlying motives) that lead some to aggress will often be shaped by optimism about outside involvement.[13] We should not assume that the forces of globalization that justify U.S. activism and incline the international community toward intervention do not also play into the strategies of regional adversaries. It is naïve to think that they, with survival at stake, do not gird for war keenly aware of the opportunities as well as dangers posed by intervention by the United States or other outside actors.

There is thus no reason to assume that forward U.S. engagement will reinforce regional stability and promote peaceful change. Because the United States may significantly influence the outcome of many conflicts, that potential must be seen for what it is; something that, by looming so large, may encourage as well discourage revisionism. If the massive risks of running afoul of U.S. power are a deterrent "shaping" the intentions of some regional antagonists, the potential windfall of securing U.S. support will shape the intentions of others. Because the benefits of enlisting U.S. support in a war may be enormous, even the slim chance of doing so may goad a party to act provocatively, become inflexible in negotiations, or otherwise do things that make war likely. In sum, forward U.S. engagement may fuel disintegrative as well as integrative tendencies in world politics and "jiggle loose" as many deadly conflicts as it knits back together.

In this light, it is important to grasp the potential to deter some revisionists through restraint, noncommitment, and the preservation of freedom of action and the danger of emboldening others by applying the simplistic prescriptions of traditional deterrence theory—that is, by defining one's role in their conflict early, clearly, and forcefully. Statesmen have long appreciated the utility of calculated inaction in preventing war as well as achieving other goals. But when it comes to thinking about deterrence, it has often been narrowly conceived as something requiring "positive" action. This is frequently the case for policy makers caught in situations where they risk losing traction over events and must "do something" that will make others take them more seriously. In relation to distant conflicts, the answer will often be to use such commitment mechanisms as declaratory threats to intervene and shows of force in order to generate political momentum for their diplomacy.

Students of strategic theory have less excuse for limiting their conception of deterrence techniques to such assertive measures. By doing so, the theoretical range of deterrence theory is unduly circumscribed, and, more important, our understanding of the variety of deterrence techniques available to (and sometimes used by) policy makers is impoverished. David Baldwin has stressed that "doing nothing" is often an efficient foreign policy choice because the costs of other feasible options are too high.[14] More to the point here, in certain contexts, it may also be true that doing nothing is the most *effective* and influential response.[15] By not committing to intervene or otherwise influence the outcome of a conflict prematurely, a country may deter those who would be more likely to run risks if it did commit. A country may also deter escalation, and impel compromise, by informing a potential belligerent (usually in private) that it will "do nothing" to rescue or aid them if they go recklessly into war. This was an ingredient in Bismarck's efforts to prevent war between Austria and Russia in the 1870s, in U.S. diplomacy in the 1960s Cyprus crises, and in its efforts to defuse the South Asia crisis of 1990 and the Aegean crisis of 1996.

To sum up, pivotal deterrence may not be easy for the United States in a unipolar world precisely because it harbors so much potential control over the fate of others. To exercise such influence effectively requires a facility for both exertion and repose. And while the necessity for repose increases as power does, so too do the temptations to "do something." For the United States to achieve pivotal deterrence in many contexts today will require that which does not come naturally to preponderance—restraint. In many pressing debates over the U.S. role abroad, however, to suggest inaction as a policy option is to invite scornful accusations of "isolationism" and a flagging faith in U.S. leadership in world affairs. These canards must be rebuffed. What is at issue is not whether the United States must play a role in deterring wars that threaten its widespread interests but rather a serious consideration of the variety of ways that it may do so.

Preponderance, Pivotal Deterrence, and Strategic Clarity

Many are uneasy with the ambiguity, equivocation, and temporizing of pivotal deterrence, which run counter to two important trends in current thinking about international relations. More narrowly, they clash with a key postulate of mainstream coercion theory, which stresses that clarity is *the* necessary antidote to the danger that those you wish to compel or deter may doubt your resolve, or miscalculate or think wishfully about your intentions. More broadly, they jibe poorly with the basic thrust of much international relations theorizing, which points to the benefits for decision making of transparency and full information.[16] Thus, it is not surprising that many who advocate deterring conflicts end up stressing, in one way or another, the need to eliminate ambiguity, to reduce uncertainty, and to offer credible commitments in order to create peace.

As we saw in Chapter 7, this is an important line of argument in the debate over the U.S. policy toward the Taiwan Strait. Such calls for highly specific and clearly contingent pivotal commitments are not limited, however, to that conflict. For example, a former U.S. national security advisor recently argued that, in relation to India and Pakistan, "the United States must . . . be prepared to make commitments to both countries concerning how we would respond to a threat of conflict between them."[17] Similarly, a former special Cyprus coordinator at the State Department has argued that a "cardinal requirement" for ending Greek-Turkish hostility is that the United States take more "forthright positions" that "force the parties to recognize that they will not win decisive U.S. support for certain of their positions" and make "clear what both sides have to do to enjoy continued American support."[18]

Here, then, we come up against a fundamental puzzle of pivotal deterrence: If there is truly a need to impose restraint on both sides in a conflict, why all the elusiveness and equivocation? Why cloak your intentions, and retain your freedom of action, when you can declare up front what actions you will take and what costs you will impose if either or both sides transgress? This study has helped to crystallize the problem, but it has not resolved it. Nevertheless, here I will give three reasons why, for a unipolar power like the United States, strategic clarity in pivotal deterrence is easier to prescribe than to actually create.

First, as I explained in Chapter 2, a potent pivotal posture is hard for a preponderant power to sustain in conflicts of secondary interest. At the most fundamental level, this is because the outcome of such a war will not directly menace its vital interests. Because it will remain preponderant and relatively secure regardless of who wins, it will be hard-pressed to convey to the adversaries the strength of its motivation to prevent war. Firm one-sided alliances are the key method by which states demonstrate (and generate) such a motivation in areas where their intrinsic interests are otherwise weak. Reputational concerns—the fear that failing to stand behind commitments in one place will undermine the credibility of commitments in others—do not do all the work here. More important are "system effects" that, as a consequence of a state's commitments, lead others to react in ways that erect more substantial barriers to its reneging on them later.[19] In this light, making starkly defined and offsetting deterrence threats, which signal contradictory allegiances, will not carry the same systemic consequences for locking-in commitment. Doing this will beg rather than answer the question of your commitment. What it amounts to, in other words, is a more *formal* expression of the pivot's equivocal loyalties; a more *concise* declaration that it remains undecided about how it will respond in the event of war and is therefore keeping its options open. In this broad sense, greater clarity is unlikely to eliminate strategic ambiguity in pivotal deterrence.

Let us get to the kernel of the problem. Formalized pivotal deterrence commitments embody the genetic threat-formula of collective security. Whichever side is deemed the "aggressor," so the logic goes, must face both its victim's resistance and the pivot's punishment. As in all collective security schemes, the hitch here is politics. Even in theory, it is often hard to determine "objectively" just who is the aggressor—the one that attacks first, or the one that provoked it? In the real world, it will come down to a subjective political judgment by the one that must mete out the punishment. In making that judgment, a pivotal state will weigh not only the "facts" of the conflict but also its wider interests in relation to the adversaries, other actors, and other goals. If in light of those factors, it is expedient for the pivot not to retaliate against one side, it may very well decide to blame the other side, regardless of who "started it." Even if it does not behave so cynically, it may decide that although one side is clearly to blame, it will respond only with cosmetic sanctions. Or it may decide that it is best to blame both, and wash its hands of the matter. When a weighty pivotal response hangs on the question of who is to blame for starting or escalating a war, the pivot will reserve unto itself the right to make that determination as it sees fit in the circumstances at hand. Its prior declarations on the matter may help it to navigate and justify the path it has chosen, but they will not constrain it to punish a side that it otherwise would not. The adversaries are likely to know—or at least suspect—this, and for that reason, are unlikely to find a clarified pivotal policy much more edifying than an intentionally ambiguous one.

To this intrinsic problem we may add one that seems uniquely to curse the preponderant power. It is hard enough for any country to convince another that it will stand behind its commitments. But what is a preponderant power to do when its very mightiness means that it can break promises with little to fear by way of consequences?[20] Reputation, again, is a slender reed to lean on. If the things a preponderant power can impart or withhold are important enough to others, its reputation for unreliability is unlikely to dissuade them from striking bargains with it in the future—especially if they have no choice. As should be clear by now, a pivotal policy is by nature a rickety contraption. Let us assume, however, an ideal scenario in which the adversaries are utterly bereft of alignment options. And let us grant that one can make the policy sturdier by declaring, perhaps even setting down in print, clearly contingent two-way threats. The problem remains—such commitments will be the least credible when coming from a grossly preponderant power, like the United States today.

So far, we have explored the implications of unipolar power, and the built-in ambiguity of a pivotal policy, for the prospects of strategic clarity in pivotal deterrence. What remains, then, is to consider the natural inclinations of most political leaders. Pivotal deterrence is a bargaining situation. It may have its three-way peculiarities, but it does not differ from other such situations in a very important way. To whit: if you want to get what you want, it is better to not fully or prematurely divulge your bottom line to the other bargainers. As Ben Franklin wrote in *Poor Richard's Almanac:* "Let all Men know thee, but no man know thee thoroughly; men freely ford that see the shadows." For any politician or businesswoman worth her salt, this is so obvious as to seem trivial. The reticence of political leaders to disclose their bottom line, even among close friends and allies, pervades all aspects of politics, international or otherwise. Statesmen engaged in a diplomatic contest as fraught with complexity and dangers as pivotal deterrence will be wary indeed of setting forth explicit commitments that expose their bottom lines to two contending parties with whom they must bargain, and continue to bargain, simultaneously. In such circumstances, they will bridle at making formally contingent two-way threats that commit them to taking active measures in the event of war, just as they will avoid firm engagements to "do nothing" in such circumstances.

In the United States in particular, the executive branch instinctively recoils from tying its hands in such ways. Congress, for its part, scarcely has the political unity or agility to support contingent threats toward both sides of a conflict, and, in all likelihood, it would be unwilling to ratify such commitments. Thus, in the context of pivotal deterrence, the potentially self-constraining aspects of America's democratic institutions do not appear to offer an escape from the curse of its preponderance. America's freedom of action is a factor that cannot easily be constrained, or disguised, by cleverly fine-tuned pronouncements or domestic "ratification" commitment mechanisms. Which returns us to the broader point: When it comes to pivotal deterrence, preponderance is no panacea.

Preponderance, Pivotal Deterrence, and the Blame Game

Maneuvers designed to "put the other side in the wrong" are a predictable response to pivotal statecraft. When either or both sides believe that the pivot's policy may be determined not by what they do but instead by whether the other side appears to do worse, then they may act more to incite and inflate their adversary's menacing aspect than to address the pivot's concerns. Here we come to what may be another drawback to pivotal deterrence by a unipolar power. The reasoning is straightforward. The more powerful a pivot is, and the more able it is to determine the outcome of a conflict, the greater are the adversaries' incentives to win the blame game.

This drawback must be borne in mind when the United States seeks to restrain adversaries, or to propel them forward in negotiations, by forcing them to compete for its support. Indeed, the very fact of U.S. engagement in regional conflicts may encourage adversaries to take positions and use tactics that tend to obstruct compromise, in order to induce the United States to corner their adversary.

There were shades of this in President Lee Teng-hui's inflammatory "two state" campaign in the summer of 1999, after the United States began quietly to pressure Taiwan to begin cross-Strait negotiations (see Chapter 7). Tensions were already running high after the United States bombed China's Belgrade embassy. By provoking China into taking actions that would widen the breach between it and the United States, Taiwan could release the U.S. pressure on it to negotiate. The hazards of the blame game increase when the adversaries try to bait the other side into taking actions that call forth forceful retaliation from the pivot. This pattern played out in bold strokes in Kosovo (see Chapter 7). There, in the winter of 1998–99, the KLA successfully subverted international efforts to achieve a political settlement that would keep Serbia intact, and triggered forceful NATO intervention, by provoking increasingly harsh Serb violations of the cease-fire. Yet again, we should beware of the notion that preponderance promises greater success in U.S. pivotal diplomacy.

Domestic Politics and Pivotal Deterrence

The abstract logic of pivotal deterrence theory may help to highlight the strategic dilemmas that the United States must face in seeking to manage regional conflicts. But the structural emphasis of the theory omits the important domestic political forces that shape U.S. involvement in such conflicts in the first place. Bismarck may have "had it easy" deterring war between Austria and Russia, not only because they lacked attractive allies but also because he was in a uniquely powerful and insulated position domestically. It may be harder for democratic leaders lacking Bismarck's control over foreign policy to employ the temporizing tactics and diplomatic jujitsu needed for pivotal deterrence. Nevertheless, U.S. leaders, facing considerable domestic political hurdles, have managed to succeed at pivotal deterrence. In fact, it is important to recognize that the offsetting interests that make pivotal deterrence desirable and doable in a particular conflict often comprise both domestic political and international considerations.

One interesting dimension of this fact appears in the "tied hands" ploy that democratic leaders have used to persuade parties in a conflict that their country will be unable to come to their aid, or will be forced to withdraw support, if they do not behave moderately.[21] Britain's Foreign Minister Edward Grey, recall, used the lack of domestic support for a war on the Continent to preach restraint in France (see Chapter 4). Similarly, Presidents Kennedy and Johnson both stressed the difficulties of maintaining congressional support for military aid to India, Pakistan, Greece, and Turkey in their efforts to curtail provocations and induce concessions in those conflicts (see Chapters 5 and 6).[22] The domestic constraints in these cases were sometimes real; but, this does not detract from the fact that the leaders in question found it expedient to amplify them in their pivotal deterrence parlays. Whether such domestic political considerations give democratic leaders an advantage in pivotal deterrence, compared to say, a less constrained leader like Bismarck, is doubtful. The point is that exposure to domestic political constraints is no more a guarantee of pivotal deterrence failure than is freedom from such constraints a guarantee of success.

The interplay of domestic politics in pivotal deterrence is most evident today in U.S. policy toward the Taiwan Strait (see Chapter 7). The conflicting impulses of the "China lobby" and supporters of the fledgling democracy Taiwan are considerable. Each expresses important dimensions of U.S. national interest, and because they do, they pull America back and forth between allegiance to Taiwan and cooperation with China, and have constrained it to pursue pivotal deterrence between the two sides. The way in which these countervailing impulses have congealed in the competition between the executive and legislative branches, and are expressed through unratified executive agreements and domestic laws, has actually given impetus to pivotal deterrence. China must worry that acting too aggressively will strengthen Taiwan supporters in Congress and undermine the executive agreements, while Taiwan must worry that acting too recklessly will weaken popular support for Taiwan and give Presidents more freedom to favor China's interests. Here then, far from subverting pivotal deterrence, democratic politics in the United States serve both to motivate the policy and to infuse it with some dynamism and agility.[23]

Still, the Taiwan Strait dispute may be unique among the pivotal deterrence scenarios facing the United States today in that there are strong domestic constituencies favoring both sides. In less conducive circumstances, we may wonder whether U.S. leaders can generate domestic support for active involvement in conflicts abroad and yet strike a balance in the policy that recognizes both sides as potentially aggressive. It will certainly be easier for the executive branch to sell policies that distort the complex realities of a conflict—by portraying one side as the aggressor—than it will be to convince Congress and the public that, though both sides are making trouble, the United States must intermeddle. Depending on the adversaries' incentive structures (Are they more likely to be restrained or emboldened by U.S. reticence?), it is not necessarily the case that popular reluctance to intervene must spell pivotal deterrence failure. If both sides of a conflict will be more likely to escalate if they believe the United States will intervene quickly, such popular reticence may in fact strengthen the hand of U.S. leaders. And even if just one side will be emboldened by the prospect of U.S. intervention, their doubts that it will do so may encourage them to settle for an outcome that serves U.S. interests in peace. For example, the understanding of Greek leaders in the 1996 war of flags that the United States was unlikely to shield them from Turkey encouraged Athens to become more flexible and to negotiate with Ankara a mutual stand-down (see Chapter 7).

But in situations, such as Kosovo, where the conflicts of interests are starker, and the trade-off between emboldening one side with reticence and goading the other with progressive involvement is more severe, striking a balance is both more important and more difficult. Ultimately, tragic choices may become unavoidable, and the best alternative may be either to back away from the conflict—as the Johnson administration did in South Asia in 1965—or to intervene decisively on one side. Then, the domestic political incentives to portray the conflict as one involving "good guys" and "bad guys" are, at that point, likely to become overriding. The real dilemma arises in the prologue to such a decision, when leaders still have a wider range of policy choices. The danger arises from the opportunity costs of imposing simplistic characterizations of the conflict in order to mobilize public opinion and allies for the future possibility of decisive intervention. Doing so prematurely will undermine the United States' ability to maintain offsetting restraints on both sides and broker a political compromise between them that may make decisive intervention unnecessary. It is difficult to impose, much less justify domestically, sanctions on a party that you have declared an innocent victim of aggression; likewise, it is hard to induce cooperation from a party that you have declared a die-hard aggressor. What we have here is the danger of self-fulfilling prophecy.

CONCLUSION

Unipolar preponderance enables the United States to play the pivot—for good or ill—unlike any power in modern history. But we should not exaggerate America's ability to make pivotal deterrence work. To say that the United States has better chances to succeed than have many pivots before is a relative judgment. For the reasons surveyed above, the opportunities for success may still be quite limited. And to them we must add one other crucial reason: The targets of American pivotal deterrence will be as clever about thwarting its policies as U.S. leaders will be about constructing them. This is especially true in light of the fact that the parties to the conflict will almost always have greater interests at stake than the United States. So even preponderant power must have its limits, and it is no guarantee against the need to choose among lesser evils. But what preponderance does offer—especially when other outside powers are less able to interfere—is more lesser evils to choose from, more carrots and sticks to deal out, and more room to maneuver in dealing them and, thus, more opportunities to work toward outcomes that avert war and preserve peace in a manner that conforms to U.S. interests.

When pivotal deterrence is done well, it frustrates the ambitions of both sides, often in defiance of legitimate grievances that will consequently go unmet. It is therefore a tawdry vehicle for justice to the parties to the conflict. It is an *imposition* of order and peaceful change that, above all else, suits the pivot's interests. From this perspective, the best that can be said for the potential antagonists is that they may avoid the costs of war and end up better off than if they had fought and the pivot had abandoned or aligned against them. Pivotal deterrence is a form of statecraft that appeals neither to the evangelists of Pax Americana nor to the subjects of it. But in a world where the bounties of peace mount daily and the horrors of war tax generations, pulling it off is no mean feat.

Abbreviations

AFP	*Agence France Presse*
AP	*The American Papers: Secret and Confidential: India-Pakistan-Bangladesh Documents, 1965–1973*
BD	*British Documents on the Origins of the War, 1898–1914*
CID	Committee of Imperial Defense
DOS	Department of State
FRUS	*Foreign Relations of the United States*
GD	*Outbreak of the World War: German Documents*
GDD	*German Diplomatic Documents, 1871–1914*
GPO	Government Printing Office
HMSO	Her Majesty's Stationary Office
PRO	(British) Public Records Office
PSM	*Primary Source Microfilm*
RFE/RL	*Radio Free Europe/Radio Liberty Newsline*
SE	Southeastern Europe
VOHI	*Vance Oral History Interview*
VP	*Vance Papers*

Notes

1. See Aesop's fable, "The Bat, the Birds, and the Beasts."

2. See Paul Kennedy, "In the Shadow of the Great War," *New York Review of Books*, 12 August 1999, 38.

3. For a revealing insider account of U.S. efforts in the 1999 Kargil war, see Bruce Reidel, "American Diplomacy and the 1999 Kargil Summit at Blair House," *Policy Paper Series 2002* (Philadelphia: University of Pennsylvania Center for the Advanced Study of India, 2002). Also see Andrew C. Winner and Toshi Yoshihara, "India and Pakistan at the Edge," *Survival* 44 (autumn 2002): 69–86.

4. On China-Taiwan, Greece-Turkey, and Serbia-Kosovo, see Chapter 7 below. On Serbia-Montenegro, see Ivo Daalder, "Another Balkan War," *Washington Post*, 22 August 2000.

5. On Ethiopia-Eritrea, see Jane Perlez, "U.S. Did Little to Deter Buildup as Ethiopia and Eritrea Prepared for War," *New York Times*, 22 May 2000. On Spain-Morocco, see "Morocco, Spain Decide to Leave Islet Alone," *San Francisco Chronicle*, 23 July 2002. On Russia-Georgia, see Steven Lee Myers, "Georgia Hearing Footsteps from Russia's War in Chechnya," *New York Times*, 15 August 2002.

6. Carlotta Gall, "Warring Afghan Factions Fire on Green Berets, but They Pay a Price," *New York Times*, 2 December 2002.

7. Alan Kuperman coined the phrase "muscular mediation" to describe the tactics of a third party that "simply proposes his own solution and threatens to use his considerable resources against whichever side rejects the agreement." "Rambouillet Requiem: Why the Talks Failed," *Wall Street Journal*, 4 March 1999.

8. See Saadia Touval and I. William Zartman, eds., *International Mediation in Theory and Practice* (Boulder: Westview, 1985), 7; Saadia Touval, "Biased Intermediaries: Theoretical and Historical Considerations," *Jerusalem Journal of International Relations* 1 (fall 1975), 51–52. For recent work in this vein, see Robert Rauchhaus, "Third Party Intervention in Militarized Disputes: Primum Non Nocere," (Ph.D. diss., University of California Berkeley, 2000), chap. 3; James A. Wall, John B. Stark, and Rhetta L. Standifer, "Mediation: A Current Review and Theory Development," *Journal of Conflict Resolution* 45 (June 2001): 370–91; Jacob Bercovitch, "Meditation in International Conflict: An Overview of Theory, a Review of Practice," in I. William Zartman and J. Lewis Rasmussen, eds., *Peacemaking in International Conflict: Methods and Techniques* (Washington D.C.: U.S. Institute of Peace, 1997), 127–8; and Thomas Princen, *Intermediaries in International Conflict* (Princeton: Princeton University Press, 1992).

9. Lawrence Freedman, "Strategic Studies and the Problem of Power," in Freedman, Paul

Hayes, and Robert O'Neill, eds., *War, Strategy, and International Politics* (Oxford: Clarendon Press, 1992), 288.

10. Most recent attempts to revive and revise traditional deterrence theory ignore the political problem behind pivotal deterrence. For the most rigorous example, see Frank C. Zagare and D. Marc Kilgour, *Perfect Deterrence* (Cambridge: Cambridge University Press, 2000). Also see Vincenzo Comporini, "Rethinking Deterrence," *Aspenia*, nos. 14–15 (2001): 98–104; Keith B. Payne, *The Fallacies of Cold War Deterrence and a New Direction* (Lexington: University of Kentucky Press, 2001); Max G. Manwaring, *Deterrence in the 21st Century* (London: Frank Cass, 2001); Naval Studies Board, *Post–Cold War Conflict Deterrence* (Washington D.C.: National Academy Press, 1997); Robert Harkavy, "Triangular or Indirect Deterrence/Compellence: Something New in Deterrence Theory," *Comparative Strategy* 17 (1998): 63–81. Two older studies that explore deterrence in multipolar contexts but ignore the problem of pivotal deterrence are Richard Rosecrance, "Deterrence in Dyadic and Multipolar Environments," in Rosecrance, ed., *The Future of the International Strategic System* (San Francisco: Chandler, 1972), chap. 8; R. J. Yalem, "Tripolarity and World Politics," *Yearbook of World Affairs 1974* (New York: Praeger, 1974), esp. 33–36.

11. Robert Jervis, "What Do We Want to Deter and How Do We Deter It?" in *Turning Point: The Gulf War and U.S. Military Strategy*, ed. L. Benjamin Edington and Michael J Mazarr (Boulder: Westview, 1994), 122–24.

12. An important recent work that *does* take up the problem, and stresses the role of alignment options, is Benjamin Miller, "Between War and Peace: Systemic Effects and Regional Transitions From the Cold War to the Post-Cold War," *Security Studies* 11 (autumn 2001): 1–52, esp. 14–16.

13. Barbara F. Walter, *Committing to Peace: The Successful Settlement of Civil Wars* (Princeton: Princeton University Press, 2002); also see Daniel L. Byman, *Keeping the Peace: Lasting Solutions to Ethnic Conflict* (Baltimore: Johns Hopkins University Press, 2002), chap. 8.

14. On this point, see Stephen M. Saideman, "Overlooking the Obvious: Bringing International Politics Back into Ethnic Conflict Management," *International Studies Review* 4 (fall 2002): 74–75.

15. See Joshua S. Goldstein, Jon C. Pevehouse, Deborah J. Gerner, and Shibley Telhami, "Reciprocity, Triangularity, and Cooperation in the Middle East, 1979–97," *Journal of Conflict Resolution* 45 (October 2001): 594–620; Joshua S. Goldstein and Jon C. Pevehouse, "Reciprocity, Bullying, and International Cooperation: Time-series Analysis of the Bosnia Conflict," *American Political Science Review* 91 (September 1997): 515–29.

16. For highlights of this debate, see Michael E. Brown, Owen R. Coté, Sean M. Lynn Jones, and Steven E. Miller, eds., *America's Strategic Choices*, rev. ed. (Cambridge: MIT Press, 2000).

CHAPTER 1. THE PROBLEM AND THEORY OF PIVOTAL DETERRENCE

1. On the concept of the pivot, see Robert Jervis, *System Effects: Complexity in Political and Social Life* (Princeton: Princeton University Press, 1997), 181–91, 232–38; on alignment consistency, 210–11.

2. Phillip Shenon, "Iran-Iraq Battles Lead US to Rush Carrier to Gulf," *New York Times*, 4 October 1997.

3. William Shakespeare, *Henry V*, ed. Gary Taylor (Oxford: Oxford University Press, 1984), 126, 128.

4. See W. E. Mosse, *The European Powers and the German Question, 1848–71* (Cambridge: Cambridge University Press, 1958), 312–17. There was a similar logic to the British government's Locarno policy of the 1920s, in which Britain pledged to intervene against *either* France or Germany if they violated the demilitarized zone in the Rhineland. See Jon Jacobsen, *Locarno Diplomacy: Germany and the West, 1925–1929* (Princeton: Princeton University Press, 1972).

5. A related discussion of how outside powers, by refusing to intervene, restrained both sides from escalating the Italian-Turkish war of 1911 appears in Charles H. Fairbanks, "War-

Limiting," in *Historical Dimensions of National Security Problems*, ed. Klaus Knorr (Lawrence: University of Kansas Press, 1976), 192–95.

6. Glenn Snyder coined the phrase "straddle strategy." See *Alliance Politics* (Ithaca: Cornell University Press, 1997), 332–34.

7. *The Prince and the Discourses* (New York: Modern Library, 1950), chap. XXI, 83.

8. See Catharin Dalpino and Bates Gill, eds., *Brookings Northeast Asia Survey, 2001–02* (Washington D.C.: Brookings Institution, 2002), 48–49; also see Chapter 7.

9. Paul Huth, *Extended Deterrence and the Prevention of War* (New Haven: Yale University Press, 1988).

10. Dulles remarks recorded in Memorandum of Conversation, (9 May 1954), *Foreign Relations of the United States, 1952–1954*, vol. 12, pt. I (Washington, D.C.: GPO), 465.

11. Minutes of Committee of Imperial Defense (CID) Meeting, (19 February 1925), British Public Records Office (PRO): Cabinet Papers (CAB) 2/4/196, 119.

12. See Oran Young, *The Politics of Force: Bargaining during International Crises* (Princeton: Princeton University Press, 1968), 217–18.

13. As a means of restraint, George Liska noted that "alignment itself may be subject to withholding." *Nations in Alliance: The Limits of Interdependence* (Baltimore: Johns Hopkins University Press, 1962), 139.

14. Memo: Churchill to the CID (24 February 1925), PRO: CAB 4/12/590–B, 2–3.

15. Quoted in Campbell Craig, *Destroying the Village: Eisenhower and Thermonuclear War* (New York: Columbia University Press, 1998), 83; also see Young, *Politics of Force*, 224–29.

16. Richard N. Lebow, *Between Peace and War* (Baltimore: Johns Hopkins University Press, 1984), 84–85; John M. Rothgreb, Jr., *Defining Power: Influence and Force in the Contemporary International System* (New York: St. Martins, 1993), 144; Phil Williams, "Deterrence," in *Contemporary Strategy: Theories and Policies* (New York: Holmes and Meier, 1975), 70–71; Lawrence Freedman, "Strategic Coercion," in *Strategic Coercion, ed.* Lawrence Freedman (Oxford: Oxford University Press, 1998), 25; Paul Gordon Lauren, "Ultimata and Coercive Diplomacy," *International Studies Quarterly* 16 (June 1972), 160. These quotes were largely drawn from Gary Schaub, Jr., "Compellence: Resuscitating the Concept," in Freedman, ed., *Strategic Coercion*, 54–57, which provides an excellent discussion of the role of "clarity of demands" in coercion.

17. Glenn H. Snyder, *Deterrence and Defense: Toward a Theory of National Security* (Princeton: Princeton University Press, 1961), 27–30; Thomas Schelling, *Arms and Influence* (New Haven: Yale University Press, 1966), 92–125; Alexander L. George and Richard Smoke, *Deterrence in American Foreign Policy: Theory and Practice* (New York: Columbia University Press, 1974), 527–30; Patrick M. Morgan, *Deterrence: A Conceptual Analysis* (Beverly Hills: Sage, 1977). The causal importance of ambiguity in pivotal deterrence and nuclear deterrence theory calls attention to the contrast with the theory of conventional military deterrence, which places much greater emphasis on fine-grained calculation and clarity: see John J. Mearsheimer, *Conventional Deterrence* (Ithaca: Cornell University Press, 1982). For a related discussion on the relationship between uncertainty and stability in multipolar international systems, see Bruce Bueno de Mesquita, *Principles of International Politics: People's Power, Preferences, and Perceptions* (Washington, D.C.: CQ Press, 1999), chap. 15.

18. Alexander George, *Forceful Persuasion: Coercive Diplomacy as an Alternative to War* (Washington, D.C.: United States Institute of Peace, 1991), 76; Peter Karsten, Peter D. Howell, and Artis F. Allen, *Military Threats: A Systematic Historical Analysis of the Determinants of Success* (Westport: Greenwood Press, 1984), 13.

19. James Fearon, "Domestic Political Audiences and the Escalation of International Disputes," *American Political Science Review* 88 (September 1994), 577–92.

20. Schelling, *Arms and Influence*, 83–84. Also see David A. Baldwin, *Paradoxes of Power* (New York: Basil and Blackwell, 1989), 52–55; Robert Jervis, *The Logic of Images* (Princeton: Princeton University Press, 1970), 113–38.

21. On this distinction between general and immediate deterrence, see Morgan, *Deterrence*, 38–42, and Huth, *Extended Deterrence*, chap. 2.

22. On the role of the balancer, see Michael Sheehan, "The Place of the Balancer in Balance of Power Theory," *Review of International Studies* 15 (1989), 123–34. Classic treatments include Edward Vose Gulick, *Europe's Classical Balance of Power* (New York: Norton, 1955), 65–70; Hans J. Morgenthau, *Politics Among Nations*, 3d ed. (New York: Knopf, 1960), 194–97, 352–53. The best critiques of the concept remain A. F. K. Organski, *World Politics*, 2d ed. (New York: Knopf, 1968), and Kenneth Waltz, *Theory of International Politics* (Reading, Mass.: Addison-Wesley, 1979), 163–64.

23. Gulick, *Europe's Classical Balance*, 65.

24. Martin Wight, *Power Politics*, 2d ed. (New York: Penguin Books, 1986), 169.

25. Henry Kissinger, *A World Restored: Castlereagh, Metternich, and the Problem of Peace, 1812–22* (Boston: Houghton Mifflin, 1957), 31.

26. Morgenthau, *Politics Among Nations*, 194. Also see Wight, *Power Politics*, 172.

27. Randall Schweller, *Deadly Imbalances: Tripolarity and Hitler's Strategy of World Conquest* (New York: Columbia University Press, 1998), 48; John J. Mearsheimer, *The Tragedy of Great Power Politics* (New York: Norton, 2001), 153–54. Also see Snyder, *Alliance Politics*, 318–20.

28. Quoted in Plutarch, *The Rise and Fall of Athens*, trans. Ian Scott-Kilvert (London: The Folio Society, 1967), 280. Also see Martin Wight, *Systems of States* (Leicester: Leicester University Press, 1977), 66, 194–95.

29. Lord Macaulay, *Historical Essays* (New York: Macmillan, 1926), 432.

30. Schweller, *Deadly Imbalances*, 48.

31. Wight, *Systems of States*, 89, 194. Also see Mearsheimer, *Tragedy*, 154–55.

32. "Only in America," *New York Review of Books*, 27 March 2003, 49.

33. Kissinger, *A World Restored*, 34.

34. Sheehan, "The Place of the Balancer," 125.

35. See Bernard Brodie, *Strategy in the Missile Age* (Princeton: Princeton University Press, 1959), 274–81.

36. On the difference between "hostile" and "friendly" balancers, see Robert Strausz-Hupe and Stefan T. Possony, *International Relations: In the Age of Conflict between Democracy and Dictatorship*, 2d ed. (New York: McGraw-Hill, 1954), 43–44.

37. Gulick, *Europe's Classical Balance*, 66–67. Also see Mearsheimer, *Tragedy*, 126–27; Wight, *Power Politics*, 171.

38. Morgenthau, *Politics Among Nations*, 354.

39. George Liska, *International Equilibrium* (Cambridge: Harvard University Press, 1957), 38. For a recent statement of this view, see Emerson M. S. Niou, Peter C. Ordeshook, and Gregory F. Rose, *The Balance of Power: Stability in International Systems* (Cambridge: Cambridge University Press, 1989), 202–3.

40. For this reason, Britain's unimpressive record deterring wars as a balancer does not surprise Schroeder: "trying [to do so] from Britain's position by her methods is like operating a jewelers balance by occasionally throwing weights onto the scales from a position across the room." Paul Schroeder, *Austria, Great Britain, and the Crimean War: The Destruction of the European Concert* (Ithaca: Cornell University Press, 1972), 425, 402.

41. Kurt Wolff, trans. and ed., *The Sociology of Georg Simmel* (Glencoe, Ill.: The Free Press, 1950), 157–59.

42. See Theodore Caplow, *Two-Against-One: Coalitions in Triads* (Engelwood Cliffs: Prentice Hall, 1968), esp. 18–19.

43. John von Neumann and Oskar Morgenstern, *Theory of Games and Economic Behavior* (Princeton: Princeton University Press, 1964), 227.

44. Ibid., 222; see also, 260–61.

45. Robert Powell, "Bargaining Theory and International Conflict," *Annual Review of Political Science* 5 (2002), 14–15.

46. See Niou, Ordeshook, and Rose, *The Balance of Power;* R. Harrison Wagner, "The Theory of Games and the Balance of Power," *World Politics* 38 (July 1986), 554–59; Urs Luterbacher, "A Theory of Cooperation in the Triad," in *Cooperative Models in International Rela-*

tions Research, ed. Michael D. Intriligator and Urs Luterbacher (Boston: Kluwer, 1994), 75–102, esp. 79–81.

47. James D. Morrow, "A Spatial Model of International Conflict," *American Political Science Review* 80 (December 1986), 1136; T. Clifton Morgan, *Untying the Knot of War: A Bargaining Theory of International Crises* (Ann Arbor: University of Michigan Press, 1994), 128.

48. See Jeffry A. Frieden, "Actors and Preferences in International Relations," in *Strategic Choice and International Relations,* ed. David A. Lake and Robert Powell (Princeton: Princeton University Press, 1999), 45.

49. Robert Powell, *In the Shadow of Power: States and Strategies in International Politics* (Princeton: Princeton University Press, 1999), chap. 5

50. Another problem with many of these models is that they assume away uncertainty and "private information" by postulating common knowledge among the players about the distribution of power and how it will determine the outcome of wars. See R. Harrison Wagner, "Peace, War, and the Balance of Power," *American Political Science Review* 88 (September 1994), 599. But the adversaries' uncertainty about how the balance of power will stack up if they go to war is a key mechanism in the theory of pivotal deterrence.

51. Lowell Dittmer, "The Strategic Triangle: An Elementary Game-Theoretical Analysis," *World Politics* 33, no. 4 (July 1981): 485–515. The literature on the U.S.-China-Soviet strategic triangle is massive. For good coverage, see Robert Ross, ed., *China, the United States, and the Soviet Union: Tripolarity and Policymaking in the Cold War* (New York: Sharpe, 1993); Joshua S. Goldstein and John R. Freeman, *Three-Way Street: Strategic Reciprocity in World Politics* (Chicago: University of Chicago Press, 1990); and Richard K. Ashley, *The Political Economy of War and Peace: The Sino-Soviet-American Triangle and the Modern Security Problematique* (London: Francis Pinter, 1980).

52. Dittmer, "Strategic Triangle," 490.

53. See Snyder, *Alliance Politics,* 192–99.

54. In a related discussion of "benevolent neutrality," Kissinger writes "[it] is always a tenuous role, for it requires precisely the degree of pretense which will disquiet one's friends, while it may not suffice to reassure the foe. To succeed too completely may involve the loss of allies; to fail prematurely may provoke a sudden attack. *A World Restored,* 68.

55. Snyder, *Alliance Politics,* 334.

56. I start with estimates of the adversaries' willingness to go to war against each other under differing conditions of pivot alignment (P_{A1}, P_N, P_{A2}) and then deduce the appropriate mix of abandonment and opposition threats. Snyder starts with underlying alignments (ally and adversary) and then deduces the appropriate type of restraining threats.

57. Jervis, *System Effects,* 185.

58. I have compressed together two quotations that are far apart in the original text; see Henry Kissinger, *White House Years* (Boston: Little Brown, 1979), 165, 712. Also see William Burr, ed., *The Kissinger Transcripts: The Top-Secret Talks with Beijing and Moscow* (New York: The New Press, 1998).

59. Quoted in Nicholas der Bagdasarian, *The Austro-German Rapprochement, 1870–1879* (London: Associated University Presses, 1976), 316.

60. Jervis, *System Effects,* 185.

61. Carl Sandburg, *Abraham Lincoln: The Prairie Years and The War Years,* one-vol. ed. (San Diego: Harcourt, 1959), 429.

62. See Chapter 5.

63. Jervis, *System Effects,* 183.

64. Ibid., 191–93.

65. This last point taps into a rich body of literature on bargaining and, more specifically, into the key insight that a party's bargaining power in a relationship is a function of its access to alternatives or, in other words, of "the availability of similar or substitutable outcomes from other relationships." Samuel B. Bacharach and Edward J. Lawler, *Bargaining: Power, Tactics, and Outcomes* (San Francisco: Jossey-Bass, 1981), 59–65, esp. 61. Also see Peter Blau, *Exchange and Power in Social Life* (New York: Wiley, 1964), 118–25; Baldwin, *Paradoxes of Power,*

chaps. 6, 7, 8; Albert O. Hirschmann, *National Power and the Structure of Foreign Trade* (Berkeley: University of California, 1945); R. M. Emerson, "Power-Dependence Relations," *American Sociology Review* 27 (1962): 31–40; J. Pen, "A General Theory of Bargaining," *American Economic Review* 42 (1952): 24–42, esp. 30.

66. Geoffrey Blainey, *Causes of War* (New York: Free Press, 1988), 57, also 44. Similarly, Caplow observed that all "social interaction is essentially triangular [because] it is always influenced by an audience, present or nearby" (*Two-Against-One*, v).

67. See Fred Charles Ikle, *How Nations Negotiate* (New York: Praeger, 1964), 55–58.

68. I am indebted to Richard Ashley for this term and for his careful explication of the logic of isolation avoidance, which much informs my argument here. See *The Political Economy of War and Peace*, 42–43.

69. Saul Bellow, *The Adventures of Augie March* (New York: Penguin Books, 1999), 444.

70. Samuel Huntington, "Patterns of Violence in World Politics," in *Changing Patterns of Military Politics* (Glencoe: Free Press, 1962), 21. Making a similar point, Kissinger noted "the assumption of the opponent's perfect flexibility leads to paralysis of action." *A World Restored*, 74.

71. Buchanan (ambassador to St. Petersburg) to Grey (25 July 1914), *British Documents on the Origins of the War, 1898–1914*, ed. G. P. Gooch and Harold Temperly, vol. 11, no. 125 (London: Her Majesty's Stationary Office [HMSO], 1926), 95.

72. I borrow this term from Brian Healy and Arthur Stein, "The Balance of Power in International History," *Journal of Conflict Resolution* 17 (March 1973), esp. 41–42, who, however, use it quite differently. On ingratiation as a form of influence ("skill in invoking affection"), see Harold D. Lasswell and Abraham Kaplan, *Power and Society: A Framework for Analysis* (New Haven: Yale University Press, 1950), 91.

73. Rusk to Galbraith (15 January 1963), *Foreign Relations of the United States, 1961–63*, vol. 19, no. 239 (Washington, D.C.: GPO). Italics added. For an account of how Egypt's and Israel's efforts to improve their relations with the United States were used by Washington to propel the Camp David peace process, see Shibley Telhami, *Power and Leadership in International Bargaining: The Path to the Camp David Accords* (New York: Columbia University Press, 1990).

74. Jon Elster, *Nuts and Bolts for the Social Sciences* (Cambridge: Cambridge University Press, 1989), 22.

75. See Daniel Ellsberg, "Theory of the Reluctant Duelists," in *Bargaining: Formal Theories of Negotiation*, ed. Oran R. Young (Urbana: University of Illinois Press, 1975), 38–52; and Kenneth J. Arrow, "The Theory of Risk Aversion," in *Essays in the Theory of Risk Bearing* (Chicago: Markam Publishing, 1971), esp. 90–91.

76. Kenneth J. Arrow, "Insurance, Risk and Resource Allocation," in *Essays*, 142. For a general discussion of moral hazard and adverse selection, see Thrain Eggertson, *Economic Behavior and Institutions* (Cambridge: Cambridge University Press, 1990), 44–45, 304.

77. For important work on the role of moral hazard in third-party intervention, see Alan J. Kuperman, "The Moral Hazard of Humanitarian Intervention," (Ph.D. diss., Massachusetts Institute of Technology, 2002), chap. 1; Robert Rauchhaus, "Third Party Intervention in Militarized Disputes: Primum Non Nocere," (Ph.D. diss., University of California Berkeley, 2000); and Mia Bloom, "Failures of Intervention: The Unintended Consequences of Mixed Messages and the Exacerbation of Ethnic Conflict" (Ph.D. diss., Columbia University, 1999). On moral hazard in alliances, see David A. Lake, *Entangling Relations: American Foreign Policy in its Century* (Princeton: Princeton University Press, 1999), 5; Alistair Smith, "To Intervene or Not to Intervene: A Biased Decision," *Journal of Conflict Resolution* 40 (March 1996), 16–40, esp. 17; Snyder, *Alliance Politics*; Paul W. Schroeder, "Alliances, 1815–1945: Weapons of Power and Tools of Management," in *Historical Dimensions of National Security Problems*, ed. Knorr, 227–62; Liska, *Nations in Alliance*, 138–39; Robert E. Osgood, *Alliances and American Foreign Policy* (Baltimore: Johns Hopkins University Press, 1968), 22; McDonald coined the term "commitment trap" to describe the moral hazard problem for the United States in its efforts to prop-up anticommunist third-world allies in the Cold War. Douglas MacDonald, *Ad-

ventures in Chaos: American Intervention for Reform in the Third World (Cambridge: Harvard University Press, 1992).

78. Memo: Rusk to Johnson (9 September 1965), in *The American Papers: Secret and Confidential India, Pakistan, and Bangladesh Documents, 1965–1973,* comp. Roedad Khan (Oxford: Oxford University Press, 1999), 54.

CHAPTER 2. POWER, INTERESTS, AND ALIGNMENT OPTIONS

1. Robert Jervis, *System Effects: Complexity in Political and Social Life* (Princeton: Princeton University Press, 1997), 210–11.

2. Randall Schweller is the foremost contemporary advocate of this approach. See his *Deadly Imbalances: Tripolarity and Hitler's Strategy of World Conquest* (New York: Columbia University Press, 1998), chap. 1, and "Neo-Realism's Status Quo Bias: What Security Dilemma?" in *Realism: Restatements and Renewal, ed.* Benjamin Frankel (London: Frank Cass, 1996), 90–121. For critique, see Jeffrey W. Legro and Andrew Moravcsik, "Is Anybody Still a Realist?" *International Security* 24 (fall 1999): 5–55.

3. Stephen Walt, *Origins of Alliances* (Ithaca: Cornell University Press, 1987).

4. *Deadly Imbalances,* chap. 1.

5. For our purposes here, we must specify the pattern of status quo and revisionist preferences in this context-specific way, for most states most of the time are revisionists toward some actors and issues, and favor the status quo with respect to others. For a nice illustration of this point, see Matthew Rendall, "Restraint or Self-Restraint of Russia: Nicholas I, The Treaty of Unkiar Skelessi, and the Vienna System, 1832–1841," *International History Review* 24 (March 2002): 37–63, esp. 60. In Schweller's systemic model, "for the purpose of simplifying the analysis," revisionism is treated as a property rather than a relational concept. Consequently, in his abstract scenarios, a revisionist will attempt conquests wherever it can rather than where it most prefers. Elsewhere, however, Schweller does distinguish between revisionists with "unlimited" and "limited" aims, which, in the latter instance, implies some relational contingency (*Deadly Imbalances,* 45, 49, 83, 77). On the distinction between property and relational concepts, see David Baldwin, *Economic Statecraft* (Princeton: Princeton University Press, 1985), 22–23.

6. Josef Joffe, "Europe's American Pacifier," *Foreign Policy* 54 (spring 1984): 64–82; Robert Art, "Why Europe Needs the United States and NATO," *Political Science Quarterly* 111 (spring 1996): 1–39.

7. See Schweller, *Deadly Imbalances,* 48; Robert Strausz-Hupe and Stefan T. Possony, *International Relations: In the Age of Conflict between Democracy and Dictatorship,* 2d ed. (New York: McGraw-Hill, 1954), 43.

8. Paul Schroeder, "Historical Reality vs. Neorealist Theory," *International Security* 19 (summer 1994), 108–48; Schweller, *Deadly Imbalances,* 54.

9. Schweller argues that "given the animosity directed against the balancer [by the two revisionists it seeks to frustrate] one would expect this role to be played by a state that was considerably stronger than the other two, not by the weakest member" (54). These are two distinct propositions: I agree with the second, but not the first.

10. Martin Wight, *Power Politics,* 2d ed. (New York: Penguin Books, 1986), 159. For the core logic of offensive realism, see John J. Mearsheimer, *The Tragedy of Great Power Politics* (New York: Norton, 2001), 21 and chap. 1.

11. William T. R. Fox, *The Super-Powers* (New York: Harcourt Brace and Co., 1944), 4.

12. See Richard Betts, *Nuclear Blackmail or Nuclear Balance?* (Washington, D.C.: Brookings Institution, 1987); Robert Jervis, *The Illogic of U.S. Nuclear Strategy,* (Ithaca: Cornell University Press, 1984); Alexander George and Richard Smoke, *Deterrence in American Foreign Policy: Theory and Practice* (New York: Columbia University Press, 1976), 558–61.

13. The literature on this thesis is vast. Prominent works supporting the superior capabilities thesis include Bruce Bueno de Mesquita, *The War Trap* (New Haven: Yale University Press, 1981) and Paul Huth, *Extended Deterrence and the Prevention of War* (New Haven: Yale University Press, 1988).

14. A good study on this point is Vesna Danilovic, "The Sources of Threat Credibility in Extended Deterrence," *Journal of Conflict Resolution* 45 (June 2001): 341–69 and idem, *When the Stakes Are High: Deterrence and Conflict among Major Powers* (Ann Arbor: University of Michigan Press, 2002).

15. Quoted in Charles Beard, *The Idea of National Interests* (New York: MacMillan, 1934), 43, n. 16.

16. Bernard Brodie, *War and Politics* (New York: Macmillan, 1973), 343.

17. Nicholas J. Spykman, *America's Strategy in World Politics* (New York: Harcourt, Brace, 1942), 17.

18. This hypothesis requires another assumption about the actors beyond those already mentioned. Though we do not assume that all of a state's interests are situationally determined, we will assume that in many circumstances, the intensity—if not the detail—of a state's interests can be inferred from its situation and that states will estimate the intensity of each other's interests, and the commitments they make concerning them, in this manner. See Franklin B. Weinstein, "The Concept of a Commitment in International Relations," *Journal of Conflict Resolution* 13 (March 1969): 39–55.

19. K. J. Holsti, *International Politics*, 3d ed. (Inglewood Cliffs: Prentice Hall, 1977), 145. Also see Richard Smoke, "National Security Affairs," in *International Politics*, ed. Fred Greenstein and Nelson Polsby (Reading, Mass.: Addison-Wesley, 1975), 249; Michael C. Desch, "Why Realists Disagree About the Third World," in *Realism*, ed. Frankel, 368–70.

20. On this point, see Alexander L. George and Robert O. Keohane, "The Concept of National Interests: Uses and Limitations," in *Presidential Decisionmaking in Foreign Policy*, by Alexander L. George (Boulder, Colo.: Westview Press, 1980), 227; Stephen Krasner, *Defending the National Interest: Raw Materials Investments and U.S. Foreign Policy* (Princeton: Princeton University Press, 1978), 41.

21. This follows from the assumption that the adversaries are revisionists with respect to each other.

22. I hold constant the adversaries' intensity of interests, assuming that they both have vital interests at stake. This follows from a strong interpretation of the necessary condition that the adversaries are revisionist toward each other, that each wishes to aggrandize itself at the expense of something the other holds dear.

23. See Gary King, Robert Keohane, and Sidney Verba, *Designing Social Inquiry: Scientific Inference in Qualitative Research* (Princeton: Princeton University Press, 1996), 135–37.

24. It is also worth noting that this distribution suggests our initial predictions about the *outcomes* in the overdetermined cases may have to be qualified. More to the point, because cases at the two ends of the spectrum [(A) and (D)] are likely to be "outliers," there is a good chance that either the adversaries or the pivot will be motivated by variables not adequately captured in the typology, and for that reason our predictions about the outcomes may be wrong. In particular, the prediction for column (D) is indeed likely to be wrong. Here we would only be likely to find extraordinarily motivated adversaries—that is, those willing to hazard the wrath of a preponderant power with vital interests at stake—and thus, if the pivot does attempt to deter them (which is improbable because it will be taken by surprise), it will in all likelihood fail. For a full and seminal exposition of this line of reasoning, see James Fearon, "Signaling versus the Balance of Power and Interests," *Journal of Conflict Resolution* 38 (June 1994): 236–69.

25. On this view of relative military capabilities, see Charles Glaser, "Realists as Optimists: Cooperation as Self-Help," in *Realism*, ed. Frankel, 130–34, n. 22; Glenn Snyder, *Alliance Politics* (Ithaca: Cornell University Press, 1997), 28–30.

26. Only an offensive posture will permit the peer pivot to come to the aid of either of the adversaries without committing to one side in advance. This scenario is not covered in Stephen Van Evera's list of conditions under which offensive doctrines and capabilities cause peace, but it follows from his logic. See Van Evera, *Causes of War: Power and the Roots of Conflict* (Ithaca: Cornell University Press, 1999), 152–54.

27. Snyder, *Alliance Politics*, 149, 352; David A. Lake, *Entangling Relations* (Princeton: Princeton University Press, 1999), 53–54.

28. If the forces are interposed in a "neutral zone," their fighting effectiveness will decrease as their political value as hostages increases because, when vulnerably deployed between adversaries, they will be poorly positioned to fight either side. In the unlikely event that the pivot's forces can occupy a highly defensible position that each side must cross before attacking the other, those forces may also achieve deterrence by defense pure and simple. A final military option—though one available in very limited circumstances—would be to project military power near enough to the adversaries that they must reallocate their own forces to meet the new threat in a way that makes it impossible for them to attack each other. Note, however, that this makes the pivot a common threat to the adversaries, if not more menacing than the threat they pose to each other.

29. See Henry Kissinger's remarks on the role of U.S. forces interposed in the Sinai: *Middle East Agreements and the Early Warning System in Sinai,* Hearings of the Committee on International Relations, House of Representatives, 94th Congress (Washington D.C.: GPO, 1975), 7.

30. On the utility of arms transfers as a policy instrument, see John Islin, "Arms as Influence: The Determinants of Successful Influence," *Journal of Conflict Resolution* 38 (December 1994): 665–89.

31. See Peter Blau, *Exchange and Power in Social Life* (New York: Wiley, 1964), 116–18.

32. Jervis, *System Effects,* 191–93.

33. See Adam Smith's seminal discussion of the "Water-Diamond Paradox" in *An Inquiry into the Nature and Causes of the Wealth of Nations,* ed. R. H. Campbell and A. S. Skinner (Oxford: Clarendon Press, 1976), 1:44–46, n. 31; Paul A. Samuelson, *Economics,* 11th ed. (New York: McGraw-Hill, 1980), 412.

34. *Euthydemus,* 304B in *The Dialogues of Plato* 3d ed., trans. B. Jowett (London: Oxford University Press, 1931), 1:245; *The Talmud of Jerusalem* (New York: Philosophical Library, 1956), 93.

35. Snyder, *Alliance Politics,* 6.

36. See ibid., 149, and 75–78, 166–68.

37. Similarly, Christopher C. Shoemaker and John Spanier defined "security transfers" in patron-client state relationships as "the supply of weapons, as well as security guarantees that the patron can provide." *Patron-Client State Relationships: Multilateral Crises in the Nuclear Age* (New York: Praeger, 1984), 14. On the substitutability of arms and alliances, see Kenneth Waltz, *Theory of International Politics* (Reading, Mass.: Addison-Wesley, 1979), 168; Benjamin Most and Harvey Starr, "International Relations Theory, Foreign Policy Substitutability, and 'Nice' Laws," *World Politics* 36 (April 1984): 383–406; Benjamin A. Most and Randolph M. Siverson, "Substituting Arms and Alliances, 1870–1914: An Exploration in Comparative Foreign Policy," in *New Directions in the Study of Foreign Policy,* ed. Charles F. Hermann, Charles W. Kegley Jr., and James N. Rosenau (Boston: Unwin Hyman, 1987), 131–60; James D. Morrow, "Arms versus Allies: Trade-offs in the Search for Security," *International Organization* 47 (spring 1993): 207–33; and the special issue on "Foreign Policy Substitutability," *Journal of Conflict Resolution* 44 (February 2000).

38. Thus, in the Greco-Turkish case when Turkey distanced itself from the United States after the 1964 crisis, its relations with the Soviet Union warmed dramatically (see Chapter 5). Similarly, as Pakistan's relations with the United States deteriorated in 1963–65, its security relations with China strengthened (see Chapter 6).

39. John MacMillan, *Games, Strategies, and Managers* (New York: Oxford University Press, 1992), 38.

40. For related arguments from the bargaining literature, see David A. Lax and James K. Sebenius, "The Power of Alternatives or the Limits to Negotiation," *Negotiation Journal* 1 (April 1985), 171–75.

41. For example, in the U.S.-India-Pakistan case, the United States tried to use its arms aid to India to extract concessions from New Dehli on Kashmir. Prime Minister Nehru, however, countered with the threat to take more arms from Russia, which the United States was loathe to see happen. So Washington backed away from its demands for a compromise on Kashmir (see Chapter 6).

42. Douglas Dion, "Evidence and Inference in the Comparative Case Study," *Comparative Politics* 30 (January 1998): 127–46. Also see Benjamin A. Most and Harvey Starr, "Case Selection, Conceptualization and Basic Logic in the Study of War," *American Journal of Political Science* 26 (1982): 839–41.

43. Adam Przeworski and Henry Teune, *The Logic of Comparative Social Inquiry* (New York: John Wiley, 1970).

44. See Andrew Murray Faure, "Some Methodological Problems in Comparative Politics," *Journal of Theoretical Politics* 6 (July 1994): 307–22, esp. 317.

45. These are known as the "method of agreement" and "method of difference" respectively. Here they are combined in a framework that "mirror images" the two approaches. See Faure, "Some Methodological Problems in Comparative Politics," 316–18.

46. See Alexander George and Andrew Bennett, "Process Tracing in Case Study Research," in *Case Studies and Theory Development* (Cambridge: MIT Press, forthcoming); Andrew Bennett and Alexander L. George, "Case Studies and Process Tracing in History and Political Science: Similar Strokes for Different Foci," in *Bridges and Boundaries: Historians, Political Scientists, and the Study of International Relations*, ed. Colin Elman and Miriam Fendius Elman (Cambridge: MIT Press, 2001), chap. 4; Stephen Van Evera, *Guide to Methods for Students of Political Science* (Ithaca: Cornell University Press, 1997), 64–67.

47. John D. Stephens, "Historical Analysis and Causal Assessment in Comparative Research," *APSA-CP Newsletter* 9 (winter 1998), 22–25.

48. Van Evera, *Guide to Methods*, 61–63, 69–70; George and Bennett, "The Role of Congruence Method in Case Study Research," in *Case Studies and Theory Development*. Also see S. Bartolini, "On Time and Comparative Research," *Journal of Theoretical Politics* 5 (April 1993): 131–67.

CHAPTER 3. PIVOTAL DETERRENCE IN THE EASTERN CRISIS, 1875–78

1. Henry A. Kissinger, "The White Revolutionary: Reflections on Bismarck," *Daedalus* 97 (summer 1968): 888–924, esp. 921; Ludwig Dehio, *The Precarious Balance: Four Centuries of the European Power Struggle* (New York: Knopf, 1962), 220–30. On Bismarck's political acumen broadly, see Isaiah Berlin's "Political Judgement" in *The Sense of Reality: Studies in Ideas and Their History* (New York: Farrar, Straus and Giroux, 1996), 47, 49. For an illuminating discussion of Bismarck's mastery of the "middle ground" and pivotal policy in particular, see Otto Pflanze, "Bismarck's *Realpolitik*," in *Imperial Germany*, ed. James J. Sheehan (New York: Franklin Watts, 1976), chap. 6.

2. See Josef Joffe, "Bismarck's Lessons for Bush," *New York Times*, 29 May 2002; idem, "How America Does It," *Foreign Affairs* 76 (September/October 1997): 13–27; idem, "Bismarck or Britain: Toward an American Grand Strategy After Bipolarity," *International Security* 19 (spring 1995): 94–117.

3. On this point, see Brian Healy and Arthur Stein, "Balance of Power in International History," *Journal of Conflict Resolution* 17 (March 1973): 33–61, esp. 48; Paul W. Schroeder, "Alliances, 1815–1945: Weapons of Power and Tools of Management," in *Historical Dimensions of National Security Problems*, ed. Klaus Knorr (Lawrence: University of Kansas Press, 1976), 242–44.

4. A. J. P. Taylor, *Struggle for Mastery in Europe, 1848–1918* (London: Oxford University Press, 1957), 235.

5. Bismarck to Bülow (14 August 1876), in *German Diplomatic Documents, 1871–1914*, comp. and trans. E. T. S. Dugdale (London: Methuen and Co., 1928) [hereafter *GDD*], 1:24.

6. The czar's comment is quoted in Gordon A. Craig, *Germany 1866–1945* (New York: Oxford University Press, 1978), 113.

7. Nicholas der Bagdasarian, *Austro-German Rapprochement, 1870–1879* (London: Associated University Presses, 1976), 267–70.

8. On these developments, see W. N. Medlicott, *The Congress of Berlin and After: A Diplomatic History of the Near Eastern Settlement, 1878–1880* (London: Methen & Co., 1938), chaps. 3–6; Bagdasarian, *Austro-German Rapprochment*, 273–77.

9. E. Malcolm Carroll, *Germany and the Great Powers, 1866–1914: A Study in Public Opinion and Foreign Policy* (Hamden, Conn.: Archon Books, 1966), 157, n. 121.

10. William L. Langer, *European Alliances and Alignments*, 2d ed. (New York: Knopf, 1956), 172–73.

11. Quoted in Bagdasarian, *Austro-Russian Rapprochement*, 273.

12. Quoted in Carroll, *Germany*, 155 (my translation from French).

13. Quoted in ibid.

14. To a French diplomat; quoted in Craig, *Germany*, 114.

15. For good general discussions, see Bagdasarian, *Austro-German Rapprochement*, chap. 14; Glenn Snyder, *Alliance Politics* (Ithaca: Cornell University Press, 1997), chap. 3.

16. Langer, *European Alliances*, 176.

17. On Bismarck's aversion to premature commitments, see Gordon A. Craig, *From Bismarck to Adenauer: Aspects of German Statecraft* (Baltimore: Johns Hopkins University Press, 1958), 13–14.

18. See W. N. Medlicott, "Bismarck and the Three Emperor's Alliance, 1881–87," *Transactions of the Royal Historical Society* 27 (1945): 61–83; J. V. Fuller, *Bismarck's Diplomacy at Its Zenith* (Cambridge: Harvard University Press, 1922).

19. See Snyder, *Alliance Politics*, chap. 3.

20. James Joll, *Europe Since 1870: An International History* (London: Weidenfeld and Nicolson, 1973), 2, 6, 14.

21. Raymond J. Sontag, *European Diplomatic History, 1871–1932* (New York: Appleton-Century-Crofts, 1933), 3.

22. Langer, *European Alliances*, 15. Disraeli's remark was that "this war [Franco-Prussian] represents the German revolution, a greater political event than the French revolution . . . The balance of power has been completely destroyed." See George Earl Buckle, *The Life of Benjamin Disraeli, Earl of Beaconsfield* (New York, 1920), 5:133–34.

23. Otto Pflanze, *Bismarck and the Development of Germany* (Princeton: Princeton University Press, 1990), 2:261.

24. On the role of the rail system in the Austro-Prussian war of 1866 and in the Prussian General Staff's strategic planning during the 1870s, see Colonel Maurice, *The Balance of Military Power in Europe* (Leavenworth, Kans.: George A. Spooner, 1891), 129; Dennis Showalter, *Railroads and Rifles: Soldiers, Technology, and the Unification of Germany* (Hamden, Conn.; Archon, 1975), chaps. 3 and 7; E. A. Pratt, *The Rise of Rail Power in War and Conquest* (London: P.S. King and Son, 1915); Hajo Holborn, "Moltke and Schlieffen: The Prussian German School," in *The Makers of Modern Strategy*, ed. Edward Mead Earl (Princeton: Princeton University Press, 1943), 177–78.

25. Pflanze, *Bismarck* 2:252.

26. Paul Kennedy, *The Rise and Fall of the Great Powers: Economic Change and Military Conflict from 1500–2000* (New York: Random House, 1987), 213, 190.

27. Langer, *European Alliances*, 101; see also 80.

28. William A. Gauld, "The *Dreikaiserbundnis* and the Eastern Question, 1871–6," *English Historical Review* 40 (1925): 208.

29. Cited in Pflanze, *Bismarck* 2:424.

30. Shuvalov Memoranda quoted in George H. Rupp, *A Wavering Friendship: Russia and Austria, 1876–1878* (Cambridge: Harvard University Press, 1941), 195, n. 27. Bismarck was not alone in this view: In 1884, even Kalnoky, the foreign minister of Austria-Hungary, admitted that there was "one thing the [Habsburg] Monarchy would not be able to survive, and that would be defeat at the hands of Russia, a slavic power." Quoted in Langer, *European Alliances*, 355–56.

31. Pflanze, *Bismarck* 2:106–14; Taylor, *Struggle*, 254. On the Polish rebellions, see Paul Schroeder, *The Transformation of European Politics, 1763–1848* (New York: Oxford University Press, 1994), 705–9, 764, 792–93.

32. Langer, *European Alliances*, 370; Sontag, *European Diplomatic History*, 4.

33. Taylor, *Struggle*, 281–82.

34. Sontag, *European Diplomatic History*, 20; see also Langer, *European Alliances*, 70.

35. On the logic of contingent necessity, see George Kennan, *American Diplomacy*, expanded ed. (Chicago: University of Chicago Press, 1984), 16.

36. Rupp, *Wavering Friendship*, 42.

37. Rupp, *Wavering Friendship*, 35; Pflanze, *Bismarck* 2:416; Langer, *European Alliances*, 70.

38. Rupp, *Wavering Friendship*, 38.

39. David MacKenzie, "Russia's Balkan Policies Under Alexander II, 1855–1881," in *Imperial Russian Foreign Policy*, ed. Hugh Ragsdale and Valerii Nicolaevich Ponomarev (Cambridge, 1993), 223–26.

40. Langer, *European Alliances*, 66; Pflanze, *Bismarck* 2:416. On Pan-Slavism, also see B. H. Sumner, *Russia and the Balkans, 1870–1880* (Hamden, Conn.: Archon, 1962 (1937), 56–80.

41. Rupp, *Wavering Friendship*, 22.

42. Taylor, *Struggle*, 233.

43. Langer, *European Alliances*, 66–69; Rupp, *Wavering Friendship*, 22–23.

44. Taylor, *Struggle*, 229.

45. Rupp, *Wavering Friendship*, 56; also see Richard G. Weeks, "Russia's Decision for War with Turkey, May 1876–April 1877," *East European Quarterly* 24 (September 1990): 307–33, esp. 308, 327.

46. David MacKenzie, *The Serbs and Russian Pan-Slavism, 1875–1878* (Ithaca: Cornell University Press, 1967), esp. 335.

47. Matthew Rendal, "Restraint or Self-Restraint of Russia: Nicholas I, the Treaty of Unkiar Skelessi, and the Vienna System, 1832–1841," *International History Review* 24 (March 2002): 37–63.

48. Barbara Jelavich, *Russia's Balkan Entanglements, 1806–1914* (Cambridge: Cambridge University Press, 1991), 28.

49. Taylor, *Struggle*, 62–86.

50. Rupp, *Wavering Friendship*, 53, 55, 57.

51. Langer, *European Alliances*, 468, 464.

52. See Sumner, *Russia*, 580–82.

53. According to René Albrecht-Carrié "German Austrians . . . and Magyars, together constituted a minority of the population [of Austria Hungary], some twenty million out of fifty in 1914. The rest were predominantly Slavic." *Europe After 1815*, 5th ed. (Tottowa, N.J.: Littlefield, Adams and Co., 1972), 107.

54. See Alfred Francis Pribram, *The Secret Treaties of Austria-Hungary, 1879–1914* (Cambridge: Harvard University Press, 1921), 2:185–87.

55. Rupp, *Wavering Friendship*, 29.

56. Quoted in Gauld, "The *Driekaiserbundnis* and the Eastern Question, 1871–6," 213.

57. Pribram, *Secret Treaties*, 189–91. For the details of the Reichstadt negotiations, see David Harris, *A Diplomatic History of the Balkan Crisis of 1875–1878: The First Year* (Stanford: Stanford University Press, 1936), 432–38.

58. Pribram, *Secret Treaties*, 221.

59. R. W. Seton-Watson, *Disraeli, Gladstone, and the Eastern Question* (London: Frank Cass, 1962), 31–35; Rupp, *Wavering Friendship*, 88. For details on the Andrássy Note and Berlin Memorandum, see Harris, *Diplomatic History of the Balkan Crisis*, chaps. 3–6.

60. Quoted in Weeks, "Russia's Decision for War with Turkey," 309.

61. Ibid., 314–15.

62. Sumner, *Russia*, 200–1.

63. Rupp, *Wavering Friendship*, 354.

64. Wilhelm to Alexander, (2 September 1876), quoted in Carroll, *Germany*, 137.

65. Sumner, *Russia*, 202–4; Rupp, *Wavering Friendship*, 190; Mihailo D. Stojanovic, *The Great Powers and the Balkans, 1875–1878* (Cambridge: Cambridge University Press, 1939), 102–103.

66. Pflanze, *Bismarck* 2:423; Rupp, *Wavering Friendship*, 191–92.

67. Sumner, *Russia*, 204; Werder Report, (8 October 1876), *GDD*, 33–34.

68. Seton-Watson, *Disraeli*, 92–93. Also see Stojanovic, *Great Powers and the Balkans*, 111–12.

69. Pflanze, *Bismarck* 2:424; Rupp, *Wavering Friendship*, 168–84.

70. Sumner, *Russia*, 209.

71. Werder Report (8 October 1876), *GDD*, 33–34; Pflanze, *Bismarck* 2:423; Sumner, *Russia*, 206–7, n. 2; Otto von Bismarck, *Reflections and Reminiscences* (New York: Harper and Row, 1968), 224.

72. Sumner, *Russia*, 207.

73. Emil Ludwig, *Bismark: The Story of a Fighter*, trans. Eden and Cedar Paul (Boston: Little, Brown, 1927), 513.

74. Rupp, *Wavering Friendship*, 201–2; Langer, *European Alliances*, 97; Pflanze, *Bismarck* 2:424; Stojanovic, *Great Powers and the Balkans*, 105.

75. Carroll, *Germany*, 137.

76. Cited in Taylor, *Struggle*, 236.

77. Gorchakov quoted in Carroll, *Germany*, 138.

78. Seton-Watson, *Disraeli*, 120–21; Carroll, *Germany*, 139; Bülow to Munster, (27 November 1876), *GDD*, 41.

79. Andrássy quoted in Seton-Watson, *Disraeli*, 141; Rupp, *Wavering Friendship*, 293–95.

80. Sumner, *Russia*, 210; Rupp, *Wavering Friendship*, 194.

81. Carroll, *Germany*, 132.

82. Rupp, *Wavering Friendship*, 194–5.

83. Münch to Andrássy, (8 October 1877), quoted in Bagdasarian, *Austro-German Rapprochement*, 200; see also Rupp, *Wavering Friendship*, 196.

84. Rupp, *Wavering Friendship*, 197.

85. Bismarck Memorandum (2 October 1876), cited in Seton-Watson, *Disraeli*, 93. On the Münch episode, also see Stojanovic, *Great Powers and the Balkans*, 113–14.

86. Bagdasarian, *Austro-German Rapprochement*, 200–2.

87. Quoted in ibid., 207 (italics added).

88. Rupp, *Wavering Friendship*, 199, 242–46, 369.

89. Seton-Watson, *Disraeli*, 97.

90. Ibid., 107; Rupp, *Wavering Friendship*, 235.

91. Weeks, "Russia's Decision for War," 319.

92. On the Constantinople Conference, see Stojanovic, *Great Powers and the Balkans*, chap. 6.

93. Rupp. *Wavering Friendship*, 233–34, 240–41

94. Sumner, *Russia*, 210; Rupp, *Wavering Friendship*, 236.

95. See "Treaty of Budapest (January/March 1877)," in *Key Treaties for the Great Powers, 1814–1914*, ed. Michael Hurst (New York: St. Martins, 1972), 2:511–15; Stojanovic, *Great Powers and the Balkans*, 145–51. On the continuing Anglo-Russian negotiations over a protocol, see Weeks, "Russia's Decision for War," 322–24.

96. Weeks, "Russia's Decision for War," 326.

97. See Pribram, *Secret Treaties*, 191–203.

98. Langer, *European Alliances*, 128.

99. Quoted in Rupp, *Wavering Friendship*, 431.

100. Seton-Watson, 198–203; Sumner, *Russia*, 320–21; Rupp, *Wavering Friendship*, 390–98; Stojanovic, *Great Powers and the Balkans*, 168–73.

101. Salisbury to Lytton, (9 March 1877), quoted in Seton-Watson, *Disraeli*, 157.

102. Andrássy to Beust, (29 May 1877), quoted in Seton-Watson, *Disraeli*, 200.

103. This is a quote of Bagdasarian's paraphrase in *Austro-German Rapprochment*, 213. He cites Harriss-Gastrell to Buchanan, Budapest, (13 May 1877), British Public Records Office: Foreign Office Papers (FO) 7/910/30/confidential.

104. Layard to Beaconsfield, (28 November 1877), cited in Seton-Watson, *Disraeli*, 213.

105. William A. Gauld, "The *Dreikaiserbundnis* and the Eastern Question, 1877–8," *English Historical Review* 42 (1927): 562–63.

106. Ibid., 564–65.

107. According to Rupp, "The Military Group . . . were inclined to believe that . . . the appearance of the Austrian Army [in Turkey] would suffice to force Russia to evacuate Turkey and Rumania, as she had done in 1855." *Wavering Friendship*, 433. See also Stojanovic, *Great Powers and the Balkans*, 193.

108. Stojanovic, *Great Powers and the Balkans*, 194; Seton-Watson, *Disraeli*, 268–69; Barbara Jelavich, *The Ottoman Empire, the Great Powers, and the Straits Question, 1870–1887* (Bloomington: Indiana University Press, 1973), 94–106.

109. Langer, *European Alliances*, 138.

110. William Gauld, "The Anglo-Austrian Agreement of 1878," *English Historical Review* 41 (1926): 108–12; Stojanovic, *Great Powers and the Balkans*, 198.

111. Quoted in Seton-Watson, *Disraeli*, 269–70, 382.

112. Munster to Bülow, (25 February 1878), *GDD*, 67.

113. Bagdasarian, *Austro-German Rapprochment*, 221–23.

114. Bülow to Stolberg, (24 February 1878) (communication from Bismarck to Andrássy), cited in Bagdasarian, *Austro-German Rapprochement*, 221.

115. Rupp, *Wavering Friendship*, 455–57.

116. Gauld, "The Dreikaiserbundnis and the Eastern Question, 1877–8," 566. As Sumner describes Andrássy's attitude at this time, "for all his negotiations with London, [he] placed no full reliance on the intentions of the British government; he doubted whether they really intended to fight; he was not impressed by their military preparations; he feared they might leave him in the lurch" *Russia*, 456–57.

117. Langer, *European Alliances*, 134.

118. Bismarck, *Reflections and Reminiscences*, 231–32; Sumner, *Russia*, 490.

119. On Bismarck and the Congress of Berlin, see Medlicott, *The Congress of Berlin and After*, chap. 2; Sumner, *Russia*, chap. 18; Seton-Watson, *Disraeli*, chaps. 10–11; and Henry A. Kissinger, *Diplomacy* (New York: Simon and Schuster, 1994), 154–57.

120. Bülow to Münster, (27 November 1876), *GDD*, 42.

121. Carroll, *Germany*, 140.

122. Quoted in Seton-Watson, *Disraeli*, 139.

123. Quoted in Gauld, "The *Dreikaiserbundnis* and the Eastern Question, 1871–6," 219.

124. Seton-Watson, *Disraeli*, 416; Bagdasarian, *Austro-German Rapprochement*, 227.

125. Gauld, "The *Dreikaiserbundnis* and the Eastern Question, 1877–8," 561.

126. Bismarck Memorandum (2 October 1876), cited in Seton-Watson, 93.

127. Gauld, "The *Dreikaiserbundnis* and the Eastern Question, 1871–6," 218.

128. Quoted in Seton-Watson, *Disraeli*, 413; and Rupp, *Wavering Friendship*, 195, n. 27.

129. Rupp, *Wavering Friendship*, 96–102, esp. n. 66.

130. Stojanovic, *Great Powers and the Balkans*, vii.

131. For discussion of Austria's and Russia's planning and preparations for war with each other see, Sumner, *Russia*, 319, 390, 393, 398, 427–28, 432–33; Rupp, *Wavering Friendship*, 501 n. 18, 521; and Stojanovic, *Great Powers and the Balkans*, 193.

CHAPTER 4. PIVOTAL DETERRENCE AND THE CHAIN GANG

1. Hew Strachan, *The First World War* (Oxford: Oxford University Press, 2001), 1:97.

2. Ibid., 1:100.

3. Luigi Albertini, *The Origins of the War of 1914*, 3 vols. (London: Oxford University Press, 1957), 3:189.

4. Glenn Snyder, "The Security Dilemma in Alliance Politics," *World Politics* 36 (July 1984): 482. Also see David Calleo, *The German Problem Reconsidered* (Cambridge: Cambridge University Press, 1978), 34; Karl Dietrich Erdmann, "War Guilt 1914 Reconsidered: A Balance of New Research," in *The Origins of the First World War: Great Power Rivalry and German War Aims*, ed. H. W. Koch, 2d ed. (London: Macmillan, 1984), 368.

5. Jack S. Levy; Thomas J. Christensen; Marc Trachtenberg, "Correspondence: Mobilization and Inadvertence in the July Crisis," *International Security* 16 (summer 1991): 189–203, at 201. Trachtenberg quotes Albertini, *Origins*, 2: 518.

6. Albertini, *Origins*, 2:332, 336, 514. Among historians, Albertini is probably the

most optimistic about Grey's ability to shape events if he had acted differently. More cautious is Bernadotte Everly Schmitt, *The Coming of the War, 1914,* 2 vols. (New York: H. Fertig, 1930), 1:409. For other optimistic views, see Jack S. Levy, "Preferences, Constraints, and Choices in July 1914," in *Military Strategy and the Origins of the First World War,* ed. Steven E. Miller, Sean M. Lynn-Jones, and Stephen Van Evera (Princeton: Princeton University Press, 1991), 245; Scott D. Sagan, "1914 Revisited: Allies, Offense, and Instability,"in *Military Strategy,* 127; Sean M. Lynn-Jones, "Detente and Deterrence: Anglo-German Relations, 1911–1914,"in *Military Strategy,* 188. Levy; Christensen; Trachtenberg; "Correspondence," 193–94, 200.

7. Samuel L. Williamson, *The Politics of Grand Strategy: Britain and France Prepare for War, 1904–1914,* 2d ed. (London: Ashfield Press, 1990), 368; Byron Dexter, "Lord Grey and the Problem of an Alliance," *Foreign Affairs* 30 (January 1952): 304; Henry Kissinger, "Coalition Diplomacy in the Nuclear Age," *Foreign Affairs* 42 (July 1964): 529.

8. Robert Jervis, letter to author, April 1999.

9. On a July 29 cable from the German ambassador to London, the kaiser scribbled, "a serious word to St. Petersburg and Paris to the effect that Britain will not help them would at once calm the situation down." Lichnowsky to Jagow (29 July 1914), in *Outbreak of the World War: German Documents,* ed. Max Montegalas and Walther Schucking, collected by Karl Kautsky (New York: Oxford University Press, 1924) [hereafter *GD*], no. 368, p. 321. Similarly, German Chancellor Theobald von Bethmann Hollweg asserted that "Grey could have prevented the war had he declared at the beginning that Britain would not participate." Konrad Jarausch, "The Illusion of Limited War: Chancellor Bethmann Hollweg's Calculated Risk, July 1914," *Central European History* 2, no. 1 (March 1969): 76, n. 98. After the war, German Secretary of State Jagow echoed the refrain: "The neutrality of Britain would . . . have signified the preservation of peace." Albertini, *Origins,* 2:507.

10. For example, Sidney B. Fay, *The Origins of the World War,* 2 vols. (New York: Macmillan, 1930), 2:557.

11. A. J. P. Taylor, *Struggle for Mastery in Europe, 1848–1918* (London: Oxford University Press, 1957), 525.

12. Fritz Fischer, *Germany's Aims in the First World War* (New York: W. W. Norton, 1967), 86–88; Immanuel Geiss, *July 1914: The Outbreak of the First World War, Selected Documents* (London: Batsford, 1967), 138; Williamson, *Politics of Grand Strategy,* 368. Erdmann, "War Guilt 1914 Reconsidered," 363–64.

13. Dale Copeland, *The Origins of Major War* (Ithaca: Cornell University Press, 2000), 79–117. That Germany simply ignored Britain is argued by Hermann Kantorowicz, *Gutachten zur Kriegsschuldfrage, 1914,* ed. Immanuel Geiss (Frankfurt: Europaische Verlagsanstalt, 1967), 345–53. See Robert Kann's review in *Central European History* 1 (1968): 383–89.

14. Zara Steiner, *Britain and the Origins of the First World War* (New York: St. Martins, 1977), 227, 245, 256.

15. Thomas J. Christensen and Jack Snyder, "Chain Gangs and Passed Bucks: Predicting Alliance Patterns in Multipolarity," *International Organization* 44 (spring 1990), 137–68. Precisely this problem seemed to arise on 24 July, when the British ambassador cabled from St. Petersburg that "it looked as if France and Russia were determined to make a strong stand even if we declined to join them." Buchanan to Grey (24 July 1914), in *British Documents on the Origins of the War, 1898–1914,* ed. G. P. Gooch and Harold Temperly (London: HMSO, 1926), vol. 11, no. 101 [hereafter *BD;* all citations are from vol. 11 unless otherwise indicated].

16. Williamson, *Politics of Grand Strategy,* 368.

17. On multipolarity, see Kenneth Waltz, *Theory of International Politics* (Addison-Wesley, 1979). On offensive strategic beliefs, see Robert Jervis, "Cooperation Under the Security Dilemma," *World Politics* 31 (January 1978): 167–214; Jack Snyder, *Ideology of the Offensive* (Ithaca: Cornell University Press, 1984); Stephen Van Evera, "The Cult of the Offensive," in *Military Strategy and the Origins of the First World War,* ed. Miller, Lynn-Jones, and Van Evera. On multipolarity and offensive strategic beliefs together, see Christensen and Snyder, "Chain Gangs and Passed Bucks." On arms racing, see David Hermann, *The Arming of Eu-*

rope and the Making of the First World War (Princeton: Princeton University Press, 1996); David Stevenson, *Armaments and the Coming of the War, 1904–1914* (Oxford: Clarendon, 1996); Paul Kennedy, *The Rise of Anglo-German Antagonism* (London: Allyn-Unwin, 1980). On domestic politics, imperialism, and the "mood of 1914," see James Joll, *The Origins of the First World War*, 2d ed. (New York: Longman's, 1992), chaps. 5, 7, 8. On psychological biases in 1914, see Richard Ned Lebow, *Between Peace and War: The Nature of International Crises* (Baltimore: Johns Hopkins University Press, 1981), 119–47. On social revolution, see Elie Halevy, *Era of Tyrannies: Essays on Socialism and War* (Garden City: Anchor Books, 1965), chap. 2.

18. Snyder, "Security Dilemma in Alliance Politics," 482–83.

19. Stephen Van Evera, "Why Cooperation Failed in 1914," *World Politics* 38 (October 1985): 80–117.

20. Cf. Levy; Christensen; Trachtenberg, "Correspondence," 200–01.

21. Paul Kennedy, "The First World War and the International Power System," *International Security* 9 (summer 1984): 20–23. Of the major Continental powers, Britain had by far the smallest peacetime military. With 192,144 peacetime effectives in 1913, it represented less than 1/10 of Russian (1,300,000) and French (700,000), and less than 1/5 of German (782,344) and Austrian (~391,297) men under arms. Hermann, *Arming of Europe*, app. A, table A.1, 234.

22. Williamson, *Politics of Grand Strategy*, 224.

23. Ibid., 340; Keith M. Wilson, *The Policy of the Entente: Essays on the Determinants of British Foreign Policy, 1904–1914* (Cambridge: Cambridge University Press, 1985), 117; Gerhard Ritter, *The Sword and the Sceptre: The Problem of Militarism in Germany* (Coral Gables: University of Miami Press, 1970), 217–19.

24. Van Evera, "Cult of the Offensive," 60–61.

25. Kurt Riezler's diary records Bethmann saying on 14 July: "If in case of war, Britain starts at once, then Italy will under no circumstances come in." Fritz Stern, "Bethmann Hollweg and the War: The Limits of Responsibility," in *The Responsibility of Power: Historical Essays in Honor of Hajo Holborn*, ed. Leonard Krieger and Fritz Stern (London: Macmillan, 1968), 264. Similarly, Wilhelm noted in the margin of a 1 August cable advising of a possible neutrality deal with Britain: "Inform Rome at once of this . . . as Italy will go timidly with Triple Alliance so long as there is any fear of Britain's opposing her." Lichnowsky to Jagow (1 August 1914), *GD*, no. 570.

26. Williamson, *Politics of Grand Strategy*, 226.

27. Cf. Strachan, *First World War*, 100.

28. Snyder, "Security Dilemma in Alliance Politics," 482–83. Christensen and Snyder, "Chain gangs and passed bucks"; Waltz, *Theory of International Politics*, 165–69.

29. Van Evera, "Why Cooperation Failed," 87–88.

30. For the argument that domestic politics, not strategic logic, was the primary motivation for Britain's weak commitments to France and Russia, see Strachan, *First World War*, 100; Kenneth N. Waltz, *Foreign Policy and Democratic Politics; the American and British Experience* (Boston: Little Brown, 1967), 9. Against this view is Herbert Butterfield, "Sir Edward Grey in July 1914," *Historical Studies* 5 (1965): 20; Snyder, "Security Dilemma in Alliance Politics," 482, n. 21. For the view that Britain's policy was a function of the pattern of economic interdependence between Britain and Germany, see Paul Papayoanou, *Power Ties: Economic Interdependence, Balancing, and War* (Ann Arbor: University of Michigan Press, 1999).

31. K. A. Hamilton, "Great Britain and France, 1905–1911," and Beryl Williams, "Great Britain and Russia, 1905 to the 1907 Convention," in *British Foreign Policy Under Sir Edward Grey*, ed. F. H. Hinsley (Cambridge: Cambridge University Press, 1977), 113–47; C. J. Lowe and M. L. Dockrill, *Mirage of Power: British Foreign Policy, 1902–14*, 3 vols. (London: Routledge and Kegan Paul, 1972), 1:1–11.

32. Williams, "Great Britain and Russia," and D. W. Sweet and R. T. B. Langhorne, "Great Britain and Russia, 1907–1914," in *British Foreign Policy*, ed. Hinsley, 133–47, 236–55.

33. Viscount Grey of Fallodon, *Twenty Five Years, 1892–1916*, 2 vols. (New York: Frederick A. Stokes Co., 1925), 1:11.

34. Robert Jervis, *System Effects: Complexity in Political and Social Life* (Princeton: Princeton University Press, 1997), 245–52.

35. G. P. Gooch, *Before the War: Studies in Diplomacy*, 2 vols. (New York: Russell and Russell, 1967), 2:58–59; Steiner, *Britain*, 48.

36. Robert A. Kann, "Alliances Versus Ententes," *World Politics* 28 (July 1976): 621. For a useful critique, see G. R. Berridge, "Ententes and Alliances," *Review of International Studies* 15 (1989): 251–60.

37. Enclosure to Buchanan to Grey (25 July 1914), *BD*, no. 125 (italics added).

38. Kann, "Alliances Versus Ententes," 621; Pierre Renouvin, "Britain and the Continent: The Lessons of History," *Foreign Affairs* 17 (October 1938): 111–27.

39. Wilson, *Policy of the Entente*, 46.

40. Bertie to Nicolson (14 May 1911), in Lowe and Dockrill, *Mirage*, 3:433.

41. Williamson, *Politics of Grand Strategy*, 330; Wilson, *Policy of the Entente*, 48; Steiner, *Great Britain*, 123. Prime Minister Asquith had similar concerns. After learning of the Anglo-French military conversations in September 1911, he thought the talks to be "rather dangerous; especially the part which referred to possible British assistance. The French ought not to be encouraged in present circumstances, to make their plans on any assumptions of this kind." Ibid., 123.

42. Bertie to Grey (30 July 1914), quoted in Wilson, *Policy of the Entente*, 47.

43. Minute by Crowe (31 July 1914), *BD*, no. 318.

44. Jonathan Mercer, *Reputation in International Politics* (Ithaca: Cornell University Press, 1996), 74–109; Lowe and Dockrill, *Mirage*, 1:11–28.

45. Mercer, *Reputation*, 154–63; Lowe and Dockrill, *Mirage*, 1:37–47; M. L. Dockrill, "British Policy during the Agadir Crisis," in *British Foreign Policy*, ed. Hinsley, 271–87.

46. Renouvin, "Britain and the Continent," 115; D. C. B. Lieven, *Russia and the Origins of the First World War* (New York: St. Martins, 1983), 35.

47. R. J. Crampton, *The Hollow Detente: Anglo-German Relations in the Balkans, 1911–14* (London: George Prior Publishers, 1979); Lowe and Dockrill, *Mirage*, 1:118–26; Steiner, *Great Britain*, 110–15.

48. Strachan, *First World War*, 101; Lynn-Jones, "Detente and Deterrence," 165–94; Snyder, *Alliance Politics*, 248.

49. Grey to Rumbold (9 July 1914), *BD*, no. 4.

50. Grey to Bertie, Ambassador to Paris (8 July 1914), *BD*, no. 38; Grey to Buchanan, Ambassador to St. Petersburg (8 July 1914), *BD*, no. 39.

51. Grey to Buchanan (20 July 1914), *BD*, no. 67; Grey to Buchanan (22 July 1914), *BD*, no. 79; Grey to de Bunsen, Ambassador to Vienna (23 July 1914), *BD*, no. 86.

52. Buchanan to Grey (22 July 1914), *BD*, no. 76.

53. Pourtales to Bethmann (21 July 1914), *GD*, no. 120, 159; Renouvin, *Immediate Origins*, 83; Buchanan to Grey (23 July 1914), *BD*, no. 84.

54. De Bunsen to Grey (23 July 1914), *BD*, no. 90. Eyre Crowe, for one, very much doubted "the wisdom of our making any representations at Vienna. It is for the German Government to do." "Any such communication at Vienna," he thought "would be likely to produce intense irritation, without any beneficial other effect." Minute by Eyre Crowe on Buchanan to Grey (22 July 1914), *BD*, no. 76; Minute by Eyre Crowe on Buchanan to Grey (23 July 1914), *BD*, no. 84.

55. Lichnowsky to Jagow (22 July 1914), *GD*, nos. 118 and 121.

56. Cf. Snyder, *Alliance Politics*, 251–53.

57. Joll, *Origins*, 23.

58. Bethmann to Pourtales, Schoen, and Lichnowsky (21 July 1914), *GD*, no. 100.

59. John F. V. Keiger, *France and the Origins of the First World War* (New York: St. Martins, 1983), 155–56.

60. Buchanan to Grey (25 July 1914), *BD*, no. 125.

61. A record summarizing the Council's decisions can be found in Geiss, *July 1914*, no. 59.

62. On this point, see Albertini, *Origins*, 2:371, 350–61; Gale Stokes, "The Serbian Docu-

ments: A Preview," *Journal of Modern History* 48 (September 1976): on demand supplement, 69–77; Lieven, *Russia,* 144. Opposing is Mark Cornwall, "Serbia," in *Decisions for War 1914,* ed. Keith Wilson (London: University College London Press, 1995), 78–81.

63. Lieven, *Russia,* 144.

64. Buchanan to Grey (18 July 1914), *BD,* no. 60; Albertini, *Origins,* 2:292; L. C. F. Turner, "The Russian Mobilization in 1914," *Journal of Contemporary History* 3 (January 1968): 71.

65. Buchanan to Grey (18 July, 1914), *BD,* no. 60. Grey confirmed the position: "you spoke quite rightly . . . I entirely approve, and I cannot promise more on behalf of HMG (Her Majesty's Government). I do not consider that public opinion here would or ought to sanction our going to war in the Serbian quarrel." Grey to Buchanan (25 July 1914), *BD,* no. 112.

66. Lieven, *Russia,* 142.

67. Ibid., 143–44.

68. Grey to Rumbold (25 July 1914), *BD,* no. 116.

69. Jagow to Lichnowsky (25 July 1914), *GD,* no. 192; Lichnowsky to Grey (26 July 1914), *BD,* no. 145.

70. Grey to Bertie (24 July 1914), *BD,* no. 98; Grey to Buchanan (25 July 1914), *BD,* no. 132.

71. Bertie to Grey (27 July 1914), *BD,* no. 194; Renouvin, *Immediate Origins,* 115; Albertini, *Origins,* 2:403. A good indication of what the official response to the proposal would have been if Poincaré had been in Paris to receive it is found in his reaction to it on the 27: "why [mediation] between Austria and Russia? Russia has not yet said anything and hasn't budged. So far she is in no way involved in the conflict. On the other hand, are we going to leave Austria alone with Serbia?" Gerd Krumeich, *Armaments and politics in France on the eve of the First World War: the Introduction of three-year conscription, 1913–1914,* trans. Stephen Conn (Dover, N.H.: Berg Publishers, 1984), 222.

72. Albertini, *Origins* 2:341–2; Fischer, *Germany's Aims,* 69.

73. Grey to Lichnowsky (25 July 1914), *BD,* no. 115; Lichnowsky to Jagow (25 July 1914), *GD,* no. 186.

74. Rumbold to Grey (26 July 1914), *BD,* no. 149. Eyre Crowe minuted: "Very insidious on the part of the German Government . . . [a] somewhat peculiar way of treating our suggestion that Germany should join in making a communication at Vienna." Albertini, *Origins* 2:342; Geiss, *July 1914,* no. 95.

75. Buchanan to Grey (25 July 1914), *BD,* no. 125; Nicolson to Grey (26 July 1914), *BD,* no. 139; Grey to Bertie (26 July 1914), *BD,* no. 140. Michael Ekstein and Zara Steiner, "The Sarajevo Crisis," *British Foreign Policy,* ed. Hinsley, 401.

76. Bertie to Grey (27 July 1914), *BD,* no. 183; Buchanan to Grey (27 July 1914), *BD,* no. 198; Communication by Beckendorff (27 July 1914), *BD,* no. 206; Albertini, *Origins* 2:403–8; Lieven, *Russia,* 145.

77. Lichnowsky to Jagow (26 July 1914), *GD,* no. 201.

78. Lichnowsky to Jagow (26 July 1914), *GD,* no. 236.

79. Bethmann to Lichnowsky (27 July 1914), *GD,* no. 248.

80. Lichnowsky to Jagow (27 July 1914), *GD,* nos. 258, 265.

81. Bethmann to Tschirschky (27 July 1914), *GD,* nos. 277, 278.

82. Fischer, *Germany's Aims,* 71; Geiss, *July 1914,* 221–23.

83. Szögyeny's letter appears in Geiss, *July 1914,* no. 95; Albertini, *Origins* 2:445–46.

84. Tschirschky to Jagow (29 July 1914), *GD,* no. 400.

85. Jarausch, "Illusion of Limited War," 65.

86. Buchanan to Grey (27 July 1914), *BD,* no. 170.

87. Albertini, *Origins* 2:538.

88. Renouvin, *Immediate Origins,* 162.

89. Bethmann to Pourtales (29 July 1914), *GD,* no. 342.

90. Albertini, *Origins* 2:541–55.

91. Goschen to Grey (27 July 1914), *BD,* no. 185, 128; J. Cambon to Bienvenu-Martin (27 July 1914), in Geiss, *July 1914,* no. 103; Albertini, *Origins* 2:481–82, 550; Turner, "Russian Mobilization," 85–86.

92. Albertini, *Origins* 2:555–61, 564–81.
93. Williamson, *Politics of Grand Strategy*, 347; Grey to Bertie (29 July 1914), *BD*, no. 283.
94. John F. V. Keiger, *Raymond Poincaré*, (Cambridge: Cambridge University Press, 1997). 174.
95. Albertini, *Origins*, 2:604; Viviani to P. Cambon (30 July 1914), *BD*, no. 294.
96. Keiger, *France*, 160.
97. Krumeich, *Armaments*, 226 (italics added).
98. Keiger, *France*, 167; Albertini, *Origins* 2:611–13.
99. Strachan, *First World War*, 95, 93.
100. Grey to Bertie (31 July 1914), *BD*, no. 352; Grey to Bertie (31 July 1914), *BD*, no. 367.
101. Keiger, *France*, 157.
102. Albertini, *Origins* 2:628.
103. Keiger, *Poincaré*, 180.
104. Viviani to P. Cambon (30 July 1914), enclosure, *BD*, no. 319.
105. Bethmann to Schoen (31 July 1914), *GD*, no. 491; Schoen to Jagow (31 July 1914), *GD*, no. 528.
106. Viviani to P. Cambon (31 July 1914), *BD*, no. 338; Bertie to Grey (31 July 1914), *BD*, no. 363; Albertini, *Origins* 3:70.
107. Keiger, *Poincaré*, 181.
108. Albertini, *Origins* 3: 185.
109. Keiger, *Poincaré*, 183.
110. As late as 31 July Grey himself—sincerely or not—alluded to the possibility of British Neutrality to Lichnowsky. Lichnowsky to Jagow (31 July 1914), *GD*, no. 489.
111. Marc Trachtenberg, "The Meaning of Mobilization in 1914," *International Security* 15 (winter 1990–91), 211.
112. Contrary to the argument in Richard Ned Lebow, *Between Peace and War: The Nature of International Crises* (Baltimore: John Hopkins University Press, 1981), esp. 132.
113. The need to "put Russia in the wrong" was also dictated by German domestic politics. Fischer, *Germany's Aims*, 72–78; V. R. Berghahn, *Germany and the Approach of War in 1914*, 2nd ed. (New York: St. Martins, 1993), 214–18.
114. Wilhelm to Jagow (28 July 1914), *GD*, no. 293. Copeland, *Origins of Major War*, 93–94 (see also Albertini, *Origins* 2:470–71, 653) argues forcefully that the Wilhelmstrasse's 28 July revisions to the kaiser's "Halt in Belgrade" proposal reflect a hardened determination to provoke war "on three fronts"—that is, against Russia, France, and Britain. "This had nothing to do with keeping Britain neutral," writes Copeland, "war with Britain is assumed as a given" (94). He charges that Bethmann and Jagow altered the spirit of the proposal, delayed its transmission to Vienna, and appended many qualifications indicating that Germany did not want to "hold Austria back" from declaring war on Serbia. Copeland makes a strong, but to my mind not convincing, case that Germany was hell-bent on world war at this point. Mainly, he goes too far in ruling out any inclination on Bethmann's part to separate Britain from the entente. For example, he claims that Bethmann's "only goal was to so alter the original Halt formula as to placate Wilhelm while shifting world and German public opinion against Russia." (94) To support this point, he quotes Bethmann who writes that if Russia rejected the plan "it would have against it the public opinion of all Europe, which is now in the process of turning away from Austria. As a result, the general diplomatic, and probably the military, situation would undergo material alteration in favor of Austria-Hungary and her allies [i.e., Germany]." By inserting Germany in brackets at the end of this line, Copeland appears to exclude Austria's other nominal ally, Italy. This is unwarranted. These lines suggest that Bethmann still harbors hope that putting Russia in the wrong will "probably" materially alter the "general diplomatic" and "military" situation in Germany and Austria's favor by keeping Britain on the sidelines, which in turn will keep Italy from bolting. How else could making Russia appear the aggressor materially alter the general diplomatic and military contours of a European war? At the end of the day, to reconcile his claim that Berlin was intent on launching a "successful war on three fronts" (100) with his formidable mass of ev-

idence that Berlin was also exacting in its efforts to put Russia in the wrong, Copeland stresses the domestic political incentive—to rally popular support for world war from the working classes—above all else (102–3). But there is no reason to believe that the international incentive (to neutralize Britain) was any less compelling than the domestic one; common sense suggests that the two went hand in hand.

115. Bethmann to Tschirschky (28 July 1914), *GD*, no. 323.

116. These warnings are recorded in the following: Lichnowsky to Jagow (29 July 1914), *GD*, no. 357; Grey to Goschen (29 July 1914), *BD*, nos. 263, 284, 285, 286; Lichnowsky to Jagow (29 July 1914), *GD*, no. 368. Historians who point to Lichnowsky's last message of 29 July as the trigger for a dramatic, if short-lived, reversal in Bethmann's attitude include Albertini, *Origins* 2:502, 520–27; Fischer, *Germany's Aims*, 78–80; and Geiss, *July 1914*, 269. Trachtenberg disagrees, arguing that by 29 July German leaders had serious doubts about British neutrality and that what most caused Bethmann's reversal was the news of Russian partial mobilization that he received that evening. "The Meaning of Mobilization in 1914," 211–12. For a detailed debate of Trachtenberg's thesis, see Levy; Christensen; Trachtenberg; "Correspondence," 190–93, 197–200. One should not go too far in separating Bethmann's reaction to Grey's warnings from his reaction to Russia's mobilization. When the latter occurred, localization was gone for good, and that, in turn, magnified for Germany the importance of Britain's attitude.

117. Albertini, *Origins* 2:498.

118. Cf. Levy; Christensen; Trachtenberg; "Correspondence," 191.

119. The statement is by Falkenhayn, Prussian Minister of War, quoted in Albertini, *Origins* 2:502.

120. Bethmann promised that "in the event of a victorious war, Germany aimed at no territorial acquisitions at the expense of France" though not her colonies. He also promised to respect Dutch neutrality so long as it was similarly respected by Germany's adversaries, which Germany intended to do anyway in order to keep a "windpipe" open on the Continent for overseas trade. With respect to Belgium, he could promise no more than that if Belgium did not take sides against Germany "her integrity would be respected after the war." In addition to these assurances, Bethmann tried to sweeten the deal with the vague promise of a "general neutrality agreement between the two countries, the details of which it would, of course, be premature to discuss at the present moment." Bethmann to Goschen (29 July 1914), *GD*, no. 373; Goschen to Grey (29 July 1914), *BD*, no. 293. On German intentions regarding Holland, see Ritter, *The Sword and the Sceptre*, 152.

121. Lichnowsky to Jagow (29 July 1914), *GD*, no. 357; Pourtales to Jagow (29 July 1914), *GD*, no. 365.

122. Bethmann to Tschirschky (29 July 1914), *GD*, no. 377; Bethmann to Tschirschky (30 July 1914), *GD*, nos. 384, 385.

123. Albertini, *Origins*, 3:18; Bethmann to Tschirchky (2:55 A.M., 30 July 1914), *GD*, no. 395; Bethmann to Tschircky (3:00 A.M., 30 July 1914), *GD*, no. 396. Also see, Levy; Christensen; Trachtenberg; "Correspondence," 192–93.

124. Kaiser Wilhelm to Emperor Francis Joseph (30 July 1914), *GD*, no. 437; Albertini, *Origins*, 3:29.

125. Albertini, *Origins*, 2:666–67; 3:19–20.

126. Bethmann to Tschirschky (30 July 1914), *GD*, no. 441. Lebow describes this as a "timorous message" that "merely urged Austria to accept mediation," *Between War and Peace*, 137, n. 105. Albertini, similarly observes "a distinct softening of tone between this document and those of the previous night." *Origins* 3:22. It is true that the message lacks a threat to abandon Austria, but it is still strongly worded. It can only be considered timorous in comparison to the harsh message we, in hindsight, might wish Bethmann had sent.

127. A message from Moltke strongly urging general mobilization may have come too late to influence this decision, but it figured prominently in Berchtold's arguments before the Imperial Council of Ministers the next day in which the decision to announce general mobilization and to reject Grey's proposal was ratified. Ritter, *Sword and the Sceptre*, 258.

128. Bethmann to Tschirschky (11:20 P.M., 30 July 1914), *GD*, no. 450.
129. Goschen to Grey (31 July 1914), *BD*, nos. 336, 337.
130. Grey to Goschen (31 July 1914), *BD*, no. 340; Lichnowsky to Jagow (31 July 1914), *GD*, no. 489.
131. Goschen to Grey (31 July 1914), *BD*, no. 385.
132. Albertini, *Origins*, 3:39.
133. The best discussions are found in: Albertini, *Origins* 3:171–78, 380–86; Stephen J. Valone, "There Must Be Some Misunderstanding: Sir Edward Grey's Diplomacy of August 1, 1914," *Journal of British Studies* 27 (October 1988): 405–24; Harry F. Young, "The Misunderstanding of August 1, 1914," *Journal of Modern History* 48 (December 1976): 644–65.
134. Lichnowsky to Grey (31 July 1914), *BD*, no. 372.
135. Lichnowsky to Jagow (1 August 1914), *GD*, no. 562.
136. King George V to Kaiser Wilhelm (1 August 1914), *GD*, no. 612.
137. See Young, "Misunderstanding of August 1, 1914," 656–63; Valone, "There Must Be Some Misunderstanding," passim.
138. Trachtenberg, "The Meaning of Mobilization," 216; Albertini, *Origins*, 3:171–81, 380–85.
139. Valone, "There Must Be Some Misunderstanding," 422.
140. (20 July 1914), *BD*, no. 67; Grey, *Twenty Five Years*, 1:299.
141. Williamson, *Politics of Grand Strategy*, 330.
142. Bertie to Nicolson (14 May 1911), quoted in Lowe and Dockrill, *Mirage*, 3:433.

CHAPTER 5. HURTING THE ONE WHO LOVES YOU MOST
1. On the many dimensions of Greek-Turkey conflict see, Monteagle Stearns, *Entangled Allies: U.S. Policy Toward Greece, Turkey, and Cyprus* (New York: Council on Foreign Relations, 1992), chap. 8.
2. Alvin Z. Rubinstein, *Soviet Policy Toward Turkey, Iran, and Afghanistan: The Dynamics of Influence* (New York: Praeger, 1982), 33; Suha Bolukbasi, *The Superpowers and the Third World: Turkish-American Relations and Cyprus* (Lanham, Md.: University Press of America, 1988), 209–11.
3. Bolukbasi, *Superpowers*, 199.
4. Theodore Coloumbis, *The United States, Greece, and Turkey: The Troubled Triangle* (New York: Praeger, 1983), 96–97; Christopher Hitchens, *Hostage to History: Cyprus from the Ottomans to Kissinger* (New York: Farrar, Straus, and Giroux, 1984), 99. On the Geneva negotiations, see Bolukbasi, *Superpowers*, 200–7.
5. See Van Coufoudakis, "United States Foreign Policy and the Cyprus Question: A Case Study in Cold War Diplomacy," in *U.S. Foreign Policy Toward Greece and Cyprus: The Clash of Principle and Pragmatism*, ed. Theodore A. Coloumbis and Sallie M. Hicks (Washington D.C.: Center for Mediterranean Studies, 1975), 106–38.
6. T. W. Adams, "The American Concern in Cyprus," *Annals of the American Academy of Political and Social Sciences* 401 (May 1972): 95, 99; Edward Weintal and Charles Bartlett, *Facing the Brink: An Intimate Study of Crisis Diplomacy* (New York: Scribner's, 1967), 37; Glen D. Camp, "Greek-Turkish Conflict Over Cyprus," *Political Science Quarterly* 95 (spring 1980): 53.
7. Johnson quoted in Hitchens, *Hostage*, 61.
8. Quoted in Sharon A. Wiener, "Turkish Foreign Policy Decision-Making on the Cyprus Issue: A Comparative Analysis of Three Crises" (Ph.D. diss., Duke University, 1980), 115, n. 3.
9. Stockholm International Peace Research Institute, *SIPRI Yearbook of World Armaments and Disarmament, 1969/70* (New York: Humanities Press, 1970), 267, table 1A.2.
10. During the period 1960–67, the figures are 29 percent for Greece and 30 percent for Turkey. Figures computed from data in ibid., 282, table A.
11. Ibid., 267, table 1A.2.
12. More specifically, 6.3:10. The annual figures are as follows: 1960, 11:10; 1961, 5:10; 1962, 2:10; 1963, 4:10; 1964, 8:10; 1965, 9:10; 1966, 8:10; 1967, 4:10. Figures cited in Stearns, *Entangled Allies*, 167, nn. 7, 8, 9.

13. Ronald R. Krebs, "Perverse Institutionalism: NATO and the Greco-Turkish Conflict," *International Organization* 53 (spring 1999): 363.

14. Parker T. Hart, *Two NATO Allies at the Threshold of War* (Durham, NC: Duke University Press, 1990), 36.

15. John F. Kennedy, National Security Action Memorandum No. 71, 23 August 1961, *Foreign Relations of the United States* [hereafter *FRUS*], 1961–63, vol. 16 (Washington D.C.: GPO, 1994), no. 248; Rusk and McCloskey, *Department of State Bulletin* 50 (24 February 1964): 283–84.

16. Memo from Battle to Bundy (7 September 1961), *FRUS*, 1961–63, vol. 16, no. 249; Memo from Brubeck to Bundy, (13 July 1962), ibid., no. 262.

17. Joseph S. Joseph, *Cyprus: Ethnic Conflict and International Politics* (New York: St. Martin's, 1997), 59.

18. For various statements to this effect, see *FRUS*, 1964–68, vol. 16, nos. 80, 188, 211, 221, 257, 295.

19. As Rusk wrote to his embassies in Greece, Turkey, and Cyprus during the 1967 crisis, "The issues in Cyprus itself are, strictly from the point of view of US national interest, trivial compared to peace between Greece and Turkey. Our responsibility is to support that central US national interest." (23 November 1967), *FRUS*, 1964–68, vol. 16, no. 318.

20. Rusk to embassy in Cyprus (9 January 1963), *FRUS*, 1961–63, vol. 16, no. 268.

21. See Sir George Hill, *A History of Cyprus* (London: Cambridge University Press, 1952), 4:488–568.

22. Bolukbasi, *Superpowers*, 30–32.

23. Joseph, *Cyprus*, 20.

24. London-Zurich Treaties of 1959, Annex I, Treaty of Guarantee. Reproduced in Hart, *Two NATO Allies*, 143–58.

25. Joseph, *Cyprus*, 23.

26. *Keesings Contemporary Archives* (London: Keesings Ltd.) [hereafter *Keesings*](1963), 19257, 20113; *FRUS*, 1961–63, vol. 16, nos. 267, 277. On Makarios' decision to revise the constitution, see Thomas Ehrlich, *Cyprus, 1958–1967: International Crises and the Role of Law* (New York: Oxford University Press, 1974), 43–60.

27. Telegrams from embassy in Cyprus (Wilkins) to Department of State (DOS), (12 January 1962 and 16 January 1963), *FRUS*, 1961–63, vol. 16, nos. 255, 270.

28. Two months later, calling attention to Makarios' moves, Erkin appealed for U.S. "advice and assistance" and probed its attitude toward Turkey using force to defend the London-Zurich bargain. Telegrams from embassy in Turkey (Hare) to DOS, (14 February and 1 April 1963), ibid., nos. 273, 277.

29. Hare to DOS, (6 November 1963), ibid., no. 294, n. 3; Memcon, Secretary's Delegation to the 18th Session of the UN General Assembly (1 October 1963), ibid., no. 289.

30. Hare to DOS (20 October 1963), ibid., no. 291.

31. Wilkins to DOS, (26 November 1963), ibid., no. 295; Rusk to Wilkins, (27 November 1963), ibid., no. 296.

32. Makarios' Thirteen Points reproduced in Joseph, *Cyprus*, app. 4, 146–47.

33. DOS (Ball) to Wilkins, (4 April 1963), *FRUS*, 1961–63, vol. 16, no. 278.

34. Wilkins to DOS (13 February 1963), ibid, no. 272.

35. National Security Action Memorandum No. 71, ibid., no. 248; Memo from DOS (Battle) to the President's Special Assistant for National Security Affairs (Bundy), (7 September 1961), ibid., no. 249.

36. Rusk to Embassies in Nicosia, Ankara, Athens, and London, (9 January 1963), ibid., no. 268. Rusk's instructions were faithfully carried out. When asked for U.S. support, Briggs, Wilkins, and Hare (ambassadors to Greece, Cyprus, and Turkey respectively), responded that the United States urged moderation on all sides and hinted that those who were most willing to cooperate would be most likely to win U.S. favor. For example, when Erkin called Hare's attention to Makarios' provocations in April 1963 and asked for U.S. support, Hare replied that "if [Turkey] felt Makarios' statements excessive, [the] thing to avoid would be to

reply in kind. To do so would merely escalate problem . . . and would also not reflect favorably on the position of reasonableness which Turkey asserts to be its purpose." Hare to DOS (1 April 1963), ibid., no. 277.

37. Rusk to London embassy (16 February 1963), ibid, no. 274. When Erkin appealed directly to Rusk for U.S. pressure on Makarios in December, Rusk was "noncommittal." The United States "already had enough problems on its agenda without taking on the Cyprus dispute." Rusk Memo (15 December 1963), ibid., no. 397.

38. Ball wrote in April 1963, "we believe [a] Turkish attempt at direct military intervention most unlikely . . . Move against Cyprus by Turkish military might mean clash with Greece and might also bring down great pressure by interested outside powers. This does not mean, of course, that [the government of Turkey] will not continue [to] hint darkly at [the] possibility [of] such intervention when it considers such a tactic useful." DOS to Nicosia and Ankara (4 April 1963), ibid., no. 278.

39. Wiener, "Turkish Foreign Policy," 126; Keesings (1964), 20114–15; Bolukbasi, Superpowers, 67.

40. George W. Ball, The Past Has Another Pattern: Memoirs, (New York: Norton, 1973).

41. Keesings (1964), 20116, 20118.

42. T. W. Adams and Alvin J. Cotrell, Cyprus between East and West, (Baltimore, Md: Johns Hopkins University Press, 1968), 35.

43. Khruschev to Johnson, (7 February 1964), in Joseph, Cyprus, 155–57; Keesings (1964), 20017.

44. Ball, Past, 342–46.

45. Keesings (1964), 20118–19.

46. Andreas Papandreou, Democracy at Gunpoint: The Greek Front (New York: Doubleday, 1970), 132.

47. Keesings (1964), 20119.

48. "Presidential Decision Study: The Cyprus Crises," State Department Report, NEA/Cyprus (24 October 1968)[hereafter "PDS"], 15. Document electronically reproduced on Primary Source Microfilm [hereafter PSM]. This and all other PSM documents were accessed at Columbia University Library, Declassified Documents Reference System-US, 11 November 2001.

49. Keesings (1964), 20120.

50. Ibid., 20121; Ball, Past, 350.

51. Papandreou, Democracy, 133; Joseph, Cyprus, 107; "PDS," 20.

52. Coloumbis, United States, 62; Keesings (1964), 20125.

53. "PDS," 18.

54. Hare to DOS, (5 June 1964), quoted in Wiener, "Turkish Foreign Policy," 115.

55. Ibid., 119.

56. Ibid., 117.

57. "PDS," 18.

58. Ball, Past, 350.

59. Johnson to İnönü (5 June 1964), FRUS, 1964–68, vol. 16, no. 54.

60. İnönü to Johnson, (13 June 1964), quoted in Hart, Two NATO Allies, 167–75. Some accounts suggest that Turkey did not seriously mean to invade because it did not have the capability and because İnönü had personal misgivings about invading. Therefore, Johnson's letter was more an excuse for Turkey to back down than the cause of it. See Nur Bilge Criss, "A Short History of Anti-Americanism and Terrorism: The Turkish Case," Journal of American History 89 (September 2002): 475, n. 9, citing 1999 remarks by George Harris, who made the case more subtly in Troubled Alliance: Turkish-American Problems in Historical Perspective, 1945–1971 (Washington D.C.: American Enterprise Institute, 1972), 113–14. The capabilities argument relies on reports in Turkish newspapers, shortly after the crisis, that Turkey did not have adequate landing craft for an invasion. See Bolukbasi, Superpowers, 68–69. But Turkey had overwhelming air and land power, as well as a formidable navy, which made an invasion feasible even without specialized landing craft. With regard to İnönü's intentions, what many have described as his

risk-averse personality probably facilitated Turkey's back-down (see Harris, *Troubled Alliance,* 114; Wiener, "Turkish Foreign Policy," 131; Bolukbasi, *Superpowers,* 66). But even if İnönü was inwardly reluctant to invade, he was also under tremendous pressure from his National Security Council (i.e., the Turkish military) to do so. Turkey had succumbed to military dictatorship in 1960, returning to civilian rule in 1961, and the military's commitment to civilian rule was still in doubt. If Johnson's letter helped İnönü to overcome the military's determination to invade (see Harris, *Troubled Alliance,* 114), then it makes sense to say that it restrained Turkey. In the declassified documents pertaining to U.S.-Turkey diplomacy after the crisis, there are many references by officials on *both* sides—in conversations and correspondence that were presumed at the time to be confidential—to the letter's critical role in Turkey's decision not to invade. See *FRUS, 1964–68,* vol. 16, nos. 59, 60, 70, 118, 230, 266, 311. I found no references in the documentary record to the landing craft issue. Quite to the contrary is a 7 July 1964 NSC meeting, in which a U.S. General briefed Johnson on "the military forces that would participate in any hostilities on Cyprus." After the briefing, according to the memorandum for the record, Johnson "summarized his understanding in these terms: The Turks have substantially greater forces than the Greeks in every respect [and] they could *land and maintain a beachhead . . .* General Burchinal confirmed the President's understanding, estimating Turk Army superiority at 3–1 and air force at 4–1." Ibid., no. 82. Given the tight relationship between the U.S. and Turkish militaries at the time, it is very unlikely that U.S. intelligence would attribute to Turkey an invasion capability that it did not have.

61. Ball, *Past,* 353.

62. Weintal and Bartlett, *Facing,* 25–26; Papandreou, *Democracy,* 133.

63. U.S. Ambassador to Greece (Labouisse) to DOS (14 June 1964) *FRUS, 1964–68,* vol. 16, no. 68.

64. Harris, *Troubled,* 117.

65. In Johnson's words, "If I can't get you to talk [with Turkey], I can't keep the Turks from moving." Memcon: President's Meeting with Greek Ambassador Matsas (11 June 1964), *FRUS, 1964–68,* vol. 16, no. 62; also see nos. 70, 74, 75.

66. Papandreou, *Democracy,* 134–35. Also see *FRUS, 1964–68,* vol. 16, nos. 75, 81.

67. *Keesings* (1964), 20268; Ball, *Past,* 355.

68. As Papandreou put the formula to U.S. officials: "[T]he only possible solution is unrestricted independence. This would be followed by a plebiscite and enosis." Memcon: Cyprus Situation and Greek-Turkish Relations (24 June 1964), *FRUS, 1964–68,* vol. 16, no. 75. Wrote Rusk two years later, Athens "clearly hopes that unfettered independence for Cyprus will ultimately lead to union with Greece." Rusk to United States' United Nations Mission (USUN) (29 January 1966), ibid., no. 220.

69. Ball described Grivas as a "fanatic, fortunately anti-communist." Memo for Record: NSC Meeting on Cyprus (7 July 1964), *FRUS, 1964–68,* vol. 16, no. 82. On Papandreou's covert plan for "instant enosis" and its evolution, see ibid., nos. 94, 97, 99, 103, 131–33, 154; Hart, *Two NATO Allies,* 183–87; Ball, *Past,* 357; Weintal and Bartlett, *Facing,* 31–32.

70. "PDS," 17.

71. On Acheson's negotiations, see *FRUS, 1964–68,* vol. 16, nos. 73, 74, 77, 83, 85–91, 124–39; Coufoudakis, "United States Foreign Policy and the Cyprus Question," 113–17; Bolukbasi, *Superpowers,* 81; Ball, *Past,* 357; Coloumbis, *United States,* 46–47; Harris, *Troubled,* 117; Weintal and Bartlett, *Facing,* 31.

72. Bolukbasi, *Superpowers,* 81.

73. Quoted in Hedrick Smith, "Makarios Refuses to Yield," *New York Times,* 31 August 1964.

74. Memo: Komer and Bundy to Johnson (18 August 1964), in Hart, *Two NATO Allies,* 185; also see Memo for Record: NSC Meeting (4 August 1964) *FRUS, 1964–68,* vol. 16, no. 102, n. 2.; *Keesings* (1964), 20269.

75. Talbot to DOS (31 July 1964) *FRUS, 1964–68,* vol. 16, no. 97. Makarios made essentially the same point: "Papandreou will accept anything I agree to but I don't necessarily accept any decision he may make." Belcher to DOS (18 August 1964), ibid., no. 130.

76. A Greek-Cypriot agent informed the U.S. embassy in Nicosia of Makarios' intention to escalate on 31 July 1964. On 9 August Papandreou admitted that "Makarios had probably planned the operation . . . for some time." *FRUS, 1964–68*, vol. 16, nos. 96, 117.

77. Bolukbasi, *Superpowers*, 82; Wiener, "Turkish Foreign Policy," 121.

78. Hare to DOS (7 August 1964), Rusk to Talbot (7 August 1964) *FRUS, 1964–68*, vol. 16, nos. 104, 105.

79. Telcon: Johnson and Ball (9 August 1964), ibid., no. 111; *Keesings* (1964), 20265.

80. Joseph, *Cyprus*, 45; *Keesings* (1964), 20266.

81. As Ball reported to Johnson that day, "the Makarios government has just told our people in Nicosia that unless they [Turkish air strikes] stop within a half an hour, they're going to turn on the whole Turk Cypriot population on the island and attack them all over the island with just a general massacre." Telcon: Johnson and Ball (9 August 1964) *FRUS, 1964–68*, vol. 16, no. 111.

82. As the first bombs fell, Makarios called on Greece to provide air cover to Cyprus. The response of the Greek air force amounted to what George Papandreou, at the time, described as a "theatrical demonstration of four planes." Talbot to DOS (9 August 1964) *FRUS, 1964–68*, vol. 16, nos. 112, 117. In Andreas Papandreou's words, Greece did not respond to Nicosia's appeal, "not because we did not wish to, but because it was technically impossible. Cyprus was far from Greek air bases, and our fighters would have had only two minutes flying time over Cyprus." Papandreou, *Democracy*, 136.

83. As Johnson put it in July, his "understanding" was that "the Soviets would not intervene" against a Turkish use of force. Memo for Record: NSC Meeting on Cyprus (7 July 1964) *FRUS, 1964–68*, vol. 16, no. 82. On 9 August Ball told Johnson that he didn't "think for a minute that [the Soviets were] going to respond to Makarios' call" for military intervention. In fact, said Ball, the Soviets had "told the Turks, within the last week, that if the Turks intervened they wouldn't do anything about it." Telcon: Johnson and Ball (9 August 1964), ibid., no. 111. The same day, Labouisse informed Papandreou that "direct and immediate Soviet or UAR [United Arab Republic] intervention seemed rather unlikely," Labouisse to DOS, ibid., no. 112. In September, Ball repeated his estimate that Moscow would not answer Makarios's appeal "in any serious way," Bundy to Johnson (8 September 1964), ibid, no. 155.

84. *Keesings* (1964), 20266; Hedrick Smith, "Makarios Scores West to Nasser: At Egypt Meeting Cypriote Asks All-Out Arab Aid," *New York Times*, 30 August 1964, 28.

85. Belcher to DOS (9 August 1964) *FRUS, 1964–68*, vol. 16, no. 116, n. 2; DOS to Embassy Greece (9 August 1964), ibid., no. 114; Embassy Greece to DOS (9 August 1964), ibid., no. 112; DOS to Hare (9 August 1964), ibid., no. 115, n. 2.

86. Rusk to Acheson (15 August 1964), ibid., no. 125.

87. See especially, Embassy Greece to DOS (21 August 1964), ibid., no. 136; Bolukbasi, *Superpowers*, 86.

88. Erkin to Acheson (28 August 1964), in Weintal and Bartlett, *Facing*, 221.

89. *Keesings* (1964), 20266.

90. At the time, Athens claimed that Grivas had gone to Cyprus "on his own initiative and as an ordinary citizen." Ibid., 20270.

91. For U.S. assessments of Soviet reluctance to back Cyprus, see *FRUS, 1964–68* vol. 16, nos. 151, 174.

92. Hart, *Two NATO Allies*, 28.

93. Adams and Cotrell, *Cyprus*, 38.

94. "Turks Delay Troop Move in Cyprus 'for short time,' " *New York Times*, 30 August 1964, 1.

95. *Keesings* (1964), 20371; Adams and Cotrell, *Cyprus*, 40, 44.

96. George Harris, "Cross Alliance Politics: Turkey and the Soviet Union," *Turkish Yearbook of International Affairs* 12 (1972): 24.

97. Mehmet Gonlubol, "NATO and Turkey," in *Turkey's Foreign Policy in Transition, 1950–1974*, ed. Kemal H. Karpat (Leiden: E. J. Brill, 1975), 29; Duygu Bazoglu Sexer, *Turkey's Security Policies*, Adelphi Paper no. 164 (London: Institute for International Security Studies, 1981), 23–24.

98. Wiener, "Turkish Foreign Policy," 133–34, 145.

99. Kemal Karpat, "Turkish Soviet Relations," in *Turkey's Foreign Policy*, 92.

100. For early indications of a thaw in Soviet-Turkish relations in August and September 1964, see *FRUS, 1964–68*, vol. 16, nos. 138, 140, 156.

101. "The tone of the Turk-Soviet communiqué," observed Rusk, "could be somewhat sobering for the Greek-Cypriots." Memcon: DOS and Galo-Plaza (9 November 1964) *FRUS, 1964–68*, vol. 16, no. 164.

102. *Keesings* (1965), 20500; Adams and Cotrell, *Cyprus*, 41.

103. On the origins of the MLF, see John D. Steinbrunner, *The Cybernetic Theory of Decision-making: New Dimensions of Political Analysis* (Princeton, N. J.: Princeton University Press, 1974), chap. 8. On Moscow's reaction to Turkey's withdrawal, see Karapat, "Turkish Soviet Relations," 93.

104. Robert H. Estabrook, "20 to 40 Missiles Reported on Cyprus," *Washington Post*, 7 May 1965, A28.

105. *Keesings* (1965), 20936; Bolukbasi, *Superpowers*, 117.

106. *Keesings* (1965), 20936; Rubinstein, *Soviet Policy*, 2.

107. Karpat, "Turkish Soviet Relations," 96–97.

108. As Talbot cabled to Hart, "the Turks . . . now see tactical advantage in involving [the U.S.] in [the] morass of internal problems on the island at the moment when they have also opened question of U.S. military facilities for discussion," (20 April 1966), *FRUS, 1964–68*, vol. 16, no. 229. That month, in an Ankara meeting between Demirel, Rusk, and their staffs, the Turkish foreign minister said "the [government of Turkey] wants the U.S. to come forward and say yes, the Turks are right." Demirel followed up: "we want you to influence Makarios and the Greek Government . . . we cannot always be the ones to give." Another Foreign Ministry official posed the question to Rusk "if something should flare up on the island, then what? Would there be another ["Johnson"] letter from the U.S.? If the Turks should react, and if there were a threat from the outside, would Turkey get NATO help?" Memcon: Rusk and Demirel (22 April 1966), ibid., no. 230. Also see nos. 232, 233, 249; Harris, *Troubled*, 161; Coloumbis, *United States*, 67.

109. Adams and Cotrell, *Cyprus*, 47.

110. Harris, "Cross Alliance Politics," 26; Rubinstein, *Soviet Policy*, 26.

111. Hart, *Two NATO Allies*, 24.

112. Labouisse to DOS (16 September 1964), *FRUS, 1964–68*, vol. 16, no. 157.

113. Labouisse to DOS (21 March 1965), ibid., no. 183. In March 1965, Papandreou wrote Washington complaining that while Greece was a "sincere and faithful ally," Turkey was engaged in a "courtship" with Moscow, and yet, Turkey had not received "any allied criticism which seems to be reserved as a prize of the steadfastness of Greece." Ibid. (16 March 1965), no. 180, n. 5. Also see nos. 187, 195, 243, 252.

114. On the development of these talks, see ibid., nos. 195, 198.

115. On the coup plot, U.S. knowledge of it, its opposition to such a "constitutional deviation," and its decision *not* to give covert support to the right wing in the May 1967 elections that triggered the coup, see ibid., nos. 224, 245, 255, 259–61, 264, 266–69, 271–73. Cf. Maurice Goldbloom, "United States Policy in Post-War Greece," in *Greece Under Military Rule*, ed. Richard Clogg and George Yannopoulos (London: Secker and Warburg, 1972), 237–39; Papandreou, *Democracy*; Hitchens, *Hostage*, 62–64; Laurence Stern, *The Wrong Horse* (New York: Times Books, 1977); Stephen Rousseas, *The Death of Democracy* (New York: Grove Press, 1967).

116. For example, in February 1967, Talbot was contacted by various members of the Greek Crown Council probing for a statement on what the U.S. government "would do in case of Turkish attack." Talbot to DOS (10 February 1967), *FRUS, 1964–68*, vol. 16, no. 254. For earlier efforts to enlist U.S. pressure on Turkey in the context of bilateral talks, see nos. 231, 235, 239, 243, 257.

117. Talbot to DOS (23 April and 5 May 1967), ibid., nos. 279, 284. Or, as an official in the junta put it to Talbot, "we are with you whether you want us or not." Ibid., no. 282, n. 6.

118. Coloumbis, *United States*, 53–54.

119. Hart, *Two NATO Allies*, 31; Wiener, "Turkish Foreign Policy," 151–53; *FRUS*, 1964–68, vol. 16, no. 232, 242.

120. Hart, *Two NATO Allies*, 178. On the September talks, see *FRUS*, 1964–68, vol. 16, nos. 299, 302; Coufoudakis, "United States Foreign Policy and the Cyprus Question," 121, n. 108; A. G. Xydis, "The Military Regime's Foreign Policy," in *Greece Under Military Rule*, ed. Clogg and Yannopoulos, 201.

121. Wiener, "Turkish Foreign Policy," 152, 179–80.

122. *Keesings* (1967), 22335.

123. Ehrlich argues that Athens orchestrated Grivas' offensive (*Cyprus*, 97). But a State Department report at the time noted that "the junta leadership is unanimously agreed that General Grivas overstepped his authority in precipitating" the 15 November fighting. Unsigned Memorandum. DOS (18 November 1967), *PSM*. A later State Department assessment argued that "hawkish elements in the [Athens] power structure bear some responsibility for the Ayios Theordoros-Kophinou incident. Memo: DOS (5 December 1967), *PSM*.

124. Xydis, "Military Regime's Foreign Policy," 202. Ehrlich says that "most estimates were in the 10,000 to 12,000 range." *Cyprus*, 90, n. 1. Similar estimates appear in *FRUS*, 1964–68, vol. 16, nos. 152, 169, 179.

125. *Keesings* (1967), 21948; Hart, *Two NATO Allies*, 22.

126. Hart, *Two NATO Allies*, 49.

127. Wiener, "Turkish Foreign Policy," 181–82.

128. *Keesings* (1967), 22435.

129. See Telcon: Hart to DOS (15 November 1967) *FRUS*, 1964–68, vol. 16, no. 308; "United States Efforts to Resolve the Cyprus Crisis of November-December 1967," DOS Report: Historical Studies Division, Bureau of Public Affairs, Research Project No. 939B (October 1968)[hereafter "United States Efforts"], 5. *PSM*.

130. *Keesings* (1967), 22435.

131. Wiener, "Turkish Foreign Policy," 185–88; "United States Efforts," 7.

132. Johnson to Embassies (17 November 1967) *FRUS*, 1964–68, vol. 16, no. 310.

133. Unsigned Memo: DOS (18 November 1967), *PSM*.

134. "A Comparison of Turkish Five Points, GOG [government of Greece] Proposal November 25, and GOT [government of Turkey] Proposal November 25," 26 November 1967, *Vance Papers*, Sterling Library, Yale University, box 2, folder 16 [hereafter *VP*]. Hart, *Two NATO Allies*, 61.

135. Belcher to DOS (22 November 1967) *FRUS*, 1964–68, vol. 16, no. 314.

136. Talbot to DOS (23 November 1967), ibid., no. 317; Vance Crisis Summary Notes (handwritten—yellow pad), *VP*; Transcript, Cyrus R. Vance Oral History Interview II 12/29/69, by Paige E. Mulhollan, Internet Copy, Lyndon Baines Johnson Library [hereafter *VOHI*], 3; Hart, *Two NATO Allies*, 65.

137. Hart, *Two NATO Allies*, 66; "United States Efforts," 9.

138. Wiener, "Turkish Foreign Policy," 192; Final Report of Vance Mission to Turkey, Greece, and Cyprus, 22 November–4 December 1967, *PSM*, 4.

139. "United States Efforts," 11.

140. NSC Report (n.d.): The President and the Cyprus Crisis: December 1963–December 1967, *PSM*, 9.

141. Memorandum for the President: NSC Discussion of Cyprus—The Broader Issues (28 November 1967), *PSM*.

142. "United States Efforts," 11.

143. Vance notes on meeting with Lucius Battle at John F. Kennedy airport (handwritten—yellow pad), *VP*; *VOHI*, 2.

144. Wiener, "Turkish Foreign Policy," 193.

145. First Meeting with the GOT—Opening Statement of Vance (notes on typescript), n.d.; and Vance notes (yellow pad—heading "yesterday at brink of war"), n.d., *VP*.

146. Hart, *Two NATO Allies*, 70–71, 73.

147. Talbot to DOS (23 November 1967) *FRUS, 1964–68*, vol. 16, no. 319.
148. Vance Notes on Negotiations with Turkey (handwritten—white pad), n.d., *VP.*
149. Wiener, "Turkish Foreign Policy," 191.
150. Talbot to DOS (24 November 1967), *FRUS, 1964–68*, vol. 16, no. 320.
151. Athens' 6–point "phased withdrawal" proposal, n.d., *VP;* "United States Efforts," 13.
152. Talbot to DOS (24 November 1967), *FRUS, 1964–68*, vol. 16, no. 320.
153. "United States Efforts," 12.
154. Hart to DOS (25 November 1967) *FRUS, 1964–68*, vol. 16, no. 322.
155. Talbot to DOS (25 November 1967), ibid., no. 324.
156. Wiener, "Turkish Foreign Policy," 196.
157. Vance Notes (handwritten—yellow pad: heading "yesterday at brink of war"), n.d., *VP.*
158. "A Comparison of Turkish Five Points, GOG Proposal November 25, and GOT Proposal November 25," 26 November 1967; and "Turkish Proposal of November 25, 1967 Revised by Mr. Vance After Taking Into Consideration the Suggestions of Mr. Rolz-Bennett," *VP;* Hart, *Two Nato Allies,* 79–80.
159. "United States Efforts," 14.
160. Talbot to DOS (27 November 1967) *FRUS, 1964–68*, vol. 16, no. 325; Hart, *Two NATO Allies,* 80–81.
161. Text of Agreement Proposed by Government of Greece (26 November 1967), *PSM;* "United States Efforts," 15.
162. Hart to DOS (27 November 1967) *FRUS, 1964–68*, vol. 16, no. 326.
163. Talbot to DOS (27 November 1967), ibid., no. 325; *VOHI,* 4–5.
164. Vance Four-Point Proposal, n.d., *VP;* "United States Efforts," 16.
165. Talbot to DOS (28 November 1967), ibid., no. 328; Vance notes (handwritten-photocopy), n.d., *VP; VOHI,* 6. After accepting the Vance plan, Athens submitted an "interpretive query" regarding "upward flexibility" on the forty-five–day withdrawal period. Demirel gave Çağlayangil the authority to "take responsibility for technical extension of fifteen days, if it proves necessary, for evacuation of equipment (not personnel), assuming of course that Greeks have been withdrawing troops in good faith and continuously." That day, in a note to the NATO Secretary General, Çağlayangil indicated that he would be willing "to envisage" a fifteen-day extension for Greece under these terms. Hart to DOS, Athens, and Nicosia, (29 November 1967), *VP;* Çağlayangil to Brosio (29 November 1967), *PSM.* All this amounted to meeting Vance's request for a two-month withdrawal period.
166. Wiener, "Turkish Foreign Policy," 198.
167. Talbot to DOS (28 November 1967), *FRUS, 1964–68*, vol. 16, no. 329.
168. Talbot to DOS (28 November 1967), ibid., no. 330; Pipinellis to Vance (28 November 1967).
169. *VOHI,* 6; Telcon: Talbot and Belcher, (29 November 1967), *VP.*
170. Hart to DOS, Athens, and Nicosia, (29 November 1967), *VP.* Two days earlier, Rusk urged his diplomats in the region to brainstorm tactics "to deter Makarios from reverting to his classic waltz around [the] ring tightly clutching the UN." Rusk to Talbott (27 November 1967), *FRUS, 1964–68*, vol. 16, no. 327.
171. Belcher to DOS (29 November 1967), ibid., no. 333; Vance notes on Negotiations with Makarios (handwritten—yellow pad), n.d., *VP.*
172. "United States Efforts," 18–19, 20–24.
173. Telcon: Talbot and Belcher, (29 November 1967), *VP; Keesings* (1967), 22437.
174. In a NSC meeting on 29 November, Director of Central Intelligence Richard Helms stated that the "Russians are fishing in troubled waters by egging on the Turks and telling the Cypriots that Turkey was bluffing." However, it is clear that Turkey needed no encouragement from Moscow to press its case. Moreover, there does not appear to be evidence of a concerted or sustained Soviet effort to convince Cyprus that, as Rusk put it, "Turks are bluffing." An official State Department postmortem of the crisis cautiously notes that the *"alleged* Soviet assertion" that Turkey was bluffing "may have been made by Soviet Ambassador [to

Cyprus] who saw Makarios before a Cabinet meeting on November 24." Summary of Notes of 579th NSC Meeting (29 November 1967), *FRUS, 1964–68*, vol. 16, no. 332; Rusk to Belcher (29 November 1967), ibid., no. 331; "United States Efforts," 18.

175. Hart, *Two NATO Allies*, 82.

176. *VOHI*, 7; also see Weiner, "Turkish Foreign Policy," 203.

177. Memcon: Rusk and Venizelos (26 November 1963), *FRUS 1961–63*, vol. 16, no. 357.

178. Rusk to DOS (18 December 1963), ibid., no. 300.

179. Rusk to Nicosia, Ankara, Athens, and London Embassies (9 January 1963), ibid., no. 268.

180. Wiener, "Turkish Foreign Policy," 105.

181. Quoted in Krebs, "Perverse Institutionalism," 363.

182. Athanasios Platias, "Greece's Strategic Doctrine," in *The Greek-Turkish Conflict in the 1990s*, ed. Dimitri Constas (London: Macmillan, 1991), 91–108.

183. Wiener, "Turkish Foreign Policy," 152; Hart, *Two NATO Allies*, 31.

184. Krebs, "Perverse Institutionalism," 353.

CHAPTER 6. PLAYING THE PIVOT IN A CROWDED MARKET

1. For details on the war, see Sumit Ganguly, *Conflict Unending: India-Pakistan Tensions Since 1947* (New York: Columbia University Press, 2001), chap. 2.

2. Yaacov Vertzberger, *The Enduring Entente: Sino-Pakistani Relations, 1960–1980* (New York: Praeger, 1983), 36.

3. John W. Garver, *Protracted Contest: Sino-Indian Rivalry in the Twentieth Century* (Seattle: University of Washington Press, 2001), 200; Rasul Bux Rais, *China and Pakistan: A Political Analysis of Mutual Relations* (Lahore: Progressive Publishers, 1977), 62.

4. G. W. Choudhury, *India, Pakistan, Bangladesh, and the Major Powers: Politics of a Divided Subcontinent* (New York: The Free Press, 1975), 189; Herbert Feldman, *From Crisis to Crisis: Pakistan 1962–1969* (London: Oxford University Press, 1972), 152.

5. People's Republic of China (PRC) to Indian Embassy, Beijing (16 September 1965), in *American Foreign Policy: Current Documents, 1965* (Washington: GPO, 1968), 752–54.

6. Choudhury, *Major Powers*, 190–91; *FRUS, 1964–68*, vol. 25, nos. 208, 212; *FRUS, 1964–68*, vol. 30, no. 204.

7. The best review of this debate is Garver, *Protracted Contest*, 201–4, esp. n. 47. Garver citing a declassified CIA assessment that military action was likely (201) concludes that Choudhury's claim (in *Major Powers*) that China was serious is reliable.

8. William J. Barnds, *India, Pakistan, and the Great Powers* (New York: Praeger, 1972), 207. Indonesia also gave material and moral support to Pakistan, although much less consequential. See K. B. Sayeed, "Southeast Asia in Pakistan's Foreign Policy," *Pacific Affairs* 41 (summer 1968): 237.

9. Barnds, *Great Powers*, 206.

10. Robert J. McMahon, *The Cold War on the Periphery: The United States, India, and Pakistan* (New York: Columbia University Press, 1994), 328.

11. Figures are calculated from annual tables in *SIPRI Yearbook: World Military Armaments and Disarmament: 1972* (New York: Humanities Press, 1973), 82–83, 88–89.

12. The yearly ratios are: 1960, 10:3.5; 1961, 10:3.2; 1962, 10:2.2; 1963, 10:1.4; 1964, 10:1.7; 1965, 10:2.8. Figures are calculated from annual tables in ibid., 88–89.

13. The 1954–65 figure for Pakistan defense spending is calculated from ibid. For the $1.5 billion estimate for U.S. military aid to Pakistan for the same period, see *SIPRI Yearbook: World Military Armaments and Disarmament: 1968/69* (New York: Humanities Press, 1970), 77, n. 43.

14. B. K. Mohapatra, *United States–Pakistan Military Alliance: A Study of Stresses and Strains* (Delhi: Ajanta Publications, 1998), 147.

15. Wayne Wilcox, "Political Role of Army in Pakistan: Some Reflections," *South Asian Studies* 7 (January 1972): 30–44, esp. 36.

16. On the history of the Kashmir conflict, see Sumit Ganguly, *The Crisis in Kashmir: Por-*

tents of War, Hopes of Peace (Cambridge: Cambridge University Press, 1999); idem, *The Origins of War in South Asia: Indo-Pakistani Conflicts Since 1947*, 2d ed. (Boulder, Colo.: Westview Press, 1994); Josef Korbel, *Danger in Kashmir* (Princeton: Princeton University Press, 1954); Alistair Lamb, *The Kashmir Problem: A Historical Survey* (New York: Praeger, 1966).

17. Sumit Ganguly, *Origins*, 41–42; Lamb, *Kashmir*, 39.

18. V. P. Menon, *The Story of the Integration of the Indian States* (London: Longman's, 1956), 394.

19. Sumit Ganguly, *Origins*, 39.

20. "Reply to Nehru and Menon," Statement at Lahore (14 July 1963), in Zulfikar Ali Bhutto, *Reshaping Foreign Policy* (Rawalpindi: Pakistan Publications, n.d.), 192.

21. For Indian leaders' opposition to Pakistan's raison d'être, see Barnds, *Great Powers*, 72; Lamb, *Kashmir*, 41; Korbel, *Danger*, 127–30. In March 1963, Nehru stated publicly that Indo-Pakistani "[c]onfederation remains our ultimate end." *Washington Post*, 19 December 1962. Just before his death on 24 April 1964, Nehru affirmed his wish that India and Pakistan would be "constitutionally closer." Sarvepalli Gopal, *Jawaharlal Nehru: A Biography* (New Delhi: Oxford University Press, 1984), 3:262.

22. McMahon, *Cold War*, 13–19; Shivaji Ganguly, *U.S. Policy Toward South Asia* (Boulder, Colo.: Westview Press, 1990), 26; Dennis Kux, *India and the United States: Estranged Democracies* (Washington: National Defense University Press, 1992), 57.

23. McMahon, *Cold War*, 73; Barnds, *Great Powers*, 100–101; Khalid B. Sayeed, "Pakistan and China: The Scope and Limits of Convergent Policies," in *Policies Toward China: Views From Six Continents*, ed. A. M. Halpern (New York: McGraw Hill, 1965), 232.

24. Barnds, *Great Powers*, 91–97; McMahon, *Cold War*, 123–71.

25. See note 32 below.

26. McMahon, *Cold War*, 19, 47.

27. Nehru to Mrs. Pandit (14 November 1946), *Selected Works of Jawaharlal Nehru* 14 (New Delhi: Jawaharlal Nehru Memorial Fund, 1984), 457–58.

28. Eisenhower assured Nehru that the United States would support India "both within and without the United Nations" if Pakistan used U.S. arms "in aggression against it." Eisenhower to Nehru (24 February 1954), in Rajendra K. Jain, ed., *US-South Asian Relations 1947–1982*, vol. 1 (New Delhi: Radiant Publishers, 1983). Eisenhower also offered India U.S. arms. Nehru derided the assurance and rejected the offer on the grounds that India could not avail itself of that which it condemned in Pakistan. Barnds, *Great Powers*, 96–97; McMahon, *Cold War*, 171–72.

29. On other sore points in U.S.–India relations, see Timothy W. Crawford, "Kennedy and Kashmir, 1962–63: The Perils of Pivotal Peacemaking in South Asia," *India Review* 1 (July 2002): 4–5.

30. Mohammad Ayub Khan, *Friends Not Masters: A Political Biography* (New York: Oxford University Press, 1967), 145. Kennedy assured Ayub that he presently had "no intention to give India any arms aid" and that if "a situation, such as impending war with China, should arise" the United States would "would talk with President Ayub and see what was the best course of action . . . If there should be a change in U.S. policy, [he] would talk with President Ayub first." Memcon: Kennedy and Ayub (11 July 1961), *FRUS*, 1961–63, vol. 19, no. 30; Kaysen to Kennedy (9 November 1962), ibid., no. 192. As Rusk later put it: The "President has given [a] personal commitment [to] Ayub to discuss with [Pakistan] prior [to a] U.S. government decision [to] provide military aid to [India]. DOS to Rountree (8 December 1961), ibid., no. 67.

31. DOS to Rountree (26 January 1962), ibid., no. 99.

32. Kennedy to Ayub (26 January 1962), ibid., no. 100. In November 1957, Secretary of State Dulles assured Firoz Noon, Pakistan's minister of foreign affairs, that consistent with its SEATO, CENTO, and UN obligations, the United States "would promptly and effectively come to the assistance of Pakistan if it were subjected to armed aggression which, however, the United States did not anticipate." For this assurance, and the U.S. government's endorsement of the exact language quoted above, see: Memcon: Dulles and Noon (23 November

1957), *FRUS*, 1955–57, vol. 13, no. 71, n. 3; DOS to U.S. Ambassador to Pakistan (7 April 1959), *FRUS*, 1958–60, vol. 15, no. 348.

33. For a thorough account of the war, see Steven Hoffman, *India and the China Crisis* (Berkeley: University of California Press, 1990).

34. McMahon, *Cold War*, 287.

35. Kennedy to Nehru (28 October 1962), *FRUS*, 1961–63, vol. 19, no. 187; John Kenneth Galbraith, *Ambassador's Journal: A Personal Account of the Kennedy Years* (Boston: Houghton Mifflin, 1969), 444–45.

36. Kennedy to Ayub (28 October 1962), *FRUS*, 1961–63, vol. 19, nos. 186, 197.

37. Kennedy to Ayub (28 October 1962), ibid., no. 186; Ayub, *Friends*, 141.

38. See Crawford, "Kennedy and Kashmir," 6.

39. Ayub to Kennedy (5 November 1962), *FRUS*, 1961–63, vol. 19, no. 195.

40. McConaughy to Rusk (5 November 1962), ibid., no. 191, n. 6. On 17 November, the State Department released a public statement saying that if U.S. military "assistance to India should be misused and misdirected against another country in aggression, the United States would undertake immediately, in accordance with constitutional authority, appropriate action both within and without the UN to thwart such aggression." See Rajendra K. Jain, ed., *US-South Asian Relations 1947–1982*, vol. 2, no. 220; Ayub, *Friends*, 148; Dennis Kux, *The United States and Pakistan, 1947–2000: Disenchanted Allies* (Washington D.C.: Woodrow Wilson Center Press, 2000) [hereafter *US and Pakistan*], 132.

41. Ayub to Kennedy (5 November 1962), *FRUS*, 1961–63, vol. 19, no. 195.

42. Shirin Tahir-Kheli, *The United States and Pakistan: The Evolution of an Influence Relationship* (New York: Praeger, 1982), 17.

43. McConaughy to Rusk (5 November 1962), *FRUS*, 1961–63, vol. 19, no. 191.

44. Rusk to Galbraith (25 November 1962), ibid., no. 211; Komer to Kennedy (16 December 1962), ibid., no. 226. Galbraith was more skeptical. See Memcons (20 December 1962), ibid., nos. 230, 231; Galbraith, *Journal*, 518, 536, 538, 554, 574.

45. Harriman's team included Paul Nitze from the Department of Defense, Roger Hilsman from the State Department, Carl Kaysen from the NSC, and General Paul D. Adams.

46. On Harriman's mission, see *FRUS*, 1961–63, vol. 19, nos. 208, 211–215; McMahon, *Cold War*, 293–95; Shivaji Ganguly, *U.S. Policy*, 81–89; Roger Hilsman, *To Move a Nation* (Garden City, N.Y.: Doubleday, 1967), 327–39; Paul Nitze, *From Hiroshima to Glastnost* (New York: Grove Weidenfeld, 1989), 240–42; Galbraith, *Journal*, 494–503. For overviews of the subsequent talks, see Kux, *US and Pakistan*, 134–44; Ganguly, *Conflict Unending*, 32–35; Denis Wright, *India-Pakistan Relations, 1962–1969* (New Delhi: Sterling Publishers, 1989), 16–21; Gopal, *Nehru*, 3:256–60.

47. Rusk to Galbraith and Harriman (25 November 1962), *FRUS*, 1961–63, vol. 19, no. 211.

48. Rusk to Galbraith (8 December 1962), ibid., no. 219; Memcon: Kennedy and B. J. Nehru (17 December 1962), ibid., no. 227; Kaysen to Kennedy (16 November 1962), ibid., no. 198.

49. The UK Prime Minister summed up this dilemma in Macmillan to Kennedy (13 December 1962), ibid., no. 224.

50. Rusk to Galbraith and Harriman (25 November 1962), ibid., no. 211; Kaysen to Kennedy (3 November 1962), ibid., no. 190.

51. Rusk to Galbraith and Harriman (25 November 1962), ibid., no. 211; see also McConaughy to Rusk (20 November 1962), ibid., no. 207.

52. Rusk to Embassies in New Delhi, Karachi, London, and United States Mission to the United Nations (USUN) (8 December 1962), ibid., no. 219.

53. On 22 December, Kennedy explained to Ayub that "to deny India the minimum requirements of defense would encourage further Chinese Communist aggression . . . Therefore, the supply of arms for this purpose should not be made contingent on a Kashmir settlement. Beyond this stage, however, *we will certainly take any one-sided intransigence on Kashmir into account as a factor in determining the extent and pace of our assistance*" (italics added). Kennedy to Ayub (22 December 1962), ibid., no. 232.

54. Ayub, *Friends*, 149.

55. Quoted in Wright, *India-Pakistan*, 15.

56. Galbraith, *Journal*, 501–2; Ayub, *Friends*, 149.

57. S. M. Burke, "Sino-Pakistani Relations," *Orbis* 8 (summer 1964): 396; Vertzberger, *Enduring Entente*, 17.

58. United Nations Commission on India and Pakistan (UNCIP), Resolutions of 13 August 1948 and 5 January 1949. See K. Arif, *America-Pakistan Relations*, vol. 2, nos. 18, 34 (Lahore: Vanguard Books, 1984).

59. Ganguly, *Conflict Unending*, 25.

60. McConaughy to Rusk (27 December 1962), *FRUS*, 1961–63, vol. 19, no. 234, n. 3; Wright, *India-Pakistan*, 16–17.

61. "While there [is] no question of linking between emergency phase military aid to India and progress on Kashmir," Ball wrote, "it should be made clear to Indians [that] there [is a] *definite* relationship with longer run aid" (italics added). Ball to Galbraith (4 January 1963), *FRUS*, 1961–63, vol. 19, no. 235.

62. Galbraith, *Journal*, 530.

63. As early as 11 January, Kennedy figured "the odds that the Indians and Chinese will get engaged again on a scale which might involve U.S. seem to be declining." Kennedy to Macmillan (11 January 1963), *FRUS*, 1961–63, vol. 19, no. 236. Galbraith, *Journal*, 523, 532.

64. The Colombo proposals were offered by six Asian and African states (Ceylon, Burma, Cambodia, Indonesia, Egypt, and Ghana). On the Columbo proposals, see M. Fisher, "India in 1963: A Year of Travail," *Asian Survey* 4 (March 1964): 737–40.

65. Robert Litwak, "The Soviet Union in India's Security Perspective," in *Security in Southern Asia*, by Zalmay Khalilzad, Timothy George, Robert Litwak and Shahram Chubin (New York: St. Martin's, 1984), sec. 2, pt. II, 81; Ian C. C. Graham, "The Indo-Soviet MIG Deal and Its International Repercussions," *Asian Survey* 4 (May 1964): 830.

66. Abdur Razzaq Khan Abbasi, "Pakistan's Relations with the People's Republic of China," in *Pakistan-US Relations: Social, Political, and Economic Factors*, ed. Noor A. Husain and Leo E. Rose (Berkeley, Calif.: Institute of East Asian Studies, 1988), 139.

67. Ball to Galbraith (4 January 1963), *FRUS*, 1961–63, vol. 19, no. 235.

68. Bhutto attached significant conditions for any acceptable partition plan. The partition should take into account the "composition of the population" and "be acceptable to [the] people of the state"—which essentially reasserted Pakistan's original position. Similarly, India hedged that "any territorial readjustments [must] take into account geography, administration, and other considerations and involve least disturbance to life and welfare of people." Galbraith to DOS, ibid., no. 242.

69. Komer to Kennedy (26 January 1963), ibid., no. 247.

70. Memcon: Kennedy and Ahmed (4 February 1963), ibid., no. 249.

71. Ibid.; Kennedy to Ayub (7 February 1963), ibid., no. 252.

72. Kennedy to Nehru (6 February 1963), ibid., no. 251; Komer to Kennedy (26 January 1963), ibid., no. 247; Galbraith, *Journal*, 543.

73. Talbot to NSC, attached to Komer to Kennedy (16 February 1962), *FRUS*, 1961–63, vol. 19, no. 253; Kux, *US and Pakistan*, 138–39; Wright, *India-Pakistan*, 18–19.

74. By 16 February, U.S. outlays under the $60 million dollar ceiling set at Nassau amounted to roughly $38 million. Talbot to NSC, attached to Komer to Kennedy (16 February 1962), *FRUS*, 1961–63, vol. 19, no. 253; Telegram from Kennedy to Galbraith (22 March 1963), ibid., no. 267.

75. Crawford, "Kennedy and Kashmir," 14; Rusk to Kennedy: Kashmir, attached to Komer to Kennedy (20 February 1963) *FRUS*, 1961–63, vol. 19, no. 257; Rusk to Galbraith (16 February 1963), ibid., no. 254; Galbraith, *Journal*, 549–50.

76. Memcon: Ahmed and Rusk (23 February 1963), ibid., no. 259, and n. 1.

77. Ganguly, *Conflict Unending*, 33; Vertzberger, *Enduring Entente*, 15; W. M. Dobell, "Ramifications of the China-Pakistan Border Treaty," *Pacific Affairs* 37 (fall 1964): 288; Burke, "Sino-Pakistani Relations," 396. The text of the boundary agreement appears in Rais, *China and Pakistan*, app. 1, 142–46.

78. Kennedy to Ayub (9 March 1963), *FRUS, 1961–63*, vol. 19, no. 263; Kennedy to Nehru (9 March 1963), ibid., no. 264 (italics added); Gopal, *Nehru*, 3:258.

79. Notes on Discussion with President on Kashmir Negotiations (21 February 1963), *FRUS, 1961–63*, vol. 19, no. 258; Komer to Kennedy (2 March 1963), ibid., no. 261; Kux, *US and Pakistan*, 139–40.

80. Wright, *India-Pakistan*, 20; Joint Communique (15 March 1963), in *50 Years of Indo-Pak Relations*, ed. Verinder Grover and Ranjana Arora (New Delhi: Deep & Deep, 1998), 3:583.

81. Telegram from Kennedy to Galbraith (22 March 1963), *FRUS, 1961–63*, vol. 19, no. 267. That Kennedy was still thinking explicitly in terms of using military aid to India as a prod in the Kashmir talks is shown in a memo Komer wrote to Kennedy on 23 March, noting that "our aid [to India] has been at about the right pace, considering our desire to use its rate of flow as leverage on Kashmir." Komer to Kennedy (23 March 1963), ibid., no. 268.

82. Galbraith to DOS (25 March 1963), ibid., no. 269.

83. "Scenario for Kashmir Negotiations," Rusk to Kennedy (31 March 1963), ibid., no. 270. Among these elements were the following: (1) Both India and Pakistan must have a substantial position in Kashmir Vale; (2) both must have assured access to and through the Vale; (3) outside the Valley, the economic and strategic interests of the parties must be accounted for; (4) inside the Valley, the settlement must have (a) clearly delineated sovereignty arrangements; (b) political freedom and self-rule for locals; (c) free movement of people within Valley; (d) rapid development of Valley by both parties for tourism and through use of development funds from external sources. See: "Elements of a Settlement," attachment to ibid.

84. Memcon (1 April 1963), ibid., no. 271.

85. Komer to Kennedy (24 April 1963), ibid., no. 280.

86. Galbraith, *Journal*, 564; Galbraith to DOS (15 April 1963), *FRUS, 1961–63*, vol. 19, no. 276; Nehru to Kennedy (21 April 1963), paraphrased by Gopal, *Nehru*, 3:259.

87. Shivaji Ganguly, *U.S. Policy*, 92–93.

88. Rusk to Kennedy (19 April 1963), *FRUS, 1961–63*, vol. 19, no. 278.

89. Komer to Kennedy (24 April 1963), ibid., no. 280; Kux, *US and Pakistan*, 140.

90. *New York Times*, 17 April 1963.

91. Joint Communique (25 April 1963), in *50 Years*, 3:384.

92. Wright, *India-Pakistan*, 21; Komer to Kennedy (24 April 1963), *FRUS, 1961–63*, vol. 19, no. 280.

93. Rusk to Galbraith (24 April 1963), ibid., no. 281. For more of Rusk's thinking on the need to de-link military aid to India from a Kashmir settlement, see Crawford, "Kennedy and Kashmir," 20.

94. Memo: President's Meeting on India (25 April 1963), *FRUS, 1961–63*, vol. 19, no. 283; Bundy Memo (26 April 1963), ibid., no. 285; Chester Bowles, *Promises to Keep: My Years in Public Life, 1941–1969* (New York: Harper and Row, 1971), 439–40.

95. Memo: President's Meeting on India (25 April 1963), *FRUS, 1961–63*, vol. 19, no. 283.

96. Rusk to DOS (2 May 1963), ibid., no. 286.

97. Rusk to DOS (4 May 1963), ibid., no. 288. Also see Crawford, "Kennedy and Kashmir," 21, n. 88.

98. The sentence ends: "but it is also Karachi which gains from changes in the status quo." Notes by Rusk on Karachi-New Delhi Visit (5 May 1963), *FRUS, 1961–63*, vol. 19, no. 290.

99. Rusk to Kennedy (8 May 1963), ibid., no. 292.

100. Summary Record: NSC meeting (9 May 1963), ibid., no. 293.

101. Kennedy to Macmillan (13 May 1963), ibid., no. 295.

102. Joint Communique (16 May 1963), in *50 Years*, 3:384.

103. Ayub quoted in Wright, *India-Pakistan*, 36; McConaughy to DOS (17 May 1963), *FRUS, 1961–63*, vol. 19, no. 298; Galbraith, *Journal*, 574.

104. Galbraith, *Journal*, 574; McConaughy to DOS (17 May 1963), *FRUS, 1961–63*, vol. 19, no. 298, and n. 3. For Ayub's skepticism toward the mediator proposal, see McConaughy to DOS (6 May 1963), ibid., no. 291.

105. Shivaji Ganguly, *U.S. Policy,* 92–93; Rusk to Galbraith (18 May 1963), *FRUS,* 1961–63, vol. 19, no. 299.

106. Memo: President's Meeting on India (17 May 1963), ibid., no. 297.

107. Memo: Conversation Between the President and Indian Defense Coordination Minister T. T. Krishnacmachari (20 May 1963), ibid., no. 300; Memo: Visit of President of India, Sarvepalli Radhakrishnan (3 June 1963), ibid., no. 304.

108. Quoted in Choudhury, *Major Powers,* 111.

109. Rusk to Galbraith (18 June 1963), *FRUS,* 1961–63, vol. 19, no. 305.

110. The Birch Grove Communiqué is printed in DOS *Bulletin* 49 (22 July 1963). On the administration's estimates for the five-year package to India, see Memo: President's Meeting on India (25 April 1963), *FRUS,* 1961–63, vol. 19, no. 283; Bundy Memo (26 April 1963), ibid., no. 285.

111. Bowles, *Promises,* 439–40, 477–84.

112. Bowles to DOS (30 July 1963), *FRUS,* 1961–63, vol. 19, no. 313; Nehru to Kennedy (11 August 1963), ibid., no. 317; DOS to Bowles (15 August 1963), ibid., no. 319, n., 3; Bowles to DOS (17 August 1963), ibid., no. 321; Kux, *US and Pakistan,* 142.

113. DOS to McConaughy (11 July 1963), *FRUS,* 1961–63, vol. 19, no. 308; Kux, *US and Pakistan,* 142–43.

114. Bhutto's speech reported in *Dawn,* 18 July 1963; Ayub's remarks in *Washington Post,* 12 September 1963. For Ayub's earlier official denial of a formal alliance with China, see McConaughy to DOS (8 August 1963), *FRUS,* 1961–63, vol. 19, no. 315. China was nevertheless encouraging Pakistan to view it as an ally: Mao told visiting Pakistani journalists in June 1963 that China "would defend Pakistan throughout the world"; quoted in Burke, "Sino-Pakistani Relations," 398, n. 18.

115. Memo: President's Meeting on Pakistan (12 August 1963), ibid., no. 318; McMahon, *Cold War,* 304.

116. McConaughy to DOS (23 August 1963), *FRUS,* 1961–63, vol. 19, no. 323.

117. Nehru to Kennedy (27 August 1963), paraphrased in Gopal, *Nehru,* 3:261. On the Sino-Pak Civil Air agreement, see Rais, *China and Pakistan,* 40–43; Kux, *US and Pakistan,* 143; Nehru's statements to Raja Sabha reported in *Times of India,* 4 September 1963.

118. George W. Ball, *The Past Has Another Pattern: Memoirs* (New York: W. W. Norton, 1982), 283–85; Ball Report to DOS on Conversation with Ayub (5 September 1963), *FRUS,* 1961–63, vol. 19, no. 328; Ball to DOS (6 September 1963), ibid., no. 330.

119. Ball to DOS (6 September 1963), ibid., no. 330; Ayub, *Friends,* 153.

120. President's Meeting on Ball Mission to Pakistan (9 September 1963), *FRUS,* 1961–63, vol. 19, no. 331.

121. Statement by Talbot (17 September 1963), in Jain, *US-South Asian Relations, 1947–1982,* vol. 2, no. 233.

122. On these measures, see Sumit Ganguly, *Crisis in Kashmir,* 51–52.

123. Rusk to Bowles (20 October 1963), *FRUS,* 1961–63, vol. 19, no. 334; Grant to Rusk (4 November 1963), ibid., no. 335. Nehru's statement paraphrased in Wright, *India-Pakistan,* 44.

124. Komer to William Bundy (14 November 1963), ibid., no. 338; Bowles, *Promises,* 481.

125. McMahon, *Cold War,* 306; Shivaji Ganguly, *U.S. Policy,* 95.

126. Rusk to McConaughy (2 December 1963), *FRUS,* 1961–63, vol. 19, no. 341; McMahon, *Cold War,* 307.

127. Bundy and Komer to Johnson (11 December 1963), *FRUS,* 1961–63, vol. 19, no. 342, and attached Rusk Memo.

128. Ball to Bowles (19 December 1963), ibid., no. 344; Choudhury, *Major Powers,* 32–33.

129. Memcon: Taylor and Ayub (20 December 1963), *FRUS,* 1961–63, vol. 19, no. 345.

130. Memcon: Ayub and Taylor (20 December 1963), ibid., no. 346; McConaughy to Rusk (16 January 1964), *FRUS,* 1964–68, vol. 25, no. 5; Ayub, *Friends,* 152–53; McMahon, *Cold War,* 310.

131. Taylor to McNamara (23 December 1963), *FRUS,* 1961–63, vol. 19, no. 348.

132. National Security Action Memorandum No. 279 (8 February 1964), *FRUS,* 1964–68, vol. 25, no. 13; McMahon, *Cold War,* 313.

133. On the Kashmir unrest, see *FRUS*, 1964–68, vol. 25, nos. 10, 16; Sumit Ganguly, *Origins*, 67.

134. Ayub, "The Pakistan-American Alliance," *Foreign Affairs* 64 (January 1964): 195–209; Sayeed, "Pakistan and China," 247; Barnds, *Great Powers*, 199; Feldman, *Crisis*, 93; McMahon, *Cold War*, 311, 313; Burke, "Sino-Pakistani Relations," 398–99; Choudhury, *Major Powers*, 183; *FRUS*, 1964–68, vol. 25, nos. 5, 9, 10, 14, 15; Bhutto, "Self Determination and Kashmir," Address to United Nations General Assembly (28 September 1965) in Bhutto, *Reshaping Foreign Policy*, 241.

135. Talbot to Rusk (23 February 1965), *FRUS*, 1964–68, vol. 25, no. 89.

136. McMahon, *Cold War*, 314. Vertzberger, *Enduring Entente*, 29–31; Barnds, *Great Powers*, 191; Sayeed, "Pakistan and China," 256.

137. McMahon, *Cold War*, 315–16; Norman Palmer, "The Defense of South Asia," *Orbis* 9 (winter 1966): 914; Choudhury, *Major Powers*, 36. See also Sumit Ganguly, *Origins*, 65–66; Thomas F. Brady, "Figures on Soviet Arms for India Indicate That U.S. Sends Less," *New York Times*, 13 May 1964.

138. McMahon, *Cold War*, 318–19; Sayeed, "Pakistan and China," 258; Choudhury, *Major Powers*, 182.

139. McConaughy to DOS (14 January 1965), *FRUS*, 1964–68, vol. 25, no. 84.

140. Sumit Ganguly, *Origins*, 67; Korbel, *Danger*, 320–22.

141. DOS to McConaughy (14 December 1964), *FRUS*, 1964–68, vol. 25, no. 80.

142. McConaughy to DOS (16 March 1965), ibid., no. 93.

143. Choudhury, *Major Powers*, 178, 182, 184; Garver, *Protracted Conflict*, 196; McMahon, *Cold War*, 321; Abbasi, "Pakistan's Relations with the People's Republic of China," 137; Memcon: Kennedy-Ayub Talks (11 July 1961), *FRUS*, 1963–64, vol. 19, no. 30.

144. McConaughy to DOS (16 March 1965) *FRUS*, 1964–68, vol. 25, no. 93, n. 4; Komer to Johnson (2 April 1965), ibid., no. 95, n. 3. McConaughy to DOS (16 March 1965), ibid., no. 93.

145. Ball to Rusk (6 April 1965), *FRUS*, 1964–68, vol. 25, no. 97.

146. Bowles to DOS (16 April 1965), ibid., no. 104.

147. India first warned the U.S. on 19 February of possible hostilities resulting from Pakistani advances. Bowles to DOS (19 February 1965), ibid., no. 87.

148. Indeed, in the midst of the September 1965 Kashmir war, McConaughy would report to Washington that "in retrospect the Rann of Kutch" clash looked increasingly like a Pakistani "pilot project for [the] Kashmir operation." McConaughy to DOS (7 September 1965), in *The American Papers: Secret and Confidential: India-Pakistan-Bangladesh Documents, 1965–1973*, ed. Roedad Khan (New Delhi: Oxford University Press, 2000) [hereafter *AP*], 33. On the Rann of Kutch crisis, see Sumit Ganguly, "Deterrence Failure Revisited: The Indo-Pakistani War of 1965," *Journal of Strategic Studies* 13 (December 1990): 87–89; Wright, *India-Pakistan*, 52–67.

149. Feldman, *Crisis*, 135, 149; Rais, *China and Pakistan*, 59; Vertzberger, *Enduring Entente*, 35; Barnds, *Great Powers*, 199; Wright, *India-Pakistan*, 65. For an official statement of Moscow's impartiality toward the Rann of Kutch dispute see Tass Statement (9 May 1965), in Rajendra K. Jain, *Soviet South Asian Relations, 1947–1978*, vol. 1, no. 19 (New Delhi: Radiant Publishers, 1978).

150. For India's position, see: "Facts About Sind-Kutch Boundary," in Jain, *US-South Asian Relations*, vol. 2, no. 249.

151. McConaughy to DOS (30 April 1965), *AP*, 4; Kux, *India and the US: Estranged Democracies*, 235; McMahon, *Cold War*, 324; DOS (Read) to Bundy (24 April 1965), *FRUS*, 1964–68, vol. 25, no. 107.

152. McConaughy to DOS (30 April 1965); Talbot to Rusk, (30 April 1965); in *AP*, 4, 6.

153. Komer to Bundy (26 April 1965), *FRUS*, 1964–68, vol. 25, no. 110.

154. Bhutto recalled: "December [sic] 23, 1957 Dulles-Noon assurances; November 29, 1956 assurances given to Baghdad Pact members; U.S. Ambassador Langley's reiteration to Ayub of Dulles' assurances on April 15, 1959; 1961 Kennedy-Ayub communiqué reaffirming March 5, 1959 US-Pakistani agreement, and the March 5, 1959 agreement." McConaughy to DOS (30 April 1965), *AP*, 3. For these assurances, see Memcon: Dulles and Noon (23 Novem-

ber 1957), *FRUS*, 1955–57, vol. 13, no. 71, n. 3; DOS (Herter) to U.S. Ambassador to Pakistan (Langley) (7 April 1959), *FRUS*, 1958–60, vol. 15, no. 348. Similarly, on 27 April, Pakistan's ambassador told Rusk that "this is a case where the U.S. should firmly come to Pakistan's aid" and reminded the Secretary of State of Ball's assurances to Ayub in 5 September 1963. Rusk to McConaughy (27 April 1965), *FRUS*, 1964–68, vol. 25, no. 112, esp. n. 4.

155. McConaughy to DOS (30 April 1965), *AP*, 3; Sumit Ganguly, "Deterrence Failure," 79; Choudhury, *Major Powers*, 120.

156. McConaughy to DOS (30 April 1965), *FRUS*, 1964–68, vol. 25, no. 114 (italics added).

157. Letter from the Ambassador of Pakistan to Rusk (11 May 1965), ibid., no. 120.

158. Ball to McConaughy (14 May 1965), ibid., no. 121.

159. McConaughy to DOS (11 June 1965), ibid., no. 132.

160. Rusk to Johnson (9 September 1965), *AP*, 53.

161. Talbott to Rusk (30 April 1965), *AP*, 7.

162. Komer to Johnson (8 June 1965), *FRUS*, 1964–68, vol. 25, no. 128; Komer to Bundy (11 June 1965), ibid., no. 131; Komer to Johnson (21 June 1965), ibid., no. 134; Bundy to Johnson (30 June 1965), ibid., no. 137.

163. Memcon: Johnson and B. K. Nehru (13 July 1965), ibid., no. 149; Memo of Johnson Telcon (28 June 1965), ibid., no. 135. In relation to India's request for arms, Komer worried that "we're driving the Indian military to get more from the Soviets, which doesn't serve our longer term interests." Komer to Johnson (21 June 1965), ibid., no. 134.

164. McConaughy to DOS (4 July 1965), ibid., no. 141, p. 290; Tahir-Kheli, *United States and Pakistan*, 20.

165. McConaughy to DOS (4 July 1965), *FRUS*, 1964–68, vol. 25, no. 141; Rusk to McConaughy (16 July 1965), ibid., no. 155.

166. Komer to Bundy (9 July 1965), ibid., no. 146; Rusk to McConaughy (15 July 1965), ibid., no. 151; Rusk to McConaughy (23 July 1965), ibid., no. 158.

167. McConaughy to DOS (2 August 1965), ibid., no. 162.

168. Sumit Ganguly, "Deterrence Failure."

169. Sumit Ganguly, "Deterrence Failure," 77, 91.

170. Komer to Johnson (28 August 1965), *FRUS*, 1964–68, vol. 25, no. 175, n. 2. The intelligence report is still classified. See also Garver, *Protracted Contest*, 197.

171. U.S. Embassy Rawalpindi (Spielman) to DOS (8 September 1965), *AP*, 44.

172. On 2 September, the day Pakistan armor rolled into Kashmir, Bowles urged India to assume a "reasonable posture" rather than "counter thrust" elsewhere: "even if Pakistan refused to negotiate and choose the path toward war, India's position at least would be clear and world wide support would be assured whatever might follow." Bowles to DOS, (2 September 1965), *FRUS*, 1964–68, vol. 25, no. 177.

173. Komer to Johnson (7 September 1965), ibid., no. 191, n. 2.

174. Memo: Office of Current Intelligence, CIA; Possible Sino-Pakistani Military Arrangement (6 September 1965), *FRUS*, 1964–68, vol. 25, no. 186; Garver, *Protracted Contest*, 196–97; Vertzberger, *China's Southwestern Strategy: Encirclement and Counterencirclement* (New York: Praeger, 1985), 40–41. During the war, Ayub denied any formal Sino-Pak alliance. See McConaughy to DOS (6 September 1965), *AP*, 27; McConaughy to DOS (20 September 1965), *FRUS*, 1964–68, vol. 25, no. 217.

175. Rusk to Johnson (9 September 1965), *AP*, 53; American Embassy Tehran to DOS (8 September 1965), ibid., 38–39.

176. McConaughy to DOS (6 September 1965), *AP*, 19; McConaughy to DOS (6 September 1965), *FRUS*, 1964–68, vol. 25, no. 187.

177. McConaughy to DOS (6 September 1965), *AP*, 22.

178. DOS to McConaughy (6 September 1965), *AP*, 28–29.

179. Ibid.

180. Komer to Johnson (4 September 1965), *FRUS*, 1964–68, vol. 25, no. 182, p. 354.

181. McConaughy to DOS (6 September 1965), *FRUS*, 1964–68, vol. 25, no. 187; McConaughy to DOS, (9 September 1965), ibid., no. 198.

182. Ibid.
183. Similarly, on 3 September, Rusk argued to India's ambassador that Dehli should agree to the UN's cease-fire plan because if India "accepts and Paks do not then UN machinery comes into play to get acceptance and compliance on the ground." Rusk to Bowles (3 September 1965), ibid., no. 180.
184. Rusk to Johnson (9 September 1965), *AP*, 53–54.
185. Bowles to DOS (6 September 1965), *AP*, 15–16.
186. McConaughy to DOS (10 September 1965), *AP*, 61.
187. Vertzberger, *China's Southwestern Strategy*, 38.
188. Komer to Johnson (10 September 1965), *FRUS*, 1964–68, vol. 25, no. 199, n. 3.
189. Bowles to DOS (11 September 1965), ibid., no. 201.
190. U.S. Embassy Rawalpindi to DOS (11 September 1965), *AP*, 70.
191. Special National Intelligence Estimate: Prospects of Chinese Communist Involvement in the Indo-Pakistan War, (16 September 1965), *FRUS*, 1964–68, vol. 25, no. 205.
192. Rusk to Bowles (17 September 1965), *FRUS*, 1964–68, vol. 25, no. 208.
193. Record of White House Meeting on South Asian Problems, (17 September 1965), ibid., no. 209.
194. Bowles to DOS (18 September 1965), ibid., no. 211, n. 2; DOS to Bowles (19 September 1965), ibid., no. 216.
195. See: Kosygin to Shastri, and Kosygin to Ayub (17 September 1965), in Jain, *Soviet South Asian Relations*, vol. 1, nos. 26, 27.
196. McConaughy to DOS (18 September 1965), *FRUS*, 1964–68, vol. 25, no. 212.
197. DOS to McConaughy (18 September 1965), ibid., no. 214.
198. American Consul in Dacca to DOS (23 September 1965), *AP*, 74.
199. Komer to Kennedy (26 January 1963), *FRUS*, 1961–63, vol. 19, no. 247; Rusk to Galbraith (15 January 1963), ibid., no. 239.
200. Kennedy to Ayub (7 February 1963), ibid., no. 252.
201. "Scenario for Kashmir Negotiations," Rusk to Kennedy (31 March 1963), ibid., no. 270.
202. Memo: President's Meeting on India (25 April 1963), ibid., no. 283.
203. Rusk to Johnson (9 September 1965), *AP*, 53.
204. Memo: President's Meeting on Pakistan (12 August 1963), *FRUS*, 1961–63, vol. 19, no. 318
205. Komer to Kennedy (12 November 1962), ibid., no. 193.
206. Kennedy to Macmillan (13 May 1963), ibid., no. 295; Summary Record: NSC meeting (9 May 1963), ibid., no. 293.
207. Ayub to Kennedy (5 November 1962), ibid., no.195; Ayub, *Friends*, 143.
208. See McConaughy to DOS (30 April 1965), and (6 September 1965), in *AP*, 3–5, 15–16.
209. Gilpatrick to Bowles (12 June 1961), *FRUS*, 1961–63, vol. 19, no. 27; Graham, "Indo-Soviet MIG Deal," 823.
210. See, e.g., DOS to Bowles (21 February 1964), *FRUS*, 1964–68, vol. 25, no. 18.

CHAPTER 7. U.S. PIVOTAL DETERRENCE IN THE UNIPOLAR ERA, 1990–2002

1. In their 1970s appraisal deterrence theory, Alexander George and Richard Smoke noted an important phenomenon: "The special historical context of the Cold War encouraged oversimplifications and distortions in the policy-maker's commitments that ran parallel to those to be found in [deterrence] theory that was being formulated during the same period. . . . [T]he special dynamics of international conflict during this era may have dulled the critical sensibilities of deterrence theorists and encouraged them to intuit that [their] simplifying assumptions . . . were not so unrealistic or questionable . . . Cold War 'reality' made it appear less necessary to question and elaborate upon the simplifying assumptions of the theory." This pattern held true after the Cold War as well. George and Smoke, *Deterrence Theory in American Foreign Policy: Theory and Practice* (New York: Columbia University Press, 1974), 553. Their full discussion of the limitations of commitment theory (550–61) is well worth revisiting.

2. Lawrence Martin, "Alliances and Alignments in a Globalizing World," in *The Global Century: Globalization and National Security,* ed. Richard L. Kugler and Ellen L. Frost (Washington D.C.: National Defense University Press, 2001), 2:602.

3. General Andrew Goodpaster, C. Richard Nelson, and Seymour Dietchman, eds., "Deterrence: An Overview," in *Post Cold War Conflict Deterrence* (Washington D.C.: National Academy Press, 1997), 10–36.

4. Paul K. Davis, "Protecting Weak and Medium Strength States: Issues of Deterrence, Stability, and Decision Making," in ibid.,153–73, esp. 172; also see idem "Special Challenges in Extending Deterrence in the New Era," in ibid., 132–40.

5. A notable exception appears in Helmut Sonnenfeld's contribution to *Post Cold War Conflict Deterrence,* which closes with the warning, "when aspiring powers are regional rivals of each other [and] it is in the U.S. interest to help prevent war . . . the U.S. should not tilt so far toward one of the parties as to run the risk of getting dragged in or encouraging that party to start a war." See "Notes on the Band Between 'Existential Deterrence' and the Actual Use of Force," ibid., 123–31, esp. 131.

6. The best analysis of these events is Sumit Ganguly, *The Crisis in Kashmir: Portents of War, Hopes of Peace* (New York: Cambridge University Press, 1997), chaps. 2, 5, 6.

7. The best accounts of the crisis are: Michael Krepon and Mishi Faruquee, eds., *Conflict Prevention and Confidence Building Measures in South Asia: The 1990 Crisis,* Occaisional Paper No. 17 (Washington D.C.: Stimson Center, April 1994); Stephen P. Cohen, P. R. Chari, and Pervaiz Iqbal Cheema, *The Compound Crisis of 1990: Perception, Politics, and Insecurity,* ACDIS Research Report (Urbana-Champaign: University of Illinois, 2001), chap. 5; Devin T. Hagerty, *The Consequences of Nuclear Proliferation: Lessons from South Asia* (Cambridge: MIT Press, 1998), chap. 6; C. Uday Bhaskar, "The May 1990 Nuclear 'Crisis': An Indian Perspective," *Studies in Conflict and Terrorism* 20 (October-December 1997): 317–29. More exaggerated accounts of the crisis danger appear in Seymour Hersh, "On the Nuclear Edge," *The New Yorker,* 29 March 1993; and William E. Burrows and Robert Windrem, *Critical Mass: The Dangerous Race for Superweapons in a Fragmenting World* (New York: Simon and Schuster, 1994), chap. 11.

8. Comments by Abdul Sattar, in Krepon and Faruquee, *Conflict Prevention,* 39.

9. Robert Gates, "Preventive Diplomacy: Concept and Reality," Center for Strategic and International Studies, Pacific Forum, PacNet, No. 39 (Washington, D.C.: CSIS, 27 September 1996), 1.

10. John F. Burns, "US Urges Pakistan to Settle Feud with India over Kashmir," *New York Times,* 21 May 1990.

11. Robert Oakley comments in Krepon and Faruquee, *Conflict Prevention,* 8, 7. Similarly, Oakley argues on p. 40 that "the fear that the United States would not [support] Pakistan in the event of a confrontation with India, which is the proverbial Pakistani fear, probably weighed in the balance."

12. Gates, "Preventive Diplomacy," 1.

13. B. G. Deshmukh, "The Inside Story," *India Today,* 28 February 1994, 63.

14. Cohen, Chari, and Cheema, *The Compound Crisis,* 86–87.

15. Ibid., 89.

16. Oakley comments in Krepon and Faruquee, *Conflict Prevention,* 7.

17. Ibid., 9.

18. Clark comments in ibid., 25. Also see Burns, "US Urges Pakistan to Settle Feud with India Over Kashmir."

19. Sherman comments in Krepon and Faruquee, *Conflict Prevention,* 26.

20. See Andrew Wilson, "The Aegean Dispute," *Adelphi Paper* 155 (London: International Institute for Strategic Studies, 1979/80), esp. 3.

21. "Spokesman on Demilitarized Status of the Dodecanese," Foreign Broadcast Information Service (FBIS), 4 December 1995, FBIS-WEU-95-233; Wilson, *Aegean Dispute,* 16.

22. For a thorough treatment, see Ekavi Athanassopoulou, "Blessing in Disguise: The Imia Crisis and Turkish-Greek Relations," *Mediterranean Politics* 2, no. 3 (winter 1997): 76–101.

23. "Greek, Turkey Dispute Deserted Island." *Agence France Presse* [hereafter *AFP*], 28 January 1996.

24. "Turkey: Baykal Says Greece 'Escalated' Situation," FBIS, 4 February 1996, FBIS-WEU-96–024; "Turkey Urges Greece to Pull Back Troops from Disputed Aegean Islet." *AFP*, 29 January 1996.

25. "Greek Claim to Desert Island Could Fire Turk Nationalism." *AFP*, 31 January 1996; "Crisis Deepens as Greece and Turkey Face Off Over Disputed Islet," *AFP*, 30 January 1996; "Turkey, Greece, Prepare to Quit Disputed Islet after U.S. Intervention." *AFP*, 31 January 1996.

26. "No NATO Reaction Following Greek Criticism," *AFP*, 31 January 1996; "Moscow Voices Concern Over Friction Between Greece, Turkey," FBIS, 30 January 1996, FBIS-SOV-96–021.

27. "Greece: Chief of Staff on Aegean Crisis Events," FBIS, 4 February 1996, FBIS-WEU-96–028. Theodore Pangalos later denied the chief of the general staff's description of the meeting, saying "there was no proposal by anyone for a violent confrontation with the initiation of hostilities on our part." "Greece: Greek Foreign Minister Attacks Former Armed Forces Chief," FBIS, 2 January 1998, FBIS-WEU-98–033.

28. Richard Holbrooke, Audio recording of speech before the National Press Club, Washington D.C., 31 January 1996 [hereafter NPC speech].

29. Presidential remarks on Imia/Kardak Islet, 30 January 1996, in *Public Papers of the Presidents of the United States: William J. Clinton 1996*, bk. 1 (Washington D.C.: GPO, 1997), 116–17.

30. Holbrooke, NPC speech.

31. As U.S. Congressman Michael Bilirakis complained before Congress on 7 March 1996, "at no time did they [the Clinton administration] recognize the sovereignty of Greece over the islet." *Congressional Record*, Vol. 142, 7 March 1996, H1968.

32. "No Nato Reaction Following Greek Criticism." *AFP*, 31 January 1996; Celestine Bohlen, "Greek Premier Already in Hot Water," *New York Times*, 8 February 1996.

33. For discussion of the diplomatic fallout after the January 1996 crisis, see Athanassopoulou, "Blessing In Disguise"; Heinz Kramer, *A Changing Turkey: The Challenge to Europe and the United States* (Washington, D.C.: Brookings Institution, 2000), 169–74.

34. On NATO's war, see Ivo Daalder and Michael O'Hanlon, *Winning Ugly* (Washington D.C.: Brookings Institution, 2000); Barry R. Posen, "The War for Kosovo: Serbia's Political-Military Strategy," *International Security* 24 (spring 2000): 39–84; Daniel Byman and Matthew C. Waxman, "Kosovo and the Great Air Power Debate," *International Security* 24 (spring 2000): 5–38; Dana H. Allin, "NATO's Balkan Interventions," *Adelphi Paper* 347 (London: International Institute for Strategic Studies, 2002), chap. 3; Benjamin S. Lambeth, *NATO's Air War for Kosovo: A Strategic and Operational Assessment* (Santa Monica, Calif.: Rand, 2001); Michael MccGwire, "Why Did We Bomb Belgrade?" *International Affairs* 76 (January 2000): 1–24; Michael Mandelbaum, "A Perfect Failure," *Foreign Affairs* 78 (September/October 1999): 2–8; Javier Solana, "NATO's Success in Kosovo," *Foreign Affairs* 78 (November/December 1999): 114–20; James B. Steinberg, "A Perfect Polemic," *Foreign Affairs* 78 (November/December 1999): 128–33.

35. See the January 1999 classified strategy paper composed for the principals in the White House and the Departments of Defense and State, quoted in Barton Gelman, "The Path to Crisis: How the United States and Its Allies Went to War," *Washington Post*, 18 April 1999. Also see "Excerpts from Remarks by Ambassadors Holbrooke and Hill" (15 December 1998), in *The Kosovo Conflict: A Diplomatic History Through Documents*, ed. Phillip E. Auerswald and David P. Auerswald (Cambridge: Kluwer Law International, 2000), 379.

36. Gelman, "The Path to Crisis."

37. Patrick Moore, "Why the Kosovo Crisis Now?" *Radio Free Europe/Radio Liberty Newsline* [hereafter *RFE/RL*], Russia, 2 March 1998.

38. "Washington Ready to Reward Belgrade for 'Good Will' Envoy," *AFP*, 23 February 1998. Gelbard said this in both Belgrade and Pristina.

39. Statement by the Contact Group (25 March 1998), *Kosovo Conflict*, 132.

40. UNSC Resolution 1160 (31 March 1998), in Marc Weller, *The Crisis in Kosovo 1989–1999, International Documents and Analysis* (Cambridge: Documents and Analysis Publishing, 1999), 1:188.

41. North Atlantic Council (NAC) Statement on the Situation in Kosovo (30 April 1998), in *Crisis in Kosovo*, 275.

42. Tim Judah, *Kosovo: War and Revenge* (New Haven: Yale University Press, 2000), 154–55.

43. Report by United Nations Secretary-General Annan to the Security Council (4 June 1998), in *Kosovo Conflict*, 180.

44. Statement by NATO Secretary General on Exercise "Determined Falcon" (13 June 1998), in *Crisis in Kosovo*, 276.

45. Joint Statement by the President of the Russian Federation and President of FRY, Moscow (16 June 1998), in *Crisis in Kosovo*, 292.

46. "Shuttle Diplomacy Without Results" *RFE/RL*, Southeastern Europe (SE), 7 July 1998.

47. "Rugova Aide Blames Foreigners for Kosovar Disunity," *RFE/RL*, SE, 8 July 1998.

48. "Hill Sets Deadline for Kosova," *RFE/RL*, SE, 7 July 1998. Also see Gelbard's 23 July remarks before the House Committee on International Relations, in *Kosovo Conflict*, 220.

49. Judah, *Kosovo*, 170.

50. Statement by NATO Secretary General Solana (13 August 1998), in *Kosovo Conflict*, 230.

51. 20 September 1998, in *Crisis in Kosovo*, 22.

52. UNSCR 1199 (1998), (23 September 1998), in ibid., 190.

53. Statement by NATO Secretary General Following ACTWARN Decision (24 September 1998), in ibid., 277.

54. Statement by the Government of the Russian Federation (4 October 1998), in ibid., 277.

55. For more on this, see Timothy W. Crawford, "Pivotal Deterrence and the Kosovo War: Why the Holbrooke Agreement Failed" *Political Science Quarterly* 116 (winter 2001–2): 510–11.

56. Norman Kempster and David Holley, "West Backs Last-Ditch Effort for Peaceful End to Kosovo Crisis," *Los Angeles Times*, 9 October 1998.

57. Statement by NATO Secretary General Following Decision on the ACTORD (13 October 1998), in *Crisis in Kosovo*, 278.

58. See "Serbian Government Endorses Accord Reached by President Milosevic, Belgrade 13 October 1998," in ibid., 279.

59. See ibid., 272–74, and the documents referenced therein.

60. Daalder and O'Hanlon, *Winning Ugly*, 50–52.

61. Klaus Naumann, interview, *Frontline*, Public Broadcasting System (transcript at http://www.pbs.org/wgbh/pages/frontline/shows/kosovo/interviews/naumann.html), access date 13 February 2001.

62. Klaus Naumann, "Moral Combat: NATO at War," report by Alan Little, *BBC2 Special*, British Broadcasting Corp., 12 March 2000 (transcript at http://news.bbc.co.uk/hi/english/static/events/panorama/transcripts/transcript_12_03_00.txt), access date 12 February 2001, 7; Daalder and O'Hanlon, *Winning Ugly*, 58.

63. Crawford, "Pivotal Deterrence and the Kosovo War," 512.

64. Ibid., 513–17.

65. "Kosovo: Rugova Urges Deployment of NATO Ground Troops in Kosovo," FBIS, FBIS-EEU-98-296.

66. For a full description of LDK obstruction of Contract Group initiatives, see Crawford, "Pivotal Deterrence and the Kosovo War," 517–18.

67. Craig R. Whitney, "NATO Says It's Ready to Act to Stop Violence in Kosovo," *New York Times*, 29 January 1999.

68. Judah, *Kosovo*, 215–16.

69. Statement by the Kosovo Albanian Delegation to the Rambouillet Conference, 23 February 1999, in *Kosovo Conflict*, 592.

70. Judah, *Kosovo*, 220. See also Remarks by Senator Dole and Ambassador Hill (6 March 1999), in *Kosovo Conflict*, 611.

71. Letter from the FRY/Serb Delegation to the Negotiators, Rambouillet (23 February 1999), 16.00 hrs., in *Crisis in Kosovo*, 470.

72. There is much speculation about the origins and purpose of the provocatively phrased SOF agreement in app. B, par. 8 of the Rambouillet plan. See "Interim Agreement for Peace and Self-Government in Kosovo, 23 February 1999," in *Crisis in Kosovo*, 469. For balanced discussion of it, see Timothy Garton Ash, "Kosovo: Was It Worth It," *New York Review of Books*, 21 September 2000; Posen, "The War for Kosovo," 44, nn. 10 and 80.

73. Allin, "NATO's Balkan Wars," 56–57.

74. Daalder and O'Hanlon, *Winning Ugly*, 94–96.

75. Posen, "The War for Kosovo," 51–52, 66–67.

76. Posen, "The War for Kosovo," also makes an excellent case along these lines, pp. 51–52, 66–67.

77. "Yeltsin Warns Clinton Not to Attack Yugoslavia," *RFE/RL*, Russia, 18 February 1999.

78. *RFE/RL*, Russia, 19 February 1999. Similarly, on 24 March, Speaker of the Duma Seleznev warned that if NATO went to war with Serbia, Russia would "immediately provide powerful weapons to Belgrade." Ibid., 24 March 1999.

79. See "Yeltsin Grounded for Next Two Months," and "Primakov Urged to Seize Power," ibid., 19 January 1999. On Milosevic's faith in support from Russia's security establishment, see transcripts of BBC Special, "Moral Combat: NATO at War," 29.

80. "START-II Ratification Linked to ABM Treaty," *RFE/RL*, Russia, 17 March 1999.

81. "US Senate Action Labeled Unpleasant Surprise," ibid., 19 March 1999.

82. "START-II's Fate Tied With Yugoslavia," ibid., 24 March 1999; "Anti-US Sentiment Growning Among Officials," ibid., 26 March 1999.

83. NATO-Russia Permanent Joint-Council Meeting at Ambassadorial Level (17 March 1999), in *Crisis in Kosovo*, 490.

84. "Milosevic's Aims in War and Diplomacy," *International Crisis Group (ICG) Balkans Report* 65 (New York: ICG, May 1999): 4; "Moscow Threatens to Cancel Primakov Trip in Event of NATO Air Strikes," *RFE/RL*, Russia, 23 March 1999.

85. "Russia Ends NATO Cooperation," and "Russia Warns of Deterioration in Relations With US," ibid., 25 March 1999.

86. On the diplomacy leading to Russia's abandonment of Belgrade, and Milosevic's capitulation, see Strobe Talbott, *The Russia Hand: A Memoir of Presidential Diplomacy* (New York: Random House, 2002), chap. 12.

87. On 5 January 1950, President Truman announced that the United States had "no intention" to involve its forces "in the civil conflict in China," nor would it "provide military aid or advice to Chinese forces on Formosa." See President Truman's Statement on Status of Formosa, 5 January 1950. Also see Acheson's famous Press Club speech, which made a similar point by spelling out America's vital defense perimeter in Asia in terms that excluded Taiwan (and South Korea), Dean Acheson's Speech to the National Press Club, 12 January 1950. Both in Roderick MacFarquhar, *Sino-American Relations, 1949–71* (New York: Praeger, 1972), 70–72.

88. See Truman's Statement on the Mission of the Seventh Fleet in the Formosa Area (27 June 1950); and Mutual Defense Assistance Agreement Between the United States and the Republic of China (9 February 1951), in MacFarquhar, *Sino-American Relations*, 83, 99.

89. President Eisenhower's State of the Union address(2 February 1963), in MacFarquhar, *Sino-American Relations*, 107.

90. Nancy Bernkopf Tucker, "Cold War Contacts: America and China, 1952–1956," in *Sino-American Relations, 1945–1955: A Joint Reassessment of a Critical Decade*, ed. Harry Harding and Yuan Ming (Wilmington, Del.: Scholarly Resources, 1989), 247.

91. Tucker, "Cold War Contacts," 248–49.

92. See the Mutual Defense Treaty Between the U.S. and the ROC (2 December 1954); and Note to Secretary of State Dulles from the ROC Foreign Minister (10 December 1954), in MacFarquhar, *Sino-American Relations*, 108–11.

93. Wang Jisi, "The Origins of America's 'Two China' Policy," in *Sino-American Relations, 1945–1955*, ed. Harding and Yuan, 205.

94. Campbell Craig, *Destroying the Village: Eisenhower and Thermonuclear War* (New York: Columbia University Press, 1998), 78–89.

95. *FRUS*, 1961–63, vol. 22, nos. 113, 92, and 94, n. 2.

96. See Henry Kissinger, *White House Years* (Boston: Little Brown, 1979), passim; William Burr, ed., *The Kissinger Transcripts: The Top Secret Talks with Beijing and Moscow* (New York: New Press, 1998), chaps. 1 and 2.

97. Burr, *Kissinger Transcripts*, 297.

98. Raymond Cohen, *International Politics: The Rules of the Game* (London: Longmans, 1981), 33; Fred Charles Ikle, *How Nations Negotiate* (New York: Harper and Row, 1964), 15; Christopher Honeyman, "In Defense of Ambiguity," *Negotiation Journal* 3 (January 1987): 81–86.

99. For the 1972 Shanghai Communique, see Gene T. Hsiao and Michael Witunski, *Sino-American Normalization and Its Policy Implications* (New York: Praeger, 1983), 237–40. Also see Robert S. Ross, *Negotiating Cooperation: US-China Relations, 1969–1989* (Stanford: Stanford University Press, 1995).

100. President Nixon to Premier Zhou Enlai (22 February 1972), *Kissinger Transcripts*, 66.

101. Joint Communique on the Establishment of Diplomatic Relations Between the United States of America and the People's Republic of China (15 December 1978), 1 January 1979; and U.S. Government Statement (15 December 1978), in Hsiao and Witunski, *Sino-American Normalization*, 241–43.

102. Memcon: Kissinger & DOS Staff (29 October 1976), *Kissinger Transcripts*, 416.

103. Taiwan Relations Act (10 April 1979), in Hsiao and Witunski, *Sino-American Normalization*, 468–75.

104. For an in-depth look at this period, see Hsiao, "A Renewed Crisis over Taiwan and Its Implications on Sino-American Relations," in ibid., 102–13.

105. Joint Communique of the People's Republic of China and the United States of America (17 August 1982), in ibid., 283–84.

106. James Mann, *About Face: A History of America's Curious Relationship with China, from Nixon to Clinton* (New York: Knopf, 1999), 127; Andrew J. Nathan and Robert S. Ross, *The Great Wall and the Empty Fortress* (New York: Norton, 1997), 69.

107. John W. Garver, *Face Off* (Seattle: University of Washington Press, 1997), 13–34.

108. For an insightful study of the pivotal U.S. role in 1990s cross-Strait relations, see Yu-Shan Wu, "Exploring Dual Triangles: The Development of Taipei-Washington-Beijing Relations," *Issues and Studies* 32 (October 1996): 26–52.

109. Phillip Y. M. Yang, "From Strategic Ambiguity to Three No's," in Barry Rubin and Thomas Keaney, eds., *U.S. Allies in a Changing World* (London: Frank Cass, 2001), 235.

110. Robert S. Ross, "The 1995–96 Taiwan Strait Confrontation," *International Security* 25 (fall 2000): 87, 91–94; Garver, *Face Off*, 35–46.

111. See Jih-wen Lin, "Two-Level Games Between Rival Regimes: Domestic Politics and the Remaking of Cross-Strait Relations," *Issues and Studies* 36 (November/December 2000): 1–26, esp. 21; Steven Goldstein, "The Cross-Strait Talks of 1993—The Rest of the Story: Domestic Politics and Taiwan's Mainland Policy," in *Across the Taiwan Strait: Mainland China, Taiwan, and the 1995–96 Crisis*, ed. Suisheng Zhao (New York: Routledge, 1999), 197–228; Hung-mao Tien, "Taiwan in 1995: Electoral Politics and Cross-Strait Relations," *Asia Survey* 36 (January 1996): 33–40, esp. 35.

112. On Taiwan's pragmatic diplomacy, see Nathan and Ross, *The Great Wall*, 217–19; Garver, *Face Off*, chap. 3.

113. Wu, "Exploring Dual Triangles," 48.

114. David S. Chou, "Cross-Strait Relations and U.S. Roles in the Taiwan Strait Crisis," *Issues and Studies* 32 (October 1996): 11.

115. Ross, "The 1995–96 Taiwan Strait Confrontation," 91; Garver, *Face Off*, chap. 8.

116. Ross, "The 1995–96 Taiwan Strait Confrontation," 93–94.

117. Ibid., 103–4.

118. Ibid.; Andrew Scobell, "Show of Force: Chinese Soldiers, Statesmen, and the

1995–1996 Taiwan Strait Crisis," *Political Science Quarterly* 115 (summer 2000): 232; Suisheng Zhao, "Changing Leaders Perceptions: The Adoption of a Coercive Strategy," in Zhao, *Across the Taiwan Strait*, 99–126;

119. Ross, "The 1995–96 Taiwan Strait Confrontation," 104–12.

120. Ashton B. Carter and William J. Perry, *Preventive Defense: A New Security Strategy for America* (Washington, D.C. : Brookings Institution, 1999); Chou, "Cross-Strait Relations and U.S. Roles," 16, 20; Yang, "From Strategic Ambiguity to Three No's," 236.

121. Ross, "The 1995–96 Taiwan Strait Confrontation," 119, 121.

122. "Military's Muscle-Flexing in a Chinese Political Game," *International Herald Tribune*, 18 March 1996, 4.

123. Ross, "The 1995–96 Taiwan Strait Confrontation," 113.

124. Quoted in Yang, "From Strategic Ambiguity to Three No's," 239.

125. Ibid., 241.

126. Clinton quoted in Yang, "From Strategic Ambiguity to Three No's," 239.

127. Chas W. Freeman, "Caught Between Two Chinas," *New York Times*, 2 August 1999.

128. Excerpts from Interview of Taiwanese President Lee, July 9, 1999, in *Foreign Policy Bulletin* (September/October 1999), 153–54. On the evolution of Lee's nationalist rhetoric, from 1994 to 1999, see Xu Shiquan, "The One-China Principle: The Positions of the Communist Party of China (CCP), the Kuomintang (KMT), and the Democratic Progressive Party (DPP)," *American Foreign Policy Interests* 22 (December 2000): 27–28.

129. Statement by the Taiwanese Mainland Affairs Council (12 July 1999), *Foreign Policy Bulletin* (September/October 1999): 154–55.

130. Denny Roy, "Tensions in the Taiwan Strait," *Survival* 42 (spring 2000): 92.

131. See Shirley A. Kan, *CRS Report RL30957, Taiwan: Major U.S. Arms Sales Since 1990* (Washington D.C.: Congressional Research Service, 1 June 2001), 9.

132. Eric Schmitt, "Clinton Threatens Veto of Closer Military Ties to Taiwan," *New York Times*, 2 February 2000.

133. "The One China Principle and the Taiwan Issue," Statement by the People's Republic of China, 21 February 2000, (http://www.nytimes.com/library/world/asia/022200china-taiwan-text.html) access date 12 March 2003; "China's Jiang Renews Taiwan Threat," *Reuters* on-line, 4 March 2000.

134. Thomas J. Christensen, "Chinese *Realpolitik*," *Foreign Affairs* 75 (September/October 1996): 45–48; Bonnie S. Glaser, "China's Security Perceptions: Interests and Ambitions," *Asian Survey* 33 (March 1993): 263–64.

135. Roy, "Tensions in the Taiwan Strait," 80.

136. James A. Robinson and Deborah A Brown, "Taiwan's 2000 Presidential Election," *Orbis* 44 (fall 2000): 611–12; Yu-Shan Wu, "Taiwanese Elections and Cross-Strait Relations: Mainland Policy in Flux," *Asian Survey* 34 (July/August 1999): 565–87; Evan Feigenbaum, *Change in Taiwan and Potential Adversity in the Strait* (Washington D.C.: Rand, 1995).

137. Chen Shui-bian, "Taiwan Stands Up: Advancing to an Uplifting Era," Inaugural Speech (20 May 2000), in *Seeking Constructive Cross-Strait Relations: Taipei's Current Mainland Policy Documents* (Taipei: Mainland Affairs Council, June 2001).

138. "The DPP's Position on Cross-Strait Relations," Remarks by Wilson Hsin Tien, Democratic Progressive Party, Director of the Department of International Affairs, The Atlantic Council, Washington, D.C., 25 April 2001; Yu-Shan Wu, "Taiwan in 2000: Managing the Aftershocks from Power Transfer," *Asian Survey* 41 (January/February 2001): 43–45; Julian Jengliang Kuo, "Taiwan's New Policy Toward Mainland China," *American Foreign Policy Interests* 22 (December 2000): 32–35; Dalpino and Gill, *Brookings Northeast Asian Survey 2000–01*, 37–38.

139. On 2 March 2001, the United States notified Taiwan that it would sell $202 million in arms; beginning in July, it notified Taiwan of $1.6 billion more for the year. Kan, *Taiwan: Major U.S. Arms Sales Since 1990*, 9–10.

140. "Beijing as a Conservative Power," *Foreign Affairs* 76 (March/April 1997): 40.

141. "Does China Matter?" *Foreign Affairs* 78 (September/October 1999): 33.

142. Russian weakness also meant that the United States had less incentive to court Beijing as a counterweight to Moscow. Wu, "The Development of Taipei-Washington-Beijing Relations," 51.

143. Erik Eckholm "Power of U.S. Draws China and Russia to Amity Pact," *New York Times*, 14 January 2001; "Jiang, Putin Sign 'Beijing Declaration' on Deepening Sino-Russian Relations," Xinhua, FBIS, 18 July 2000, FBIS-CHI-2000–0718.

144. Gilbert Rozman, "A New Sino-Russian-American Triangle?" *Orbis* 44 (fall 2000): 541–56; Andrew C. Kuchins, "Russia's Strategic Partnerships and Global Security," *Program on New Approaches to Russian Security, Policy Memo No. 165* (New York: Council on Foreign Relations, 2000), 103–7; Jennifer Anderson, "The Limits of Sino-Russian Strategic Partnership," *Adelphi Paper*, No. 315 (London: International Institute of Strategic Studies, 1998); Rajan Menon, "The Strategic Convergence Between Russia and China," *Survival* 39 (summer 1997): 101–25.

145. Gerald Segal, "East Asia and the Constrainment of China," *International Security* 20 (spring 1996): 128.

146. Nakai Yoshifumi, "Policy Coordination on Taiwan," in Nishihara Masashi, *The Japan-US Alliance: New Challenges for the 21st Century* (Tokyo: Japan Center for International Exchange, 2000), 72–80, esp. 76. On Japan's weak inclination to balance more generally, see Christopher Twomey, "Japan, A Circumscribed Balancer," *Security Studies* 9 (summer 2000): 167–206.

147. See J. Mohan Malik, "China-India Relations in the Post-Soviet Era: The Continuing Rivalry," *The China Quarterly* 142 (June 1995): 317–55.

148. John P. McClaran, "US Arms Sales to Taiwan: Implications for the Future of the Sino-US Relationship." *Asian Survey* 40 (July/August 2000): 622–40.

149. Yitzhak Shichor, "Israel's Military Transfers to China and Taiwan," *Survival* 40 (spring 1998): 72–73; Robinson, "America in Taiwan's Post Cold-War Foreign Policy," 1349.

150. See Michael O'Hanlon, "Why China Cannot Conquer Taiwan," *International Security* 25 (fall 2000): 51–86. For the argument that what deters China from using force to impose reunification is not Taiwan's defense capability but, rather, the much larger threat of U.S. intervention, see Robert S. Ross, "Navigating the Taiwan Strait: Deterrence, Escalation Dominance, and U.S.–China Relations," *International Security* 27 (fall 2002): 48–85.

151. Robert S. Ross argues that, more than any other factor, China's missile threat is what deters Taiwan from declaring independence. See "The Stability of Deterrence in the Taiwan Strait," *National Interest* 65 (fall 2001): 67–76.

152. Open Letter to President Clinton, 24 August 1999, (http://www.heritage.org/news/99/nr082499_letter.html), access date 3 April 2001.

153. Wolfowitz, "Remembering the Future," 44–45. Also see Jaw-ling Joanne Chang, "Lessons from the Taiwan Relations Act," *Orbis* 44 (winter 2000): 65. This position was echoed in author's interviews in Taiepei with Dr. Hung-mao Tien, Taiwan's Minister of Foreign Affairs, 2000–2002 (26 March 2002), and Chiou I. Jen, the Secretary General of Taiwan's National Security Council (27 March 2002). When asked, however, neither Tien nor Chiou could describe what level of security commitment from the United States would be sufficient to inspire in Taiwan the confidence necessary to begin reunification talks with PRC.

154. Shirley A. Kan, *CRS Report RL30957, Taiwan: Major U.S. Arms Sales Since 1990* (Washington D.C.: Congressional Research Service, 1 June 2001); Jason Sherman, "Proposal Gives Taiwan Defense Privileges," *Defense News*, 21 May 2001, 4.

155. "US Refuses Taiwan Request for JDAM, HARM, and PAC-3 Missiles," *Aerospace Daily*, 25 April 2001.

156. Predictably, Democratic congressmen countered this executive decision by proposing legislation requiring annual meetings between the President or his senior aides, and Taiwan's top military chiefs, and for treating Taiwan as the "equivalent of a major non-NATO ally"—although not actually designating it as such—for arms transfers under the Arms Export Control Act and the Foreign Assistance Act. See Kan, *Taiwan: Major U.S. Arms Sales Since 1990*, summary.

157. Cf. Kruschev's similarly vague promise to "help Cyprus to defend her freedom and independence" in August 1964, just before Moscow shifted to favoring Turkey; see Chapter 5.

158. John Pomfret, "In Fact and in Tone, U.S. Expresses New Fondness for Taiwan," *Washington Post*, 30 April 2002.

159. Chen is quoted in "Chen on Taiwan: It's the Democratic Republic of China," interview with Mike Chinoy, 23 May 2001, CNN.com. See http://www.cnn.com/2002/WORLD /asiapcf/east/05/23/taiwan.chen/index.html, access date 12 March 2003.

160. Charles Snyder, "Wolfowitz Clarifies Taiwan Stance," *Taipei Times*, 31 May 2002; Chris Cockel, "US Opposed to Taiwan Independence: Wolfowitz," *China Post*, 31 May 2002.

161. See, e.g., remarks by Michael Swaine, Michael O'Hanlon, and Henry Rowen in "Facing China," *Commentary* 111 (February 2001): 17, 21. This has also been a key contention of Taiwan officials who argue that it is premature to begin political negotiations with Beijing. For example, the Secretary General of Taiwan's National Security Council argued that Taiwan could expect to obtain a political agreement with much more democratic "content" through negotiations with a democratic regime in Beijing than through negotiations with the present one (Chiou I. Jen, interviewed by author, Taipei, Taiwan, 27 March 2002). One also often hears the convenient argument that only a democratic China could credibly commit to abide by any agreement it reached through negotiations with Taipei.

162. Jack Snyder, *From Voting to Violence: Democratization and Nationalist Conflict* (New York: W. W. Norton, 2000); Edward D. Mansfield and Jack Snyder, "Democratization and the Danger of War," *International Security* 20 (summer 1995): 5–38. Alan P. L. Liu argues that domestic politics within China are the *primary* driver of China's revisionist goals; see "A Convenient Crisis: Looking Behind Beijing's Threats Against Taiwan," *Issues and Studies* 36 (September/October 2000): 83–121.

163. Richard Betts and Thomas Christensen, "China: Getting the Questions Right," *National Interest* (winter 2000/01): 25; Snyder, *From Voting to Violence*, 339. Also see Avery Goldstein, "Great Expectations: Interpreting China's Arrival," *International Security* 22 (winter 1997/98): 67; Nancy Bernkopf Tucker, "China-Taiwan: U.S. Debates and Policy Choices," *Survival* 40 (winter 1998–99): 156.

164. Wilson Tien, DPP Director of International Affairs, "The DPP's Position on Cross-Strait Relations," Presented to the Atlantic Council, Washington D.C., 24 April 2001. As the director of the Policy Council and the Department of Propaganda of the DPP recently put it, "independence is . . . the ultimate and the most effective counterweight to the PRC's use of force in Cross-Strait bargaining." Julian Jengliang Kuo, "Taiwan's New Policy Toward Mainland China," *American Foreign Policy Interests* 22 (December 2000): 32.

165. Mike M. Mochizuki, "American and Japanese Strategic Debates: The Need for a New Synthesis," in *Toward a True Alliance: Restructuring US-Japan Security Relations*, ed. Mochizuki (Washington D.C.: Brookings Institution, 1997), 76; Zbigniew Brzezinski, "A Geostrategy for Asia," *Foreign Affairs* 76 (September/October 1997): 59; Daniel I. Okimoto, Henry S. Rowen, Michel Oksenberg, James H. Raphael, Thomas P. Rohlen, Donald K. Emerson, and Michael H. Armacost, *A United States Policy for the Changing Realities of East Asia: Toward a New Consensus* (Stanford: Asia/Pacific Research Center, 1996), 24.

166. Joseph S. Nye, Jr., "A Taiwan Deal," *Washington Post*, 8 March 1998.

167. Thomas J. Christensen, "Clarity on Taiwan: Correcting Misperceptions on Both Sides of the Strait," *Washington Post*, 20 March 2000. Christensen's argument is fully fleshed out in "The Contemporary Security Dilemma: Deterring a Taiwan Conflict," *Washington Quarterly* 25 (autumn 2002): 7–21.

168. See Betts and Christensen, "China: Getting the Questions Right," 25–26; Mochizuki, "American and Japanese Strategic Debates," 76; Chou, "Cross-Strait Relations and U.S. Roles in the Taiwan Strait Crisis," 21.

169. As Richard Haass put it, the problem with a policy that "inform[s] both China and Taiwan that only if Taiwan declared independence would there be any question of American" intervention is that "it might prompt Taiwan to take every step short of indepen-

dence—steps that might provoke a Chinese attack that in turn would require a U.S. response." "Digging for a China Policy," *IntellectualCapital.com*, 23 March 2000. Similarly, China would be expected to increase pressure tactics that skirt the limit allowed by a clear U.S. threat. Ross argues that China has already begun to do this, "The 1995–96 Taiwan Strait Confrontation," 119. For a formal analysis of this dynamic, see Suzanne Werner, "Deterring Intervention: The Stakes of War and Third-Party Involvement," *American Journal of Political Science* 44 (October 2000): 720–32.

170. On this point, some have suggested drawing a line between "strategic clarity" and "tactical ambiguity," with *strategic* referring in the limited sense to high-level goals and *tactical* referring to the ways and means of achieving them. See, e.g., Andrew J. Nathan, "What's Wrong with U.S. Taiwan Policy?" *Washington Quarterly* 23 (spring 2000): 105.

171. Thomas Christensen, letter to author, 4 June 2001.

172. Christensen, "Contemporary Security Dilemma," 19.

173. For historical background on this point, see Thomas Christensen, *Useful Adversaries: Grand Strategy, Domestic Mobilization, and Sino-American Conflict, 1947–1958* (Princeton: Princeton University Press, 1996), 254.

CONCLUSION

1. See John J. Mearsheimer, *The Tragedy of Great Power Politics* (New York: Norton, 2001).

2. See, e.g., Martin Wight, *Power Politics,* 2d ed. (New York: Penguin Books, 1986), 177.

3. On this point, see James D. Morrow, "Alliances: Why Write Them Down?" *Annual Review of Political Science* 3 (2000): 63–83.

4. For an overview of the broader implications, see Stephen M. Walt, "American Primacy": Its Prospects and Pitfalls," *Naval War College Review* 55 (spring 2002): 9–28.

5. William T. R. Fox, *The Super-Powers: The United States, Britain, and the Soviet Union— Their Responsibility for Peace* (New York: Harcourt, Brace, 1944).

6. See Samuel P. Huntington, "The Lonely Superpower," *Foreign Affairs* 78 (March/ April 1999).

7. Fox, *The Super-Powers,* 7.

8. Jim Hoagland highlighted this when he noted that, after 11 September 2001, "Russia and China spend their time trying to leverage American power for their goals rather than opposing its exercise." Hoagland, "Managing America's Superiority," *Washington Post,* 7 March 2002, A21.

9. "Forward engagement" was a main plank in the Democratic Party's foreign policy platform in the 2000 presidential campaign; "global leadership" is a close Republican analogue (especially in neoconservative circles). The former places greater stress on multilateral action, the latter on unilateral action. Rhetorical differences aside, they both commend proactive U.S. engagement on a global scale, backed by a strong forward-deployed military. For the Democratic Party's vision of forward engagement, see: http://www.issues2000.org /Celeb/Democratic=Party=Foreign=Policy.htm (accessed 6 August 2002). For the conservative's take on global leadership, see The Project for the New American Century, Statement of Principles (3 June 1997): http://www.newamericancentury.org/statementofprinciples.htm (accessed 6 August 2002). For a critique of both, see Barbara Conry, "US Global Leadership: A Euphemism for World Policeman," *CATO Policy Analysis* 267 (5 February 1997).

10. William Sanderson, *Statecraft: A Treatise on the Concerns of Our Sovereign Lord the King* (London: Constable & Co., 1932), 124.

11. See Bush's cover letter to *The National Security Strategy of the United States of America, September 2002,* iv. At http://www.whitehouse.gov/nsc/nss.pdf, access date 14 March 2003.

12. Michael Hirsh, "Bush and the World," *Foreign Affairs* 81 (September/October 2002), 39.

13. This is the flaw in Walter's argument that "outside intervention [in civil wars] provides important information about what type of opponent each side is facing, distinguishing predators from nonpredators. Domestic groups who are intent on aggression are unlikely to accept outside interference since this would jeopardize their ability to carry out any mali-

cious plans. Peace loving groups, on the other hand, should eagerly agree to such involvement and thus signal their benign intentions." See Barbara F. Walter and Jack Snyder, eds., *Civil Wars, Insecurity, and Intervention* (New York: Columbia University Press, 1999), 306. For a lucid and succinct theory that explains why weak and aggressive domestic groups seek outside intervention in civil wars, see George Modelski, *The International Relations of Internal Wars*, Research Monograph no. 11 (Princeton University: Center of International Studies, 1961), esp. 6–7.

14. David A. Baldwin, *Economic Statecraft* (Princeton: Princeton University Press, 1985), 123–26, esp. n. 32.

15. As Stanley Hoffmann once noted, "By its weight alone, a great power influences and acts whether it wants to or not; self-restraint may (or may not, depending on the circumstances) be the most productive way of keeping control of men and events." *Gulliver's Troubles, or the Setting of American Foreign Policy* (New York: McGraw Hill, 1968), 192. Similarly, Martin Wight remarked "non-intervention in a particular case may be as positive a policy as intervention." *Power Politics*, 199.

16. For example, an important and growing body of formal theory conceives of and explains war as a bargaining failure caused by uncertainty and "asymmetric information" among the adversaries. See Robert Powell, "Bargaining Theory and International Conflict," *Annual Review of Political Science* 5 (2002): 1–30; Erik Gartzke, "War Is in the Error Term," *International Organization* 53 (fall 1999): 567–87; James D. Fearon, "Rationalist Explanations for War," *International Organization* 49 (summer 1995): 379–414.

17. Robert C. McFarlane, "Infertile Ground," *New York Times*, 14 October 1999.

18. M. James Wilkinson, *Moving Beyond Conflict Prevention to Reconcilliation: Tackling Greek-Turkish Hostility*, A Report to the Carnegie Commission on Preventing Deadly Conflict (New York: Carnegie Corp., 1999), 39, 42.

19. See Robert Jervis, *System Effects: Complexity in Political and Social Life* (Princeton: Princeton University Press, 1997); Glenn Snyder, *Alliance Politics* (Ithaca: Cornell University Press, 1997), 149, 352; and Chapter 2 herein.

20. This is an aspect of what John Ikenberry calls the "classic problem of political order," how to establish stable relations "between strong and weak states." See *After Victory: Institutions, Strategic Restraint, and the Rebuilding of Order after Major Wars* (Princeton: Princeton University Press, 2001), chap. 1, esp. 17. Ikenberry argues that liberal international institutions and democratic polities have helped to solve the problem by allowing the U.S. to "bind" itself in ways that make its commitments credible to others. As I explain below, I doubt that such factors can do much to solve the two-way commitment problem of pivotal deterrence by a grossly preponderant power.

21. On the use of "tied-hands" logic in international bargaining, see *Double-edged Diplomacy: International Bargaining and Domestic Politics*, ed. Peter Evans, Harold K. Jacobsen, and Robert Putnam (Berkeley: University of California Press, 1993), esp. 28, 442.

22. A caveat to the point about the weakness of democratic ratification as a means for locking in credible two-way threats may be in order. It could be argued that while such mechanisms add little to the credibility of pivotal deterrence threats to intervene directly, those mechanisms may do better if the operative threats are to abandon one side or both if they transgress.

23. For more on this point, see Timothy W. Crawford, "Alexander Hamilton's Revenge: Executive Power and American Foreign Policy Revisited," *Security Studies* 11 (autumn 2001): 148–50.

Index

Cornell Studies in Security Affairs

A series edited by Robert J. Art, Robert Jervis, *and* Stephen M. Walt

The Sacred Cause: Civil-Military Conflict over Soviet National Security, 1917–1992,
    by Thomas M. Nichols
Liberal Peace, Liberal War: American Politics and International Security, by John M. Owen IV
Bombing to Win: Air Power and Coercion in War, by Robert A. Pape
A Question of Loyalty: Military Manpower in Multiethnic States, by Alon Peled
Inadvertent Escalation: Conventional War and Nuclear Risks, by Barry R. Posen
The Sources of Military Doctrine: France, Britain, and Germany between the World Wars,
    by Barry Posen
Dilemmas of Appeasement: British Deterrence and Defense, 1934–1937, by Gaines Post, Jr.
Crucible of Beliefs: Learning, Alliances, and World Wars, by Dan Reiter
Eisenhower and the Missile Gap, by Peter J. Roman
The Domestic Bases of Grand Strategy, edited by Richard Rosecrance and Arthur Stein
Societies and Military Power: India and Its Armies, by Stephen Peter Rosen
Winning the Next War: Innovation and the Modern Military, by Stephen Peter Rosen
Vital Crossroads: Mediterranean Origins of the Second World War, 1935–1940,
    by Reynolds Salerno
Fighting to a Finish: The Politics of War Termination in the United States and Japan, 1945,
    by Leon V. Sigal
Corporate Warriors: The Rise of the Privatized Military Industry, by P. W. Singer
Alliance Politics, by Glenn H. Snyder
The Ideology of the Offensive: Military Decision Making and the Disasters of 1914, by Jack Snyder
Myths of Empire: Domestic Politics and International Ambition, by Jack Snyder
The Militarization of Space: U.S. Policy, 1945–1984, by Paul B. Stares
The Nixon Administration and the Making of U.S. Nuclear Strategy, by Terry Terriff
The Ethics of Destruction: Norms and Force in International Relations, by Ward Thomas
Causes of War: Power and the Roots of Conflict, by Stephen Van Evera
Mortal Friends, Best Enemies: German-Russian Cooperation after the Cold War,
    by Celeste A. Wallander
The Origins of Alliances, by Stephen M. Walt
Revolution and War, by Stephen M. Walt
The Tet Offensive: Intelligence Failure in War, by James J. Wirtz
The Elusive Balance: Power and Perceptions during the Cold War, by William Curti Wohlforth
Deterrence and Strategic Culture: Chinese-American Confrontations, 1949–1958,
    by Shu Guang Zhang